# AFTER THE VOTE

Feminist Politics in La Guardia's New York

Elisabeth Israels Perry

OXFORD
UNIVERSITY PRESS

**OXFORD**
UNIVERSITY PRESS

Oxford University Press is a department of the University of Oxford. It furthers
the University's objective of excellence in research, scholarship, and education
by publishing worldwide. Oxford is a registered trade mark of Oxford University
Press in the UK and certain other countries.

Published in the United States of America by Oxford University Press
198 Madison Avenue, New York, NY 10016, United States of America.

CIP data is on file at the Library of Congress.
ISBN 978–0–19–934184–9

9 8 7 6 5 4 3 2 1

Printed by Sheridan Books, Inc., United States of America

For Michael Jozef Israels,
who knows why

# CONTENTS

# PREFACE

This book is about the women who went to my grandmother's funeral. On January 2, 1933, Belle Lindner Israels Moskowitz, adviser and political strategist to former New York State governor Alfred E. Smith, died unexpectedly of an embolism. Her funeral at Temple Emanu-El in Manhattan attracted some three thousand mourners. Among them were dozens of prominent men, many of them members of New York's political and reform elites. Dozens of prominent women were there too. Newspapers listed some of them: Eleanor Roosevelt, Democratic Party activist and wife of President-Elect Franklin D. Roosevelt; Frances Perkins, New York State commissioner of labor, soon-to-be US secretary of labor, the first woman to serve in a presidential cabinet; Pauline Morton Sabin, a Republican and founder of the National Organization of Women for Prohibition Reform, a key player in winning repeal of the Eighteenth Amendment; popular novelist, screenwriter, and civic activist Fannie Hurst; Jane Hoey, head of the New York City Welfare Council and later a bureau head in the Social Security Administration; and attorney Anna Moscowitz Kross, soon to be one of Manhattan's first women magistrates and twenty years later the city's commissioner of corrections.

Though not all of New York City's women political activists shared Moskowitz's partisan loyalties, they had admired her tenacity, political skills, and accomplishments. Like her, they were passionate reformers—of political parties, women's status, labor-industrial relations, municipal government, health care, education, and criminal justice, to name just a few of their causes. Now that they were voters, a status they had gained in 1917, they were increasingly involved in partisan politics. Most of them disliked political parties. But they had all come to realize that partisanship was the only way they could win the authority they needed to enact the public policies they believed in.

This book illustrates five interrelated aspects of their stories. It shows first how their participation in the New York woman suffrage movement trained them to use the political process to achieve the vote

and after suffrage to apply that training toward making an impact on current political issues. It then shows how they gradually carved out roles for themselves in
political parties at all levels—from the city's assembly district party clubhouses
to county, state, and finally national party committees. It turns next to concrete
examples of how, during the 1920s and 1930s, these women introduced, and
sometimes won, progressive feminist reforms—that is, reforms that embodied
the feminist principles of sex equality and the social and economic reforms
sought by Progressive Era reformers. It explores how, starting in the early 1930s,
New York women used their rising political muscle to help a progressive politician, Fiorello La Guardia, win an unprecedented three mayoral terms. Finally, it
explains why La Guardia appointed dozens of these women to administrative and
judicial posts, appointments that not only were groundbreaking but also paved
the way for later generations of accomplished New York City women to become
leaders at higher levels of American government.

I first encountered some of these women in the 1970s while I was in the early
stages of work on a biography of Belle Moskowitz. I was astounded that, except
for Eleanor Roosevelt (whom I knew primarily as the president's widow), I had
never heard of any of them. Trained in French history in the 1960s, I had only
minimal experience in American history and none in women's history, a field
then just beginning to make its mark. By the time the Moskowitz biography was
finally done—it was published by Oxford University Press in 1987—I had become familiar with Moskowitz's colleagues in New York City's world of women's
politics and decided that my next research and writing project would be about
them. Though other projects intervened, I continued to collect original source
materials for what I at first called "From Belle to Bella," a phrase that linked Belle
Moskowitz's world of New York City women activists to that of Bella Abzug,
New York City's redoubtable US congresswoman in the 1970s. I still needed a
larger narrative arc that would link the women not only to one another but also
to New York City's history.

In hindsight, I probably had found my arc earlier than I had thought. In the
mid-1980s, I was invited to an informal meeting with visiting women scholars
from India. As we went around the room introducing ourselves, I said I was
working on a book about the political career of my grandmother, a powerful
behind-the-scenes Democratic Party activist in the 1920s. One visitor asked,
cryptically, "What happened?" She was wondering, if a woman like my grandmother had been so powerful in the 1920s, why was women's political power so
negligible now? I found myself saying: "Two things: first, men kept women out;
second, women kept themselves out."

Since that meeting, my answer has not changed. My work on both Moskowitz
and her community of politically active women, and even on those who came

after, has only confirmed it. Again and again, I encountered capable, talented, strategically smart New York City women—women with advanced leadership skills, deep subject knowledge, and strong political convictions—sidelined either by the men who still held the reins of political power or by their own adherence to traditional norms of appropriate behavior for women with political interests. It appeared that the passage of the Nineteenth Amendment to the US Constitution in 1920, authorizing woman suffrage, had done little to change the culture of centuries of men's political dominance and women's socialization to be subservient to them.

Despite the persistence of this culture, New York City produced some powerful counterexamples of women who developed meaningful political careers. These were the "firsts"—the first woman lawyer, county register, legislator, magistrate, alderwoman, congresswoman, deputy commissioner, commissioner, government bureau head, party coleader, party leader, and presidential cabinet secretary. In telling their stories, this book pays tribute to their accomplishments but does not ignore the constraints they faced, some of which were of their own making, while many were made by others. Because of those constraints, they rarely climbed as high as they wanted to, and many did not stay in their posts for long. Of those who won elective office, few won re-election. Most faced criticism purely because of their sex. Using individual women as exemplars of "all women," critics implied they held posts that never should have gone to them in the first place, or that a woman's failure meant that no woman could ever succeed. Many women found the pressure hard to take. Dreading scrutiny and public attack, they kept clear of competitive politics entirely, sometimes accepting appointive offices they hoped might protect them but abandoning even those when the arrows got too sharp.

A statement by Charles Poletti, former New York lieutenant governor (and briefly governor), which he made to an interviewer from Columbia University's Oral History program in 1978, clarified for me some of the complexities in the story of New York City women in politics in the mid-twentieth century. His interviewer asked him whether the government he had served in the 1930s and 1940s had discriminated against women. "No," he replied emphatically. He himself had not only "supported women" but also gotten most of his "inspiration for new ideas" from women. Through such New York City organizations as the Women's Trade Union League and the Consumers' League, he had "encountered a group of very learned and intelligent and public-spirited women." Whenever he could, he had brought them up to Albany to meet with his boss, Governor Herbert H. Lehman, as they "had much more creative ability than men." "If you talked to the ordinary fellow in business or banking you never got any new ideas," he said further, "but these women had new ideas and proposals whether it was in housing or whatever, they just came up with new ideas." New York City at that time "had a lot of capable women," he recalled; it "was bubbling over with women's organizations. There were scores of them with superlative people."[1]

Here was my smoking gun. Someone at the top of state government had appreciated the knowledge and creative thinking of New York City women activists. Not only were they well known to the public at large, but also Poletti and his colleagues had listened to their counsel. Still, few of these women had ever held office, elective or appointive.

Another indication of the actual importance in government of mid-twentieth-century New York women came from a 1953 National Association of Women Lawyers survey of women attorneys holding public office. Thirty-one states and the District of Columbia responded to the association's questionnaire. New York State had the highest number: eighty-four (the closest runners-up were California with thirty-four and Illinois with thirty-one). When I looked up one of them, a judge who had come from the Bronx, I happened on a letter written to the *Washington Post* in 1993 that responded to a description of US Supreme Court Justice Ruth Bader Ginsburg as "mentor, role model and heroine" for the "first generation of feminist lawyers." "This is incorrect," one Moe Greenberg of Silver Spring, Maryland, wrote, adding that had the reference been to the "second generation," it would have been correct. "I must go back to the late 1920s and 1930s when a group of young women lawyers, graduates of New York University Law School, friends and members of the same sorority, banded together and formed the Bronx Women's Bar Association as a result of having been ignored by the New York State Bar Association," Greenberg wrote. He named some of them: Nettie Rosenblatt Reese, Clara Tepper, Rose Schnep (for many years assistant corporation counsel in New York City), Marlie Margulies Berk, Bertha Schwartz (later a judge), and Henrietta Greenspan Margulies (later assistant to several of the city's judges). This group, Greenberg averred, "set the stage for the wonderful role Ruth Ginsburg played in later years in helping to open the door much wider for participation of women in this important field."[2] Of course Greenberg cited only the Bronx women attorneys he had known personally. Hundreds more had already held prestigious posts across the five New York City boroughs.

Where had all these women—those in appointive or elective office or serving as informal public policy advisers—come from? What had made their careers possible in an era generally hostile to women wielding power? What, if any, was their impact on the public policies and laws of mid-twentieth-century New York or beyond? In answering these questions, this book emphasizes three interlocking themes: women's entry into partisan politics, their continuing commitments to progressive feminist reform, and their lasting contributions to the modernization of New York City's government. It explores not only how, when, and where the city's women activists had influence in these three areas but also how events and developments in those areas made their political careers possible long before the modern feminist movement of the 1960s and 1970s.

The book begins with the New York woman suffrage movement itself. Most historians see the woman's vote as a "glass half empty," and in many ways it was. The suffrage movement fractured over many issues, most notably war preparedness, the National Woman's Party's proposed Equal Rights Amendment, sex-specific protective labor laws, and Prohibition. Moreover, fewer women than hoped went to the polls, and the women who did vote seemed to be voting similarly to men. Most men (along with many women) opposed the equal integration of women into the nation's political life, and negative stereotypes about women's political abilities persisted. Finally, for decades after the passage of woman suffrage, women won pitifully few positions of authority. And so (some have argued), since woman suffrage neither immediately nor sufficiently changed the American political landscape, it was far from a major turning point for the nation.

For women, though, it was huge. In the New York City context alone, it allowed an impressive number of women to construct political careers, a result they never could have achieved without the ballot. For sure, after winning the vote, women experienced frustrations trying to fulfill their personal and public policy ambitions. Nonetheless, the vote allowed many New York City women to make places for themselves in political parties and eventually government. Many of the causes they pursued were continuous with their presuffrage social justice commitments. The causes were also feminist, in the sense that they assumed women and men should enjoy civil rights equal to those of men, and they aimed to correct the gender imbalances of power that kept women subservient. Determined to affect local government, they gradually built on their political experiences and networks to win positions of public authority. In short, though the woman's vote may not have immediately transformed national politics, winning it was nothing short of transformative . . . for women, especially (and at first) at local levels. Even if it failed to realize all the hopes envisioned for it, it opened doors that would never again close. Moreover, New York City's woman suffrage movement was foundational to women's later political activism. After suffrage, when they looked for guidance on how to achieve policy goals, they turned to the tactics, role models, and networks they had inherited from the past.

Though I had been slowly collecting sources on this topic for some thirty years, it was only after the advances of twenty-first-century digitization that my progress accelerated. When I was working on the Moskowitz biography in the 1970s and 1980s, I had access only to the printed indexes and microfilms of the *New York Times*. Working with these sources was a tedious and time-consuming process. Today, digitized copies of many of the city's old newspapers and magazines reveal that print media managers of the postsuffrage era were deeply interested in women's use of their new citizenship rights and assigned writers to cover the topic. Without these exceptional resources, I could never have done justice to the complexity of the political careers of the women I cover in this book or understood how public opinion about those careers had evolved. Of course, the journalistic record was not always accurate, but it was essential for verifying chronologies and discovering, often through obituaries of women's husbands, the birth names of many prominent women otherwise identified only as "Mrs. Husband's Name," which was not the way I wanted to identify them.

These sources had always been there, but now that they are more readily available, I hope they will stimulate others to recognize that, even if all the names on office doors and enacted bills are male, women were there too, and that their involvement still needs to be uncovered and fleshed out. I also hope that never again will the political history of New York, or of any other city or nation for that matter, be written without integrating women as ubiquitous sources of ideas and agents of change.

A word about the diversity, or apparent lack thereof, among the women I write about. While they originally came from varied socioeconomic, ethnic, religious, and racial backgrounds, by the time they were in mainstream urban politics, they were all solidly middle or upper class either by birth or marriage. All had received or worked their way through good educations, not always in colleges or universities but in institutions such as women's clubs and voluntary associations that had given them both deep knowledge about how government worked and the skills to make it better. Ambitious women also learned from these institutions how to use their social and professional networks to advance their careers. As mature adults, they were all either sufficiently successful as professionals (attorneys, businesswomen, health care professionals, educators, journalists, publicists, administrators, social welfare workers, writers, union leaders, and more) or sufficiently leisured to engage in civic and political activism. All of them developed some level of clout in city political arenas, either through their own contacts in business, cultural, and political circles or through marriages or family relationships to members of the city's male elites.

My earliest personal encounters with women like these came in the early 1980s, when I was looking for material in New York City on the political careers of Belle Moskowitz and Eleanor Roosevelt. An institution they had both belonged to, the Women's City Club of New York, was still in existence. Founded by suffragists in 1916, the club gave women a nonpartisan venue where they could talk and learn about civic affairs and engage in advocacy work. By the 1920s, a few thousand white women had joined the club, a membership surge that enabled it to take out a mortgage on a Park Avenue mansion. When I first visited the club, it no longer had the mansion and was meeting in spare and utilitarian quarters and its membership had dwindled to a few hundred well-educated professional and non-professional women, most of them retired or elderly. The club's then president graciously allowed me access to the club's bound volumes of board and committee minutes, untapped resources that provided insight into not only Moskowitz and Roosevelt but also many other New York City postsuffrage women, including Frances Perkins. I was so excited by these resources that I worried they would get thrown out the next time the club downsized, a prospect that seemed inevitable. As the club's correspondence had already been discarded, the heavy bound volumes I was paging through were sure to go next. June Farmer, later a club president and one with a special sensitivity to this issue, gave me an opportunity to address the board about my concerns. Thanks to her support, I was able to persuade them to launch an oral history project, donate their records to an archive (they are now at Hunter College), and allow a broad selection of them to be microfilmed.[3]

Since for me the Women's City Club represented a living link between Moskowitz's era and my own, I originally thought I would write its history. Although in the end I did not take that route, I used its records in my Moskowitz biography and in essays on women's political choices after suffrage, Eleanor Roosevelt's early political career, and New York women's campaigns for jury service. And so in a sense, the club, along with its sister organization, the New York City League of Women Voters (another postsuffrage group still in existence, whose fragile records are at Columbia University), played critical roles in bringing this book to life.

After a book has gestated for as long as this one has, it accumulates an enormous list of "helpers." It's easy to be oversentimental about them, but I am not holding back. My feelings are deep and I express them joyfully.

I must begin with Nancy Toff, senior history editor at Oxford University Press, who did not want to retire before she had "midwived" this book. She has stood by me all the way. Without her encouragement, help, and pressure, I doubt I would ever have finished. Thank you, Nancy. You are a treasure not only to me but also to the entire historical profession.

Research assistants are only as good as the instructions they receive. In my early days with this project its shapelessness meant I could not be precise. Even so, assistants compiled wonderful materials, and as my questions became more focused, what they found got better. I am grateful for all the work they did, mostly scrolling for needles in microfilm haystacks (a seasick-causing chore). Thank you, Randy Page, Stacy Braukman, Ann Vandevelde, Emily Walker, Paul Lubotina, Kris Smith, Jennifer Ann Price, Josh Sopiarz, and Jamie Schmidt Wagman.

Joshua Hideo Mather brings up the rear: by the time I hired him I knew exactly what I needed, and so his work was exemplary. Reference librarians and the Interlibrary Loan staff at Saint Louis University often got me the most obscure article or text in less than twenty-four hours. I am especially grateful to Jamie Emery and Miriam Joseph, who helped with searches and answered questions expeditiously and with patience.

Members of the Women's City Club have always been supportive. I appreciate their cooperation, invitations to speak, and participation in my thought processes as I tried to figure out how to approach this topic. The following stand out: Susan Alt, Stuart Buice, Anna Clark, June Farmer, Adele Filene, Edythe First, Carol Leimas, Elizabeth Lubetkin Lipton (our grandmothers were charter members and we are still in touch), Carole Lubin, Ethel Paley, Dorothy Fisch Thomas, Nina Untermyer, Blanche Lawton, Jacqueline Ebanks, and Marjorie Shea (also a League of Women Voters stalwart, who read early chapter drafts). Thank you, all, for your faith in me.

I was lucky enough to meet a few of the women who appear in this book or are relevant to its story: Eleanor Roosevelt (whose hand I shook after a speech she gave at Bard College when I was in my first year there and who spoke admiringly of Belle Moskowitz), Anna Rosenberg (who confirmed some anecdotes about Moskowitz), Caroline Klein Simon (still tall and elegant, and going daily to her office, where she was "of counsel," late into her nineties), Congresswoman Shirley Chisholm (serendipitously seated next to me on a flight from New York City to Buffalo), Eleanor Clark French (who entered Democratic Party politics in the 1950s, ran unsuccessfully for Congress in 1964, and during an afternoon encounter in her Manhattan home told me stories of her life in politics), and Ruth Messinger (then Manhattan borough president and a reader of my Moskowitz biography). In 1984 at the Vassar College celebration of Eleanor Roosevelt's centennial, someone said to me, "That's Pauli Murray!" I did not meet her but will never forget the sight of her thin, slight figure and penetrating gaze as she passed me by. I treasure my memories of these all-too-brief encounters.

Early research support for this project came from the Arthur and Elizabeth Schlesinger Library on the History of Women in America, the American Council of Learned Societies, and the Vanderbilt University Research Council. A Loewenstein-Weiner Fellowship in 2004 from the Jacob Rader Marcus Center of the American Jewish Archives facilitated my work in the Anna Moscowitz Kross papers. The center's Kevin Proffitt, Fred Krome, and Dorothy Smith were all especially welcoming and helpful. Other archivists and librarians who at various points led me in good directions include Lucinda Manning, Martha Foley, the Schlesinger Library's Eva Moseley, Pat King, and Sarah Hutcheon; all went the extra mile to find me the materials I was looking for, as did Linnea Anderson of the University of Minnesota Social Welfare Archives and Thai Jones of the Rare Books and Manuscripts Collection, Butler Library, Columbia University.

Many conversations with friends and colleagues convinced me the project was worth pursuing and sharpened my ideas about it. The list has grown unwieldy, but here it is, to the best of my memory: Kathryn Anderson, Jo Ann and Peter Argersinger, Gretchen Arnold, Joan Bertin, Randy Boehm, Charlotte Borst, Howard Brick, Carole Bucy, Eloise Buker, Miriam Cohen, Blanche Wiesen Cook, Nancy Cott, Kathleen Dalton, Roger and Judith Daniels, Anne Dean, Tom Dublin, Rebecca Edwards, Kathleen Farrell, Andrea Friedman, Lorri Glover, Susan Goodier, Susan Goodman, Ron Grele, Melanie Gustafson, Vivien Hart, Dirk Hartog, Amanda Izzo, Linda K. Kerber, Chuck and Anne Korr, Kriste Lindenmeyer, Marcia McCormick, Evelyn Meyer, Kristie Miller, Wynne Moskop, Robyn Muncy, Jill Norgren, Phyllis Palmer, Bill Paul, Elizabeth Payne, Daniel Prosterman, Mae Quinn, Lauren Saintangelo, Debra Schwartz, Dawn Scibilia, Marty and Sue Sherwin, Kathryn K. Sklar, Karen Manners Smith, Philippa Strum, Connie Wagner, Susan Ware, Penny Weiss, and Rafia Zafar. Special thanks go to my Women's and Gender Studies colleagues at Saint Louis University, and to Kitty Sklar, Jill Norgren, Marcia McCormick, Mae Quinn, Miriam Cohen, Susan Ware, and Linda Kerber for critiquing early chapter drafts and assuring me I had a story to tell.

My family. I begin with my late mother, Irma Commanday Bauman: as fraught as our relationship was, I must acknowledge she was a major source of this book. It was my husband, Lewis Perry, who first suggested I write a book about Moskowitz, but around the same time my mother alerted me to an excerpt from Robert Caro's forthcoming biography of public works builder Robert Moses that appeared in the *New Yorker* ("Your grandmother is in it!"). The excerpt, which described how "Mrs. M" fostered Moses's career, made me think I could (and should) undertake her biography, even though my late father had once told me, "No one can write about her because she didn't save her papers."[4] My mother then dug up the first resources I needed to start the research for the biography. My late stepfather, Mordecai Bauman, loved the idea of a follow-up book called "La Guardia's Women" ("It'll sell!"), a title I was then using as a fun shorthand but whose message was ambiguous and focused too much on "the man." Thanks to my cousin Ramah Commanday, who, when I answered her question "What is your book about?" said, "That has to be your first sentence!" And so it is. Family members who encouraged and read early drafts: my partner-historian, Lewis Perry (more on him in a moment); my son and other partner-historian, now also journalist, David Mordecai Perry: his insights were always honest, and his insistence I keep my eye on the ball was spot on; my brother, Michael Jozef Israels, in so many ways now my "life manager," faithful cheering section, and corrector of errors about the law and lawyers; my daughter, Susanna Perry Gilmore, who makes our hearts sing with her violin and love . . . you all played critical parts in the book's completion.

And then there's my "elective affinity group," who took such loving care of me during recent health crises: Anne Dean, "doula" extraordinaire, and Kathleen Farrell, who organized our lives. I don't know how we would have endured without you. You are in our hearts forever.

A special thanks to Lew, who through years of pillow, kitchen, and dog-walking talks kept telling me I could do it, I was the *only* person who could do it, and I'd better hurry up and just do it. I believed him, and here we are. Still.

## PEARL BERNSTEIN, A WOMAN IN NEW YORK POLITICS

Shortly before his inauguration as mayor in January 1934, Fiorello La Guardia asked Pearl Bernstein, a young woman then working for the New York City League of Women Voters, to come see him. She had voted for him but never met him before. Wasting no time, he asked her straight out: "How would you like to be Secretary of the Board of Estimate and Apportionment and Director of the Budget?" This was a new position he hoped would rationalize the board's chaotic budget procedures. "What they did," Bernstein recalled later, "was to put some figures together and then every week they would add or subtract or multiply or divide—and nobody knew in the middle of the year how much had been spent." The mayor chaired the board, but the borough presidents also submitted budgetary proposals, "and so it was a very unsatisfactory situation." The League of Women Voters, where Bernstein had worked for the previous seven years monitoring municipal affairs, had advocated the city's adoption of an executive budget prepared solely by the mayor. In the end she persuaded La Guardia to separate the two jobs he offered her, and because she knew nothing about accounting or budgets, she took the post of secretary. In January, the new board of estimate confirmed her appointment.[1]

Born in 1904, the eldest of six in a family that had come from Russian Poland in the 1870s, Bernstein grew up around Mount Morris Park in Harlem, then a predominantly Jewish section of Manhattan. Her attendance at Hunter College High School's annex at 108th Street and Amsterdam Avenue brought her into contact with a "bigger world" and helped her "blossom." Unlike most of her friends, who went to Hunter College to become teachers, Pearl won a Regents Scholarship to Barnard College. She graduated Phi Beta Kappa in 1925 with a degree in history and political science.

Her favorite Columbia University political science professor, Raymond Moley, asked her, "What do you want to do?" "Well, I'd like to get a job in some kind of civic or city work, some sort of government activity," she answered. At the end of the summer, one of Moley's colleagues, Joseph McGoldrick, recommended her for a three-month job at the Citizens Union, a nonpartisan reform organization, keeping track of its pamphlets and books during the 1925 mayoral campaign.[2] When that job ended she supported herself as a substitute teacher and volunteered at the League of Women Voters. Attorney Dorothy Strauss enlisted her to monitor legislation. Other league members—Agnes (Mrs. Henry Goddard) Leach and Caroline (Mrs. F. Louis) Slade—soon asked her to attend and report on board of estimate meetings. They donated her starting salary. When she first started going to city hall, she recalled,

> there were no women at all at the Board of Estimate Meetings or any of the
> other meetings that I attended and being a brash young woman and also
> knowing that I could get away with things that a man probably couldn't,
> I got up and asked for information that wasn't available and I wanted a
> copy of the city budget – and who had a copy of the city budget? Nobody
> had that – not even the members of the Board – but finally I got one and
> the League became quite respected grudgingly because of its knowledge
> of and interest in a non-partisan way in City affairs.[3]

Next thing she knew, the *New York Sunday World* was asking her to write a series of front-page articles on the city budget for its magazine. "Well, that set the League up no end," she concluded, and it "became quite a force in local political affairs."

In addition to coordinating the league's municipal affairs committee, Bernstein also joined the Women's City Club and Citizens Budget Commission. Then came the 1930–32 investigations led by Judge Samuel Seabury of corruption in city government. This "aroused everybody's interest," Bernstein said, and culminated in the determination of Fiorello La Guardia to run for mayor. She could not join his campaign, as she was holding a nonpartisan job, but whenever campaign staff asked for information she provided it. When the mayor-elect decided that the board of estimate needed an administrator, Bernstein's league mentors Agnes Leach and Caroline Slade, who had both contributed to his campaign, nominated her. Commenting on the paucity of women in government posts at that time, Bernstein said,

> there were very few women in local positions of responsibility at that time.
> And La Guardia was the first Mayor to really give women a very important

role in municipal affairs. He appointed quite a number of women to important posts ... and there were quite a number of women who were very close advisors of his.[4]

One was Republican Rosalie Loew Whitney, who according to Bernstein "nudged" La Guardia to appoint more women. That he appointed so many was "quite an advance over what took place previously."[5]

In 1938, after La Guardia had appointed several women to the board of higher education, one of them, Ruth Shoup, another league colleague, recommended Bernstein to direct the board's professional staff. Bernstein got the job. At the time, the city's four municipal colleges (Brooklyn, Queens, City, and Hunter) all had different standards and ways of doing business, including budgets. None issued annual reports or kept statistics on enrollments or expenditures. As "administrator of the board," Bernstein coordinated and systematized their affairs and regularized their faculty tenure system, which because of imprecise language had led to lawsuits. Other colleges later emulated the system, which she got incorporated into state law. As chair of a committee looking to the future, Bernstein became a critical guiding force in the creation of the City University of New York (CUNY). After 1957, she was its de facto chancellor until the board appointed a man to the post in 1960.[6] She retired in 1969.

Bernstein's career encapsulates this book's three themes: how women moved from a generally nonpartisan suffrage movement into partisan politics, sustained progressive agendas through conservative times, and were instrumental in the city's modernization. Bernstein's own sense of her place in the larger history of women's relationship to the city's government is also exemplary. In her remembrances she cites the Seabury investigation, La Guardia's decision to run for mayor, and women's support for him as critical signposts of women's increasing importance in city politics. Bernstein was in the vanguard of their rise. Though she never rose to the "top," she made lasting, and mostly unsung, contributions to the city's emergence as a modern metropolis. She was far from the only one.

# 1 PRECEDENTS

The American woman suffrage movement inspired women to take actions unprecedented for their sex. Starting in 1910, thousands of suffragists marched almost every year down city avenues carrying banners and signs demanding votes for women. The parades were huge successes, attracting publicity for the cause and millions of new supporters. A few years later, smaller bands of suffragists went even further into uncharted territory. They picketed the White House, seeking to embarrass President Woodrow Wilson for going to war to save democracy abroad while denying it to half his nation's citizens. In all kinds of weather, relays of picketers stood silently, holding aloft banners that asked such questions as, "MR. PRESIDENT, HOW LONG MUST WOMEN WAIT FOR LIBERTY?" Both parades and picketing had dark sides. The parades drew hostile onlookers who, unrestrained by police, heckled marchers and pelted them with stones. The picketers got even worse treatment. Arrested and convicted for "obstructing the sidewalk," they landed in the workhouse, where they endured brutal force-feedings and permanent damage to their health.

Marching and picketing were not the only actions suffragists undertook to win the vote. They also engaged in political action, much of it at state levels, where women had to persuade legislators—at the time all male—to pass resolutions to amend state constitutions removing the word "male" or "men" as a descriptor of voters. To do this, suffragists had to harness their local political processes. New York suffragists pioneered in perfecting a response to this challenge. Their methods not only turned the tide in New York State but also provided a model that suffragists in other states followed.

New York suffragists' political work demanded patience, persistence, and personal sacrifice. First they had to get state legislators to propose a state constitutional amendment to remove the word "male." Then they had to get the proposal reported out of the appropriate committees of both legislative houses and convince a majority of lawmakers to pass it. Before amendments could go to voters, state law required legislators to pass them again in their next consecutive session. Suffragists thus had to repeat the entire process the following year, after which they still had to persuade the state's voters to ratify the change. They came close in 1915, losing by fewer than two hundred thousand votes. Since state law required them to wait two years before trying again, they had to keep up their work through most of 1917. The state amendment finally passed that year by more than one hundred thousand votes statewide, with New York City tipping the balance. Because New York State had the highest number of Electoral College votes, this victory increased the pressure on Congress to approve a resolution in favor of national woman suffrage, the step that led to the ratification of the Nineteenth "Suffrage" Amendment to the US Constitution in 1920.

By the time of their state victory in 1917, New York suffragists had become experts in using politics to achieve their goal. They knew the strengths and weaknesses of the state's entire cast of political characters. They knew how to mine data to sharpen their rhetoric and master the complexities of the legislative process. They learned how to write propaganda, speak in public, and canvass registered voters, and received training in how to brave street-corner hecklers and enter unwelcoming neighborhoods without fear. Many among New York City's first generation of women voters, and most of its political activists, had either done this kind of work or knew someone who had.

The story of how New York City's women activists used the political process after 1917 begins with the suffrage movement itself. The movement produced the role models, tactical traditions, and personal networks of New York City women's subsequent political activism. It also set the fault lines that soon opened up in New York women's postsuffrage women's political culture.[1]

According to tradition, the New York State woman suffrage movement began in July 1848, when more than three hundred antislavery and temperance workers convened in Seneca Falls, New York, to discuss women's rights. Elizabeth Cady Stanton, a young Seneca Falls abolitionist, articulated a broad vision that called for "the sacred right of the elective franchise."[2] Over time, this call would become the movement's core demand.

Beginning in 1850, activists held almost annual women's rights conventions at local, state, and national levels. In 1851, Stanton met Susan Brownell Anthony, a teacher and antislavery and temperance worker from Rochester, New York. Forming a powerful political partnership, the two women were soon establishing activist traditions that postsuffrage women would continue. In 1854, they made the first appeal ever to a legislature for woman suffrage. The following year Anthony gave suffrage lectures in all sixty of New York State's counties. Later activists would travel repeatedly to Albany to testify before legislators. In addition, in the 1920s New York City activists (including Eleanor Roosevelt) would emulate Anthony's tours. In a series of trips they called Trooping for Democracy, Democratic women would visit every one of the state's counties on behalf of their party.

Stanton also launched the tradition of women entering political races, no matter how hopeless. After the Civil War, women's rights agitators expected Congress to enfranchise both former slaves and women. Stanton was so angered by Congress's decision to continue to define voters as "male" that when she moved to New York City she stood for Congress. Though no political party endorsed her and she received only twenty-four votes, as the nation's first female candidate for national office, her example may have inspired some of the city's future women office seekers, who also entered "hopeless" races if only to prove that they could.

New York suffragists also established a tradition of civil disobedience. Arguing that women, as US citizens, already had the right to vote, in the late 1860s and early 1870s, several hundred women across the country attempted to register to vote. Anthony's attempt to do so in Rochester got her arrested, and this action would inspire women to undergo arrest in defiance of laws they considered unjust. In that spirit, many New York women would later join the White House picketers and endure harsh imprisonment.

When the National American Woman Suffrage Association (NAWSA) was formed in 1890, it set up its base in New York City. The city would soon see the birth of many local suffrage organizations and become the state's chief hub for woman suffrage agitation. Also based in New York were multiple organizations founded to bring about social and economic reform. All of these organizations boasted prominent women founders, leaders, and members. Their activism fed the suffrage movement with ideas about how to harness the political process to bring about women's right to vote.

Though based upstate, the New York temperance movement is an early example of one such organization. The quest for temperance in the consumption of alcoholic beverages was the most popular reform movement at the turn of the twentieth century. New York's movement had taken on new life in the 1870s, when health reformer Diocletian Lewis persuaded women to breach the doors of local saloons and hold prayer vigils. After women in Fredonia organized vigils, women elsewhere in the state followed suit. In fall 1874, temperance workers in Syracuse formed the Woman's Christian Temperance Union of the State of New York. By 1894, it had twenty-two thousand members.

The state temperance movement resorted to political methods that later women political activists would draw upon. Using "memorial, petition, and protest," New York temperance workers appealed to legislative bodies, asking them to enact new laws or better enforce old ones.[3] They accumulated victories important to them, such as a requirement that teachers include "scientific" temperance instruction in school curricula (1884); prohibitions against alcohol on fairgrounds (1886); raising the age of consent for girls from ten to sixteen (1887); and the use of police matrons and separate houses of detention for women in cities of over twenty-five thousand (1888). In 1891 their protests against a bill to legalize prostitution forced legislators who had proposed the bill to withdraw it. Some of their initiatives failed. An 1890 ban on tobacco sales to children under sixteen was never enforced. They never won a requirement that a majority of adult male and female residents approve liquor licenses proposed by specific localities. The union supported suffragists' quest for women's right to vote for school officers: a school suffrage law passed in 1880 but after many challenges in 1893 was ruled unconstitutional. Most disappointing, despite having received thousands of signatures for prohibition and woman suffrage, the New York State constitutional convention of 1894 failed to approve either.[4]

Despite these setbacks, by 1900 the state's temperance organization was fully invested in women's political empowerment. As early as 1876, it urged members to support only "total abstinence candidates." In 1884 it followed its national leader Frances Willard in formally endorsing the Prohibition Party. The next year, New York's temperance leader, Mary Towne Burt, commanded her followers to pledge "our influence to that party, by whatever name called, which shall furnish us the best embodiment of prohibition principles, and will most surely protect our homes," a goal that anticipated by a decade the national temperance movement's adoption of "Home Protection" as its motto. Burt observed that, "distasteful though the word 'politics' may be to many in connection with our work, we can none of us ignore the fact that the strength of the saloon system, which is an open menace to our homes, is vested in political power." The temperance workers who, inspired by Burt, later ran for public office were rarely successful, but their races demonstrated powerful links between nineteenth-century temperance movements and women's later pursuit of government office.[5]

The temperance movement was only one aspect of a larger political ferment at the turn of the twentieth century. In the latter 1800s, women were deeply involved in four overlapping reform efforts—the social settlement, labor, consumer, and municipal reform movements. The nation's rapid industrial growth after the Civil War had created a raft of social and economic ills. Male and female workers of all ages toiled in unsafe, exploitative conditions. Cyclical economic downturns brought periods of mass unemployment and widespread misery, punctuated by violent national strikes. Cities, in many cases led by the corrupt or incompetent, were increasingly overcrowded and unhealthy. Unregulated corporate monopolies were depleting the nation's natural resources. In response, a growing number of social critics, including many women, began arguing for more government protection of the nation's human and natural resources. Although they did not agree on all the specifics, these "progressives," as they began to call themselves, sought such reforms as government regulation of industrial workplaces and the environment, an end to child labor, the legalization of labor unions, the professionalization of government bureaucracies, and public control over essential city services.

New York City had a large population of vulnerable residents. The 1898 consolidation of its five boroughs—Manhattan, the Bronx, Brooklyn, Staten Island, and Queens—brought almost 3.5 million people under one government. Thirty-seven percent of its population was foreign born. Ten years later, the foreign-born had grown to 40.8 percent and the general population to almost 5 million, with almost half in Manhattan alone. By 1900, the city employed 11 percent of the nation's factory workers producing nondurable consumer goods such as clothing, printed materials, and textiles. Most of these workers were recent immigrants working in low-wage, unsafe factories and sweatshops and living in equally unsafe tenements. These conditions made the city a hub for social and economic reform movements in which the woman's vote was seen as central.

Settlements—inhabited at first by university students who "settled" into working-class neighborhoods to learn about the poor—appeared in London in the 1880s. The first American settlement was Lower Manhattan's Neighborhood Guild (later, the University Settlement), founded by an Amherst College graduate in 1886. Women quickly founded their own settlements and came to be powerful leaders in the settlement movement. In New York City, Lillian Wald, a graduate of the New York Hospital Training School for Nurses, founded the Nurses' (later, Henry Street) Settlement on New York's Lower East Side in 1893. Her colleague, New York's Greenwich House founder Mary Kingsbury Simkhovitch, described settlements as "not a mission, not a school, not a charity, but a group of persons living a common life, learning the meaning of life by which they are surrounded, interpreting this life to others and acting on what they have learned." Both Wald and Simkhovitch were active suffragists and, in the postsuffrage era, campaigned for partisan candidates and progressive reforms. They also inspired colleagues to run for office. Wald explained that she originally thought politics "concerned itself with matters outside [women's] realm and experience." As she became involved in community work she realized that she was "really in politics." Simkhovitch came to politics through the woman suffrage campaign, which showed her "that politics as such—that is, the bringing to pass of social change through the activities of legislators and court decisions . . . was a practical responsibility" she had to undertake. Simkhovitch testified frequently before governing bodies, served on and led multiple committees and commissions, and in 1937 ran for office.[6]

Women had long been leaders in the labor movement. The Women's Trade Union League (WTUL), founded in 1903 by unionists, socialists, and settlement leaders, was the first organization to focus on unionizing women. Financed by so-called allies, or pro-union women of means, the WTUL supported New York City women garment workers during their massive strikes of 1909–11, marching with them, bailing them out of jail, and paying for their lawyers. When the horrendous 1911 Triangle Shirtwaist Factory fire took the lives of 146 garment workers, most of them young women, the WTUL was at the forefront of agitation for factory reform. The WTUL pushed hard for woman suffrage. Its leaders, who included union women Rose Schneiderman and Maud Swartz and their ally Mary Elisabeth Dreier, all became influential city political figures in the postsuffrage era. The Women's Trade Union League would remain a leader in agitation for protective labor legislation throughout the mid-twentieth century.

The consumer movement was closely linked to the labor movement. It began in 1888, when Leonora O'Reilly, a New York garment worker, appealed to philanthropist Josephine Shaw Lowell and suffragist Maud Nathan to help improve women's working conditions in factories. They set up a committee, in 1890 renamed the Consumers' League of New York, to convince shoppers to patronize only those employers who treated workers fairly. After consumer advocates founded similar leagues in other cities, in 1899 a National Consumers' League (NCL) formed in New York City, with industrial reformer Florence Kelley as general secretary. The NCL drew up "white lists" of decent employers, who were then allowed to display labels showing league approval, a tactic some labor unions later adopted. Kelley eventually moved the NCL to support a legislative approach, lobbying for laws legalizing minimum wages, limits on work hours, and bans on child labor. Like the settlements and the Women's Trade Union League, the NCL gave major support to woman suffrage and launched many women, most notably Frances Perkins, Mary (Molly) Dewson, and Elinore Morehouse Herrick, into national political careers. It would join the WTUL and other women's voluntary associations in continuing to work for protective labor legislation for women and children in the industrial workforce.

Women participants in the city's municipal reform movements also contributed political experience to the suffrage movement. During the 1890s, the city's Republicans and dissident Democrats were determined to wrest control of local government from Tammany Hall, the powerful political machine that had become synonymous with the city's Democratic Party. After the Civil War, Tammany members enriched themselves by collecting graft on contracts to serve the city's growing population. Tammany sank deep roots into the city's immigrant communities by providing informal welfare to distressed families and support for cheap entertainments, such as saloons, dance halls, gambling houses, and brothels. In return, immigrants supported Tammany with their votes.

Middle- and upper-class women became fixtures in anti-Tammany campaigns. They formed associations, such as a "ladies committee" that raised money for the cause, and independent groups, such as the Woman's Health Protective Association of Brooklyn (WHPA), organized in 1890 to keep streets clean and health laws enforced. In 1893 the WHPA's founder and president, Ellen Hastings Scrimgeour, announced "it was time women's influence was felt in municipal affairs." Campaigning for Brooklyn Republican mayoral candidate Charles A. Schieren, the WHPA distributed eight thousand copies of an *Appeal to Voters* asking women to "arouse indifferent citizens to a sense of their duty as voters." Schieren won. A few years later, the *New York Times* referred to the WHPA as a "power," saying, "There is nothing it will not undertake, from the disposition of political questions to the disposal of garbage."[7]

Worried about being criticized for interfering in city politics—still an exclusively male sphere—some women municipal reformers denied they were interested in suffrage. A Woman's Municipal Purity Auxiliary led by philanthropist Josephine Shaw Lowell promised to avoid all discussion of votes for women in her campaigns for reformer William L. Strong, who ran for Manhattan mayor in 1894. This stance must have mollified the city's antisuffrage male voters, as Strong won.

Renamed the Woman's Municipal League, Lowell's auxiliary produced a sixteen-page pamphlet, *Facts for Fathers and Mothers*, in support of Columbia University president Seth Low's 1901 mayoral campaign. The league distributed 900,000 copies of the pamphlet, which accused Tammany of protecting young men (called "cadets"), who lured women into prostitution. A political cartoonist depicted the league's campaign as a giant "Motherhood of New York," sweeping away Tammany, brothels, corrupt police, and the "spoils system" that awarded government jobs to party loyalists regardless of qualifications.

In 1905 the league backed antivice independent William Travers Jerome, then seeking re-election as district attorney, by distributing 350,000 copies of *Why New York Women Stand Back of Jerome*. It also set up a pro-Jerome committee led by consumer activist Maud Nathan, settlement leaders Lillian Wald and Mary Simkhovitch, Women's Trade Union League leader Margaret Dreier, and social worker Frances Kellor, all future New York political leaders. This committee waged a campaign with, as a *New York Herald* reporter put it, the "forethought of a political party," issuing a huge amount of campaign literature and plastering the city with posters. At the same time as some anti-Tammany women felt they needed to calm fears of women voting, others were functioning as political actors fully conscious of their potential for power.[8]

In addition to their work in reform movements, in this period women were also engaged in direct political party work. Since 1892, for example, New Yorker Helen Varick Boswell had been hiring women speakers for mass Republican Party meetings. After Strong's victory, Boswell formed women's Republican clubs in New York, such as the West End Woman's Republican Association. In 1897, when the newly consolidated city of New York was getting ready to elect its first mayor for the five boroughs, Strong declined to run, whereupon municipal reformers formed the Citizens Union and drafted independent Republican Seth Low as their candidate. Since Low opposed woman suffrage (as well as women's higher education), the association campaigned for a rival, Benjamin F. Tracy. The result was a divided Republican vote that gave victory to Tammany's Robert A. Van Wyck. His two-year term was so corrupt that in 1901 Republican women set aside their misgivings about Low's antisuffrage stand and campaigned for him. Their canvassing in Tammany districts, where Republican men would have been unwelcome, helped Low squeak to victory.[9]

Democratic Party women were less well organized. Tammany officials' wives would campaign for their husbands, but a woman's Democratic club was not founded until 1905. Its founder, Nellie Fassett Crosby, was an unorthodox Democrat who believed in Henry George's "single tax" movement yet wanted Democrats elected. In 1906 her club of eighty members endorsed William Randolph Hearst for governor and in 1908 raised money for William Jennings Bryan. Unlike the municipal reformers, Crosby openly endorsed woman suffrage.[10]

The lesson some members of the public learned from women's campaign work in this era was that women's political activity did not destroy the social fabric. Journalist and municipal reformer Oswald Garrison Villard made this point in 1902, when he spoke to the National American Woman Suffrage Association about women's work for Seth Low. He noted that "extremely interesting changes in the attitude of the New York public towards women in politics" had taken place. "Twenty-five years ago such a thing as a woman's headquarters distributing pamphlets, raising money, getting up meetings, supplying speakers, and furnishing one of the most effective arguments of the entire campaign, would have aroused . . . announcements that . . . the unsexing or . . . masculinization of women was at hand." In 1894, he went on, many still thought women should not concern themselves with the city's political conditions; in 1897, the Citizens Union welcomed women, albeit still treating them as "curiosities"; by 1901, women's participation in the battle against Tammany had become a "matter of course [and] the most public-spirited women in New York believe that they are in politics to stay."[11] By the time the New York suffrage movement was ready to be more deeply involved in the political process, these activists were well supplied with techniques, ideas, and leaders.

Participation in social and economic reform movements, municipal reform, and party politics all provided women with groundbreaking opportunities for leadership. But it was the emergence of new leaders in the early 1900s that completed the suffrage movement's "political turn." These leaders would model their methods on those used, in the past, only by men. Some of these new leaders came out of traditional, white, upper-middle and upper-class backgrounds; others represented more marginalized groups, including middle-class African Americans and white working women.

For African Americans, ending lynching and racial discrimination in employment took precedence over woman suffrage, but in the late 1880s black women in New York City began to organize for the vote. Brooklyn's Sarah J. Smith Tompkins Garnet, the city's first African American female school principal, founded an Equal Suffrage League. In the early 1900s, as superintendent of the Suffrage Department of the National Association of Colored Women (NACW), she sought to erase the discriminatory treatment of "colored" teachers and championed equal pay for women. Inspired by antilynching crusader Ida B. Wells's New York City speaking tour, Victoria Earle Matthews, a journalist for the *New York Age*, cofounded the Woman's Loyal Union and helped collect ten thousand signatures for woman suffrage. Frances Reynolds Keyser, the first president of the Empire State Federation of Women's Clubs, founded in 1908 and then affiliated with the NACW, also campaigned for women's full citizenship rights. Keyser, a Hunter College graduate, was superintendent of the White Rose Home, which Matthews had founded in 1897 to assist young black women new to the city. She was also a board member of the YWCA and a founding member of the National Association for the Advancement of Colored People (NAACP).[12] Their actions laid a foundation for New York black women's suffrage and postsuffrage political work, especially in Brooklyn and Harlem.

Other new leaders included society women, whose wealth funded the movement. In 1905 Katherine Duer Mackay had run for the school board in Roslyn, Long Island; won; and served on the board until 1910. In 1908 she started an Equal Franchise Society, decorated a Manhattan office to resemble a French drawing room, and invited her society friends to hear woman suffrage lectures. Socialite Alva Belmont brought both money and organizational skills to the cause. She financed the National American Woman Suffrage Association's state and national headquarters, as well as a press bureau and eleven branches of the Political Equality League charged with recruiting young working women, including African Americans. After meeting with Belmont in January 1910, Sarah Garnet and Irena Moorman (later, Blackstone), president of the Negro Women's

Business League, brought more than a hundred new members into Belmont's league. Socialists rebuffed Belmont's offers of funding because of its links to capitalist exploitation.[13]

Most important for the movement's political turn, Harriot Stanton Blatch, one of Elizabeth Cady Stanton's daughters, entered the campaign. Born in 1856, Harriot Stanton grew up in a household where politics was "the breath of my nostrils." After graduating from Vassar College in 1878, she traveled in Europe as a tutor until 1882, when her mother called her home to help her and Anthony prepare the second volume of their monumental *History of Woman Suffrage*, a compendium of hundreds of suffrage documents. On the ship home she met English businessman William Henry Blatch, whom she later married. Living outside London for two decades, she bore two daughters, studied working women in English villages, and was active in suffrage and social reform.[14]

In 1902 her husband retired and Blatch brought her family home. She found the New York suffrage movement "in a rut." To revive it, she urged the recruitment of working women, street actions, and the targeting of specific politicians to act on a state constitutional amendment. She began this work herself, using her contacts in the Women's Trade Union League to reach out to wage-earning women. In 1907 she brought some forty professional friends into the Equality League of Self-Supporting Women, the goal of which, Blatch said, was to "guide the suffrage ship into political channels." Many early members of the league would later enter politics either as activists, candidates for office, or government officials.[15]

Charging a one-time membership fee of twenty-five cents, the league soon had nineteen thousand members. One of its first acts was to follow in Blatch's mother's footsteps by testifying at a legislative hearing on the amendment. Blatch took garment workers Mary Duffy and Clara Silver to Albany to explain to legislators how women's political rights would deter men from mistreating them in the workplace. On Election Day, league members in decorated automobiles bore down on the polls, distributing literature and making speeches. In 1908, after celebrating the sixtieth anniversary of the Seneca Falls convention, Blatch and a colleague traveled by trolley from Seneca Falls to Poughkeepsie, stopping for open-air meetings in each town along the way. Back in New York City, league workers catalogued the membership according to political districts, a step that presaged the suffrage movement's final political turn.[16]

Meanwhile, the league's profile was rising. In October 1909 it sponsored a highly publicized visit of Emmeline Pankhurst, the charismatic leader of England's Women's Social and Political Union (WSPU). Representing militant suffragettes, as English suffrage workers were called, the WSPU performed "deeds," some law-breaking, to embarrass a government that refused to take their demands seriously. Many American suffragists disapproved; Katherine Mackay, for one, declined to attend Pankhurst's speech. Blatch recalled that Pankhurst's audience, at first unsympathetic, was charmed by this "slight woman with curly, graying hair, dressed in soft violet . . . looking as if she were ready to pour a cup of tea in an English vicarage."[17] The league also won positive publicity from poll watching. After attorney Bertha Rembaugh, the league's legal adviser (and later one of the city's earliest candidates for elective office), discovered that no law forbade women from poll watching, in 1909 the league sent five members to watch. In the 1910 primaries, twenty-five members watched. The police arrested some of them but because they were legal had to let them go. Newspapers loved the story, and by the November elections women poll watchers were accepted as normal.[18]

"What could be more stirring than hundreds of women, carrying banners, marching—marching—marching!" wrote Harriot Blatch, recalling the May 21, 1910, New York City suffrage parade, the nation's first major women's march. When news broke of the plan, both national and state suffrage associations warned that a parade would harm the movement. It did not. Despite rain and hecklers, thousands of New York women marched, banners held high. For Blatch's Equality League, which that fall saluted Pankhurst's organization by changing its name to the Women's Political Union (WPU), the only disappointment was that some suffragists rode in automobiles. In the future, Blatch decreed, with the exception of women riding horseback, all marchers would use "their own two feet."[19]

The WPU now expanded its political work. Katherine Mackay financed a WPU headquarters in Albany, as well as the salaries of Caroline Lexow as executive secretary and Hattie Graham as lobbyist. After Graham tallied how few legislators favored woman suffrage, Blatch got prominent women to show their representatives the number of citizens in their districts who approved of suffrage.[20] In the fall 1910 election campaign, the WPU targeted antisuffrage legislators. Despite the WPU's campaign against Republican assemblyman Artemas Ward Jr., he won, but only by 260 votes. In 1911 it went after Democratic assemblyman Louis A. Cuvillier. On Election Day teams hung fifteen thousand "Votes for Women" banners across the city, distributed copies of its publication *The Woman Voter* to newsstands, and formed "flying squadrons" of women in automobiles to spread the suffrage message. Cuvillier won, but another arch-enemy of woman suffrage, Brooklyn Democrat George F. Carew, lost.[21]

By 1912, six western states had enfranchised women. To make more progress in New York, suffragists formed a cooperative committee that hired Montana suffragist Jeannette Rankin as a paid Albany lobbyist. On March 12, the WPU brought three hundred determined members to Albany to prod pro tem senate president Robert F. Wagner, a Democrat, to bring the suffrage resolution to the floor. Trapped by a crowd of women in a committee room, he gave in.

Marshaling its forces for a March 19 floor vote, suffrage opponents argued that women's highest duty was to "motherhood," not the "wicked world" of business and politics. Proponents ridiculed such views, citing the growing number of women earning wages. From the gallery, Blatch and her cohort sent down a stream of notes containing advice on how to proceed. In the end, suffrage lost, but by fewer votes than before. The assembly debated the resolution the same day and also voted it down. Disappointed, the WPU regrouped, holding a mass meeting in New York City's Cooper Union the following day and a parade of ten thousand on May 4.[22]

A brash young suffragist, Rosalie Gardiner Jones, then added a new spectacle to the movement. Born in 1883 into a family of prominent Long Island landowners, Jones graduated from Adelphi College and then visited England, where she became a militant suffragist. Upon her return in 1912, she took over the presidency of the Nassau County suffrage association. She teamed up with British-born Elisabeth Freeman to travel around Long Island in a horse-drawn wagon painted "suffrage yellow" and decorated with flags and banners. Then she organized a "hike" to Albany that garnered tremendous publicity. On December 16, two hundred women carrying Boy Scout–type knapsacks and wooden staffs gathered at the end of the subway line in the Bronx and set off. Followers dubbed Jones the "General" and her assistants Ida Craft "Colonel," Katharine Stiles "Corporal," and Lavinia Dock (or "Little Doc Dock," a nurse and mentor to Lillian Wald) "Surgeon General." When asked how they were holding up, hiker Jessie Hardy Stubbs said their effort paled in comparison with the daily treks of women industrial workers, forced to stay on their feet twelve to fourteen hours a day. After almost two weeks of walking 170 miles in winter weather, by the end only five marchers had stayed the full course, but crowds greeted them in every town and in Albany Governor-Elect William Sulzer promised to help their cause, which he did.[23]

Urged by the governor, on January 23, 1913, the senate passed the suffrage resolution by a vote of forty to two. The assembly passed it with only five against. At the same time as Blatch celebrated this result, she worried about the timing. The resolution would have to be repassed the next year and then go before the voters in 1915, when a constitutional convention would take place. Blatch feared that voters, having to consider both a new constitution *and* woman suffrage, would lose sight of the latter. Her fears were well founded.

The Women's Political Union now focused on keeping voters aware of the upcoming vote. It started a semimonthly newspaper, *Women's Political World*, an eight-page sheet with a cartoon on the first page, a format that later women's publications would emulate. The WPU also started mixed-class balls and theater parties and mounted more parades. The latter were now national events. In 1913 Blatch assisted militant suffragists Alice Paul and Lucy Burns, soon to become national figures, in putting on their spectacular March 3, 1913, parade, held in Washington, DC, on the eve of President Woodrow Wilson's inauguration.

New Yorkers, including attorney Crystal Eastman Benedict, helped raise money for the Washington parade. The Women's Political Union sent seventy-five delegates. Rosalie Gardiner Jones organized a second suffrage hike, this time to Washington, planning to present a petition to President-Elect Wilson. On February 12, she mustered an "army of the Potomac," dressed in long, brown, hooded cloaks to evoke images of the pilgrims. Though their numbers soon dwindled, a steady stream of publicity followed. In the end, fourteen suffragists (including some men) marched almost three hundred miles. The flamboyant Jones would remain a memorable figure in the New York City suffrage legacy.[24]

New York suffragists followed up the Washington march with their own massive procession on May 3. Inez Milholland, who carried an American flag on horseback at the head of the parade, became a dramatic icon of the movement. The Women's Political Union gained greater visibility with new offices on West Forty-Second Street opposite the great New York Public Library. Over the summer it reached across the state, sending out speakers and opening up new branches. Paul and Burns asked Blatch to come work with them, but for the time being Blatch stuck to her goal of first winning a New York victory.[25]

A herculean effort went into the 1915 New York State suffrage referendum. In the process, the political techniques of the woman suffrage movement developed further. An organization founded by Carrie Chapman Catt played a major role in the movement's final political turn. Born in Wisconsin in 1859, Catt grew up in Iowa and then worked as a newspaper reporter, teacher, and school administrator. In the late 1880s she honed her skills as a suffrage organizer, in 1900 succeeding Susan B. Anthony as president of the National American Woman Suffrage Association. By 1907, she was in New York, where she took over the Interurban Woman Suffrage Council, a group that coordinated the city's suffrage organizations. She then conceived of a woman suffrage "party" constructed along the lines of Tammany Hall. Tammany had a boss at the top and district leaders who got out the vote at election time. The city then had 63 assembly districts (ADs) and 2,217 election districts (EDs). After locating suffragists in as many of these districts as possible, Catt had them elect delegates to a city-wide convention. On October 29, 1909, 804 delegates and 200 alternates met at Carnegie Hall, where they formed the Woman Suffrage Party of Greater New York (WSP). An elected board of officers appointed a leader for each AD and a captain for each ED, charging them with raising suffrage to the "status of an acknowledged political issue."[26]

The Woman Suffrage Party started out with a membership of twenty thousand; by 1917 it had more than five hundred thousand. Its various departments issued daily bulletins, held press parties, and printed literature. After the 1910 election, members made detailed maps and surveys of each ED; organized mothers, school, church, and street meetings; and distributed "rainbow fliers" (printed in ten colors and seven languages) containing Catt's "suffrage evangel" in large print and simple terms. They held occasional mass meetings in Carnegie Hall or Cooper Union, and raised money with bazaars, rummage sales, teas, theater parties, plays, picnics, card parties, and dances. A suffrage school taught workers the new methods. So "unquestioned became the results of the system," Catt claimed, "that students attended from twenty-eight states."[27]

Catt's system gave birth to a capstone document in the New York suffrage campaign's political transformation: *Organizing to Win by the Political District Plan* (1914). Its author, Harriet Burton Laidlaw, had grown up in Albany, worked as a teacher, and graduated from Barnard College in 1902. In 1905 she married banker James Lees Laidlaw (he would later lead the Men's League for Woman Suffrage) and in 1909 became chair of the Manhattan division of the Woman Suffrage Party. Her *Organizing to Win* offered thirty-five pages of precise instructions on how to win legislative approval for woman suffrage.[28]

Laidlaw structured her handbook around five areas of work: political, legislative, propaganda, education for civic life, and reform. Political work, she wrote, entails walking "step by step" with the dominant political parties. At every meeting, suffragists must deliver an "undeviating demand for the submission of the woman suffrage amendment to the voters." They need to get into district party "designation" meetings that nominate candidates and then insist on prosuffrage pledges from all nominees. In the legislative arena, state suffrage societies need to agree on which legislators should introduce a suffrage bill, hiring a legislative agent ("some earnest woman"). This agent should be friendly with the bill's introducers and a "student of the political combinations and of the whole legislative procedure"; she must always be at the state capital, keeping track of everything, even gossip. Finally, suffragists must keep the bill from dying in committee, get it reported out, and then get it placed favorably for prompt first and second readings.

On propaganda work, Laidlaw advised ingenuity, suggesting events from silly to serious, from "votes for women dog and cat shows" to exploiting holidays to get attention and raise money. Remember, she wrote, "no time or place can detract from the dignity of the cause as long as the suffragist who represents it is dignified, gracious, tactful and earnest." Participating in a suffrage party is "education for civic life," she continued. It trains women in a "real" (not theoretical) democracy, fostering in them an ethical development and a desire to relieve oppression. In sum, it makes women good citizens, "vital factors in the world life of to-day."

How far should suffrage organizations pursue social reforms? While stressing "that the Woman Suffrage Party must keep free of all political alliances," Laidlaw admitted it cannot ignore the day's burning questions. Suffrage organizations need to sympathize with union rights, an end to child labor, suppression of smoke nuisances, improving police protection, reforming criminal courts and prisons, and abolition of "White Slave" (forced prostitution) traffic. She ended the handbook with a list of goals suffragists could win if they had the vote: equal pay for equal work, a minimum wage, shorter work hours, steady employment, better housing, women judges and magistrates, and extensive public recreation.

Laidlaw's handbook marked the peak of suffragists' efforts to politicize their campaign. By laying out the concrete steps any participant could take to win, it gave specific direction to Blatch's vision of guiding "the suffrage ship into political channels." In addition, it solidified the links between suffrage and the progressive reforms that the first generation of postsuffrage New York women activists would continue to pursue. Finally, it highlighted the first major challenge these activists would have to face once they could vote: shaping their relationship with political parties. Early on in the handbook Laidlaw used boldface to enjoin a suffrage party "never [to] work for a candidate nor ally itself with any political party or organization." She did not need to explain this injunction, as most suffragists disdained political parties. But enfranchised women would soon realize they would have to come to terms with partisanship. For them, the learning curve would be steep.

As plans for the 1915 New York State constitutional convention went forward, Lillian Wald led a committee to urge political parties to nominate women as at-large delegates. Single-mindedly focused on the referendum, Harriot Blatch opposed this step, sure that a women's campaign for seats would only distract from the referendum. Although a few women ran, none were elected, but they established a precedent for New York women to keep trying.

Throughout the summer of 1914, suffragists held demonstrations and mass meetings, buttonholed legislators across the state, and won prosuffrage planks at the Progressive, Republican, and Democratic state party conventions. In February 1915 the legislature passed the suffrage resolution the required second time, this time without dissent. The statewide vote was set for November. In June, Blatch's Women's Political Union carried a "Torch of Liberty" by automobile from Montauk Point to Buffalo, and in the fall commemorated the hundredth anniversary of Elizabeth Cady Stanton's birth. As Election Day neared, all the suffrage organizations marched. On the day itself, more than six thousand women were poll watchers.

The Woman Suffrage Party was also busy. After dividing the state into twelve campaign districts, Catt took charge of the state campaign and named Mary Garrett Hay as New York City chair. Soon called "Suffrage Big Boss" (a nod to Tammany's "bosses"), Hay had grown up in an Indiana doctor's Republican family and become a suffragist. She directed her followers to identify voters in every possible profession, craft, or job—from barbers to firemen, street cleaners to bankers, factory workers to clergy—and to create special days for each group. When Lyda D. Newman opened a Negro suffrage headquarters in Manhattan, Hay sent Dr. Mary Halton and Portia Willis to represent the WSP. With the goal of keeping woman suffrage before the public "every hour of every day," the WSP organized rallies for Irish, Syrian, Italian, and Polish populations and held bonfires, torchlight processions, street dances, concerts, theatrical events, hikes, and automobile tours. Hay sent hundreds of canvassers to make personal appeals in tenement shops, factories, banks, restaurants, department stores, and office buildings. Beginning in January, the WSP under Hay's direction held 60 district conventions, 170 canvassing suppers, 4 mass meetings, 27 canvassing conferences, and a Carnegie Hall convention. By Election Day, it had canvassed almost 400,000 male voters and more than 60,000 women; printed and distributed almost 3 million leaflets; held over 5,000 outdoor meetings, 660 indoor meetings, and 93 mass meetings; provided 80 newspapers (English and foreign) with news; and gotten clergy to preach 64 prosuffrage sermons.[29]

Oreola Williams Haskell, head of the party's press bureau, fictionalized these activities in her short story "Suffrage Switchboard." Written in the voice of a telephone operator, the story describes a hectic day at party headquarters. When a friend asks the operator to go out to lunch, she says she does not have time. "Why not?" he asks. She replies that an endless stream of questions keeps her too busy. Caller: "Why haven't I received literature yet?" Operator: "You're at the end of the alphabet." Caller: "Can you get me a speaker for my next event?" Operator: "Soap box or hall?" Caller: "Will voting give women so much liberty that they'll drink more cocktails, or refuse to sew on a man's suspender buttons?" The operator ignored that question. Caller: "[Don't] only a minority of women want the vote?" Operator: "We've got the names and addresses of one million.... Yes, you can come here and look at them," and it will take a week to get through them. Caller: "Suffs are unsexed!" The operator warns the caller against reviling a million women, including perhaps the caller's own mother or wife.

The story continued by describing the spirit of Hay's party. She ran it like an army. Because every worker believed so deeply in the cause, none disobeyed a command. They worked overtime without complaint, on one night sending out five thousand letters, on another a hundred thousand pamphlets. The telephone operator herself took a public speaking class, using her lessons to squelch a heckler at a meeting. She reported that "Some of our street speakers, why they can only yell in a whisper now." But the "time has passed for women to be doormats for politicians," she asserts. Women are taxed, "legislated for and against," and suffer from bad laws and conditions, so "haven't we a stake in the government the same as men? Sure we have."[30]

On November 2, both the suffrage resolution and a new constitution went to the voters. Because the constitution contained features on government reorganization, apportionment, and home rule that Democrats opposed, Tammany urged its defeat. Woman suffrage went down with it. Although more than 500,000 voters approved suffrage, the amendment lost by 194,984 votes. Tammany "swamped us," Blatch recalled, and thereafter gave up on New York. On January 28, 1916, the board of the Women's Political Union voted unanimously to amalgamate with Alice Paul's new organization, the Congressional Union, and from then on to work only for the federal amendment in Washington, DC.[31]

The Woman Suffrage Party stuck with the New York fight. Workers at its headquarters wept, but vowed not to surrender. Their leaders fired them up anew. After midnight women from the state and city party organizations flooded a public square for a rally. At an overflow meeting at Cooper Union two days later, they raised $100,000 for a new campaign. When in March 1916 the legislature voted to resubmit the amendment, suffragists representing all sixty-three New York City assembly districts took trains to Albany to ensure a positive vote. It passed, with ten nays in the assembly, seven in the senate.

The Woman Suffrage Party opened its 1917 state referendum campaign in March. Not everything went smoothly. As the United States anticipated entering the Great War, fault lines opened up over "war preparedness." In February, pacifists, including Elinor Byrns, who would later be among the first New York women to run for Congress, resigned their suffrage party offices in protest. A rift also opened up over the White House picketing actions of Alice Paul's newest organization, the National Woman's Party. Calling the picketing "foolish and unpatriotic," Mary Garrett Hay dissociated her party from picketing. It disturbed her, she wrote to the *New York Tribune*, that the actions of "a misguided minority," a "few militant women who in no wise represent the great army of working suffragists, should have the power to cause discredit" of suffragists. At the party's August state convention in Saratoga, with the sole dissent of labor leader Rose Schneiderman, who could never condemn a picketer, WSP leaders unanimously passed a resolution rebuking the picketers for harassing the nation "in its time of great stress."[32]

Tensions also arose between the Woman Suffrage Party and black suffragists, who felt slighted in Saratoga and called for a separate suffrage movement. Annie K. Lewis, then president of the Colored Women's Suffrage Club of New York

City, denied that any discrimination had taken place. Insisting that the New York WSP "is one of the most democratic organizations in town," she noted that its membership included "women from every class of society and from every nationality." A white WSP leader then addressed Lewis's club, explaining that, as the party had abandoned the idea of being a mere "union of clubs," Lewis's followers need only elect leaders according to the party's rules and they would be fully integrated. The following week, Lewis resigned as her club's president and won election as a WSP vice leader for the Nineteenth AD.[33] African American women would be in the suffrage fight to stay.

The WSP forged on. By September it had collected almost a million signatures to prove that women wanted the vote. It revived its attention-getting stunts, including *tableaux vivants* (or "Walkless Parades") in public parks, billboard-wearing riders on subways, and white-haired ladies playing hurdy-gurdies and then making suffrage speeches. The party distributed more than two million leaflets in several languages and trained thousands of poll watchers. "Big Boss" Hay kept a "Suffrage Book" on her desk that detailed political conditions: vote tallies in 1915 and 1916 for every district, how individual male leaders voted, and which districts were strong, lukewarm, or opposed. In a final huge parade on October 27, twenty thousand marched from Washington Square to Fifty-Ninth Street, some carrying banners repudiating the National Woman's Party's "unpatriotic" picketers. The *Times* reported that uptowners applauded these banners more than downtowners, who were the more politically radical. The paper also noted that several "negro" women were in evidence, including an elderly woman on crutches who walked the entire route.[34]

On Election Day, November 6, the Woman Suffrage Party placed 6,180 women as poll watchers. Women who would later play roles in the city's political life served as supervisors and inspectors: Ethel Eyre Dreier, Mary Dreier's sister-in-law and future La Guardia campaign leader; Alice Duer Miller (Katherine Duer Mackay's cousin), a novelist, screenwriter, and writer of satiric verses about antisuffragists; and criminologist Katharine Bement Davis, now chair of the city's parole board. Their work was critical to the outcome: suffrage lost outside New York City by 1,150 but won in the city by 103,863.[35]

In some ways the journey proved more thrilling than the results. Suffragists were now trained political operatives. They possessed well-honed skills in propaganda, data collection, canvassing, street action, and lobbying. Armed with the vote, they were optimistic about finally achieving some of their public policy goals: temperance, if not outright prohibition; an end to prostitution; a modern welfare system; industrial health and safety; collective bargaining; improved maternity and infant care; greater access for women to higher education and the professions; a "modernized" city government; and more. Some suffragists even thought they would now be welcomed into party and government posts.

They would be disappointed. While a few male allies supported women's participation, most "party men" made only a few organizational concessions. They had no intention of making women equal players or nominating them for significant posts. Some suffragists accepted this, saying that women were by nature unsuited for "men's" politics and that women were more interested in causes than personal reward. Others, who fought the stereotype and pushed against the barriers that kept them marginalized, experienced frustrations but nevertheless constructed political careers unimaginable before they could vote. Most important, as they developed those careers, they would apply what they had learned through the suffrage movement to their future political campaigns, whether for reforms or to win offices for themselves or others. The suffrage legacy lived on.

# PART I | AT THE MARGINS

# 2 NEGOTIATING PARTISANSHIP

In May 1915, a columnist writing under the pen name Just Gone for the African American *Philadelphia Tribune* took a cynical view of woman suffrage. He said suffragists claimed that better legislation would come from giving them the vote. Men, they say, do not care about child labor, sanitation, pure food and milk, factory regulation, or prostitution: "Give women the ballot, and all these things will be taken care of by the 'mothering influence' of women." "If all this is true," the columnist then asked, "why have all the suffrage states failed to give women a conspicuous share in the work of lawmaking?" In Wyoming, where women have voted for forty-six years, the legislature has no woman senator and only one woman House member. Colorado, where women have voted for twenty-two years, has only one woman senator and one woman in the House.[1]

Just Gone's comments were apt for post-1917 New York. Only a few women won seats in the state legislature in the 1920s, and only one served more than one term. A few women won other posts in the decade—register of New York County (because this post maintained the city's public records, it was considered a woman's job) and one alderwoman. A few others won appointive government and judicial posts, and many were elected to local and state political party committees. But again, though these victories encouraged other women to keep trying, in the 1920s their political impact on state and city appeared minimal.

In a 1923 essay that compared American and British women in politics, former New York Progressive Party leader Frances Kellor suggested why. She wrote that American women did not pursue public office because they saw politics as an uninspiring "game, a scramble for jobs, and a party reward for services." In a privately circulated essay, she went even further, accusing former suffragists of having "disinherited women by regulations forbidding them to engage in political activities" and by clinging to a "non-partisan doctrine in the face of a victory in which the only fruit could be partisanship."[2]

Indeed, after their victory, a number of leading suffragists discouraged partisanship. "We have won a land called Political Emancipation," Woman Suffrage Party (WSP) boss Mary Garrett Hay declared at the party's annual convention in January 1918. "Now we must work harder than ever before to be worthy of its occupancy." She asked her followers to focus now on winning national woman suffrage, teaching women to be good citizens, and lifting politics "to a higher plane." To Hay, the only way this would happen was if women remained nonpartisan, at least at first, and thus she urged them to refrain from enrolling in a party until they had studied its principles. She also warned them not to let the WSP become a woman's political party. She wanted it to remain nonpartisan so that it could "solve problems impartially for women Democrats, Republicans, Socialists, and Prohibitionists." She closed her speech with the imperative, "Let us change the old adage, 'Every man has his price,' into 'Every woman has her principle.'"[3]

Such a transformation would not be easy. Women activists who dreamed of careers in politics, as well as those who wanted to influence public policies, would find this out early in the postsuffrage era. Without substantial support from both the parties' male leadership and their ongoing women's networks (both partisan and nonpartisan), their effectiveness would at best be short lived, at worse nonexistent.

Hay's instruction to go slow on party enrollment was particularly problematic for New York City women. When a Republican gerrymander created vacancies in four city congressional districts, the governor called a special election for March 5, 1918. No woman wanting to vote that day could do so without first registering, and in the state all registrants had to enroll in a political party. Since suffragists were among the women most likely to vote in a special election, partisan women urged them to ignore Hay's order.[4] The number of women who went ahead to register shows that many did.

Still, a number of obstacles made casting that first vote problematic. The law on special elections provided only one day for new voter registrations. Worried that women in the four vacant congressional districts could not all register on the allotted day, at the end of January, veteran suffragists Mary Hay, Harriet Laidlaw, Rosalie Loew Whitney, and Helen M. Leavitt went to Albany to demand three days. Contending that three would be too costly, legislators authorized a day and a half, plus a day in May for new voters to register for the September primaries. The suffragists accepted this compromise.

Officials set the special election registration for Friday, February 22, from 5:00 to 10:00 p.m., and Saturday from 7:00 a.m. to 10:00 p.m. Suffragists predicted that more than 131,000 women would register. By the end of the first day, only 5,000 had done so. Snow and the fact that Friday was a holiday and the start of the Jewish Sabbath kept many away. In addition, officials had promised registration stations comfortable for women, such as florist shops. But barbershop stations remained in service. A *Times* reporter saw married women accompanied by their husbands entering the latter with confidence but observed women walk away, unnerved by the sight of men in barber chairs. Some women found questions from all-male election boards about their ages, marital status, and citizenship embarrassing. None of these conditions deterred former suffragists. Neither afraid nor embarrassed, they lined up early in hope of being first.[5]

After discarding faulty forms, in the end officials counted only 35,205 women enrollees for the special election. Suffragists excused the poor showing by citing special election apathy. Promising better results in May, they demanded that in the future one of two required poll watchers be female. At the special election itself, female turnout exceeded male: over 90 percent of eligible women (31,958) voted, in contrast with only 45,134 out of an eligible 130,866 men. Prohibitionist Ella A. Boole, the second woman to vote in the Eighth District, reported that men had been most courteous, even clearing out the smoke in the polling place before women arrived. Democrats won all four vacant seats, a result that, because Republicans held only a one-seat majority, changed Congress's balance of power. Democrats now extolled the virtues of women voters.[6]

Because the special election registrations were valid only for that day, all city women had to reregister in May for the primaries. This time the Woman Suffrage Party predicted a tally of 350,000; party organizers hoped for more. Helen Boswell, now head of the Women's Division of the New York County Republican Committee, sent a delegation of forty-two women to the theater district to remind women leaving matinées and picture shows to be good citizens. Fearing a loss of control over primary outcomes, some male party leaders said they hoped few women would turn out. Not all party men agreed. Supporters of a third term for Republican governor Charles S. Whitman counted on a large woman vote to offset primary challengers. Attitudes toward women voting depended on predictions of party loyalties.

In the end, 283,873 women registered—fewer than suffragists had wanted, but a good result. The largest numbers were in Brooklyn and Manhattan. Republican Ethel Dreier was "pleased beyond measure," saying that the result "should end the theory that a woman's party, separate and distinct from any other party, would be set up in this State." Democrat Isabel M. Pettus echoed the point, saying, "We have urged consistently against women segregating themselves into a separate political group for independent action as women."[7] The future would be with women political partisans.

Enrollment went even better in the run-up to the general election in November. Stations were open daily for a whole week in October from 5:00 to 10:00 p.m. and all day Saturday. When more than 414,760 women registered, analysts predicted women's votes would determine the outcome of the 1918 gubernatorial contest. Women had reasons for supporting both candidates. Governor Whitman had favored both Prohibition and woman suffrage; his Democratic challenger, Alfred E. Smith, former Speaker of the assembly and now president of the city's board of aldermen, was a fan of neither but had championed factory worker protections. In November, 350,000 women turned out. Smith won the city by a plurality of 258,544. Whitman, who failed to carry a single city borough, lost the state.[8]

Women voters who wanted to do more in politics than just vote joined political clubs. Every political party in every assembly district had at least one. Alderman Henry Curran said that, since the clubs led to nominations for office and party rewards, they were more important than campaign committees. He called them the "armies that give us our government."[9]

For the first few years after suffrage, women disagreed over whether to integrate with the men's or form their own single-sex clubs. In July 1918, a Woman's Suffrage Party leader in one district asserted that "women should work with the men, to give their co-operation and support, and not in separate organizations."[10] The women's non-Tammany Democratic organization resolved to seek equality in choosing state committeemen and local candidates. Republican women in one district believed that only by entering the "men's club" could they learn how to play the political game. These women simply showed up at the men's meetings and declared themselves members.

As every club had its own rules, each responded differently to the challenge. Some clubs invited women in, but then ignored them at meetings. Others demanded that women apply for membership, a request that irked them. Were they not, the women asked, already members by being enrolled in the party? When clubs took months to respond to applications, women grew angry. At one point fifty Republican women in Brooklyn's Twelfth Assembly District (AD) announced they were tired of waiting and formed their own club. When Democratic women in the Thirteenth District had to postpone electing a woman club coleader three times because too few men showed up for the vote, they threatened to adjourn and elect their own leader. Democratic leader John H. McCooey apologized:

> There are a few older men, steeped in the traditions of centuries, who do not take kindly to the new order of things. But the franchise for women is in the Constitution of the State of New York to stay. The Democratic party has established the principle of dividing everything with the women on a fifty-fifty basis. The Assembly District clubs are political and social organizations and are purely local in their regulations. The individual

attitude of any club has nothing to do with the big principle of absolute political equality.[11]

By September 1918, in Brooklyn alone Republicans had thirteen integrated and thirteen single-sex clubs. Democratic women in the borough counted twenty-five separate organizations, a fact that led some party men to accuse women of fomenting "sex wars."

African American women in New York City politics faced similar issues, but their concerns revolved more around race than sex. Hundreds of black women organized "colored" clubs and leagues. Some were explicitly nonpartisan. In March 1918, for example, the Woman's Non-Partisan Political League in Harlem planned to make black women voters a "factor in politics." In April, Gertrude E. McDougald, an African American organizer of black laundry workers and a member of the Women's Trade Union League (WTUL), presided over a mass meeting to introduce women to the political parties. By May, black women voters were showing a growing interest in partisanship, inviting "colored official representatives" of the Republican, Democratic, and Socialist Parties to present their party's views. Former suffragist Annie K. Lewis organized a Harlem "get out the vote" campaign. In September, "colored Republican women" met for the first time with the male Brooklyn members of the B. K. Bruce Republican Club.[12]

The 1920 election year saw many cross-race activities. In July, the Committee of Forty-Eight, a national effort to revive the Progressive Party, made a point of advocating "political and legal rights for all irrespective of sex or color." In August, Dr. L. Adele Cuinet and Mabel T. S. Falco helped form the Colored Women's Division of the Brooklyn First AD Republican Club. Still separating themselves out as women, the following month this group dropped the word "colored" and became, simply, Women's Division No. 2 of the First AD Republican Club, a development that presaged more interracial cooperation to come.[13]

Gradually, men adjusted to women's presence in the clubs. Still, women complained of being excluded from clubs' inner councils. When it became clear that male party leaders were not going to offer women preferment, some suffragists argued that qualified women ought to have as much chance at rewards as men. Yet when male party leaders got together to pick candidates, they still doubted women's suitability for office and picked men. When party leaders did nominate women, they often aggrieved suffragists by choosing non- or even antisuffragists, or by entering them in hopeless races.

Complaints about being ignored heated up. Women wanted the men to recognize their efforts. In fall 1918, a Democratic organizer in Brooklyn's Sixth AD complained the men never acknowledged that she had enrolled some 4,000 women, 2,176 of whom were Democrats. The Republican organizer in the Third

AD charged that though women had paid club dues, they never received meeting notices or were offered posts, even minor ones. Gertrude Maclin of Brooklyn's Eighteenth AD Republican Club complained that the men refused women's campaign help, not realizing "what a potential force they are allowing to go to waste." Women "did not work for the franchise merely to vote once a year," she protested.[14]

By early 1919, Republican women were restless. Brooklyn suffrage leader Rebecca C. Talbot-Perkins warned that the party would find itself unpopular unless it began to show more "cordiality and comradeship" with women. Men "have had things political all their own way since the beginning of time," she noted, and they need to change. In June, Lillian M. Sire, who had managed Mary Lilly's 1918 campaign for the state assembly, said,

> Women are capable of doing much more than they are allowed to do. We do not care for bouquets. So far, few of the hard workers have been consulted. I regard politics as a sacred duty. I do not approve of special laws for special classes. If we give of our best to politics, we will make it a higher and cleaner thing. We need to educate women and also men to their political responsibilities. We want the opportunity to serve on an equality.[15]

Henrietta Livermore, chair of the Republican women's state executive committee, declared: "We want to know what is going on from the inside, not to be kept on the outside."[16]

The following year, the National Woman's Party (NWP), Alice Paul's Washington-based organization, formally protested the pitifully low number of women delegates at national conventions. Democrats were sending more women than Republicans, but the numbers were still negligible, and most were only alternates. The NWP labeled the women on the national party committees mere "proxies" for the men, and women's executive committees "powerless." By midsummer 1920 some Democratic women predicted that in five years women will have lost interest in politics; others warned of a coming woman's party. Journalist Esther Coster, then editor of the *Brooklyn Daily Eagle*'s "The Woman Voter," reported that such "mutterings" revive every time "women voters fail to receive the recognition they desire or the honors they think they deserve." Women do not aim to be governor or president, she wrote, but "want the chance to start."[17]

Bold words about forming a woman's party came to naught. Alice Paul hoped women would organize "as a whole," but soon the National Woman's Party was focusing almost exclusively on winning a federal Equal Rights Amendment. The League of Women Voters again disclaimed any plans for a woman's party, but as Coster noted, since its slogan was "Principle before Party," its work tended toward a "sex division." In November Coster interviewed Republican women who thought they deserved rewards for the recent re-election victory of US senator James W. Wadsworth. Men of limited achievement get all the "plums," they complained, while women—if lucky—get unpaid commission posts or low-paid jobs that require the most work. Coster warned that women were "watching the shaking of the plum tree" and were unhappy at being left out.[18] New York City women activists had made a good start at getting "inside," but their unhappiness about being excluded would only increase.

Not all New York City women seeking power in the parties rose through clubhouses. A few used their bases in single-sex voluntary associations or party women's divisions to become players. Frances Perkins, Belle Moskowitz, and Eleanor Roosevelt are three examples of Democratic Party women who rose to power by attaching themselves, in different ways, to Alfred E. Smith's rising political star. None ever ran for office.

By 1918, Al Smith had been in state politics for fifteen years. Born in 1873, he grew up on Manhattan's Lower East Side, where his father's death forced him to leave school in the eighth grade. He eventually became a bookkeeper and general factotum at the Fulton Fish Market, in his spare time performing in amateur theatricals and hanging out at Tom Foley's saloon, the center of Fourth Ward Tammany politics. Foley got Smith his first white-collar job and in 1903 sponsored him for a state assembly seat. Smith not only won but also kept his seat through a dozen more annual elections.

Smith quickly mastered the legislative process. His theatrical experience made him comfortable delivering speeches. Using the sparest of notes, he could mix hard facts with witty, homey anecdotes. At Tammany's direction, he championed progressive social legislation, such as stricter health and safety rules for factories, limits on women's and children's working hours, and a workers' compensation law, drafted by lawyer, suffragist, and social investigator Crystal Eastman, that put the burden of proof for industrial safety on employers.[19]

Work on these bills brought Smith into contact with Frances Perkins, a progressive feminist then lobbying for a fifty-four-hour workweek for women factory workers. Born in 1880 into a middle-class Boston family, Perkins graduated from Mt. Holyoke College and then taught outside Chicago, where she volunteered at social settlements, including Hull House. She moved to New York on a School of Philanthropy fellowship, and in 1910 earned a master's degree in sociology and economics at Columbia University. She also accepted the post of executive secretary of the New York Consumers' League.

A horrendous event determined her life's work. On March 25, 1911, a fire broke out at the Triangle Shirtwaist Factory in Greenwich Village. Housed on the upper floors of a twelve-story building with rusted-out fire escapes, emergency doors locked from the outside, and no sprinklers, the factory was a deathtrap. Hearing the alarms, Perkins ran to the fire. Writing almost four years later, she could still evoke a vivid image of the tragedy.

> A cry of fire fills the room. Frantic with fear, fighting in the midst of a panic-ridden mob for air, for breath, for escape—flames leaping higher, the exits blocked, the screaming crowd grows helpless.
>
> A frail girl, with clothing torn, eyes staring, choking, coughing, gasping, blinded by smoke, rushing wildly back and forth, tries to decide in the half second that remains whether to leap from the window to almost certain death on the sidewalk below, or with one more breath of the scorching air, fall suffocated to the floor with the flames ready to do their fatal work on the young body.[20]

The Triangle fire claimed 146 lives, and many more people were injured. Most of the victims were young immigrant women and girls. Perkins joined hundreds of thousands of outraged citizens who marched down Fifth Avenue, held mass meetings, and raised money for victims' families. A committee on safety formed to get the state legislature to launch an official investigation. On the advice of former president Theodore Roosevelt, who knew Perkins from the Consumers' League, the committee appointed her executive secretary.

In that role, Perkins worked closely with Assemblyman Smith and state senator Robert F. Wagner Sr., cochairs of the New York State Factory Investigating Commission (FIC) set up by the legislature to look into health and safety problems in the state's industries. Perkins's testimony led the commission to put her in charge of their investigations. She took Smith and Wagner on unannounced visits to canneries, where they saw women and children standing for hours in miserable conditions. Over the three years of its existence, the FIC won more than three dozen landmark industrial safety bills. Working with Bernard Shientag, the commission's assistant counsel, Perkins wrote many of them. Smith's unwavering support for her led her to tell her anti-Tammany friends that, if she could ever vote, she would vote Democratic. Though shocked, they too would soon follow suit.[21]

In fall 1913, at the age of thirty-three, Perkins married statistician and municipal reformer Paul Wilson, appointed the next year as budget secretary for reform mayor John Purroy Mitchel. When in 1917 Mitchel lost re-election, Wilson, who had shown signs of depression, became mentally ill. The following year, while supporting him and their baby daughter, Perkins (who had kept her birth name for feminist and professional reasons) campaigned for Smith for governor. After he won, he appointed her the first woman on the state industrial commission, a post she had neither solicited nor expected. She would lose this post after Smith failed to gain re-election in 1920 (at the time, New York governors had only two-year terms) but get it back when he returned to office in 1923. In 1926 Smith named her the commission's chair, and in 1933 President-Elect Franklin D. Roosevelt appointed her US secretary of labor. She would hold this post until FDR's death twelve years later.

Because of Al Smith's labor reforms, many progressive Republicans had supported his first gubernatorial race in 1918. Belle Lindner Moskowitz was one. Born in 1877, the daughter of Jewish immigrant shopkeepers, Lindner went into settlement work on Manhattan's Lower East Side. In fall 1903 she married architect Charles Israels, eventually bearing three children (a fourth was stillborn). As a volunteer in social reform and charitable campaigns, in 1908 she launched a drive to license New York's dance halls, the city's most popular recreational venues. She campaigned not to shut the halls down, but to regulate them. Her goal was to make them alcohol-free, chaperoned, and supervised by "dancing masters" who would teach decorous forms of dancing instead of the popular "rags" and "tangos" that, she thought, stimulated sexual appetites. Her dance hall licensing campaign gained her a national profile as an idealistic but practical social reformer.[22]

When Charles died of heart disease in 1911, Belle Israels had to find a job. Thanks to a recommendation from Henry Moskowitz, a former settlement work colleague, she began settling labor grievances for a garment manufacturers' association. After settling some thirteen thousand cases, in 1916 a new association board fired her for being too conciliatory toward labor.[23] Meanwhile, she had entered politics. In 1912, the Eighth Ward Progressive Party in suburban Yonkers, where she then lived, elected her associate leader; at the party's state convention she gave a seconding speech for gubernatorial candidate Oscar Straus. In 1914, she made her first and last foray into electoral politics as one of five women chosen by suffragists to represent senatorial districts at the upcoming constitutional convention. She ran on the Westchester County Progressive Party ticket, finishing ninth in a field of fifteen. No woman sat in the 1915 Constitutional Convention (and none in future such conventions until 1938).[24]

In fall 1914 Belle married Henry Moskowitz. A PhD in philosophy, founder of a Lower East Side settlement, and a garment industry mediator who ran for Congress in 1912, Henry became head of the municipal civil service commission under Mayor Mitchel. Unlike Frances Perkins, who kept her name, Belle changed her name to Moskowitz, explaining, "I've put two names across, I guess I can manage a third."[25]

In 1918, the Moskowitzes joined Alfred E. Smith's "independent" (i.e., non-Tammany) Democratic gubernatorial campaign committee, a third of whose members were women.[26] Worried that women's voting potential was being ignored, Belle persuaded the committee's leaders to create a women's division; they put her in charge of it. In the two weeks left before Election Day, she organized opportunities for Smith to talk to women. A plan to address university women made him nervous. How could he, a man who never finished eighth grade, talk to such "highbrows"? Advising him to speak to them as if they were men, she jotted down a short list of topics: his legislative record on health, women's working conditions, fire prevention, and woman suffrage. Asked what he should say about Prohibition, which many women wanted but Smith opposed, Moskowitz told him to handle it "without gloves." He did, focusing his remarks on the Anti-Saloon League, an organization many women considered repressive. His frank talks won audiences over. When Moskowitz came back to him later with another idea, he listened.

This idea occurred to her a week after his victory. The world war had prevented the state from acting on important issues. Now that the war was over, Moskowitz thought Smith should seize the moment to develop a systematic plan. Frances Perkins remembered Moskowitz saying to her, "We must do something. This administration of Smith's has got to mean something positive to the people of New York. We must pick up a program. Everything has drifted along previously. The war is over and the people expect something to be done, something new."[27]

The two women drew up a plan for the Reconstruction Commission of the State of New York, a bipartisan panel of experts who would outline Smith's legislative agenda. Smith approved the idea and appointed Moskowitz its executive secretary.[28] She oversaw its reports on labor and industry, the rising cost of living, public health, education, and government reorganization. For the rest of Smith's time in office (four two-year terms), these reports drove his legislative agenda. After his re-election in 1924, Smith, who had found Moskowitz's advice reliable, offered her any government post she wanted. She declined, asking instead that the Democratic state committee name her director of publicity. This post put her at the fulcrum of information going in and out of the governor's office and made her a member of his "kitchen cabinet," an informal group of advisers. Her position evolved into gatekeeper and unofficial campaign manager. While it paid half of what she might have earned as a state commissioner, it gave her a level of power unprecedented for a woman in politics.[29]

In 1928, after masterminding Smith's nomination for president on the Democratic Party ticket, Moskowitz ran the national publicity campaign. But she could not win him the presidency. Roman Catholic, anti-Prohibition, and a "provincial" New Yorker, Smith fought a losing battle against the less colorful but accomplished engineer and former US secretary of commerce Herbert H. Hoover. Devastated, Moskowitz tried to gain a foothold in the inner circle of Smith's successor in Albany, Franklin D. Roosevelt, but his friends (including both Perkins and Franklin's wife, Eleanor, who knew Moskowitz well) advised against her as too close to Smith. In 1932, Moskowitz led Smith's futile bid against FDR to retake the Democratic Party's presidential nomination. In December, she slipped on the icy steps of her Manhattan brownstone and, while recovering from fractures to her arms, a blood clot struck her heart and she died. She was fifty-five years old. Smith referred to her death as "a disaster." His political career never recovered.[30]

In the 1920s, Belle Moskowitz taught Eleanor Roosevelt the basics of running a partisan women's political campaign. Such knowledge had not been a part of Roosevelt's upbringing. Born in 1884 to wealth and privilege, she received an English boarding-school education and returned to New York City as a debutante. Upper-class society held little appeal for her. She volunteered in a settlement house and joined the Junior League and Consumers' League, organizations that made her a lifelong reformer of industrial work conditions. In 1905 she married her distant cousin Franklin, and over the next eleven years supported Franklin's political career and bore six babies (the third died at seven months). In 1910 he won a state senate seat and in 1913 became assistant secretary of the navy under President Wilson. In 1920, when he ran for vice president, Eleanor campaigned with him. By then she knew of his affair with her former social secretary, Lucy Mercer, and they almost divorced. Franklin's mother, the formidable Sara Delano Roosevelt, persuaded them to hold the marriage together as a political and business partnership.

When infantile paralysis struck Franklin in 1921, his political future seemed over, but his campaign manager, former newspaperman Louis Howe, thought Eleanor could help revive it by keeping Franklin's name before the public. Her method would be increased activity in New York City women's organizations. She was already on the board of the League of Women Voters (LWV). Its attorney, Elizabeth Read, showed her how to follow state and federal legislation; Read's partner, journalist Esther Lape, brought her into the Women's Trade Union League. She also continued in the Consumers' League and joined the Women's City Club, at the time the city's premier nonpartisan civic action group.

Roosevelt also joined the women's division of the state Democratic committee. Its leaders, Caroline O'Day, Elinor Morgenthau, Marion Dickerman, and Marion's life partner Nancy Cook, became her closest friends. In 1924, to call attention to the involvement in the "Teapot Dome" scandal of Smith's gubernatorial opponent, her cousin Theodore Roosevelt Jr., Eleanor, and her friends toured the state in an automobile topped with a canvas mock-up of a teapot that spouted steam when it entered town. On the tour she met upstate Democratic women who reported feeling ignored by the party's state committee. In response, the women's division started a newspaper they hoped would bind the state's Democrats together.

Building on its mimeographed *News Bulletin*, in May 1925 the division produced its first monthly issue, the *Women's Democratic News* (*WDN*). Its staff was entirely female: O'Day (who in the 1930s would serve four two-year terms as congressman-at-large) was president, Morgenthau vice president, Cook business manager, Roosevelt editor and treasurer, and Dickerman secretary. Its cover always featured a party message, political cartoon, or photograph of a prominent Democrat. Inside were profiles of party leaders, explanations of major issues (Moskowitz wrote some of these), reports from Democratic clubs, and sarcastic stories of male biases against women in politics. One feature captured the essence of the paper's goal. Women's division officers had pledged to visit every county organization or club once a year, tours Nan Cook called "Trooping for Democracy." The *WDN* told stories of the tours, how the women drove a little Chevrolet roadster through all kinds of weather and over rough roads, coped with mechanical breakdowns, and made speeches drowned out by passing trains.[31] Over the next twenty years the unity the women's division helped create served the party well. Democrats reaped one victory after another: Al Smith, re-elected three more times; Franklin Roosevelt, elected governor twice and president four times; Herbert Lehman, four victories as governor and then as US senator.

As Eleanor Roosevelt participated in these campaigns with articles, essays, and public addresses, she developed a national political profile that went beyond her self-presentation as Mrs. Franklin D. Roosevelt. A political career of her own never occurred to her, however. She knew where her duty lay. At that time "I still lived under the compulsion of my early training," she would write later; "duty was perhaps the motivating force of my life, often excluding what might have been joy or pleasure."[32] After Franklin won the governorship in 1928, she resigned from the boards of New York City's women's groups and moved to Albany as the state's First Lady. Duty called her to an even greater role four years later, which she would play in the nation's capital and transform into a position of national and later global power.

In the postsuffrage era, these three New York City women followed different, though related, paths to power. All three had the political skills and knowledge to have run for office. Yet apart from Moskowitz's attempt in 1914 to be a state constitutional convention delegate, none tried. Perkins denied having sought even appointive office. When an interviewer asked her to comment on her political "career," she reflected,

> It may be true that unlike many other women I have had a life of my own and a career, but I had no intentions of having that. . . . Those who have

a career have been thrown by a series of circumstances and their own energies into situations where they had to assume responsibility, did assume it, were asked to assume more, did assume more. Before they knew it they had a career.[33]

Even when she heard that friends were urging President-Elect Roosevelt to appoint her labor secretary, she told him that she hoped the rumors were untrue. While she found the letters nominating her gratifying, she wrote, "for your own sake and that of the U.S.A. I think that the appointment of some one straight from the ranks of some group of organized workers should be appointed to reestablish firmly the principle that *labor is in the President's councils*."[34] Perkins held the political needs of the nation above her own personal ambitions.

In addition, all three women denied having any interest in party patronage. They wanted to "get things done." Perkins took a government post because her family needed the income. Moskowitz could have had a state commissionership. "I have no ambitions for office holding," she told a reporter in 1926. "I am in politics only to further the causes I believe in—better housing and recreation, protection of public health." If she could not help these causes by her job as publicity director, she would have given it up. Roosevelt asserted that women reject politics as "a game played for selfish ends by a few politicians." She praised Frances Perkins's goal of improving working conditions rather than self-advancement.[35]

Beyond a distaste for "political pie," other factors kept these and other women from running for office. Men remained uncomfortable with women exercising authority. Perkins wore simple black dresses and little tri-corn hats, hoping this dowdy style would remind them of their mothers. Similarly, Moskowitz kept out of the limelight, was never photographed with Governor Smith, and during "kitchen cabinet" meetings sat against a wall, usually knitting and speaking up only when asked for her views. In the early 1930s Eleanor Roosevelt saw a dim future for women in politics. Only women who are "not too anxious and insistent upon recognition and tangible reward" can win acceptance, she wrote, but even then they should not expect to enter "the inner circle where the really important decisions . . . are made!"[36]

Despite the limitations placed on these women's careers as politicians, they nonetheless were able to exercise power in historically significant ways. As secretary of labor, Perkins would spearhead and shape two of the New Deal's most consequential laws—the National Labor Relations and Social Security Acts of 1935. Moskowitz's impact on Smith's legislative initiatives left indelible marks on New York State and established models for policies Franklin Roosevelt and his advisers incorporated into the New Deal. Eleanor Roosevelt applied all the skills she had learned in women's political groups from the 1920s onward to lead

United Nations delegates to formulate and ratify the Universal Declaration of Human Rights. Shortly before she died, she headed John F. Kennedy's Presidential Commission on the Status of Women, the body that, in part, launched the modern feminist movement. Their accomplishments demonstrate that holding elective office was not the only path to political effectiveness after suffrage.

In March 1932, Belle Moskowitz told Felix Frankfurter, then a Harvard University law professor and later a US Supreme Court justice, that she could not agree with the Democratic state committee's order that all Democrats support Franklin Roosevelt for president. "Just because I am a progressive," she wrote, "and because the Democratic party, as such, means nothing to me any more than the Republican party does, I cannot follow the Albany leadership." Frankfurter found this declaration "incredible."[37] In contrast, the women political activists of her generation would have understood completely. For many of them, their reform causes often trumped party loyalty.

This was the stance taken by the Republican women who opposed the 1920 re-election bid of New York's US senator James W. Wadsworth Jr. Wadsworth, a farmer and rancher from upstate, won election as US senator in 1914. In the Senate he opposed both woman suffrage and Prohibition, arguing that states should decide these issues. When in 1919 he announced he would seek re-election, New York suffragists sprang into action. Caroline Slade, head of the state League of Women Voters, organized a nonpartisan senatorial committee to campaign against him. Mary Garrett Hay persuaded Ella Boole, leader of the state's Woman's Christian Temperance Union, to oppose Wadsworth in the primaries.[38] At the time, Hay was rising in Republican Party ranks. In 1918 a secret meeting of state GOP leaders chose her over Nicholas Murray Butler, president of Columbia University, to head the platform committee. Will H. Hays, Republican National Committee (RNC) chair and an old friend from Indiana, appointed her to the Republican Women's National Executive Committee, of which she soon became chair.[39] She had much to lose by defying her party's command to support Wadsworth.

And lose she did. When she announced she would oppose him even if he won in the primaries, the RNC stripped her of her "delegate at large" status for the 1920 Chicago national convention. She went to Chicago anyway, where she demanded that the size of the party's executive committee be doubled, with all new seats going to women. In response, Republican men joked that the nation might as well elect two presidents, one for men and one for women. In an act of "chivalry," twelve committeemen ceded their seats to women. Hay was not impressed. The men "should be ashamed," she scolded; "they cannot toss a few crumbs to the women and then sit down to the feast table."[40]

She soon lost even those few crumbs. Party leaders removed her from both state and national women's executive committees. She now urged followers to help younger women win places in politics, regardless of party affiliation. "I rebel," she proclaimed, against the "crack of the party whip," and she accused men of holding conferences in secret and then telling women what to do. *Women* weren't making a "sex war"; *men* were maintaining a "man's party."[41]

A backlash ensued. Editorials took her to task, pointing out that suffragists themselves had opposed "sex in politics" and that many party workers, men and women alike, never penetrate party inner circles. Stand-pat Republican women also went after her. Grace Vanamee and Rosalie Loew Whitney, both on the women's state executive committee, noted that "secret conferences" were not necessarily corrupt. In 1918 just such a conference had chosen Hay over Nicholas Murray Butler as platform committee chair: they recalled "no animadversions by Miss Hay following that occasion."[42]

Other Republican women continued to support Hay. Dr. L. Adele Cuinet was among the most outspoken. Born in 1854 in Hoboken, New Jersey, Cuinet had grown up distributing handbills for her mother's suffrage meetings. After a private school education, she graduated with honors from the Pennsylvania College of Dental Surgery in 1883.[43] After suffrage, she dove into politics. In February 1918 she organized a nonpartisan women's civic league to address school health and sanitation and to free the streets of garbage and ashes. She then joined the First AD Republican Club, getting its leaders to authorize a women's division, which in June endorsed a third term for Governor Whitman. She later blamed Whitman's loss on Republican men's failure to partner with women. In 1919, calling Senator Wadsworth women's "greatest foe," she said she could not believe her party would require them to vote for him.[44]

Despite her opposition to Wadsworth, in May 1919 Cuinet, along with a number of other women, won posts on the board of Brooklyn's First AD Republican Club. When these women endorsed the direct primary, they were in a dilemma. By the end of the year, the hot question was what to do if Wadsworth won. Party regulars threatened repercussions for anyone who failed to support the ticket. Anti-Wadsworth forces replied that voting against one's conscience violated their principles. Other Republican women disagreed. At an August 20, 1920, meeting of the club's women's division, Jessie Crane asked, "Hasn't the candidate who assumes the expense of a campaign and wins the primary the right to expect the voters to support him after the primary?"[45] Henrietta L. Livermore, Mary Garrett Hay's successor as chair of the Republican women's state executive committee, said she expected Republican women to be "good sports" and work for whoever wins.

As September neared, Mary Garrett Hay, Carrie Chapman Catt, and Elizabeth Collier held a final anti-Wadsworth rally at Cooper Union. Using the slogan "Wadsworth's Place Is in the Home," they mocked his effort to get women to vote for him by pretending to use his voice to recite this doggerel:

For you to vote is very wrong,
I've said so, firmly, right along;
But since the awful fact is true
That law gives votes to such as you,
It is quite clear, you must agree,
That you should cast your votes for me.[46]

Their satire did not help. Wadsworth crushed his rivals.

Women leaders of the First AD Republican Club—Cuinet, Collier, and Mabel T. S. Falco (who would run for alderman the next year)—all abided by the primary's result. Even so, Collier was forced to resign as a member of the Kings County Republican Committee, and other Wadsworth opponents, including Clara A. Rodger (Queens vice chair) and Eva Sherwood Potter (a committee member), also lost their party posts. In November, Boole ran on the Prohibition ticket. Though she won only four counties, she claimed that her 153,000 votes were the most any woman running for office anywhere had ever received. Wadsworth was re-elected, but by a plurality of only 471,000, half of Warren G. Harding's New York State vote tally.[47] Women took credit for that.

Because of her opposition to Wadsworth, Mary Garrett Hay lost her clout not only with the GOP but also with some women activists. Some prominent Republican women resigned from the League of Women Voters, saying, "Scratch a non-partisan and you find a Democrat." Hay held on to presidencies of the New York LWV and the Women's City Club, but previous admirers, who had accepted her as "suffrage boss," now chafed under her leadership. As early as February 1920, Vira Boarman Whitehouse, who had run the state Woman Suffrage Party, wrote a colleague that "Miss Hay's great faults are vanity and egotism," and "if you disdain to use flattery it is sometimes very difficult to cope with her—she wants to control everything." In 1923 the league eased Hay out. Commenting on the ouster, Esther Lape revealed that Franklin Roosevelt called Hay "Charlie Murphy Hay," a name that conjured up the image of the current Tammany boss. Hay retired from the WCC the following year and died a few years later.[48]

Regardless of their continuing Republican Party affiliation, many anti-Wadsworth activists held on to their "principles." In 1922, when Wadsworth's name came up as a possible presidential candidate, Cuinet warned that Republican women might vote for a Democrat.[49] In 1926, however, when Wadsworth attempted a third term in the Senate, he found plenty of support from women Republicans.

Pauline Morton Sabin led the Wadsworth campaign. Born in 1887, Sabin came early to politics. Her grandfather, governor of Nebraska J. Sterling Morton, was Grover Cleveland's secretary of agriculture; her father, Paul Morton, was Theodore Roosevelt's secretary of the navy. After 1904 she attended every Republican national convention; her favorite pastime was watching Senate debates. After an early marriage that ended in divorce, in 1916 she married a Democrat, Charles Hamilton Sabin, chairman of Guaranty Trust. Though she saw no reason women should be denied the ballot, she did not work for suffrage; instead, she became involved in politics through charity work. She ran for party office only once. Owner of an estate in Southampton, Long Island, she was eligible for a seat on the Suffolk County Republican Committee. In 1919 she defeated a male opponent to take it but resigned in 1923 when the Republican National Committee chose her to be the party's first New York State committeewoman. She held memberships in the Women's City Club, the Colony Club, and, her favorite, the Women's National Republican Club (WNRC), which she helped found and presided over from 1921 to 1926. A superb organizer, she built up the WNRC to some three thousand members across forty states.[50]

In 1926 Sabin cochaired Wadsworth's 1926 re-election campaign. She organized women's campaign events and saw Wadsworth's campaign biography into press. When she spoke publicly on Wadsworth's behalf, she lauded his achievements, courage, and ability, and called him a "great asset to New York State." Pointing out that since the passage of woman suffrage Wadsworth had "urged the fullest participation by women in politics and public affairs," she begged former suffragists not to hold his former "conscientious" objection to suffrage against him. Prohibitionists had pledged their votes to state senator Franklin Cristman, an independent "dry" from Herkimer. Sabin warned Republican women that a vote for Cristman was a vote for Tammany Hall, "an organization far wetter than the Republican Party." Besides, in her view, Cristman was unelectable.[51]

Her prediction came true. The Cristman candidacy split the Republican vote and Democrat Robert F. Wagner Sr. won. The day after the 1926 election an anonymous voter, who could only have been female, sent Wadsworth a telegram boasting, "THE WOMEN OF NEW YORK STATE DID NOT FORGET." Though there were other reasons for Wadsworth's defeat, at least one woman thought women's votes had been decisive.[52]

Though no New York City party woman achieved major office in the 1920s, some established reputations that led to appointments later on. Two Republicans, Maria C. Lawton and Rosalie Loew Whitney, and one Democrat, Anna Moscowitz Kross, stand out. The two Republicans were leaders in the 1933 fusion movement that elected Fiorello La Guardia mayor. While La Guardia was her friend, Kross was at first loyal to Tammany.

Lawton, the oldest of the three, was a major leader in Brooklyn's African American community. Born in 1864, she attended Howard University and became a teacher. In 1886 she married William Rufus Lawton, a Presbyterian pastor, with whom she raised a large family. In 1892 they moved to Brooklyn, where William was a pastor and civil servant; Maria wrote for the *Brooklyn Standard Union*. Active in women's clubs in the 1910s, she lectured on race and sex discrimination, joined the borough's Equal Suffrage League and the National Association for the Advancement of Colored People (NAACP), and founded welfare programs for children and seniors. In 1916, acknowledging her expansion of the number of clubs affiliated with the Empire State Federation of Colored Women's Clubs from a handful to 103, the federation elected her president, a post she held for ten years. In 1920, she became a director of the First AD Republican colored women's club. In 1924, Republican activist Hallie Q. Brown named Lawton director of the eastern division of the RNC's Colored Women's Department.[53]

Lawton spoke out often on race. She sent a powerful letter to the *Eagle* on the paper's failure to understand community feeling about the execution of thirteen soldiers for their alleged involvement in the 1917 mutiny of black soldiers stationed at Camp Logan, Texas, who were protesting mistreatment by the Houston police. She was appalled that the soldiers' "splendid previous record counted for naught," and that they had been sent to a "section of the country so well defined in its hostility and so well organized in its propaganda against law and justice." In 1920 she reacted to the paper's editorial criticizing Ohio African Americans for their confidence in Republican presidential candidate Warren G. Harding. The editorial asked why Ohio's eighty thousand male black voters, and half as many women, see Harding as "a Moses." Lawton shot back that the black community "are not only looking to him as the Moses of the colored race, but the Moses of America."[54]

As president of the Brooklyn NAACP in 1922, Lawton argued for federal antilynching legislation and against the Ku Klux Klan and newspaperman William Randolph Hearst's "race prejudice." She became so well known that people introduced William as "the husband of Mrs. M. C. Lawton." By the end of the decade, the press was referring to her as one of the "foremost speakers of the negro race." In 1929, as vice president of the Kings County Colored Republican Organization, she formed and led the New York branch of the National League of Colored Republican Women, an organization with the slogan "We are in politics to stay and we shall be a stay in politics."[55] In the 1930s, Lawton would become a key member of an interracial group of women supporting La Guardia.

Rosalie Whitney's career path was more privileged than Lawton's. She came from a long line of Hungarian rabbis and attorneys.[56] A graduate of Hunter College in 1892, in 1895 she became one of the first women to earn a New York University law degree. Since bias against female (and Jewish) lawyers precluded her earning a living on her own, she joined her father, William Noah Loew, in a partnership, Loew and Loew. When the *Times* asked William how he felt about women lawyers, he said (in contrast to the other men interviewed), "I believe that women will be treated as minds, regardless of sex." When asked, "How about politics and the law?" he replied, "They are twins, and, logically, the woman lawyer will presently become a politician."[57] His daughter fulfilled his prophecy.

As women litigators were rare, Rosalie Loew's court appearances gained press attention. The *Times* praised her petite figure, "clear, ringing voice [and] confident, unembarrassed" demeanor. Her founding in 1899 and presidency of the Women Lawyers' Club (later, Association) also received coverage, as did the city bar association's refusal to accept her into membership in 1903.[58] Her reputation widened when in 1897 she became the first woman lawyer at the Legal Aid Society, founded in 1876 to provide free legal services to the poor. In 1901 she became its lead attorney. After marrying her colleague Travis H. Whitney, she resigned, in 1904 forming a partnership with him, Loew and Whitney.[59]

During the 1910s Whitney received political training as legislative chair for the Woman's Municipal League, director of the Brooklyn Consumers' League, and congressional committee chair for the city's Woman Suffrage Party. After suffrage, she was active in the League of Women Voters, the Women's City Club, the Citizens Union, and the Republican Party. She recruited women to work for Republicans and organized voter schools, at times sharing the dais with Fiorello La Guardia. As women's division chair of Brooklyn's First AD Republican Club, in 1918 she stumped for Governor Whitman and was a delegate to state Republican conventions. In 1919 she worked for Bertha Rembaugh's election as a judge. In 1920, as a member of the RNC's Women's Executive Committee, she testified in Washington to make the US Women's Bureau, then a temporary wartime agency, permanent.[60]

Until Wadsworth's primary victory, Whitney opposed his renomination. Afterward she lined up behind him. In fall 1920 the state Republican committee invited her to accompany Judge Nathan Miller's campaign train in his race against incumbent governor Al Smith. The first woman speaker to be so invited, she made dozens of "whistle-stop" speeches for Miller, whose wife, Elizabeth, praised Whitney for her "gift of gab." Back in New York City Whitney made many multistop trips around the county for Wadsworth, chastising the Republican women who opposed his re-election. "There is no such thing as non-partisanship," she told them, adding, "Women who claim to be independent and not tied to party are 25 years behind the times in political knowledge." Admirers called Whitney and Grace Davis Vanamee, chair of the Republican Women Speakers Bureau, the "Gold Dust Twins," a reference to images (now seen as racist) on a popular cleaning product. When both Miller and Wadsworth emerged victorious, Whitney claimed he owed his election to women.[61]

In April 1921 newly elected Governor Miller reorganized the state industrial commission into a three-person board and put Whitney in Frances Perkins's place. Hoping to defeat Tammany's Mayor Hylan in the fall, she urged Republican women to use the vote "the right way." For Whitney, that meant party loyalty. In June 1921, on the same day the Citizens Union called for a coalition mayoral ticket to get Tammany out of city hall, Whitney spoke against such a ticket. The idea of a nonpartisan city administration is "false doctrine," she said. Since coalitions lack a "set body to hold responsible, they win elections only to be booted out at the next." She urged a straight Republican ticket vote come fall.[62]

Then her own party surprised her by forming a coalition with anti-Tammany Democrats and nonpartisans to oppose Hylan and support Manhattan borough president Henry H. Curran for mayor.[63] Despite her negative view of coalitions, Whitney agreed to join a town hall women's debate on Curran's behalf. Her chief debate opponent would be noted Tammany attorney Anna Moscowitz Kross.

Kross and Whitney shared similar life experiences.[64] They both were active in the Women Lawyers' Association and defended vulnerable clients. But Kross had been born in Russia and was almost twenty years Whitney's junior. Unlike Whitney, she had grown up in a poor Lower East Side family. Her father, broken by the deaths of five of his nine children, no longer earned a living. From the age of ten Anna worked in a button factory and taught English on the side. After high school she began a teacher-training course but was soon drawn to the law. A New York University Law School scholarship won her a free three-year course. She earned a bachelor of laws in 1910 (La Guardia was her classmate) and a master's in 1911. Then only twenty, she had to wait six months to apply to the bar.[65]

Getting a job was another question. No firm wanted a woman, much less a Jew. Finally, thanks to a suffrage movement friend, she landed a clerkship. In six months she was managing the firm. Two years later she went out on her own, at first accepting cases of workers in dispute with their unions. She endured the scorn of judges and "fat attorneys" who looked down upon the diminutive young lawyer (she was only five feet two).[66] She marched in suffrage parades and volunteered on a prison committee affiliated with Greenwich Village's Church of the Ascension, then led by social gospel pastor Percy Stickney Grant. Through this committee she became aware of how plainclothes decoys lured women into offering "a good time" and then arrested them for soliciting. Anna and friends from the Women Lawyers' Association began representing such women in court. By 1915, as chair of the church's legal committee, she began calling for the abolition of the city's women's court, a place notorious for collusion among corrupt policemen, bail bondsmen, lawyers, and judges.[67]

In 1917 Anna married surgeon Isidor Kross. By then she had long been involved in party politics. In 1913 she spoke on street corners and in union halls in the re-election campaign of a Democratic general sessions judge, speeches that led the up-and-coming Alfred E. Smith to call her "my silver-tongued orator." After the 1917 state woman suffrage victory, Smith took her to Tammany's boss Murphy, who appointed her head of the machine's Women Speakers Bureau. Following the Democratic state victory of 1918, Mayor Hylan named her the city's first female assistant corporation counsel.[68]

Kross's sights soon rose higher. Former suffragists were demanding that the mayor appoint the city's first woman to the magistracy. Kross believed she was a perfect choice. In asking Reverend Grant to recommend her, she noted that contemporary laws relating to women and children had not kept up with modern criminology. A woman like herself "could do much as a magistrate to mitigate these conditions," she told him. Mayor Hylan did not choose her. Instead, in 1919 he picked Jean H. Norris, then president of the Women Lawyers' Association and assistant secretary of Tammany Hall. Kross would have to wait more than ten years to receive the judgeship she knew she deserved.[69]

Kross's debate with Whitney on the town hall stage in late October 1921 gave the press a field day. Columnist Marguerite Mooers Marshall described the event as a "free for all" with "tabasco, paprika, cayenne, horseradish, tomato catsup, chile con carne, and anything else that is sharp and biting." Anne Rhodes, the event's organizer, had promised "a quiet, sane, orderly discussion." None of those adjectives applied. Marshall wrote that the audience repeatedly interrupted speakers with hisses, hoots, "Homeric bursts of scornful laughter," cheers, pounding of fists, and loud applause. As for the speakers, they had all promised not to attack personalities, but Grace Vanamee and Rosalie Whitney flouted the promise from the start with personal criticisms of both Mayor Hylan and Anna Kross.[70]

When Democrat Emma Russell opened the debate by declaring special pride in the city's schools, laughter swept through town hall. When she boasted of the glorious police department record, the "solid new walls of the auditorium seemed to rock" with hilarity, and when she pointed with pride to the markets, the audience, aware of recent scandals in Hylan's market administration, erupted in derisive chuckles. Responding for the coalition, Whitney attacked Hylan's school policies and Grace Vanamee cited instances of corruption and scandal. Kross riposted by characterizing the coalitionists as lacking courage to stand by their own Republican party. Snickers met Kross's claim that the administration had shown care for the people's interests by removing snow swiftly. Kross then ridiculed Major Curran's "new method of disposing of garbage 'by air, water or sending it to another borough.'" She asserted that Curran's call on everyone in the city to live near where they work would require "nothing short of a miracle" and ended by impugning her opponents' social class. "The great spirit of the people rebels against dictation from Fifth Avenue," she declared.

The event drew to a tumultuous close with Emma Russell's claims of police efficiency and boasts about Hylan's preservation of the five-cent subway fare. By the time Whitney rejoined, she had "lost her academic calm," Marshall wrote. She tramped the platform, "hammering home her points with as many gestures as T. R. [Theodore Roosevelt] was wont to use." Whitney aimed her "final bolt" at Kross. "I consider it a cheap, contemptible, political gesture," she stormed,

> for one of my opponents to uphold her party as the party of the people that must lead the fight against Fifth Avenue when she herself is a member of an Administration that has more highly priced automobiles than any other that this city ever knew and the head of which has to go to Palm Beach every winter to spend his vacation![71]

"BING!" Marshall concluded, describing the wild applause that drowned out both Whitney's last words and the moderator's gavel.

Marshall reported that a Radcliffe graduate exclaimed as she left the hall, "It's as good as a theatre!" The spectacle had changed no one's mind. The audience had learned that women could wield political arguments as well (or as poorly) as men and use the same oratorical gambits to score points. Moreover, they saw women unafraid to stand up before a large, unruly crowd and give proud voice to their views. The following week the Republican-coalition ticket met defeat. "Reform" died and Tammany ruled again. Democrats would stay firmly in power until Fiorello La Guardia's inauguration in January 1934.

Many suffragists were unsure about women's potential for public office. Mary Garrett Hay had at first discouraged women from not only joining a political party but also seeking election. Better that women are "chosen after deliberation than that some woman—any woman—be thrust into office in a hasty effort to give us representation," she said. Even Sarah Stephenson, a Brooklyn attorney and the first woman to seek statewide office (she ran for secretary of state in 1918), said no woman should aim for the governorship ("too arduous") or comptroller ("too important").[72]

In this period women who managed to be nominated faced questions never asked of men. "Should women vote for you because you are a woman?" No, most replied, there should be no sex in politics. Yes, said others, "women who have never voted before will raise a sex issue and vote for her because . . . she is a woman." "Will you pursue only 'women's issues'?" If a woman candidate admitted she would, she risked losing male voters. "Would you be loyal to party even if it failed to support your causes?" Recognizing the importance of party backing, some women said yes, others, never.[73] No answer could possibly please everyone.

Even so, in the early postsuffrage years a surprising number of New York City women entered electoral contests. The vast majority lost. Of those who won, a small number had been suffrage-movement trained. Attorney Mary M. Lilly, who ran for the state assembly in 1918, was among the first.[74] Lilly earned a law degree from New York University in 1895, only to discover in widowhood that her earnings were too low to support herself and her son. She became a teacher, in the 1910s speaking out frequently in favor of woman suffrage and equal pay. She still occasionally practiced law. One of her cases drew public attention. In 1917 she represented Alice Jay, who accused a music publisher of plagiarizing her song for the blockbuster "It's a Long Way to Tipperary." After composer Victor Herbert testified that Jay's tune and "Tipperary" were similar but not identical, Lilly lost Jay's case. She also endured a judge's chastisement for wearing a hat indoors, a practice customary for women but not for lawyers arguing a case.[75]

In 1918 the Amsterdam Democratic Club decided Lilly was their best bet to defeat the incumbent Republican assemblyman, an antisuffragist who had run unopposed six times. Lilly won by 229 votes. As the district was heavily Republican, Lilly was sure that women had crossed party lines to vote for her. In January 1919 a large women's delegation accompanied her to Albany to applaud her first day on the assembly floor.[76]

In the assembly Lilly introduced bills that reflected a feminist progressive agenda. She wanted to abolish the death penalty for minors, raise the age of court jurisdiction over minors from sixteen to eighteen, and legitimize babies born out of wedlock because of the war ("war babies"). She also favored women's jury service and a women's minimum wage and introduced an election law amendment to permit political parties to select equal numbers of women and men for state committees. She cosponsored the resolution that asked New York's federal representatives to vote for national woman suffrage. Yet she opposed Prohibition, which many women favored, believing that the constitution should extend rights, not take them away. She insisted she was not "representing women." "There is no sex in work," she said.[77]

Though Lilly's major initiatives did not survive, near the end of her first term Tammany talked about making her a "leader." They hoped such a move might convince upstate Republican women to support statewide Democratic candidates. It did not. In summer 1919, after Helen Varick Boswell urged followers to vote only Republican, Lilly could no longer count on women crossing party lines when she ran for re-election. In August, the Citizens Union criticized Lilly for failing to oppose "vicious" bills, and on election eve charged her with drawing two government checks, one as assemblyman ($1,500) and a second as superintendent of women prisoners on Blackwell's Island ($2,100). Lilly explained she had competed for the prison job long before she had run for office and it had just come through. But the damage was done. She lost her seat.[78]

Other suffragists who ran for office included Mamie Colvin, who announced for Congress—the first woman to do so—in New York City's March 1918 special election. Running on the Prohibition ticket, she expected a large vote from women but polled only 382 votes. In Queens, Republicans nominated Clara A. Rodger for the lucrative post of county clerk. As a Woman Suffrage Party official, Rodger had won Queens for suffrage in 1917 by eleven thousand votes. Hoping to raise his profile among women, Governor Whitman named Rodger to the unexpired term of the incumbent, recently convicted of bigamy. Despite being called "the best man for the job," she lost the fall election to a Democratic alderman.[79]

Dozens of women tried for state office. Though they lost, they were proud of their "showing." As the September primary neared, newspapers speculated that because of "war conditions" women's votes would outnumber men's. Would women vote for women? Commentators saw the Canadian-border town of Gouverneur, New York, as a litmus test. When the town's majority female and Republican voters overwhelmingly approved an all-male Republican ticket over an all-female Democratic ticket, they concluded that women's chances for election were doomed.[80]

Some radical political activists did not see the governorship as beyond a woman's reach. In 1918 the Socialist Labor Party nominated Olive Malmberg Johnson for the post. A Swedish immigrant who grew up in Minneapolis, Johnson in the late 1890s worked as a lecturer, speaker, and writer for the party. She was unable to go to college until her forties, when she worked her way through Hunter College and graduated in 1916. In 1918 the party named her editor of its organ, *The Weekly People*, a post she held for two decades. Her gubernatorial race netted only 5,183 votes. In 1925 she was the first woman to run for board of aldermen president and in 1929 the first nominated for mayor. Described in the press as "below average height, rather rotund and genial," in her nomination acceptance speech she spoke dismissively of the mayor's position: "I have a strong right hand and can do as much hand-shaking as [Mayor James J. Walker] can." When asked what she would do in office were she elected, she admitted she would not like holding any post under capitalism, which she described as "frazzled" and unlikely to last. Though she won 646 more votes than former police commissioner

Richard E. Enright, her total of 6,602 was far from the incumbent's. Her political career never got far, but she believed she showed that women could run a good campaign.[81]

Socialist and pacifist Elinor Byrns, an attorney, ran for Congress in the fall of 1918. The press paid her little attention. A year later, *Everybody's Magazine* reported that she had run "a very creditable young fight." Byrns revealed that, when Tammany leaders in her Staten Island home district found out she was running for Congress, they asked, "Why didn't you tell us you wanted a job? We would have fixed you up." When Byrns answered, "Because I happened to have principles," the men replied, "But we have the votes!" Byrns personified the dilemma for the woman political novice in this era: machine politicians saw political posts as jobs and knew how to get them; the novice hoped to put principles into practice but lacked the know-how to win.[82]

Marion Dickerman, a woman who ran upstate but whose campaign was managed by members of the New York City women's labor reform community, later became Eleanor Roosevelt's close associate on the *Women's Democratic News*. Born in 1890 and educated at Wellesley College and Syracuse University, Dickerman earned a graduate degree in education in 1912 and then, along with classmate and partner Nancy Cook, became a teacher and suffragist in Fulton, Oswego County. During the world war, Marion worked as a nurse and Nan made wooden legs in a British hospital.[83]

By the time they came back to the United States in August 1919, labor reformers had become totally frustrated with Thaddeus C. Sweet, the assembly Speaker who refused to let minimum wage and eight-hour workday bills for women and children reach the floor. Sweet was known as "lord of Oswego County," a 70 percent Republican district that had returned him to office for ten years. The Women's Joint Legislative Conference (WJLC) was the bills' chief advocate. Mary Elisabeth Dreier, former president of the Women's Trade Union League and then industrial section chair for the state Woman Suffrage Party, had founded the conference the year before. Dreier felt their only recourse was to defeat Sweet in 1919. But how? No strong Oswego Democrat dared run against him. On the afternoon of their return from England, Dickerman and Cook received Dreier's invitation to meet with a group of suffragists. Dreier pleaded with Dickerman to run as a Democrat against Sweet. Moved by the "simplicity and forcefulness" of Dreier's words and her pledges of labor support, Dickerman, up to then a Republican, said yes.[84]

Her race was uphill. Though she received endorsements from the Democratic, Prohibition, and Socialist Parties, politicians who relied on Sweet for patronage declined to support her. Her top platform plank was Prohibition enforcement, yet even local ministers and the Woman's Christian Temperance Union thought they could get more from Sweet than from an inexperienced legislator. All but one local newspaper refused to run her paid advertisements; managers of halls would not rent to her; women's clubs (all heavily Republican) turned down her offers to speak; and the Women's League for Equal Opportunity (WLEO), a Brooklyn organization opposed to all protective labor legislation specific to women, supported Sweet. Sweet's supporters maligned Dickerman supporters like Dreier, who managed Dickerman's campaign, as "tricky outsiders," "uplifters," "society women faddists," and, most damning of all, "Bolsheviks."

Dickerman lost, but got enough votes (ten thousand, twice as much as Sweet's former opponents, to Sweet's seventeen thousand) to console herself with having made Sweet work for his victory. Dreier later recalled how friends had advised her not to waste her time on such a "quixotic" race, but after losing the labor bills she knew she had to act. She also believed the race showed suffragists that a woman could "stand square against slander and despicable lies, unflinchingly and with a serene spirit." A quixotic race, yes, but one that propelled both Dickerman and Cook into state Democratic women's networks and a relationship with Eleanor Roosevelt that profoundly shaped Roosevelt's life in politics.[85]

Attorney Bertha Rembaugh ran an equally quixotic race. A graduate of Bryn Mawr College and New York University Law School, Rembaugh had done legal work for Blatch's Equality League and volunteered as legal counsel for striking garment workers and women charged with soliciting. (Her law partner, Mary Towle, was a close college friend of actress Katharine Hepburn's mother; Katharine called both Rembaugh and Towle "Auntie.") In 1919 Republicans nominated her for a ten-year term on the municipal criminal court, where no woman had sat. A cross-section of political faiths campaigned for Rembaugh. The Bar Association of the City of New York, which still excluded women from membership, endorsed her on the ground that her opponent, Judge John Hoyer, slept during court proceedings. Rembaugh's all-female campaign committee worked out of a former saloon, from which they served tea and canvassed house to house. She polled 8,231 votes, some 500 short of the Democrat. Had she enjoyed campaigning? It was "like going to the dentist," she said. The *Tribune* editorialized that she had "blazed a trail" for other women and pushed Tammany mayor John F. Hylan to appoint Jean Norris to the magistracy.[86]

Women kept on trying to win elective office. Some—such as Democrat Sue Mulholland and Republicans Leontine C. Klein and Eva Miller in 1919—ran unsuccessfully for alderman and never tried again. In 1920, Rose Schneiderman, president of the New York WTUL, made a hopeless bid for US Senate on a new state Labor Party ticket against both Wadsworth and Boole. Thinking campaigning "might be a lot of fun," she was later annoyed to discover that philanthropist Dorothy Payne Whitney Straight's $1,000 contribution had gone to posters for Dudley Field Malone, the party's gubernatorial candidate. Her race barely made a ripple. Also in 1920, Harriet May Mills, who came from Syracuse, ran for secretary of state on the Democratic ticket, but was defeated in the year's Republican sweep. Another upstater, Florence Knapp, would win this post in 1924 but would hold it only for a year.

Others reaped later benefits from their races. Attorney Clarice Margoles-Baright, a Democrat, failed to win a seat on Manhattan's children's court but received a temporary appointment in 1925. Socialist Grace P. Campbell, a social worker, probation and later parole officer, and the city's first black woman to run for office, lost her 1919 and 1920 bids for the state assembly, but over the next two decades remained a highly respected Harlem activist. Lucy Kipper of Staten Island lost her race for the assembly to an incumbent, a war amputee. Though she too had a war-related injury, she refused to wage a "Campaign of the Lame Leg." She ended up happy when board of aldermen president Fiorello La Guardia appointed her secretary, a post she saw as having "far more interesting situations and possibilities."[87]

In acknowledging the weakness of enfranchised women's legislative power, columnist Just Gone had called the black women who were "red hot" for suffrage "poor, deluded souls," who will be worse off when white women have the vote. The columnist ended: "When that time comes, our colored sisters will surely sing, Good bye, my honey, I am... Just Gone." New York City's African American women did not respond this way. Justifying her rush to register, Harlem businesswoman Mabelle McAdoo wrote, "As a woman—and a colored woman, I felt that I would not only be doing myself an injustice by neglecting to vote, but that I would be doing my race a wrong." Optimistic that the "colored people have it in their power to do away with much of the oppression and injustice from which they now suffer," she sent out a clarion call to black women to organize.[88]

Organize they did, but not at first to field black candidates. Instead, they supported white women's races. The first was Marguerite L. Smith, daughter of Dr. J. Gardner Smith, president of the Harlem Board of Commerce.[89] Marguerite earned a master's degree from Columbia University's Teachers College and during the war chaired a Red Cross auxiliary, led Girl Scout troops, and volunteered at the draft board and canteen. In summer 1919, Republicans in the Nineteenth AD decided that her popularity made her their best choice against a powerful Tammany state assembly candidate.

Marguerite Smith—only twenty-five and lacking political experience—accepted the call. Her father managed her campaign. An African American minister and independent Republican, Richard M. Bolden, opposed her in the primary. Motivated more by gender than race loyalties, the black women members of Harlem's Roosevelt Women's Republican Club supported her. With a platform that addressed Harlem's housing congestion and rent scandals and called for increased government control of profiteering and the rising cost of living, she defeated Bolden and went on to beat the incumbent Democratic assemblyman by 631 votes. The Roosevelt Club was proud. Especially pleased she hired a black woman as secretary, the club featured her at its third anniversary celebration as one of their own and organized a mass meeting for her re-election.[90]

This support helped Marguerite Smith become the first New York woman legislator to win a second term. She was also the first to chair a committee (social welfare) and briefly wield the speaker's gavel during a tumultuous closing session, ruling forcefully and getting feuding assemblymen to return to their seats. Her legislative impact was small. She won a bill for a state bond issue to support veterans' and nurses' bonuses, but the courts ruled it unconstitutional. She defended the assembly's judiciary committee decision to expel the five Socialists elected in 1919 and irked the League of Women Voters with a bill allowing women over twenty-one to work as newspaper proofreaders at night. She then pleased labor protectionists by favoring a ban on night work by women *under* twenty-one.[91] Her status as lone woman legislator during her second term made her a popular speaker. She told Vassar students that she had not given up a "single ribbon or frill" to serve in the assembly. "I want no difference shown because I am a woman," she said. "I want to be known entirely by what I do on my own merit." Her popularity did not last. She lost her try for a third term in the Democratic landslide of 1921 to a young attorney ironically named James Male.[92]

Brooklyn Republican Mabel T. S. Falco, who in 1921 ran for alderman, also received interracial support. Both white and black women's clubs endorsed her, as did many Republican men and even some Democrats. When her choice of a man as her campaign manager raised questions about her gender loyalty, she responded, "I am not exclusively the women's candidate, but the people's." Yet she also hoped her "feminine presence" on the board would prevent fist fights and improve decorum. She won her primary against two male opponents but lost in the Democratic landslide. The *Eagle* reported that partisan loyalties trumped gender: Democratic women had spurned her because Republican-coalition candidates that year had vilified incumbent mayor John Hylan.[93]

The Democratic sweep that defeated Falco brought victory to Annie Mathews, a suffragist, social worker, and Tammany coleader in Harlem's Nineteenth AD. Mathews's race for New York County register pitted her against long-time Republican leader Helen Varick Boswell. Some women believed that pitting two women against one another eliminated the objection that "it is not right for a woman to contest an election with a man." Mathews won two to one over Boswell (their male opponent, who ran as an independent, got only a few thousand votes). The post's annual salary of $12,000 made Mathews the highest-paid female public official in the nation.[94]

Only two African American women ran for elective office in the 1920s, Dr. Julia P. H. Coleman, pharmacist, drugstore owner, and hair-care products businesswoman, and Nannie C. Burden, a coloratura soprano and clubwoman. In 1924 the National Colored Coalition Political Association, a Harlem organization supporting Senator Robert M. La Follette's revived Progressive Party, prevailed upon Coleman to stand as a Nineteenth AD Republican candidate for the state assembly. The Bethel AME Church on West 132nd Street put Burden forward. Though the district's black population was growing, its regular Republican Party leader, white attorney Abraham Grenthal, defeated both women in the primary and went on to win election. Three African American women—Republicans Eunice Hunton Carter and Jane Bolin and Socialist Alma Crosswaith—would run for the state assembly from Harlem in the 1930s, but none was successful.[95]

No woman candidate in the city for electoral office was as successful as Republican Ruth Baker Pratt, who in 1925 became the city's first woman on the board of aldermen. Four years later she was elected the state's first congresswoman. Born in 1877, Ruth Sears Baker went to Wellesley College and in 1903 married attorney John Teele Pratt. Described as "tall, with a pleasant smile, most vivacious and gracious," Ruth bore six children (the youngest died as an infant).[96] By 1920 she was participating in Republican Party affairs at all levels. A talented fundraiser, she became vice chair of the party's ways and means committee and was elected a state convention delegate and presidential elector. During the Harding-Coolidge presidential race she presided over campaign meetings and raised money nationwide. In 1922 she served as associate chair and campaign manager for New York Congressman Ogden L. Mills's re-election. In 1925, after she helped resolve a bitter factional fight as Republican coleader of the Fifteenth AD, district captains asked her to run for alderman.[97]

Pratt's experiences as a candidate and then as officeholder illustrate the challenges New York City women faced in electoral politics in this era. The first was suffragists' expectation that all women politicians should have helped the movement. Pratt confessed she had been too busy with domestic cares to have "lifted a finger" for suffrage. Discounting her five years in high-level Republican Party work, suffragists considered her "untrained." The anti-Tammany Women's Democratic Union tried to convince a Democratic woman to run against her.[98] They approached Minnie Blumenthal, wife of former deputy state attorney general and Democratic leader of the Fifteenth AD Maurice B. Blumenthal, who refused, saying her husband would not allow her to run. "Woman has the right to vote," she wrote in an open letter to the press, "the right to be in politics, the right to hold public office, but these rights must be subordinated to the duty which she owes to the home."[99] In contrast, Pratt's husband was proud of his wife's political career and accompanied her on campaigns.

Mixed gender expectations presented other dilemmas for Pratt. Some journalists described only her physical attributes. Esther Coster emphasized Pratt's "graceful carriage," "fascinating dimples," and habit of "rolling her eyes roguishly that just makes you laugh with her." Lillian Sabine wrote that a five-letter word had brought her victory: "C-H-A-R-M." In contrast, Eunice Fuller Barnard appreciated Pratt's "thorough grounding in electioneering methods . . . that Tammany might have envied." Edward Titus admired Pratt for her "advanced ideas without being a crank" (code for "radical feminist"). At the same time he called her fearless, predicted she would not "mince words," and thought she might someday be mayor. In fact, he warned that if more women were like Mrs. Pratt, "man's supposed supremacy in the world would vanish." Her aldermanic colleagues gave her a favorable, though patronizing, review. "She's a regular fellow," majority whip Charles McManus said, saying further, "And she's got brains, she attends to business." "Mrs. Pratt hasn't been a bit of trouble," said Frank Cunningham, chair of finances and a seventeen-year Tammany veteran; she's "no obstructionist."[100] In short, Pratt had to be knowledgeable about politics but remain "a perfect lady."

Pratt's win over a younger male opponent led suffragists finally to embrace her. At a dinner in her honor at the Women's City Club, Mary Garrett Hay said, "The trouble with New York City is that it has been fathered to death. What it needs is a little mothering, and I'm glad, it's going to get some now." But as one of only three Republicans on the board, Pratt had little clout. Republicans urged her appointment as the minority's representative on general welfare and finance, two of the board's most important committees, and protested when she received inconsequential assignments. Attorney Dorothy Straus of the League of Women Voters also protested Pratt's marginalization and demanded that the board's president, Joseph V. McKee, do something. McKee refused, saying Pratt lacked experience and would have to wait at least a year for a better assignment. The *Times* warned that the league's "protest cannot be expected to accomplish anything, except, perhaps, to provoke Aldermanic irritation." "The common impression," the editorial continued, "is that though the hard-boiled politicians composing the board professed to welcome Mrs. Pratt warmly when she first took her seat among them, they were not really pleased to have her there."[101]

Pratt spearheaded welfare measures, such as increasing appropriations for tenement inspectors and playgrounds, and argued for charter reform. She spent most of her energies chastising the majority for rubber-stamping budgets and wasting millions on salaries and "perks." She attacked graft and waste in Mayor Walker's administration.[102] When her husband died suddenly in 1927, she considered resigning, but acceded to party pressure to run again. She won, but this time with fewer votes. The following year her party nominated her for Representative Ogden L. Mills's congressional seat. She won and served two terms. A fiscal conservative, she supported Prohibition repeal and Books for the Blind. Her unqualified loyalty to President Hoover handicapped her in the Democratic Party sweep of 1932 and she lost her third-term bid.[103]

In just two years, New York City's political women had traveled a long way from Mary Garrett Hay's "Every woman has her principle" to Rosalie Loew Whitney's "There is no such thing as non-partisanship." Still, only a handful had won central party roles and even fewer attained elective office; surrounded by overwhelming majorities of male colleagues and bosses, those few who did win were not able to exert much authority. Voters were just not ready to accept them, no matter their party affiliation, race, age, or social class. Recognizing that voters were not ready to elect black women to office, black women's political organizations put their weight behind white women candidates, but even these had a hard time winning re-election.

Yet the number of women trying to gain office continued to rise. They did so because they believed they would perform better in office than men. Women would give more time to the job, they said. They are more gracious and even-tempered in meeting the public and have "a genius for organization," greater patience with detail, and instincts for economy. They are less easily corruptible, are less impatient of routine, look more to responsibility and less to self-interest, understand human nature, and, because of their "intuition," have greater insight into things men never sense at all. Finally, with tongue in cheek they pointed out that women "know how to manage men, for they have done nothing else all their lives."[104] In the 1920s, whether any of these stereotypes about women were true, half true, or not true at all hardly mattered. Voters might have believed them yet still not vote for a woman candidate.

Even so, women's active entry into New York City's political campaigns was transformative. In the 1920 presidential campaign observers said women had brought new "social appeal" into campaigning. Journalist Esther Coster noted that men refuse to do house-to-house canvassing, which involved climbing stairs, ringing doorbells, and making personal appeals, but suffragists were used to this kind of campaigning and did it willingly. Nor did men know how to organize meet-the-candidate teas or the myriad committees—county committees, non-partisan committees, district committees, candidate's committees—that women formed and coordinated so well. Women had even transformed the political dinner from "stag affair" to "night at the opera." A *Times* reporter noted yet another technique women had brought to campaigns: the five-minute speech. "Men have listened to endless hours of political oratory since time was, but women have refused to undergo this torture," the reporter wrote. Women introduced simple language to campaign literature; organized mass meetings, election schools, and street booths; met candidates' arrivals with parades, reached out to the foreign-born, and solicited contributions from small to large (even a dime was not too little); sent out thousands of speakers, organized motor corps to get out the vote, and enlisted Girl Scouts to babysit while mothers cast ballots.[105] All of these techniques came from the suffrage movement. Though now permanent elements of American political party life, the techniques continued to launch men, not women, into office.

# 3 SUSTAINING FEMINIST PROGRESSIVISM

On December 3, 1919, some sixty members of the state League of Women Voters (LWV) traveled from Utica to Albany on the Empire State Express. Emma Bugbee, the *New York Tribune*'s women's politics reporter, described the league members, who had just adjourned their first convention, as "exuberant."[1] Suddenly, Rosalie Loew Whitney spied a "baldheaded little man" racing through the dining car. It was Thaddeus Sweet, Speaker of the assembly. "Catch him, somebody, quick!" she cried. Three women sped off. He was nowhere to be found, they reported sadly on their return, wondering why he was going to Albany before the start of the next session. "Perhaps he read the morning papers," one chuckled, referring to articles describing women's plans to curb his power. With a wicked smile, Whitney mourned: "I wanted to introduce him to Mrs. Vanderlip." Everyone got the joke. Narcissa Cox Vanderlip, newly elected the LWV's first chair, was preparing a legislative agenda that Speaker Sweet had vowed to block.

Almost a year before this missed encounter with Speaker Sweet, many of these same women had attended Governor Alfred E. Smith's inauguration. This event had made them feel accepted into the body politic. But over the months that followed, as many of their policy initiatives went down to defeat, that status felt less secure. The 1920 national elections loomed. Vanderlip told Emma Bugbee that now was the time to show men, who were keenly interested in how women would vote, that they were still resolved to bring about progressive, feminist change. In the 1920s and 1930s, two nonpartisan groups in the city—the state and city branches of the League of Women Voters and the Women's City Club of New York—acted as catalysts for such action. Their overlapping memberships consisted primarily of middle-class, native-born, European American women. Working-class and minority members of the New York Women's Trade Union League and the Empire State Federation of Colored Women's Clubs often partnered with them. The National and New York Consumers'

Leagues, Business and Professional Women's Clubs, National Council of Jewish Women, Young Women's Christian Association, National Woman's Party, and many other women's voluntary organizations also signed on, depending on the issue or principle at stake.

The League of Women Voters began as an auxiliary of the National American Woman Suffrage Association (NAWSA) and became independent six months before the August 1920 ratification of the Nineteenth Amendment. Riding on what she called a "wave of sanguine expectation" of female political power, Carrie Chapman Catt, NAWSA's president and the league's prime mover, saw the league as reorienting suffrage toward winning long-sought reforms. When Catt and her associates could not agree on which to pursue first, they settled on goals everyone accepted as important: educating voters and encouraging women's active citizenship. Local branches focused primarily on improving the lives of women and children and modernizing municipal and state governments. The New York League of Women Voters in particular monitored the legislative and executive branches, issued policy statements, and lobbied at city hall and in Albany. In 1919 state assembly member Mary M. Lilly expressed her optimism about the league by predicting it "will be able to bring about splendid reforms in both parties."[2]

Middle- and upper-class reformers used the Women's City Club as their chief meeting place. Anticipating the passage of woman suffrage that fall, suffragists had founded the club in summer 1915 as a venue through which they could learn about and monitor civic affairs. After the suffrage vote failed, they went ahead with their plans and leased a Vanderbilt Hotel suite as a meeting place. When the 1917 victory increased its membership to about three thousand, the club leased (with an option to buy) a five-story mansion at 22 Park Avenue. Designed by famed architect Stanford White for his sister-in-law, Mrs. Preston Butler, and nicknamed "the round house" for its many oval-shaped rooms, the mansion remained in the club's hands until the Great Depression.

The club's chief activities consisted of studying civic and legislative issues, meeting with officials, providing forums for debates among political candidates, hosting public discussions of controversial topics, and honoring women's achievements. Committees that investigated city institutions reported to a board, which then authorized actions, such as publishing a report or holding a mass meeting. Frances Perkins said the club's founders envisioned making every member an expert in some aspect of city affairs. Though this never happened, Perkins said that "every now and then a perfectly brilliant person . . . would do everything that she was asked a little better than you would expect her to." Among them were women who would figure prominently in La Guardia's political campaigns and later join his administration.[3]

Over the next two decades, New York City's civic women activists expended the most energy and passion over three campaigns: winning state acceptance of federal funds for improving the health of mothers and babies, legalizing women's jury service, and passing laws to protect women wage earners. Using the tactics and networks they had developed during the suffrage movement and working through both partisan and nonpartisan voluntary associations, they led other public policy campaigns, such as legalizing the dissemination of birth control information, repealing national prohibition, and modernizing state government. The stories of these campaigns demonstrate both the possibilities and limitations of New York City women's efforts to sustain feminist progressive reform after enfranchisement.

Lowering maternal and infant death rates was a top priority. During the 1910s, 250,000 babies and 25,000 new mothers died annually, a rate that put the United States seventh in infant and seventeenth in maternal mortality in comparison with advanced European nations. The founding director of the US Children's Bureau, Julia Lathrop, proposed matching grants to states to support improvements in maternal and infant health. Jeannette Rankin, Congress's first woman member, incorporated Lathrop's proposal in a bill she introduced in 1918.[4]

The Women's City Club had already pioneered in this area. In 1917, Irene Osgood Andrews, a University of Wisconsin–trained social scientist, spurred the club to focus on the lack of prenatal care for the urban poor. As Frances Perkins put it, wealthy women experienced "infinitesimal" losses in childbirth. In contrast, the general population saw a doctor only a week or so before delivery, if then, and by that time undetected infections, kidney problems, and high blood pressure had all too often brought tragedy.[5]

In response to Andrews's initiative, the club formed a committee on maternity protection, which recruited a board of medical advisers. The committee then raised money for a maternity center, a free clinic offering prenatal care and nurse-midwife services. The center, the nation's first, opened on August 30, 1917, on East Seventy-Ninth Street in Manhattan. Club volunteers, settlement workers, and medical personnel contacted pregnant women, whom nurses would then visit. The center then provided sterile delivery outfits, layettes, and even house-keeping assistance in case of a mother's hospitalization. After managing the clinic for almost two years, the club handed it over to the Maternity Centre Association (MCA), which child welfare advocates had founded in 1918 to expand the program. Perkins, who ran the MCA for a year before becoming a state industrial commissioner, praised its work as "social justice operating in a field where nobody had thought of it before."[6]

Meanwhile, Rankin's bill lay dormant. In 1919, Senator Morris Sheppard (Democrat from Texas) and Representative Horace Towner (Republican from

Iowa) submitted a new version, the Act for the Promotion of the Welfare and Hygiene of Maternity and Infancy, later known as the Sheppard-Towner Act. After making an outright annual grant to states of $10,000, the act promised matching funds for programs to improve the health of new mothers and their babies. Keen to see the bill enacted, National Consumers' League head Florence Kelley launched the Sheppard-Towner Subcommittee of the Women's Joint Congressional Committee (WJCC), an organization founded in 1920 by the League of Women Voters' first national president, Maud Wood Park, to coordinate women's national legislative initiatives.[7] Kelley expected wide support for the bill: who could be against saving mothers and babies? Support was widespread, but so was opposition. The bill's critics argued that maternal health was best left to doctors; others objected to extending government reach into family life; physicians claimed that because infant mortality was already "trending downward" the bill was a waste of money. One writer to the *Times* linked the bill to feminism. She charged that the bill's sole purpose was "to create jobs with good salaries and considerable power for a notorious group of feminists, to whose machinations the country should by now be awake."[8]

Sheppard-Towner finally passed, and President Harding signed it into law in November 1921. Suffragists were jubilant, but their work was not done. Each state now had to pass legislation to "enable" the bill, that is, to permit it to receive and distribute federal money. In its first six months, twelve state legislatures did so and thirty more submitted provisional acceptances, but four, including New York, rejected it, citing financial "strains" and objections to "federal interference." Meanwhile, other opponents had surfaced: some senators confessed they would have voted against it if they could have done so secretly in the cloakroom, where women voters could not see them. Doctors charged that the bill would lead to socialized medicine. A loosely organized Boston-based group called the Woman Patriots, a successor to the National Association Opposed to Woman Suffrage, claimed the bill would only create political jobs for "childless suffragists" and destroy marriage by promoting birth control and "free love." When Republican governor Nathan Miller approved $125,000 for hog barns on the state fairground, Florence Kelley accused him of finding "swine shelters" more appealing than saving mothers and babies. Recalling that the state had no qualms about accepting federal funds to protect livestock, Narcissa Vanderlip suggested, "If it is constitutional to use Federal funds to save hogs from cholera, and cows from tuberculosis, it is constitutional to use them to save babies and their mothers from death." Under pressure, Miller approved $100,000 for a state bureau for infant and maternal hygiene. Kelley then pointed out that enabling Sheppard-Towner would have netted a better deal: a $10,000 grant plus $75,000 matched by an equal amount of federal money.[9]

In 1922 the New York State League of Women Voters made enabling Sheppard-Towner a primary goal. By then its relations with Governor Miller had soured. In an address to the league's annual convention at the start of the previous year, Miller had characterized the organization's attempts to exert political power as a "menace to representative government." Saying there was no more place for a "league of women voters" than one of "men voters," he cited the league's opposition to Senator Wadsworth as a sign that it was not nonpartisan. He respected "the ability, the patriotism and the capacity for public service of the high-minded women in this league," but urged them to exert influence only through a political party, which to his mind was the only way to hold political actors accountable. That political parties marginalized women's policy issues did not seem to concern him.[10]

The feminist reform community responded quickly. Carrie Chapman Catt told the governor she could not recall any party that had ever accomplished "a great reform" without pressure from nonpartisan groups. Forty-one Republican members of the league published a long letter in the *Times* saying they were humiliated when the mainstream political parties banned their exercise of "independence or judgment." They asked the governor if he thought the Dairyman's League, Grange, Citizens Union, Bar Association, American Legion, and Manufacturers' Association were also menaces. Or, "are we a menace because we are women?" They ended by listing principles they thought all Republicans embraced, including educating voters, presenting all sides of an issue, and making public office a trust, not a spoil of victory. Miller was not convinced. A year later, he reaffirmed more strongly than ever that pressure from nonpolitical groups was a menace to American institutions.

Although Narcissa Vanderlip later said the league had restored cordial relations with Miller, his critique emboldened the opposition to enabling Sheppard-Towner. In response, the league formed the United Organizations for the Sheppard-Towner Maternity and Infancy Bill (UO). Consisting of representatives from all the state branches of the national groups that had gotten the bill through Congress, the UO elected Vanderlip its chair.

She was well prepared for this role. Born in 1879, she was the wife of banker, international financier, and former assistant secretary of the treasury Frank A. Vanderlip. She had come to woman suffrage when as a young mother she realized how little say she had over conditions for raising her six children. In 1913 she organized a Scarborough, NY, civic study club, a name that camouflaged its true purpose: to work for the vote. Only in 1915 did she change its name to the Woman Suffrage Party of Scarborough, after which she became a state Woman Suffrage Party (WSP) captain. She sent out tons of mail, organized meetings and parades, and canvassed voters house to house. In 1917, as WSP congressional chair, she kept detailed card files on thousands of activists, legislators, officials, and potential supporters. Her files on speakers—noting their intelligence, "attractiveness," suitability for parlor meetings, what foreign languages they spoke, and how they had performed—put a wealth of resources at her fingertips.[11]

Many other women helped the campaign. Few were more important than Dr. S. Josephine Baker. An 1898 graduate of the Women's Medical College of the New York Infirmary, Baker began her career in private practice, but when that did not prosper she took posts first as a medical examiner for the New York Life Insurance Company and later as a city medical inspector. In 1907, assisting the city's health commissioner on vaccination and sanitation, she helped apprehend Mary Mallon (aka "Typhoid Mary"), a cook who had spread the infection. In 1908 Baker proposed that the Health Department establish a bureau of child hygiene, the nation's first. The commissioner agreed and appointed her director. When the New York University-Bellevue Hospital Medical School asked Baker to lecture in a new public health doctoral program, she enrolled in the program herself. The school granted her a doctorate in the field in 1917.

Baker's support for the Sheppard-Towner enabling campaign gave it stature. She wrote press statements, testified before the legislature, and addressed mass meetings on the need for more rural public health resources. She sent out concise summaries to legislators on what the bill was and was not and connected league members to her medical community. To counter a charge that New York City would get all of the money, she repeatedly stressed that funds would go primarily to rural areas, as her own work had already led to a 50 percent drop in the city's infant death rate.[12] Baker's support remained crucial to every step of the league's Sheppard-Towner campaign.

Vanderlip began her part of the campaign by responding to a sarcastic *Times* editorial entitled "Federal Midwifery" that began, "Governor Miller can't find among the enumerated powers of Congress 'to provide for the common defense and general welfare' the power to engage in the 'practice of medicine or midwifery.'" The editorial described the backers of the Sheppard-Towner law as sociologists and Socialists, sentimentalists, universal meddlers, and place hunters. They forced the law's passage "to promote the welfare and hygiene of maternity and infancy" in order to successfully maintain the highly modern and expensive theory that Congress has the power to legislate in regard to anything that a minority can persuade or bulldoze it into believing to involve the general welfare.[13]

Vanderlip's answer emphasized the human side of the issue. In 1920 alone, she wrote, 1,406 mothers died in childbirth along with 20,238 babies. She observed further that the cost of raising motherless babies was much higher than funding public health nurses. She ended by attacking the term "federal midwifery." During the war, she said, healthy men and women, who of course had been healthy babies, were matters of national concern and hence covered under the Constitution's general welfare provisions.[14]

She then reached out to her network, asking the United Organizations' member groups to distribute literature and arrange meetings, contact local editors, send clippings to legislators, raise money, and send telegrams, letters, petitions, and resolutions to the legislature's Public Health Committee. She circularized legislators herself, assuring them that Sheppard-Towner was not federal interference. She also got state senator Holland S. Duell to introduce an enabling bill and sent a delegation to Governor Miller to urge him to support it. Miller vowed a veto.[15]

Vanderlip's chief lieutenant in this work, the United Organizations' vice chair and suffragist Betty Wakeman Mitchell, came from Hudson Falls, a small town north of Albany. As chair of the rural problems committee of the state Woman Suffrage Party, Mitchell had seen local women mill hands face tough health challenges. For the Sheppard-Towner enabling campaign she wrote thousands of letters, surely as many as Vanderlip, corresponding frequently with state senator Nathan Straus Jr., who made strategic motions from the senate floor and warned Mitchell about what to expect at hearings. She wrote to every legislator she knew, often bantering about old personal and family connections, and encouraged others to write their own letters, saying, "You know how sometimes the fate of a bill may depend on just one person," and then thanking them for their efforts. Mitchell kept key state and national women leaders informed of every step of her progress.[16]

During the spring 1923 legislative session the United Organizations met every Tuesday afternoon in a room at Grand Central Terminal. After the senate defeated the bill twice, the women heard it was in the "grave-yard" unless they could persuade the assembly to take it up again. Assembly leaders told them to stop bumping heads "against the stone wall." The group would not stop. Unexpected pushback seemed to come from the Catholic Church. Rumors circulated that Sheppard-Towner would introduce birth control or was somehow connected to a pending Smith-Towner bill mandating an end to parochial schools. The archbishop was astonished, as he did not oppose Sheppard-Towner. The UO had to place letters (all in long-hand) on every legislator's desk attesting to his support.

On the last day of the 1923 session, the enabling bill finally passed. Promised 102 votes in the assembly, it got 104. At that point, Al Smith, now back in the governorship, sent a message that if the Democratic senate could not pass a bill already passed by the Republican assembly, they had better "pull down their shades." The bill squeaked through the senate 26 to 22. In reflecting on this experience and looking forward, Vanderlip offered important strategic advice. In the future, she said, "as many women as possible should unite each year for the passage of just one bill." She concluded, "We fought our same old fight, with our same old enemies, between progress and reaction—in both parties." Women would need to band together tightly if they had any hope of winning.[17] Single-minded focus and absolute unity were her watchwords.

The United Organizations' work was still not done. Betty Mitchell got Dr. Hermann Biggs, head of the state Department of Health, to come to New York City to explain how the federal funds would be spent. She sent letters of gratitude, adding a personal touch to each, to leading legislators, party leaders, and Governor Smith and his wife. To Helen Rogers Reid she expressed appreciation for a "glorious editorial" and for what her paper, the *Tribune*, had done for the cause. *Tribune* reporter Dennis Lynch received special praise. "It was he who first warned us of our real enemies, and who yesterday advised our getting a special message from the Governor. We never could have held the Democrats in line without it."[18]

The New York Sheppard-Towner enabling campaign showed suffragists that they could harness the power of their old networks to fight for progressive change in a time of conservative reaction. How long those networks would hold was an open question. Leaders had to select new goals carefully, reinspire troops, and recruit younger campaigners—not easy tasks. As for Sheppard-Towner, it may have lowered maternal and infant death rates by about 9 to 21 percent, but only among white rural populations. Infant mortality rates remained high in non-white families. Moreover, credit for declining rates of infant mortality seemed to be due more to trends begun early in the century through improvements in nutrition, water purity, and sanitation. Observers agreed, however, that home visits from nurses and health centers offering ongoing care were helpful. In any event, funding for Sheppard-Towner was soon threatened. As a condition of its renewal in 1926, Congress demanded it be ended in 1929, and it was.[19]

A tremendous effort for uneven results, Sheppard-Towner was nonetheless significant to the women who fought for it. For the first time they had seen federal law incorporate motherhood as a governmental concern. Moreover, the women could take pride in the selflessness of their effort. As Dorothy Kirchwey Brown, chair of the national League of Women Voters Child Welfare Committee, put it,

> Here were a group of women who were willing and glad to give their time and strength, and to work—and how they did work!—to persuade the Congress of the United States that the public welfare demanded the passage of this bill,—and not a woman there had anything to gain, individually, by its passage.[20]

While selflessness had made the suffragists feel good about their hard work, it had done nothing to win them the high level of political power many of them had hoped to achieve. Still, it showed them the enduring value of their suffrage networks and political skills. They would continue to use both in their ongoing quests for further progressive feminist change. For them, having the vote meant everything.

On the morning of April 11, 1936, a dead baby boy was found at the bottom of an airshaft of an apartment house in the Bronx. The next night, the police questioned eighteen-year-old Elizabeth Smith, who lived nearby. At first she denied knowing anything. Later she confessed she had given birth to him in the middle of the night in her parents' bathroom and then taken him up to the roof. She claimed the baby neither moved nor cried. As she rested her arms on the parapet, she fainted. When she awoke, the baby was gone. The police charged her with murder.

Smith went on trial in October. Her three attorneys—two men and one woman—argued that sedatives she had taken for pain had put her into a "twilight sleep." Thus, she had been in a "hypnotic" or sleepwalking state when the stillborn baby fell. Two physicians testified that the violence of the unattended birth had most likely killed the baby and that Smith's actions had been "automatic." Assistant District Attorney William Smith (no relation) had a different view. He said that because Elizabeth Smith had hidden her pregnancy and made no preparations for the birth, she had planned to kill her baby all along.[21]

When Bronx county judge Harry Stackell asked Smith point blank whether she had thrown her baby off the roof, she insisted she had been in a daze. "The baby was in my arms. All I thought was to kill myself. I saw blackness come over me. I fainted near the edge of the roof with my arm resting on the edge." When she came to, she went back home and fell asleep. She also claimed that a married man had attacked her and that her parents had been unaware of her condition.

Elizabeth Smith's case attracted citywide attention. Members of the Women's League of Washington Heights attended the trial, openly weeping at Smith's testimony and gathering signatures for leniency. The local press described Smith's pallor from having endured the most "sacred [yet] dangerous" experience of womanhood silently and unaided. The city's feminist reformers expressed outrage over her all-male jury. Men could never imagine what she had suffered, they claimed, whereas a "jury of mothers would have known as a certainty." Pointing to New Jersey's women jurors, they demanded to know when New York women would be entitled to a jury of their peers.

Woman suffrage did not automatically confer jury service rights on women. New York statutes, for example, retained male-specific wording in laws governing juries. The Women Lawyers' Association began lobbying the legislature to remove the wording as soon as suffrage passed, but got nowhere. In late 1919, Julia V. Grilli, a Brooklyn trial lawyer, charging that jury lists without women were "inadequate, insufficient and illegal," filed a writ of mandamus to compel the commissioner of jurors to call women. Claiming that women did not want to participate in jury service, Brooklyn supreme court justice Edward Lazansky denied Grilli's writ. The League of Women Voters, the Women's City Club, and the National Woman's Party joined with other women's organizations annually to propose jury service bills. Arguing that it was unfair for a woman to be "arrested by a man, brought into court before a jury of men, sentenced by a male Judge, and then sent to a jail that is run by men," they said that keeping women off juries made them second-class citizens. Their bills made women's service mandatory but with the same exemptions available to men. Legislators remained unmoved. All of the coalition's bills either died in committee or passed the assembly but not the senate.[22]

To buttress their arguments against women's jury service, opponents marshaled a wide set of gender stereotypes. In 1923 Frederick O'Byrne, New York County commissioner of jurors, argued that women were emotionally unfit to judge criminal behavior and would be swayed by how a defendant looked. He also insisted that "Conditions around a court house are a man's conditions and I don't think the men are ready to change them. When a man goes into the jury room he pulls out his cigar or cigarette right away, and if he isn't able to do this, you can't get him, so to speak." A state senator pointed to the hardships of sequestering, when women would be "locked in a jury room with men for possibly one, two or three days." In the 1930s, local all-male bar associations repeated these arguments. They even surmised that as lawyers they would have difficulty talking to women jurors "man-to-man."[23]

Woman juror advocates had little trouble responding. Women might be "tender-hearted," Buffalo lawyer Helen G. M. Rodgers told judiciary committees in Albany in 1926, but no more than men, who might also be swayed by a defendant's looks. One respondent to a Brooklyn *Daily Eagle* poll on the topic retorted, "Women are doing jury duty in the home every day." On the sequester point, Rhoda Fox Graves, in 1930 the sole female assembly member and a National Woman's Party spokesperson, noted she had been "locked up in the Assembly chamber with 149 men for the last five years, sometimes as late as 2 o'clock in the morning," and never had any trouble. Finally, the idea that lawyers needed to talk "man-to-man" with jurors was "prejudicial to justice," especially in moral cases involving young girls.[24]

The one argument that stumped them was the claim of women's reluctance to serve. State senator Nathan Straus, an ally on Sheppard-Towner, warned the League of Women Voters that farm women were especially resistant. In 1924, journalist Esther Coster blamed their husbands: "The thought that 'my wife' should be compelled to go away from home for perhaps a week on a murder trial and maybe 'have to be shut up all night with a lot of rough men' is anathema to the farmers who have no objection to the women staying at home all the time and working their heads off."[25] In a piece she wrote four years later she said investigators had not found that rural women objected to "getting away from home occasionally." In fact, she said, many women saw jury duty as a pleasant break in their daily lives.[26]

Some urban women also complained about prospective jury duty. A *Brooklyn Daily Eagle* survey conducted in 1924 netted only 347 replies favorable to some kind of jury service. In 1927, out of seventy-five women polled by the Women's National Republican Club, twelve favored service of any kind, while twenty-two wanted optional only; eleven opposed all service and the rest did not vote. In the late 1930s, three New York City couples wrote to Governor Lehman claiming women's jury service would work a hardship on "the average housewife" who was "already burdened down with duties at home." They characterized women jury service campaigners as those "who either haven't a home, have no intention of presiding over one, 'the spinster' or 'old maid' type or the 'daily frequenter of political Clubs.'" US district judge Frank Cooper agreed, in 1936 saying that the only women in favor of jury duty were "the militant club women and not all of them are in favor of it."[27]

Over time, new leaders emerged in the women's jury service campaign. In response to a 1924 survey on why women should serve, attorney Dorothy Kenyon, a League of Women Voters officer, said, simply, "It is their duty." Born in 1888 into a lawyer's family and raised on Manhattan's Upper West Side, Kenyon graduated from Smith College in 1908. Years later, after a trip to Mexico awakened her social conscience, she went to New York University Law School, graduating in 1917 and becoming a social activist on civil rights, labor reform, marriage equality, and birth control. In 1926 she wrote a pamphlet and designed programs on the women's jury service for women's organizations. For decades she remained on the front lines of the quest.[28]

She worked closely with another attorney, Caroline Klein Simon. Born in 1900, Simon graduated from New York University Law School in 1925 but could not find a job, perhaps (she thought) because she was Jewish, married, and a mother. Women's voluntary associations offered her a niche where she could use her knowledge of crime prevention and corrections. She became a major spokesperson for both the Women's City Club and League of Women Voters on the jury issue.[29]

The next steps in the jury service campaign demonstrated the importance of having women in legislative office. Three women in the state legislature in the

1930s played key roles in the final victory. One was attorney Doris Irene Byrne, born in the Bronx in 1905 into a family of Democratic Party activists: her father, Daniel, was a Bronx court clerk (eventually the borough's chief clerk) and her mother, Mabel, was copresident of the Bronx Assembly District (AD) Democratic Club and corresponding secretary of the Bronx County Democratic Committee. Two years after graduating from Fordham Law School in 1931, Doris Byrne ran for the state assembly on the ticket of the Recovery Party, founded by Democrats anxious to show their independence from Tammany's corruption scandals. Byrne beat all her male opponents, first winning the primary by 697 votes and then the general election by a healthy margin.

The first woman to win a seat in the assembly in years, Byrne did not self-identify as a feminist. *Eagle* journalist Isabelle Keating described her as a "product of the post-suffragist era," "distinctly New Deal," but neither looking, acting, nor talking like a typical woman politician. She offered no feminist program, no era of social reform. "There aren't any great social reforms to be accomplished any more," Byrne told Keating, implausibly. "You can't get anywhere alone in the Assembly anyway," she continued, pointing to her status as the assembly's lone female.[30] Once in the assembly, she must have changed her mind, for soon she was the woman juror bill's prime mover.

Two other women, both Republicans from outside New York City, became her allies. One was Jane Hedges Todd. A former suffragist and organizer of Republican women's clubs in Westchester County, Todd became a Republican Party committee member and frequent delegate to Republican national conventions. She won election to the assembly in 1934 and then nine more one-year terms. Rhoda Fox Graves, also a former suffragist, came from Gouverneur, the upstate town where in 1918 an electoral contest had led observers to conclude that women candidates were "doomed." Graves won election to the assembly in 1925 and annual elections thereafter until 1932, when she lost a bid for the state senate. When she made a second attempt for the senate in 1934 she won, a victory that made her the first woman in that body. Graves and Todd worked closely with Byrne in the jury service campaign.[31]

A number of factors came together in the 1930s that turned the tide toward approval of women's jury service. Court scandals of the decade's early years demonstrated the vulnerability of women brought before the magistrates' courts, often without counsel and no resources to defend themselves. Even though these courts did not empanel juries, they sent cases to courts that did, and the lack of women jurors (as in Elizabeth Smith's case) made the public think that gender diversity might lead to a fairer outcome. In addition, by the 1930s a number of women had become judges. It made little sense to exclude women from juries when women were sitting on the bench.

Factors external to New York also played a role. In January 1935, renewed attention to New York's lack of women on juries arose from publicity about the four New Jersey women jurors then trying Bruno Richard Hauptmann for the murder of Charles and Anne Lindbergh's baby. In addition, the US Department of Justice approved women jurors for all federal courts, in part because judges who could not fill panels were turning to unemployed men, whose sole interest was the three-dollar-a-day pay. Woman juror advocates pointed out the obvious: empaneling women would double the jury pool with much more qualified participants.[32]

In March 1935, Doris Byrne sponsored a bill for mandatory jury service, with exceptions for housewives, mothers, or women caring for young children. Conscious of visual symbolism, on the day of the assembly debate on the bill Republican Jane Todd crossed the aisle to sit beside Democrat Byrne, even though she did not agree with mandatory service. Rhoda Fox Graves came over from the senate to join them. The bill passed by a large majority (105 to 33), but then went down in the senate, 3 to 1. The senate continued to reject all further mandatory jury bills.[33]

Jury service advocates pressed on. The resolution of the Elizabeth Smith case helped their cause. The case had not gone well for her. After deliberating seven hours, her all-male jury returned a verdict of guilty of second-degree manslaughter, a crime punishable by up to fifteen years. After the judge revealed he had received thousands of letters and telegrams urging mercy, he stunned the court by saying he wanted to give her "another chance at life" by giving her three years' probation. He ordered her to report once a month to a probation officer and demonstrate behavior "absolutely above reproach," not to capitalize on the interest her case had aroused, and not to give interviews to the press or seek a motion picture contract. A member of the Women's League of Washington Heights took her into her home to recuperate from her ordeal.[34] Believing their efforts had helped win this result, Elizabeth Smith's supporters later referred to her case as a reason women needed to be on juries.

In the end, it was a male legislator who got a compromise women's jury service bill passed. In spring 1937, Brooklyn state senator and Democrat Philip M. Kleinfeld proposed a nonmandatory bill that allowed women—simply by virtue of their sex—automatic exemptions. Opposition was still stiff. Over thirty county and city bar associations and men's lawyers' clubs from across the state sent in objections. The Oswego County Bar Association argued that women had shown no interest in jury service. Moreover, the county would have to build extra washrooms and incur new costs, such as buying cigarettes for female jurors in the same way it buys cigars for male jurors. Local officials even worried that women would charge counties for "rouge, powder, and lipstick." The senate ignored these caveats and at the end of March passed the Kleinfeld bill thirty-four to thirteen. The assembly approved it in May and Governor Lehman signed it, effective September 1.

The first New York State women to serve jumped the gun, participating at the end of August in a short upstate trial of a woman charged with reckless driving. Declining cigarettes, they asked for ice cream, and got it. The *Amsterdam News* proudly announced that one of their long-time staff writers, Leola Lillard of Harlem, was the first African American woman to serve. New York's courtrooms would never be the same.[35]

Most jury service advocates had wanted a mandatory bill. Doris Byrne called the elective bill "simply a sop" that women accepted merely to prove they could be good citizens. Dorothy Kenyon denounced it as "not amounting to a hill of beans" and "totally inadequate." Reformers regrouped for a mandatory service campaign, with Caroline Simon leading at the Women's City Club and attorney Jane Smith Cramer at the New York State League of Women Voters. Jane Todd and Rhoda Graves also stayed on. Showing again the continuity between the suffrage movement and progressive feminist reform, Cramer organized "jury schools" modeled on the schools set up after suffrage to teach women about voting. In the jury schools, judges presided over moot trials; attorneys (including Kenyon) role-played plaintiffs; and women who had served on juries reported on their experiences, including how to resist being bullied by male jurors. Thousands of people across the state turned out for these events, which paid off, as thousands of women rejected their automatic exemption and enrolled as potential jurors.[36]

In New York, winning a woman's right to elective jury service had taken twenty years. In 1924 journalist Esther Coster had suggested that women would eventually learn that jury duty was "not such a bugbear" and husbands would find they would not be "as neglected as they feared." At that point, she guessed, mandatory service would follow.[37] It did not. Perhaps if women's jury service advocates had been willing to compromise in the 1920s, accepting the proverbial half a loaf to win the whole loaf later on, they might have won elective service earlier. Whereas some women activists were open to such an incremental approach, the advocates of mandatory service would not compromise. In their view, only a women's jury service on exactly the same terms as men would elevate women's citizenship to "first class" status.

Jury service advocates had no way of knowing how long New York's legislature would hold out against mandatory service. When the rejection continued into the 1950s, advocates gave up the quest, turning to other priorities. Events higher up brought it to pass. In 1975, the US Supreme Court ruled in *Taylor* v. *Louisiana* that juries excluding women did not represent "a fair cross section of the community" and would henceforth be illegal. Only then did the New York State legislature repeal women's automatic exemption.[38]

"When women were given the vote we had more power on our side," wrote labor activist Rose Schneiderman in her autobiography. By "our side" she meant women labor activists like herself who, after winning the vote, put more faith in laws than in strikes and collective bargaining to achieve worker protections. Schneiderman had come to this position after years as a union activist. Born in 1882 in Russian Poland and arriving in New York City with her family at age eight, when her mother could not care for her she and her siblings spent time in an orphanage. She had to leave school at thirteen. By 1903 she had become a skilled cap-maker and avid Socialist and unionist. Her passionate, impromptu speeches and keen organizational skills soon won her a seat on the United Cloth Hat and Cap Makers' general executive board, an election that made her the first woman to hold such a post. In 1908 she became vice president of the New York Women's Trade Union League (NYWTUL), and the following year she participated in the city's largest-ever garment strike. Her angry speech at the mass meeting following the Triangle fire galvanized the audience into pressuring the state to establish the New York State Factory Investigating Commission (FIC). Although ultimately disappointed in union failure to prioritize reforms specific to women's needs, Schneiderman remained a committed unionist. For her, however, the NYWTUL would be her most important labor affiliation.[39]

Schneiderman's trust in the power of women's votes would prove overconfident. Strong opposition to laws protecting labor came from many fronts. Most employers, already resistant to union demands, convinced courts that laws interfering in their business practices violated freedom of contract, workers' presumed right under the due process clause of the Fourteenth Amendment to negotiate their own terms of employment. Some unionists also rejected the legislative approach, arguing it gave excessive power to bureaucrats. Finally, some working women opposed any law that did not protect both sexes equally. They feared employers would use sex-specific laws as excuses to fire them (which they did). Protectionists like Schneiderman retorted that such laws would be an "entering wedge" leading to judicial approval of laws protecting all workers—male and female, adult and child alike.

By the time women had won the vote, New York labor reformers had already won sex-specific bills, that is, laws protecting women and children only: in 1881, suitable seating for women in mercantile and industrial establishments; in 1886, bans on women and minors under twenty-one from working over sixty hours a week; in 1889, bans on night work for women under twenty-one; in 1896, a sixty-hour workweek for women in mercantile establishments, and the same for women factory workers in 1899. In 1912, the Factory Investigating Commission won a fifty-four-hour workweek for women factory workers (canneries got seasonal rush exemptions). During World War I, the National Consumers' League (NCL), Women's Trade Union League (WTUL), and later the Women's Joint Legislative Conference (WJLC) won bans on women under twenty-one working as messengers and on street railways, and under eighteen on elevators—jobs seen as putting young women into moral danger. Not all of these laws were enforced: businesses ignored them, inspectors were stretched too thin, and workers feared reporting breaches. But after suffrage, New York's women labor reformers continued to pursue such laws, some of which went even further.[40]

On March 5, 1919, a dramatic event unfolded in the New York State Assembly chamber that exposed the deep fault lines created by their proposals. A joint labor and industry committee held a nearly five-hour hearing on sex-specific protectionist bills. One bill established an eight-hour workday for female adults and minors working in industry; another proposed a commission to study and determine a minimum, or "living," wage for these workers. The remaining bills mandated a fifty-four-hour workweek for female office workers, elevator operators, and street transportation workers, and prohibited those same groups from working after 10:00 PM. The bills were the result of intense lobbying by the members of the Women's Trade Union League working alongside representatives from over a dozen trade unions.[41]

The hearing began with the arrival in Albany of hundreds of the bills' supporters, brought in on a special train hired by the Women's Joint Legislative Conference. A band played as they marched up Capitol Hill carrying flags and banners displaying the slogan, "Give the Girls a Fighting Chance!" Opponents were there too, wearing purple badges with only one word on them: "Opposed." Once the hearing began, witnesses cross-examined one another with "verbal claws." Opponents taunted the bills' promoters by calling them "society women" and "professional uplifters"; in return, proponents labeled their critics as selfish, accusing them of sacrificing the welfare of the many to benefit a few.[42] The atmosphere was so nasty and charged that neither side could empathize with the other.

The hearing opened with the opponents. Nora Stanton Blatch, Elizabeth Cady Stanton's granddaughter, a civil engineer, and like her mother, Harriot, affiliated with the National Woman's Party, represented office workers and the Women's League for Equal Opportunity (WLEO). Founded by women printers in 1915 to oppose night-work bans, at the end of World War I the WLEO had brought in women transportation workers, who opposed limits on weekly hours. "For years," Nora Blatch began,

> we came to Albany as suffragists and asked you men not to class us with minors and not to consider us wards of the State politically, and finally

you woke up and let us stand on our own feet politically. Now, we come and beg of you not to class us with minors . . . , not to call us wards of the State . . . , but to let us stand on our own feet economically.[43]

She attacked laws that banned women conductors and ticket sellers from night work while ignoring the night-work women who swept platforms and scrubbed floors. She noted that, while no laws ban nurses, women doctors, and actresses from working at night, the state is ready to interfere "in a mischievous way with the rights of women who are receiving fairly good salaries and with the exceptional women who have climbed up the industrial scale." As chief draughtsman for a steel construction company, she herself had on occasion worked sixty, seventy hours a week, often after 10:00 p.m. Restrictions on the workweek threatened women's ability to compete with men for jobs and to avoid being "crushed" out of higher work grades.

Officers from the Women's League for Equal Opportunity took up her points, giving examples of how special legislation for women newspaper, transportation, and elevator workers limited their competitiveness and incomes. "Working at night is a personal affair entirely," former president Ada R. Wolff (an unemployed proofreader) asserted. WLEO president Ella M. Sherwin pointed to England, where "protections for women" had turned out to be "protections for men." Field secretary Margaret Kerr-Firth cited medical opinion that night work was no more harmful for women than for men and claimed that working nights made it easier for women to get childcare. Finally, she avowed that women, like men, hate being "coerced" by government.[44]

Amy Wren, president of the Brooklyn Woman's Bar Association, called the bills' advocates "professional reformers." She admitted that "there are a number . . . who are good hearted—I give them all credit—I think they try to do what is right, but there are a lot . . . whose fathers earned their money by the sweat of their brow and they are going around racked with sympathies for the working women." Insisting that working women alone should propose regulations of their labor, she noted that, since workers could not spend time in Albany, legislators thought the reformers' "paid lobby" represented women, but this was not true. She spoke derisively of the idea of women being morally at risk after dark, reminding legislators that people had once used such arguments against the idea of women lawyers and doctors. She asked if the woman doctor should tell her patient, "You cannot have your baby after ten; it will have to wait until seven in the morning." She joked about riding in a hotel elevator after ten o'clock at night and being disappointed that the men in the car had failed to solicit sex from the female operator. Night work must go on, she continued, on trolleys, subways, and elevators. Working women do not want to be told what they can and cannot do by well-meaning women "who have nothing to do but reform all the time." In her view, a greater social benefit would come from keeping men at home after ten o'clock and letting the women work.[45]

Other opponents of the bills included a hotel owner, who predicted the bills would legislate his waitresses and elevator operators out of good jobs. While praising the Consumers' League for winning worker health benefits, a mill owner argued that decreasing weekly hours would force him to hire extra shifts at increased costs, thereby lessening his ability to compete with southern factories, which had lower production costs. The heads of rural telegraph companies pleaded for exemptions on the ground that emergencies often require holding employees over. Finally, representing the Women Voters' Anti-Suffrage Party, a Mrs. LeRoy S. Blatner, wife of a Buffalo physician, predicted that soon the "working girl" would be calling around only "once a week in a limousine to collect her salary."[46]

Representing the Women's Joint Legislative Conference, Mary Elisabeth Dreier then introduced the bills' proponents. Born in Brooklyn in 1875 to inherited wealth, Dreier had devoted her entire adult life and much of her fortune to protecting working women. She was president of the New York Women's Trade Union League for almost ten years and then industrial section chair of the Woman Suffrage Party. She was the only woman appointed to the Factory Investigating Commission. Faulting labor unions for inadequate protections of working women, after suffrage Dreier focused on legislating labor reforms and defeating antireform legislators, such as Speaker Thaddeus Sweet.

Dreier introduced three government officials: James M. Lynch, state industrial commissioner; Mary van Kleeck, director of the US Women in Industry Service; and Dr. Louis I. Harris, chief of preventable diseases in the New York City Bureau of Industrial Hygiene. Lynch conveyed his colleagues' approval of the bills but warned that enforcement required larger inspection staffs. Van Kleeck pointed to the historical exploitation of women in industry (long hours seven days a week for low pay) and argued that shorter workweeks increased both efficiency and output. Harris, an expert in occupational diseases, blamed industry for rising rates of tuberculosis, especially among children and women. He claimed night work not only heightened these risks but also caused women to neglect their children. Labor leader James P. Holland of the state Federation of Labor countered the claim that "professional reformers" and "uplifters" had initiated the bills by pointing out the bills' working-class advocates in the chamber, including New York Women's Trade Union League officials Rose Schneiderman (president) and Nelle Swartz (secretary).

Florence Kelley spoke next. Born in 1859 into a distinguished abolitionist and politically renowned family, Kelley graduated from Cornell University in 1882 and then studied law and government at the University of Zurich. After marrying a Russian Socialist medical student, in 1886 Kelley moved with her family to New York City, where she joined the anti–child labor campaign. When her husband became abusive, she fled with her three children to Chicago, finding refuge with Jane Addams at Hull House and work in the field of labor statistics. Her 1892 report on sweatshop conditions led to an eight-hour law for women and children, prohibitions on tenement sweatshops, and the establishment of factory inspection in Illinois. Named the state's first chief factory inspector, Kelley held this post until 1896, at the same time as she earned a law degree from Northwestern University. In 1899, the newly formed NCL made Kelley its executive secretary. Kelley moved back to New York, where she would transform the NCL into the nation's premier lobby for protectionist labor laws.[47]

Kelley's speech was short and pointed. She began by reminding the legislators that the National Consumers' League had been pushing for minimum wage and eight-hour bills since 1910. With thirteen states already passing similar laws, New York State was lagging. If New York fails to act, she warned, strikes would follow.

> The living wage is coming now; the eight hours a day is coming now and they are coming by law if you will, by peaceable methods, otherwise they are coming by methods which will be no credit to our state, but will be the evil and painful and cruel choice forced upon the workers by the failure of our Legislature for the fifth time to take action on this very modest program.[48]

Assemblyman Bewley rebuked her for "agitating strikes." When she responded that she was only describing what would happen, he cut her off.

Dreier moved swiftly to give workers the floor. Betty Hawley, a waitress from Buffalo representing three hundred "girls," called Mrs. Blatner's image of women collecting wages in limousines unkind but added that such a sight would make her proud. Decrying the twelve-hour workday, she argued for eight hours and night-work bans for waitresses to protect them from harassment. Nelle Swartz called union members' opposition to the bills disgraceful and selfish. She admitted that although a few women might suffer, the lives of the vast majority would be better and eventually an eight-hour workday for women would convince employers to give the same to men. She wished scrubwomen could have been included, "but we must take what we can get now." She begged legislators not to listen to "a few selfish women and a woman lawyer and some anti-suffragists. Good Lord, to think that there are such to-day, and two or three trade union women who will line themselves up with the Manufacturers Association and the Anti-Suffragists. It is a disgrace."[49]

After two more workers—a paper-box maker and an upholsterer—complained of their slim earnings and long hours, Brooklyn Deputy Assistant District Attorney Helen P. McCormick (the first woman in the state to hold such a post) testified. Active in suffrage and Republican Party politics, she had drafted the final version of the transportation workers' bill. She asserted that women worked on the street railways over ten hours a day with "insufficient and inadequate accommodations" (i.e., restrooms). She then yielded her time to Anna Merritt, a Brooklyn Rapid Transit "conductorette" fired for failing to report while under suspension. Merritt testified to suspensions for refusing long hours, insufficient meal times, seven-day-a-week schedules, "indecent" assaults, and an array of health issues, including fallen arches, varicose veins, and bruises. She endured all of this, she said, for a starting wage of two dollars and forty cents a day.[50]

With time running out, the chair allowed the remaining witnesses time only to state names and endorsements. Rebuttals were short. Amy Wren derided the Women's City Club, Woman Suffrage Party, and Consumers' League, whose members had never read the bills nor studied their potential effects but merely sympathized with the "poor working girl." Commissioner Lynch said he would not allow the great Empire State to treat its labor as North Carolina did. Of the five bills discussed that day, only two passed, those banning night work for female transportation workers, printers, and elevator operators. This was the worst possible outcome for women workers, as passage coincided with city leaders' pleas to businesses to hire unemployed veterans. Employers complied by firing women and replacing them with men, a result seemingly unanticipated by protectionists, although workers had repeatedly warned it would happen. Harriet Laidlaw of the state League of Women Voters called the dismissal of women workers unjust and indefensible. Frances Perkins demanded that transit companies adjust their schedules and stop using the bills as excuses to exclude women from those jobs. Their complaints fell on deaf ears.

Hundreds of women workers held public meetings to express their wrath. Speakers accused the bills' promoters of conspiring to force them back into their kitchens as housemaids. "Are we going?" one asked. "Never!" the crowd shouted. Amy Wren, as adviser to a grievance committee, vowed she would get the night-work bans repealed. She accused the "emotional, irrational" women reformers of turning women workers into "Bolsheviki" and "developing a class of scab labor." Nora Blatch referred to reformers as "Mrs. Van Astorbilts." Victoria Phillips, a conductor in Manhattan, compared her former job in a candy factory's "ice box" for ten dollars a week with her thirty-dollar-a-week conductor job. "How many lady lobbyists are prepared to pay me that for working in their kitchen?" Former conductor Helen Maxwell said her aunt worked as a maid for the law's framer, Helen McCormick. "Many's the time she has had to stay up until late at night to serve a supper to Miss McCormick's friends after the theatre," she said. "Did Miss McCormick pay my aunt overtime? She did not." In later sessions lawmakers repealed night-work bans for women in the printing trade and made various exceptions to the bans for adult female elevator operators and street railway workers. Women in those occupations had difficulty getting their old jobs back, however.[51]

Both sides in this emotional debate held fast. Reformers' promises that the current bills would lead to protections for all workers was small comfort to the hundreds of women who now lost well-paid jobs. In the early 1920s both the National Woman's Party (NWP) and the Women's National Republican Club declared their continuing opposition to the bills. In 1924, Doris Stevens, the well-known NWP leader, told the legislature's joint labor committee that she saw no more reason for restricting women's work than for applying laws to "one particular race or one particular creed."

None of this opposition stopped labor reformers from continuing to agitate for sex-specific labor laws. Dorothy Kenyon, state League of Women Voters legislative chair, protested against the 1925 Joiner bill, proposed by the Associated Industries of the State of New York and Assemblyman Webb A. Joiner, which mandated a nine-hour workday and fifty-four-hour workweek for women while promising to investigate whether such hours truly damaged women's health. A "48-hour-week law is in force in several States, and is already the law in New York for State employees," Kenyon observed. "It is a source of mortification that after 13 years' open discussion and detailed study our legislators are still unable to make up their minds on this question without another year of investigation." The Joiner bill passed. Governor Smith, told by his labor advisers that it was a "fake," vetoed it.[52]

Still not ready to approve a "real" forty-eight-hour workweek bill, in 1926 the legislature authorized the Industrial Survey Commission to study, yet again, the health impact on women of a fifty-four-hour workweek. The commission also hoped to find out whether women "truly wanted" forty-eight-hour workweeks. By this time, both sides were worn out. A compromise looked possible. Ada R. Wolff, representing the Women's League for Equal Opportunity, announced she would support a forty-eight-hour workweek *if* the bill allowed limited periods of overtime. Accepting that some women wanted to work longer hours, the League of Women Voters agreed to overtime exceptions. State Senator Seabury C. Mastick and Assemblyman Herbert B. Shonk cosponsored a new bill, which mandated forty-eight-hour workweeks with exceptions. It passed and Governor

Smith signed it. Effective January 1, 1928, it contained complex provisions that the state labor department was supposed to administer. This worried Nelle Swartz, now chair of the state's bureau for women in industry, as the department had not received the funds necessary to do so. Still, women labor reformers felt they had won. In the fall, now presidential candidate Al Smith took credit for the victory, a claim that infuriated Republican women who had previously supported him. They said they would now vote for his opponent, Herbert Hoover.[53]

During the same period as they were fighting for shorter hours and night-work bans, labor reformers were also campaigning for a minimum wage. In the early 1920s Mary (Molly) Williams Dewson (whom friends later called "Minimum Wage Dewson") joined Florence Kelley as one of the campaign's leaders. Born in 1874, Dewson graduated from Wellesley College, did research on domestic service for the Boston Women's Educational and Industrial Union, and in 1900 became superintendent of the parole department of the State Industrial School for Girls. In 1911, the state appointed her secretary of a commission to formulate a minimum wage, the nation's first. It became law the following year, but with a weak enforcement mechanism: wage boards could merely publish "white lists" of compliant companies and urge shoppers to patronize them. After joining the woman suffrage campaign and then doing war work overseas, in 1919 Dewson became research director for the National Consumers' League. She worked closely with Harvard law professor Felix Frankfurter on his defense of the District of Columbia's minimum wage in *Adkins v. Children's Hospital*, a case he lost in 1923.[54] Dewson then moved to New York, where, after a brief stint as civic secretary of the Women's City Club, she became president of the New York Consumers' League. In collaboration with Eleanor Roosevelt, whom she had met at the club, she ran the state Democratic Party women's campaign of 1928 and in 1932 became head of the national Democratic Party women's division. Along with ending child labor, achieving a minimum wage remained among her top policy goals.

The Depression's drastic wage cuts renewed the effort for a women's minimum wage. In 1933, Dewson won a new "living wage" bill for women, only to see many business owners violate it. Convicted of violation, Brooklyn laundry manager Joseph Tipaldo appealed; his US Supreme Court victory rendered New York's bill unconstitutional. This was a bitter defeat not only for labor reformers but also for Governor Lehman, who had considered the minimum wage a key feature of his "Little New Deal." In 1937, labor reform organizations—aided by Charles Poletti, Lehman's legal adviser and Frankfurter's former student—tried a new tack. Instead of proving that a minimum wage would preserve women's health, they argued it would allow women to receive a "fair wage" for "value of services rendered." Then, unexpectedly, Supreme Court Justice Owen J. Roberts switched sides, voting to uphold a Washington State minimum wage for women and minors sufficient for the "necessary cost of living and to maintain the workers in health." New York State promptly passed a new minimum wage bill, which was upheld. In 1938, when Congress passed the Fair Labor Standards Act, minimum wages finally won nationwide legitimacy.[55]

Women's unity achieved in the suffrage movement was by then long gone. Tactical differences had always threatened that unity, as had the campaigns for Sheppard-Towner and jury service, though to a much lesser extent than the divisions over labor reforms. These latter were long-lasting. Harriot Stanton Blatch's attack on those reforms is illustrative. In January 1919, the *Tribune*'s literary editor Natalie H. McCloskey asked her what she thought of sex-specific labor bills. "The subject matter of these bills makes me boil," Blatch said. "I cannot bear to see them foisted upon working girls as laws which will bring them ideal conditions, when, in truth, it will bar them from good jobs." She accused suffragists of "mothering" the bills while working their own stenographers and file clerks "as long as they please." She charged suffragists with "approaching the industrial question in the very same way they have approached the political one since 1848." They need to get over "the long training they have had in thinking only of women," she said, and "take a broad view of the whole matter by thinking of the good of the race in general."[56]

The idea that protections for women would lead to protections for all was no consolation to Blatch for the harm protective labor bills caused, a harm, she observed, that would never affect the women "teachers, doctors, lawyers and women of leisure" who had drawn them up. Refusing to accept the excuse of judicial opposition to labor protections, she chided suffragists for failing to "use their new power to secure proper working conditions for *all* adults." "It is high time that women stop thinking as feminists, and begin thinking as humanists," she asserted.

> The women who worked so long and hard for suffrage cannot get over the long training they have had in thinking only of women. They are approaching the industrial question in the very same way they have approached the political one since 1848. It is time women began to take a broad view of the whole matter by thinking of the good of the race in general. We can't build up a happy, healthy race on health laws for women alone.[57]

Blatch admitted that she sometimes thought "all those women who have agitated the vote for women must be dead and in their graves before we have a broad, human point of view on all these questions." Her forecast, though unkind, came true. The disappearance of the suffragist generation did not cause the change, but it was only after most suffragists had passed on that the movement to end all sex discrimination gathered speed.

Looking back on the impact of ten years of New York woman suffrage, in 1927 *Times* journalist Eunice Fuller Barnard observed, "Neither the fondest hopes of the suffragists nor the jeremiads of their opponents have come true. Politics is not purified nor the home destroyed. Women have not been clamorous for public office nor party leadership. And certainly neither has been thrust upon them." While acknowledging the welfare measures women had put through, she surmised that male politicians had approved them only because they worried about losing women's votes. As Ethel Dreier, Women's City Club president, said, "Power in name, not in fact, is what the vote has thus far brought to women. To many it has been a disillusionment to find the political parties, through whom all real power comes, comparatively cold."[58]

Politically, "women asked for bread and got a stone," Barnard quipped. Psychologically, however, they got a "ten-course dinner." They won the fight to be treated as full human beings, and to live and work in a world without fear or favor. Overnight, suffrage had become an accomplished fact, accepted as is the coeducational elementary school. The boys still lead, Barnard continued, and the girls do the humble work, but women were slowly getting into the minor offices. She gave credit for raising the level of political discourse to the League of Women Voters, the only permanent forum where voters could hear both sides of political issues. As for the National Woman's Party, its goal of ending all discrimination on the basis of sex remained controversial and out of reach.[59] For Barnard, then, the glass of postsuffrage women's politics was both half full and half empty.

For many New York progressive feminists, part of the half-full side came from their victories on Sheppard-Towner, women's jury service, and protections for women wage earners. In the early postsuffrage decades they won other victories. The most important to them were legalizing information about birth control, repealing Prohibition, and modernizing state government. New York City's politically active women gave unstinting support to all three of these goals.

The 1873 Comstock Law had labeled information about birth control obscene and banned its dissemination through the US mail. In the suffrage tradition of civil disobedience, birth control campaigners Emma Goldman, Mary Ware Dennett, and Margaret Sanger and her sister Ethel Byrne were all punished for defying the law. When Goldman's public lectures on "family limitation" resulted in a choice between a fine and fifteen days in jail, she chose jail. Dennett's sex education pamphlet, which she wrote for her sons and distributed through the mail, got her fined. When Sanger publicized birth control in her journal *The Woman Rebel* and Byrne opened the nation's first birth control center in Brooklyn in

1916, they earned thirty-day jail sentences; in the workhouse, Byrne refused to eat and was force-fed for ten days until Sanger promised the governor her sister would comply with the law and convinced him to pardon her. In the early 1920s Sanger's tactical alliance with physicians brought her support from mainstream women's organizations, including the League of Women Voters and Women's City Club. In the 1930s two court decisions, one overturning Dennett's conviction, the other allowing Sanger's Committee on Federal Legislation for Birth Control to import birth control devices (*United States v. One Package of Japanese Pessaries*, 1936), ended the obscenity classification. After that, hundreds of birth control clinics sprang up around the country.[60]

The Prohibition repeal movement began in New York City, where it tapped into middle-class women's political networks. The movement further divided the suffrage community, but by the late 1920s the "drys" were so politically weak they could not stop it. Repeal's leader was Republican Party fundraiser and James Wadsworth Jr.'s campaign manager Pauline Morton Sabin. She had once supported Prohibition because of its promise to reduce alcoholism. By the mid-1920s, she had become disillusioned with it, appalled not just by rising levels of alcohol-related crimes but by "a national culture of hypocrisy": politicians promoted Prohibition in public while breaking the law in private. She campaigned for Prohibition supporter Herbert Hoover in 1928, but Hoover's view of Prohibition as a "great social and economic experiment, noble in motive, far-reaching in purpose," led her to resign as Republican committeewoman and apply her political skills to repeal.

In spring 1929 Sabin founded the Women's Organization for National Prohibition Reform (WONPR) with a small number of wealthy women in New York and Chicago. Within a year its membership of over ten thousand was enough to support a national New York City office. By the time it endorsed Franklin Roosevelt for president in 1932 its membership had grown to over a million, far exceeding the membership of the state's Woman's Christian Temperance Union (WCTU). When the drys attacked it for reflecting the values of elite, pleasure-loving, hard-drinking socialites, Sabin canvassed for support from ethnic neighborhoods, showing residents how Prohibition came down hardest on working-class, immigrant communities. Her use of new, high-profile publicity techniques—newsreels, radio spots, motorcades, and airplane sky-writers—drew in more members. The press ate up her chic appearance, intellect, and charm—a stark contrast to the WCTU's Ella Boole, whom the press depicted as "dowdy" and unrepresentative of the modern woman. Congress members thought perhaps a repeal resolution was now politically safe. When such a resolution passed, the WONPR lobbied state legislatures to ratify it. Sabin's organization was critical to the success of repeal. By severing the powerful bond between suffrage and temperance, it marked a critical turning point in women's political history.[61]

Finally, New York City women embraced reorganizing state government, long a goal of reformers who believed it would save money. Over the latter 1800s, as the state's population and industrial activities expanded, so had its administration, but without a systematic plan. The result was an administration choked with a hodgepodge of agencies, boards, bureaus, councils, departments, and commissions, many with overlapping jurisdictions, redundant functions, vague termination points, and unclear lines of authority. The legislature controlled the budget. The governor, who had only line-item veto power and served terms of only two years, often had no control over appointments of directors. Party bosses and civil servants generally opposed reorganization. The bosses wanted to retain their power to reward followers with the "spoils" of winning elections; civil servants worried that reorganization would cost them their jobs.

"Good government" activists (derisively called "goo-goos" by their opponents) found a new opportunity for reorganization when Al Smith took office as governor in 1919. Belle Moskowitz, who had convinced Smith to form a reconstruction commission to address the state's major problems in the postwar era, saw government reorganization as the key to fulfilling the commission's agenda of economic retrenchment. As the commission's executive secretary, she hired the young and ambitious Robert Moses to direct a ten-person staff for a committee on retrenchment.[62]

Moses's retrenchment plan included four main features: to reduce the executive branch's 187 separate agencies into 16 groupings, each under a single head or board; to increase the governor's term to four years and give him appointment authority over all department heads and vacancies, subject to state senate confirmation; to reduce the number of elected statewide officers from seven to three: governor, lieutenant governor, and comptroller; and to empower the governor to prepare the budget while retaining a veto on legislative appropriations. Moskowitz hoped to incorporate a "progressive" provision that the reorganized state agencies should be responsive to social needs. The labor department, for example, would have a bureau of employment and administer minimum wage and health insurance laws. The health department would emphasize rural health services and put women on its boards. The education department would run an Americanization program to help immigrants gain citizenship. The civil service would be thoroughly professionalized, removing all sex discrimination in filling civil service posts.

Though none of these changes were radical, the opposition dug in. Republican legislators were particularly opposed to a four-year term for the governor and executive control over the budget, but their counter plans never reached fruition.

Only in 1926, during Governor Smith's third term, did a reorganization amendment incorporating minor compromises with the commission's plan win both legislative and voter support. Though Smith won an executive budget in 1927, a four-year gubernatorial term (with elections held in nonpresidential years) would not go into effect for another ten years.[63]

Moskowitz kept a close watch on the plan's progress, supervising publicity, advising the governor on tactical moves with the legislature, and helping with his speeches and giving her own. She reached out to women voters for support, persuading their organizations to form reorganization committees to campaign for the changes. Calling the plan "the only basis on which economy and responsible government, consistent with good service, are possible," the Women's City Club sent a delegation to Albany to attend hearings. Moskowitz's name never appeared in these matters, but her hand guided them all.[64]

The policy campaigns of postsuffrage New York women offer a mixed picture of gains and losses. The Sheppard-Towner campaign showed that suffrage networks could still work together selflessly and effectively for a unified goal. Even though the twenty-year quest to get women on juries fell short of mandatory service, the elective service it achieved advanced women another step toward first-class citizenship. Sex-specific labor protections fractured the suffrage community but eventually led the courts to accept wage-worker protections as constitutional. Legal access to birth control for all women, married or single, still had a long way to go, but many women benefited from the small steps achieved in the early postsuffrage years. The campaigns for Prohibition repeal and government reorganization sharpened women's organizational skills and increased their knowledge of how government worked. Whether fully or only partially successful, unifying or dividing, each of these campaigns helped women become effective workers for feminist progressive change and built their confidence as enfranchised citizens. Over the coming decades a significant number of them would take the lessons they learned from their public policy campaigns into influential and sometimes powerful political roles.

# PART II MOVING TOWARD THE CENTER

**SCANDAL IN THE COURTS**

On May 12, 1930, Emma Swift Hammerstein was living alone in the Winthrop Hotel on New York's Lexington Avenue when someone knocked on her door. Expecting a messenger carrying a loan from a banker, she opened it. A man handed her $30, which she accepted. Suddenly, two other men appeared. The three men, all plainclothes detectives from the city's vice squad, then arrested her for "immoral behavior." Unable to make the $500 bail, Hammerstein was locked up overnight and, in the morning, arraigned in Manhattan's women's court.

Hammerstein was a well-known local celebrity. Fifteen years earlier, when she was a thirty-two-year-old divorcée, she had married the sixty-eight-year-old Oscar Hammerstein. Over a long career as an inventor, businessman, and opera impresario, Oscar had made, unmade, and remade several fortunes. His first wife had died; his second divorced him. Falling for the statuesque and lively Emma, he gave her at their marriage almost five thousand shares of Hammerstein Company stock.[1]

Emma thought her husband was rich. She soon discovered his finances were a mess. He was also diabetic and irascible. They fought often. In July 1919 she threw a bucket of cold water over him as he lay in bed (or so he later said). Somehow he got himself dressed and, hobbling on a cane, walked from their house in Atlantic Highlands, New Jersey, to the local train station, where he collapsed. A brother-in-law, who was driving by on his way to visit him, spotted his trademark top hat upside down on the platform, found him unconscious, and drove him to Manhattan's Lenox Hill Hospital. After two weeks in and out of a coma, Oscar died. Emma was Oscar's sole legatee and executrix, but as he had set up prior trusts guaranteeing life incomes for children from two former marriages, they sued and won.[2]

This was but the start of Emma Hammerstein's many reversals of fortune. In 1922 a reporter found her destitute, sitting on a Central Park bench with nothing but a handbag and her one remaining friend, a white collie named Teddy. "There's 38 cents in that handbag," she said. She had tried to manage her late husband's property, but all was tied up in litigation. The cheap hotel where she was living had thrown her out for unpaid rent and seized everything she had except Teddy. Betrothal to a young tenor—supposedly an Italian prince who had been her protégé—turned out to be a fantasy. Friends mounted a benefit for her in the 1,900-seat Carnegie Hall; only 128 people came. She claimed she had a right "by widow's dower and by law" to a million-dollar estate. Insisting her stepchildren had robbed her, she had filed one lawsuit after another against them and lost them all. Rescued by friends, she went abroad, where she wrote feature articles and (she claimed) Oscar's biography. She also launched a string of schemes to restore his reputation and enhance her own.[3]

Her May 1930 arrest for "immorality" ignited a firestorm of protest among New York City's white middle-class women activists. They believed her claims that the charges against her were absurd and that the "same enemies who have robbed me of all I owned, and who would have me dead if they could, must be back of this." The Winthrop Hotel staff said she had been living there for about three months with "unimpeachable" conduct. Reading about her plight in the newspapers, one of Oscar's old friends bailed her out.

Hammerstein's hearing took place on May 30. Dressed in black, carrying a green parasol and a black fan, and displaying a "dignified" bearing and an "air of detached hauteur," she swore she thought the man at her door that night was the agent of a banker delivering a $30 deposit on a promised loan of $500. Ignoring testimonials to her character from more than twenty prominent women, on June 6 Magistrate Earl Smith found Hammerstein guilty of vagrancy, the term then used against women in sex crime prosecutions (no visible means of support, no permanent residence). He remanded her to jail to await sentencing.[4]

For years the city's press had carried sensational stories of how the vice squad repeatedly hauled in innocent women on morals charges. Since it was highly unlikely that Hammerstein was engaging in prostitution, women civic leaders were convinced that hers was a similar case. Catherine Parker Clivette, a former suffragist and Greenwich Village clubwoman, called the arrest a "frame-up" and announced she would found a society to prevent unjust convictions to aid women arrested on immoral conduct charges. Mary Hamilton, former head of the New York City Police Department's Women's Bureau, promised a special investigation. Marie E. Lassell, founder of the Park Slope Women's Forum that debated issues such as Prohibition repeal and birth control, scored the detective bureau for moving "heaven and earth" to convict Hammerstein when they should be grabbing "murderers and crooks." After Hammerstein's guilty verdict, Clivette said that the corruption entailed in women's arrests had brought women "to the limit of endurance." She predicted that "the case would mark the beginning of a test fight against the dual legal standard of morality." She planned to raise money for an appeal and a trip to Albany to ask Governor Roosevelt to investigate the women's court.[5]

Hammerstein spent only one more night in jail. Anxious to get her out of town (or better yet, out of the country), her stepson Arthur offered her what he considered enough money to live on for the rest of her life. In accepting his offer (which according to her he never honored), she announced her departure for France. "After the way I have been framed, and those awful days and nights in prison, I want never to see this country again," she said.

By late summer, Governor Roosevelt had authorized an investigation into New York City's lower criminal court system. Since the women's court was part of that system, the press speculated that Hammerstein's conviction might be overturned. And so it was. On October 22, the court of special sessions voted two to one that the prosecution had failed to establish her guilt. Her supporters cheered. Despite her determination never to return, in early November Hammerstein came back to New York to demand the return of her fingerprints. In November, telling the press "Ladies must eat," she went on relief and began selling apples for a nickel, like other Great Depression sufferers, in front of one of her husband's old theaters. The following year she sued her stepson Arthur for failing to pay her a lifelong weekly stipend of forty dollars. This suit, like all the others, failed.[6]

Meanwhile, a state-authorized inquiry into the courts had begun. When the investigation's hearings were opened to the public at the end of November, the women's court became sensational front-page news. The court was, investigators said, riddled with perjury, bribery, "fixing," and "framing." A ring of dishonest vice squad officers, lying stool pigeons, greedy bondsmen, unethical lawyers, and bribery-prone court staff had systematically victimized defenseless women for profit. None of this surprised the city's feminist political community. They had been complaining about such conditions for decades, but no public official had taken them seriously.

The investigation eventually moved on to other parts of the lower court system and scrutiny of the city's entire government. Since the investigation had a dramatic impact on the city's politics and its powerful Democratic Party machine, Tammany Hall, many writers—historians, political scientists, politicians, journalists, and novelists—have told this story. Not one has ever done so from the perspective of the city's women voters. They make no mention of women's reactions to the revelations, the role women played in encouraging and later broadening the investigation, or women's participation in decisions about its consequences. Nor have they considered the investigation's impact on women's political lives. Indeed, they write about these events as if women as political actors did not even exist. An active women's political community did exist, however, and it made significant contributions to events as they unfolded.

Few people today remember that, for fifty-seven years, New York City had a special court for women. This women's court prosecuted women arrested for solicitation or other petty crimes, such as public drunkenness or pickpocketing. It was created to solve a problem in the city's night court, which had been established in 1907. By giving immediate hearings to people arrested for petty crimes after hours, the night court was supposed to end the racket of "raptorial bondsmen" who charged exorbitant fees for bailing out detainees desperate to avoid a night in jail.[7] At first, the night court seemed to accomplish this goal, but soon social workers targeted its holding pens, which mixed males and females of all ages, types of offense, and levels of sobriety. Alarmed by the impact of such mixing on young, first-time female offenders, Maude Miner, executive secretary of the New York Probation and Protective Association, suggested that a commission on the courts headed by state senator Alfred R. Page establish a separate night court for women. The commission adopted her idea, incorporating it into the 1910 Inferior Criminal Courts Act, or Page bill. Accordingly, on September 1, 1910, a women's night court opened in Manhattan's Jefferson Market Court House on Sixth Avenue and Tenth Street.[8]

The setting for the women's court was a churchlike room large enough to hold 150 to 200 people. It had a high ceiling, dark wood-paneled walls, stained-glass windows, and rows of wooden benches separated by an aisle up the middle. A low railing separated spectators from witnesses and officials—vice squad and probation officers, social workers, and lawyers—who sat in two rows in the front. The magistrate sat on a raised dais behind a higher railing. This man (and until late 1919 all were men) had summary jurisdiction over petty offenses, which meant he acted as both judge and jury. Witnesses sat in a slightly lower box on the judge's left and next to the court stenographer; the clerk of the court sat on the judge's right. The defendant, her attorney (if she had one), and a deputy district attorney sat at a long table immediately in front of the clerk. A door on one side of the room led to probation rooms and the judge's chambers; a door on the other side led to detention, fingerprinting, and physical examination rooms, all connected by a corridor to the women's jail. Because of the elevated railway on Sixth Avenue, when trains passed by and the courtroom's windows were open all proceedings stopped.[9]

Most women brought to this court were charged with vagrancy. Next came disorderly conduct, battery, pickpocketing, and petit or grand larceny. Striking garment workers, women distributing "seditious" political material, and suffragists demonstrating against President Wilson also landed in this court. Sentences varied. Magistrates generally discharged first-time offenders, or fined or suspended the sentences of others or put them on probation. "Wayward girls," a term generally applied to sexually active unmarried teenagers, got sent to rescue homes (such as Florence Crittenton or Magdalen); repeat offenders were transferred to hospitals if they had a venereal disease or the workhouse on Blackwell's (later Welfare, now Roosevelt) Island. Few defendants could afford counsel.[10]

Almost from the day of its founding, city feminists attacked the women's court. They objected fiercely to its attracting of "gawkers." "Society" folk looking for free late-night entertainment would show up in automobiles and ask door attendants, "Anything worth coming back for?" Chief Magistrate William McAdoo had ordered attendants to admit no one unconnected to a case, but "slummers" always seemed to find a way in. Frederick H. Whitin, general secretary of the Committee of Fourteen, a citizens' antiprostitution group, said that on some nights an "SRO" sign (Standing Room Only) was needed at the door.[11]

A second hated aspect of the women's court arose from the Page law's clause 79, which mandated a presentencing medical exam. The court's feminist critics noted that not only were women's customers never examined but also women with venereal disease received longer workhouse terms (one year) than those without (six months). Lavinia Dock (soon to be the "Little Doc Dock" of Rosalie Jones's Albany suffrage hike) called the medical exam a futile "procedure which treats a few diseased persons while leaving the cause and source of disease untouched." In her view, the exam was both discriminatory and a step toward introducing the European system of government regulation, which most American policymakers rejected, of the "social evil" (the era's euphemism for prostitution).[12] In November 1910, the Women's Prison Association and the Societies Allied to Secure the Repeal of Clause 79 of the So-Called Page Law challenged the exam's constitutionality. Their counsel, attorney and suffragist Bertha Rembaugh, used the case of a woman confined to the workhouse to call the exam an "undue extension of the police power." Though New York Supreme Court justice Henry Bischoff stated in his opinion that "the danger from the spread of disease by women of the class in question is greater than the danger existing from the disease in the case of men," he ruled against the exam on technical grounds: because the examining physician does not give formal evidence before a magistrate, the exam deprives an accused of due process of law. He ordered Rembaugh's client freed. The medical exam reappeared later, applied to offenders after commitment.[13]

The women's night court had ardent defenders. While deploring the court's detention pen, which mixed young with "hardened" women, the *Times* assured readers that the court was humane. In January 1911 the Charity Organization Society of New York (COS), a group that advocated a "scientific" approach to philanthropy, formed a committee on the criminal courts headed by tenement house reformer Lawrence Veiller to support the women's court's budgetary requests. In 1912, after spending two hours in the court as an observer, Louise Caldwell Jones, a prominent antisuffragist, praised the magistrate for his "spirit of fairness and absolute justice." Frederick Whitin of the Committee of Fourteen commended the court for its introduction of uniform sentencing, fingerprint identifications, and a well-run probation system. Social worker Alice D. Menken, who had been assigned to work in the women's court, wrote that the court deterred further crime and stimulated scientific studies of the "causes and the preventive and remedial measures of delinquency."[14]

Still, criticisms abounded. Early in 1912 female defendants' lack of counsel led the Women's Prison Association to hire attorney Helen J. McKeen to represent women asking for help.[15] Other attorneys volunteered their services, many affiliated with Greenwich Village's Church of the Ascension's Legal Committee of the Forum, founded in 1914 and chaired by young attorney Anna Moscowitz (later, Kross). At first Moscowitz praised the court for cutting off bondsmen's sources of revenue. By 1915 she described it as a "heartless" institution applying legal formulae to cases caused not by wickedness but by human folly or misery. She asserted that the court would never cure the "social evil."[16]

The following year, Moscowitz called for the court's abolition. When it was first established, she explained, New York City was going through a "moral clean-up" that brought in 150 "girls" each night. Now, cases had dwindled to a handful. More important, in the court sessions held during the day women were presumed innocent; in night court they were presumed guilty from the start. The defendant's word was worth nothing, while the arresting officer's word was "taken without question." Chief Magistrate McAdoo had said, "How can a magistrate accept the word of a painted and obviously vicious hussy against that of a respectable policeman?" "Judge, officer, attendants and spectators all have mentally tried and condemned the woman before she speaks," Moscowitz charged. Writer Ruth Comfort Mitchell's widely published 1916 poem, "Night Court," attested to Moscowitz's charge. Written as Mitchell rode the subway home after a night observing the court in action, her poem opens:

"CALL Rose Costara!"
Insolent she comes.
The watchers, practiced, keen, turn down their thumbs.
The walk, the talk, the face,—that shell-pink tint,—
It is old stuff; they read her like coarse print.
Here is no hapless innocence waylaid.
This is a stolid worker at her trade.[17]

In the late 1910s, anecdotes about vice squad "frame-ups" surfaced in the press. According to these stories, "stool pigeons" (*agents provocateurs*) and "crooked plainclothes policemen" were inducing women into committing, or offering to commit, sex acts. Chief Magistrate McAdoo attested he had "never known of a single case of an honest, decent, and virtuous woman being arrested by the police mistakenly for street-walking." Other magistrates accused the court's volunteer attorneys of slander. Assistant District Attorney Gerald van Casteel filed formal charges against the volunteers, saying they were exploiting the court to gain experience and take money from poor, gullible women.[18]

Sensationalist writer Frank Harris then joined the fray. In July 1916, after becoming editor of *Pearson's* (once a popular "muckraking" magazine), he began writing exposés of the city's world of commercialized sex and eyewitness accounts of women's night court proceedings. His powerful articles prompted Moscowitz to suggest that the husband of one of the court's defendants go see him.[19]

The man was Johan Silver, a German immigrant and a skilled workman at the Du Pont munitions works in New Jersey. He came home on weekends to the flat he shared with his wife on Manhattan's West Twenty-First Street. On a Saturday in April 1917, an old friend of his, a man in his sixties, came looking for him. Told by Silver's wife he would be home soon, the old friend waited. The day was hot. Three months pregnant, she was wearing a kimono. As a washerwoman had been in, money was lying on the kitchen table. Another man then arrived asking for Johan. His wife offered both men cake and a small glass of brandy. Eventually the old man said he had to leave. Shortly after that, the second visitor, who turned out to be a plainclothes detective, arrested Mrs. Silver. In court he claimed that after paying her two dollars in marked bills "the usual thing occurred."

When Mr. Silver got home, he was astonished not to find his wife. It took him hours to learn she was in the Jefferson Market jail, where he was not allowed to see her. Nor was he allowed to speak to her at her 11:00 p.m. hearing. Denied access to her after that, he learned only that her case would be tried several nights hence and that "a member of the legal committee of the Church of the Ascension" (Moscowitz) would represent her. Moscowitz helped Silver bring the old man, the washerwoman, and his wife's physician to serve as witnesses, all in vain. The magistrate found his wife guilty. Days later, after the judge had put her on three months' probation, Silver was allowed to speak to her for the first time. In shock from her ordeal, she miscarried. Later she became addicted to physician-supplied "stimulants" and then to alcohol. Silver took Harris to meet her, hoping Harris could persuade her to abandon her despair. He could not. Returning to women's court, Harris interviewed the clerk, who only vaguely remembered the case. Probation officer Alice Smith reported that Mrs. Silver had pleaded guilty only to being "improperly dressed."

At Silver's urging, Harris met Moscowitz. She described Mrs. Silver, who had since died, as "a hard-working woman, intelligent, saving, looking forward . . . to the birth of her first child." She insisted Mrs. Silver had not pleaded guilty to anything, and as a first-time offender should not have been held incommunicado for days. She told Harris about other cases and took him to observe two young women arrested along with their landlady. The women had twice engaged in "casual sex" with vice squad officers, who had arrested them only on the third occasion. Moscowitz asked what that said about the integrity of those officers. Another case concerned "medically verified virgins" charged with disorderly conduct and jailed or remanded to "utterly worthless" reformatories. Moscowitz told Harris the purpose of night court was to give immediate relief. As it no longer did, it should be shut down.[20]

Harris's "stool pigeon" stories fueled growing protests against the women's night court. Caroline Klein Simon of the Women's City Club described the court as "a public spectacle" so awful it persuaded her to become a political activist just to get the "tragic place" shut down. While denying the stories about the court were true, Chief Magistrate McAdoo finally acceded to pressure to end the night sessions, not because of false arrests but on account of its "circus-like" atmosphere. In one of its last night sessions in March 1919, six officers of the National Woman's Party, including Alice Paul and Doris Stevens, received a hearing. They had been picketing President Wilson when soldiers and sailors attacked them, tearing their banners. The women, arrested for disturbing the peace, were released for insufficient evidence. The servicemen had not even been detained.[21]

Ending the women's court night sessions did not end the problematic arrests. The police continued to bring women in simply for being out alone at night. In June, Lillian Cohen and Sally Cobin, two young Brooklyn women, went to the Metropolitan Opera House in Manhattan to hear President Wilson speak. Unable to get in, they waited for a streetcar to take them home. Two army officers asked if they wanted a drink. Though they may have flirted, in the end they declined. A policeman who was watching asked the officers if they knew the girls. When the men said they did not he arrested the girls for "soliciting." Locked up for four days, the women were subjected to a physical exam and placed on probation. In overturning their conviction, court of general sessions judge Otto A. Rosalsky charged that the city had become "an unsafe place for your sister, my sister, or anyone's woman relatives to be in if this sort of thing keeps up." He advised the arrested girls to sue the policeman and rebuked the magistrate, Francis X. Mancuso, for accepting the policeman's story without corroboration. The case had other consequences. Pressure from women's groups led Mayor Hylan to order his district attorney, Edward Swann, to appoint a woman prosecutor to the women's court, and Judge Rosalsky, for one, made sure that other women arrested on flimsy evidence for disorderly conduct were exonerated.[22]

In the ensuing months, new scandals broke, this time connected to Brooklyn's women's court. In this borough, police decoys wore military uniforms to lure young women. When political activist Rebecca Talbot-Perkins protested this practice, Navy Secretary Josephus Daniels said he could do nothing about it because the uniforms were not real. But they were. Attorney Amy Wren discovered not only that the Brooklyn Navy Yard commandant had given uniforms to the police but also that a women's court magistrate had authorized police to wear them in the exercise of their duties. Not all women activists disapproved of the practice. Saying it was a good idea to use "the khaki to trap delinquent women," antisuffragist Annie Nathan Meyer, the founder of Barnard College, accused the court's critics of making "sensational and sentimentalized" statements.[23]

Journalist Emma Bugbee felt hopeful about the new daytime women's court but believed it still did "irreparable wrong to innocent girls." They might have "flirted with strange men on the street" or allowed a man to talk to them, but since the man is never forced to testify the girls have no defense. That was supposed to change when the district attorney appointed a woman prosecutor to the women's court in July 1919. The first woman to join a district attorney's staff, Rose Rothenberg was a twenty-six-year-old Jewish immigrant from Rumania and a 1914 New York University Law School graduate. She promised to apply two mottoes to her work: first, "Old Offenders May Reform," and second, "Bring the Man into Court." She intended to help repeat offenders "go straight" and never allow a woman to be convicted on the unsupported testimony of a single policeman. More important, she ordered police not to bring in a woman charged with disorderly conduct without also bringing in the man she was with.[24] She did not always succeed, since many of the men were stool pigeons whom police officers claimed were "unknown." Moreover, the district attorney, who considered her a talented prosecutor, sent her to try cases in other courts, and thus her women's court service did not last long.

By far the most positive sign for the future of the women's court—or so it seemed at the time—was Mayor Hylan's appointment of the city's first woman magistrate. For years, women attorneys and women's voluntary organizations had been pushing for this step. Though Anna Moscowitz Kross had hoped to get the post, she lost out to Jean Hortense Noonan Norris, former suffragist and president of the National Association of Women Lawyers. More important for Hylan, Norris had cochaired Tammany judicial campaigns and was coleader of the lower section of Manhattan's Tenth District. Hylan appointed her at the end of October 1919 to a thirty-day term to replace an ailing magistrate. By December, when women's clubs petitioned him to renew her appointment, he complied.[25]

At eighteen, Jean Norris had married a man over twenty years her senior, who two years later was dead from a shooting accident. Left without resources, Norris worked her way up as a secretary to the post of assistant to a former Republican Party lieutenant governor. She then got a job in the state comptroller's office, a post that led her to the law. Graduating from New York University Law School in 1909, she earned a master's degree in 1912. During the 1910s she worked closely with Anna Moscowitz, Bertha Rembaugh, Mary Lilly, and other feminist lawyers counseling women defendants in the women's court. She saw her appointment as magistrate as an "entering wedge" for women rising to every bench in the country. When asked how she felt about women jurors, however, she said she supported them in theory but in practice did not find the idea "quite successful."[26]

Not everyone was enchanted with her appointment. Two women attorneys accused Norris of "railroading" women. Reporting on behalf of the legislative committee of the State Federation of Women's Clubs, in February 1920 Rose Falls Bres, a writer on women and the law, deplored Norris's failure to reject the word of policemen who fed women "intoxicants" and then arrested them for immorality. She called for an amendment to the vagrancy law outlawing a vice charge conviction of a woman on the uncorroborated testimony of plainclothes policemen. In March, after observing Norris's courtroom for six weeks, Hortense Lersner accused her of believing that "once a girl has 'gone wrong' she has sold her soul." Charging policemen with being "so well versed in their story that they tell it the same, detail by detail," she drew a compelling image of a railway line from Jefferson Market direct to Bedford Reformatory, filled with girls "not given even half a chance to defend themselves." As a result of Lersner's report, the city's Federation of Women's Clubs demanded proper trials for women's court defendants so that they do not have to depend on the "whim of one Magistrate" and the "unsupported testimony of arresting policemen."[27] The magistrates ignored this demand.

When the appeals court reversed some of Norris's convictions for insufficient evidence, Norris warned against disregarding police testimony. "We may as well shut up court and declare the town wide open," she said. In her eleven years on the bench, Norris tried 5,502 women, acquitting only 775. Of those she judged guilty, 713 were sentenced to the reformatory, 15 received suspended sentences, 1,551 were placed on probation, and 4 were forcibly hospitalized. The vast majority of the 2,441 she found guilty went to the workhouse. One was Billie Holiday, later a famed jazz singer but in 1929 a young teenager boarded out by her mother in a Harlem apartment that turned out to be a brothel. Working as a prostitute, Holiday displeased a powerful Harlem figure who gave her up to the police. Her mother lied in court that Holiday was eighteen to keep her out of Bedford, which could have held her for several years. Sentenced to a hundred days on Welfare

Island, Holiday considered herself lucky. She later described Norris as "tougher than any judge I ever saw in pants before or since."[28]

Stories of women claiming to have been framed continued to enflame Harlem, where young, unemployed or underemployed African American women, many of them recent migrants from the South, were easy marks. In 1924 the city's black press published dozens of their stories. Most were about Charles Dancey, aka the "Harlem Paper Dropper." Posing as an employment agent or salesman of bargain-priced "silken wearables," Dancey lured women into dark hallways where, after fondling them, he dropped marked bills. Vice squad confederates then burst in, picked up the bills as proving immorality, and arrested the women. They made a show of questioning Dancey and throwing him out. Dancey would then telephone a bondsman confederate, telling him that a "mark" was on her way to the station house. Meeting her there, the bondsman would promise to get her off on payment of a $500 bond secured by the woman's bank passbook, which the terrified woman promised to hand over. The next day, passbook in hand, the bondsman would enlist a lawyer to enter a not guilty plea and win a discharge. Later investigations revealed that the men paid a representative from the district attorney's office $25 each time he interceded with a magistrate to "go easy" on a defendant who had paid them. Stool pigeon, bondsman, vice squad officer, lawyer, and prosecutor—each got something out of the scam. The woman defendant lost everything.[29]

Calling Dancey a "reptilish stool saurian," the *New York Age* claimed that scores of fearful victims had complained to the paper about him. A four-count grand jury indictment did not stop him. At his trial, a jury took only three-and-a-half minutes to acquit him, an action that drew judicial rebuke but changed nothing.[30]

Dancey's was not the only Harlem scam. Another was the "Landlady's Racket." After gaining entry into homes advertising rooms to let, a stool pigeon used various methods to entrap the landlady. One was to lure her into his room by asking for a towel. When his confederates appeared, he would brandish the towel as a sign they had had sex, whereupon the police would arrest her for running a "disorderly" house. Another method involved the stool pigeon taking a room and saying his "wife" would be arriving shortly. Sometimes this woman would be a confederate, other times a prostitute the police were out to get. In the latter case, when the police arrived they arrested both prostitute and landlady. Well-connected landladies got their cases dismissed, but not before enduring the humiliating medical exam and blood test for venereal disease. The *New York Age* called this system of "fattening on the money extorted from women" one of "shocking depravity."[31]

The *New York Age* featured two articles on framing by Grace P. Campbell, an African American social worker who had run as a Socialist for the state assembly in 1919. As she had been a probation and parole officer, and then a court attendant, she was well qualified to comment on the "racket." She noted the disproportionately high number of young black girls arrested on morals charges and sent to the workhouse, where they had to mix with "hardened" criminals. Calling the women's court "Gethsemane," she drew a vivid picture of girls convicted solely on the word of vice squad officers. She herself tried to find the stool pigeons, but they had always vanished. When the charge was the actual act of prostitution (as opposed to its mere suggestion), the court never held the male accomplice accountable. Convicted "colored girls" rarely got probation, as the probation officers, who were all white, either declined to supervise them or pleaded inadequate to the task. White houses of refuge did not accept black girls. The result? White girls got probation and black girls went to the workhouse.[32]

None of the papers that primarily served New York's white community—the *Times, Tribune,* and *Brooklyn Daily Eagle*—showed any interest in the black press's stories about stool pigeons. Even in 1929, when Mme. Stéphanie St. Clair, Harlem's richest woman "banker" in the lucrative numbers racket, published her letters to Mayor Jimmy Walker and Governor Roosevelt pleading for action against crooked cops and framing, no response came. Because she was a part of Harlem's underworld, city officials gave her stories no credit.[33]

In the late 1920s, the city's newspapers catering to the white community were interested only in the "rat hole" conditions of Brooklyn's women's court.[34] Officials described this court as "decrepit," "squalid," and "nauseating." Its holding pens mixed young girls with "hardened" women and men who used "degraded" language; worse, no matrons (policewomen) accompanied female prisoners during transfers. Brooklyn women activists had been complaining for years about such conditions. The Brooklyn Women's Court Alliance campaigned to move it into renovated, or better yet new, quarters and get a separate house of detention built. The envisioned court would be small, so as to eliminate "leering riff-raff"; the detention house would be "a home," attorney Helen McCormick imagined,

> a place of salvage and salvation, a clinic where young girls and women held for the court on first offenses or as witnesses can be diagnosed, treated and made whole again in body and soul, ready to resume their normal functions as happy and useful members of society—not brazen Magdalens on whom the world will turn with scorn and pity.[35]

Though Brooklyn civic and philanthropic leaders supported this rosy vision, it never came to pass.[36]

Spurred by increasing public protests, in 1928 the (men's) City Club asked the Women's City Club (WCC) to join them in making a survey of court conditions. As was usual in similar joint ventures, the women did all the work. Attorney Caroline Klein Simon headed a committee on city affairs that recruited eighty-four volunteers—"the largest group of volunteers ever to engage in a single piece of club work," she recalled—to visit a courtroom for one full day's session. A joint committee then analyzed the results of the questionnaires they filled out.[37]

Their eleven-page report, released in early 1929, began by complimenting the judges' "courtesy, patience and common sense," especially toward non-English-speaking witnesses and even "ignorant or unintelligent defendants." Then came the critique, which focused less on issues of faulty administration than physical inadequacies—the courts' noise, dirt, and "unhealthy and disgraceful" ventilation. More serious, the report charged that court sessions lasted on average only three hours and eleven minutes, including recesses. Perhaps, the report speculated, the judges lacked "sufficient business to demand the full quota of time which the law requires them to be sitting" or were failing to "give adequate consideration in the interest of justice to each one of the cases which come before them." The report acknowledged that judges had "duties when not sitting on the bench" but opined that a "liberal allowance of off time seems to be made for them." It suggested that a centralized system of pooling cases would produce a better distribution of the work. Magistrates' tardiness also came under fire. On average, sessions opened nearly fifty minutes late. The cause of "much of the contempt for the administration of our courts" came, the report concluded, from keeping thousands of people waiting.[38]

The city's mainstream press praised the report. While Chief Magistrate McAdoo agreed that the courts should be centralized and open on time, he said that tardiness was "not an impeachable offense." Norman Thomas, the Socialist candidate for mayor in 1929, later observed that magistrates, unlike appellate judges, "do not have any weighty documents to examine in off-court hours," and thus the clubs' critique of truncated hours was spot on. Years later, when the Women's City Club celebrated its twentieth anniversary, both Caroline Simon and the club's president, Ethel E. Dreier, claimed their report had laid the basis for the investigations of the magistrates' courts that began the following year. This statement exaggerated the report's importance. While it led to heightened scrutiny of a few systemic problems, it represented a mere pinprick.[39]

The immediate catalyst for the official courts investigation was a gangland murder in late 1928. On November 4, gambler and racketeer Arnold Rothstein was about to enter a hotel room to play cards when he was killed. The city's police commissioner, Grover Whalen, managed to get one person indicted for the crime but lost the case for lack of evidence. The crime then slipped from the news.

In fall 1929 Republican congressman Fiorello La Guardia, then running to un-seat Mayor Walker, revived it by revealing that Magistrate Albert H. Vitale, a Bronx Tammany leader, had borrowed almost $20,000 from Rothstein. Vitale claimed an intermediary had gotten him the loan without telling him its source. La Guardia would not let go. He hammered away on Vitale's connections to gangsters and demanded that Walker either "repudiate or support" the judge.[40]

In November, Walker won re-election by almost five hundred thousand votes. Then an event occurred that rekindled interest in Magistrate Vitale. In December, members of the Bronx Tepecano Democratic Club were hosting a restaurant dinner for Vitale, their honorary life president, when masked gunmen burst in. After lining up the guests against the wall, the gunmen stole cash, jewelry, and three revolvers, one belonging to a police detective. The subsequent investigation brought out that some diners had criminal records—compromising company for a judge and a detective. In addition, shortly after the robbery Vitale got the firearms and some of the loot returned, proof (Tammany critics said) of Vitale's connections to "the boys." Concerned for the honor of the magistrates, Chief Magistrate McAdoo demanded that Vitale explain. Vitale claimed the "gangsters" were mere restaurant diners, not guests of his club, but more charges surfaced later, such as Vitale's dismissal of a case against a confessed criminal defended by a Rothstein lawyer. In response, Charles C. Burlingham, president of the city's bar association, got permission from the appellate division to investigate.[41]

Over the early months of 1930, corruption charges against other judges led to more calls to investigate. Norman Thomas demanded that legislators investi-gate the entire magistracy. Samuel H. Hofstadter, Manhattan's only Republican state senator, warned that if Mayor Walker did not investigate the courts, then the Republican-controlled legislature would. Republican leaders asked Governor Roosevelt to appoint a special commission to investigate not only the magistracy but also the police for "incompetence" (failure to solve Rothstein's murder), the board of standards and appeals (taking kickbacks), and the fire department ("neg-ligent" in a fire at Brooklyn's Pathé Studio that had taken ten lives). Roosevelt declined, saying he opposed setting a precedent that might force future governors to meddle in local affairs, including (he threatened) those of Republican-led cities. Republicans charged Roosevelt with being afraid of Tammany, an accusa-tion reiterated when Roosevelt sought re-election in the fall.[42]

Meanwhile, the press was hot on the corruption trail. From January 8 to 18, Milton MacKaye, an investigative journalist with the *Evening Post*, published ten front-page articles on the "magistrates' racket." He began by exploring the "un-holy alliance" between the underworld and politics. He then showed how party bosses controlled judicial appointments. He described the courtrooms as smelly, hot, and overcrowded, with tobacco smoke so thick one could hardly breathe;

the smell of disinfectant "only serves to accentuate the distaste into nausea." He satirized how magistrates leaped, "Minerva-like," straight from Tammany Hall into judicial wisdom. Finally, he painted an ugly picture of a parade of back-slapping "fixers" and dishonest bondsmen, who charge whatever they can get.[43]

In February, the city's bar association formally asked the appellate division to remove Vitale from the bench. At his hearing, Vitale admitted he knew the $20,000 loan had come from Rothstein but his use of an intermediary kept his conscience clear. Rejecting this excuse, the five justices of the division labeled the loan a "tainted transaction" that had put Vitale into Rothstein's and his lawyer's "vest pocket" and dragged the courts into a scandal. They voted unanimously to remove him.[44]

The clamor for investigations grew louder. At the end of March, backers of Norman Thomas's 1929 run for mayor formed a city affairs committee. At first cochaired by Thomas and the Reverend John Haynes Holmes of the Community Church, the committee later put Free Synagogue Rabbi Stephen S. Wise, Columbia University philosophy professor John Dewey, and former *Nation* associate editor Paul Blanshard at its helm. Attorney Dorothy Kenyon, then campaigning for women's jury rights, headed a subcommittee on the courts. The committee became a gathering point for the city's "good government" reformers.[45]

By midsummer, accusations that innocent women were being framed received renewed public attention. A new framing case, a nurse caught in a "Doctors Racket," brought more attention to women's court conditions. A week after Emma Hammerstein's conviction, Mary Crow, a thirty-year-old registered nurse, was in her office late at night, when a man, claiming to need immediate treatment for pain, knocked on the door. When told the doctor was not in, he insisted the nurse herself treat him. He got undressed and put five or ten dollars in a conspicuous spot. His confederates then burst in. Pointing to the money, the man told them the nurse had signified her willingness to commit an "immoral act." They arrested her. Hammerstein's chief defender, Catherine Clivette, and her Society for the Prevention of Unjust Convictions, rushed to Crow's defense. Despite their support, the magistrate found her guilty.[46]

In the meantime, financial scandals kept magistrates in the headlines. Bernard Vause, president of the Brooklyn Democratic Club and a county judge, had helped obtain pier leases for a huge fee; indicted for fraudulent use of the mail, in July he got six years in jail. The same month, investigators found proof of Magistrate George F. Ewald's leniency toward politicians and businessmen on traffic tickets; worse, bank transactions suggested Ewald had paid a Tammany leader $10,000 for his seat. For Governor Roosevelt, the Ewald case proved the tipping point. As he approached re-election he did not want to alienate the machine, but if he declined to follow through on what appeared to be gross malfeasance he would lose support upstate and from nonmachine Democrats. He now asked to see all documents relating to Ewald's conduct.[47]

To compound the drama, yet another scandal occurred: the disappearance of Judge Joseph Force Crater. Crater, president of an Upper West Side Tammany club, had served as law secretary to state senator Robert F. Wagner Sr. and recently been named to the state supreme court. On August 6 Crater left his summer cottage in Maine, telling his wife he had to take care of some business in New York City. That evening he bought a single ticket to a Broadway show, dined with his chorus-girl mistress and a mutual friend, stepped into a taxi, and vanished. For reasons of their own, both his wife and colleagues kept his disappearance quiet, not informing even the police until September 3. By then, the trail was cold. An investigation revealed that Crater had withdrawn $22,500 from his bank account and removed papers from his office. Neither money nor papers ever showed up. Tammany critics concluded Crater had been involved in corruption. The clamor for a court investigation was now a roar.[48]

Retired judge Samuel Seabury was vacationing in London when, on August 26, 1930, a reporter called him in his hotel room. Was it true that the appellate division of the New York Supreme Court named him referee of an investigation of the criminal justice system of Manhattan and the Bronx? The next morning a cable arrived, confirming the appointment. Booking passage on a fast boat, Seabury and his wife sailed home.

A descendant of the nation's first Episcopal bishop, Seabury had been admitted to the bar in 1894 and established himself as a non-Tammany Democrat. He represented poor clients, defended unionists, and spoke out against the "unjust distribution of wealth that creates a system of society in which the few get without working, while the many work without getting." At twenty-eight, he ran for a judgeship during the fusion campaign of 1901 and won a ten-year term on the city court. In 1906 he won a fourteen-year term on the state supreme court, and in 1914 a fourteen-year term on the court of appeals, the state's highest court. He resigned from the bench to run for governor in 1916 but lost to Republican Charles Whitman. He blamed the loss on Tammany's lack of support. Rumblings about future political opportunities continued, but his moral self-righteousness did not endear him to voters. He stuck to private practice until called in 1930, at Governor Roosevelt's suggestion, to lead an official probe into New York City's courts. Though Tammany Hall impugned his motives and obstructed him at every turn, his work was so meticulous and well documented that few questioned his findings.[49]

To help him in his work, Seabury recruited a staff of eager young attorneys he called "my boys" and, at the bar association's suggestion, the sharp-witted Isidor Jacob Kresel as chief counsel. Kresel contributed an investigatory method he had developed in previous cases. With the goal of uncovering bank deposits incongruent with a person's salary, he got subpoenas that allowed scrutiny of income tax returns, real estate dealings, and bank and brokerage-house records, not just of witnesses but also of their families.

At the end of September, Seabury told the bar association his intentions. He would determine the "conditions in the magistrates' courts" and find out if justice was being done. Speaking before the Women's City Club's Committee on Prevention and Correction, Joseph Corrigan, who had replaced McAdoo as chief magistrate after McAdoo's sudden death in June, insisted that the "magistrates, as a body, are honest men [*sic*] trying to do the best they can." He worried that the "wild charges" appearing in the press, such as that some forty-five took bribes to fix cases, "will break down public respect for the bench." He denied the existence of a "bail bond evil," pointing to the recent establishment of a set scale of fees that had lowered the possibility of graft. He did not address the continuing overcharges that women caught in the racket were too scared to report.[50]

Most New Yorkers of the late 1920s viewed Tammany Hall's domination of city government as a given. Few expected it ever to end. Even when anti-Tammany fusion forces elected a reform mayor, Tammany loyalists still held a majority of posts in city agencies, the police force, and the judiciary. Equally problematic, reform mayors never won re-election. Whatever improvements they put in place vanished soon after they left office. While serious probes into government corruption, especially in law enforcement, had brought about a few resignations, firings, and even jail sentences, Tammany always resurged, like the proverbial phoenix, from the ashes of scandal. Ordinary citizens who needed the machine helped it survive. Lacking public resources to assist them in hard times, they depended on its favors. In return, grateful citizens lined up on Election Day to vote the Tammany ticket. Thus reform coming from the top rarely cut into the deep layers of loyalty that Tammany commanded. A repetitive pattern emerged: waves of reform succeeded by a predictable return to the status quo ante.

Seabury's work, which went on for almost three years, disrupted this pattern. His investigations led to a permanent diminution (though not elimination) of Tammany's power. Seabury's judicial experience and absolute probity were certainly reasons for the more lasting results. There were other reasons, including the Great Depression, which aroused popular fury at public officials eating at the trough of graft, kickbacks, and payoffs while ordinary citizens went hungry. As New York City's infamous madam, Polly Adler, put it: "John Q. Public didn't give a damn how the Tammany boys were getting theirs" until the Depression hit; then it was a different story.[51] The communications revolution also had an impact. By the late 1920s, radio was so ubiquitous that even citizens who never read a newspaper had heard about the investigations, and some hearings were broadcast. Newsreels showed disgraced officials fleeing hooting crowds.

Moreover, the city's ethnic make-up was changing. Tammany's Irish base had already begun to cede dominance to newer immigrants, especially Jews and Italians. "Boss" Charles F. Murphy, a consummate politician who had held the reins for over two decades, had died in 1924. The next year a Tammany favorite, former state legislator James ("Jimmy") J. Walker, won the mayoralty. Handsome, well dressed, a wisecracking charmer and pleasure seeker, Walker was a highly popular man about town. More interested in the city's nightlife and vacations ("for his health") than in governing, he made light of corruption charges. Murphy's two successor "bosses"—George W. Olvany and John F. Curry—lacked their predecessor's political skills. By the time they saw the storm coming their corrective actions were too late.[52]

No analyst of these events has ever mentioned one other factor: women were now voters. Women not only joined movements to pressure officials to launch investigations but also initiated some of them. They also spearheaded campaigns to expand the investigations into the outer boroughs and then all city departments. During the investigations women activists followed every detail. Further, in the investigations' aftermath, they participated in, and sometimes led, campaigns to bring about permanent legal and political change.

Not all women voters were anti-Tammany. As Socialist Norman Thomas observed, many women voters had "fitted very docilely into the Tammany scheme of things" and were thus "susceptible to the . . . favors doled out by district leaders."[53] This was certainly true of former suffragists Jean Norris, Anna Moscowitz Kross, Annie Mathews, and Rose Rothenberg—all lifelong Democrats whose careers benefited from the machine. Yet, the allegations of women's mistreatment in the magistrates' courts had disgusted enough women (including Kross, who had been expressing her dismay for years) that even women Tammanyites were eager for reform.

The first, and most colorful, woman activist to respond publicly to Judge Seabury's plans for investigating the courts was Catherine Clivette, Emma Hammerstein's ardent defender. Her background differed substantially from that of the feminist lawyer critics of the women's court. In the 1890s and early 1900s Clivette had been a singer in light opera, a venue where she may have crossed paths with Oscar and Emma Hammerstein. She later performed as the Veiled Prophetess in a vaudeville mind-reading act with her equally colorful husband, Merton (his character was the Man in Black). By 1918 she had retired from the stage and taught piano and voice from her home in Greenwich Village. By the early 1920s she had become a well-known civic activist, founding the Greenwich Village Historical Society and Greenwich Village Humane League and serving as first vice president of the World Anti-Narcotic Union. In 1929, for the first and only time, Clivette let shine her political ambitions by running a futile race for president of the board of aldermen on the minor "Square Deal" Party ticket. By the time of Hammerstein's case in 1930, she had wide connections among middle-class, politically organized women whom she mobilized to campaign against the women's court.[54]

Commenting on Seabury's plans on October 9, almost two weeks before Hammerstein's acquittal, Clivette did not restrain her displeasure with both court and government officials. In a letter she wrote to Police Commissioner Edward P. Mulrooney and other city officials as representative of her Society for the Prevention of Unjust Convictions, she said,

> We are not interested in the prices paid for the position of magistrate, and we do not care whether there is any truth in the statements that magistrates bought their positions, but we do care how these magistrates act after they are in office. It is a settled legal principle that every person's house is his or her "castle," and yet daily, homes of citizens are entered without warrant, persons are seized and places searched by members of the vice squad."[55]

She enlisted Louis Waldman, then the Socialists' gubernatorial candidate, to speak before the Society for the Prevention of Unjust Convictions at a Brooklyn Heights meeting that attracted three hundred attendees, with two hundred or more turned away for lack of space. Waldman assailed the political appointments of magistrates, saying that "no person is safe in a court with back stairs which offer admittance to the politicians." Clivette pressed on with the attack: "The system is controlled by a triple alliance—politicians, police and the underworld. The politically appointed magistrate has his parasitical staff—the shyster lawyer, the runner from the underworld, the dishonest bondsman and the court clerk, who is the go-between." She accused both Mayor Walker and Governor Roosevelt of ignoring complaints about vice squad home invasions "under assumed names, under false pretense and without warrants."[56]

Representing some four hundred city women's organizations, the New York City Federation of Women's Clubs followed up on Clivette's initiatives, though in a more restrained manner. The federation asked Chief Magistrate Corrigan to make sure that all future cases involving women arrested on morals charges require testimony from the "unknown man." On October 23, the day after special sessions overturned Emma Hammerstein's conviction, 2,300 federation members met to hear his answer. Contending that the clubwomen were "confusing a moral issue with a legal one," Corrigan told them to be patient while the magistracy undertook to correct abuses. Instead of patience, the federation chose action. They appointed a committee of three lawyers—Anna W. Hochfelder, Ruth Lewinson, and Olive Stott Gabriel—to investigate the alleged framing and meet with officials on the issue.

The three lawyers all graduated from New York University Law School: Gabriel in 1903, Hochfelder in 1908, and Lewinson in 1919. Hochfelder, the committee's chair, was a Tammany Democrat from Brooklyn who for years had been a feminist activist. In 1913 she had founded the Alliance of Civil Service Women to end sex-specific restrictions on civil service jobs, a reform she finally won during Governor Al Smith's first term. New York policewomen, women court attendants, and women tenement inspectors all credited Hochfelder with opening their jobs to them. In the early 1920s, Hochfelder campaigned to have a woman appointed to the state's civil service commission so that the twenty-five thousand women civil servants would have a voice. In 1923 she became the second female assistant corporation counsel (following Anna Kross) in the city's legal department. Her husband, Julius, who had been one of Hammerstein's defense lawyers, had made her personally aware of framing.

Democratic Party activist Lewinson was an outspoken promoter of women in political office and a popular lecturer on the impact on women of recent changes in estate and property law. She became the youngest college trustee in the country when in 1921 Mayor Hylan appointed her to the board of Hunter College, from which she had graduated in 1916; in 1926, Mayor Walker appointed her to the board of higher education. Gabriel, who had moved to New York City in 1900 from Portland, Oregon, was known for opposing the so-called white slave trade and sex-specific labor legislation. As Republican coleader of Manhattan's Tenth District, she was part of the movement to oppose the re-election of Senator Wadsworth, who in her view had brought the GOP "to the brink of ruin." In 1926, she had helped Democrat Robert F. Wagner Sr. defeat Wadsworth. She was three times elected president of the National Association of Women Lawyers.

Hochfelder's committee sat in court when in early November Chief Magistrate Corrigan imposed a higher bail on three vice squad members being tried for perjury. (An elderly woman in attendance was so moved by the magistrate's action that she said she would have hugged him if judicial protocol had allowed.)[57] From then on, federation members would follow all aspects of the Seabury investigations as they unfolded and work to make sure that the investigations' consequences would endure. Hochfelder's committee would play a prominent role in winning permanent changes in the way women were treated in future "immorality" cases.

At the end of November 1930, the tall, ruddy-faced, white-haired Judge Seabury opened his hearings to the public. His staff had already gathered explosive evidence. The hearings began with a startling admission from John

C. Weston, the representative of the district attorney's office as a "deputy prosecutor" in the women's court. When confronted with bank records showing he had
accumulated $20,000 more than he could explain by his salary, Weston confessed
to having taken $25 bribes over the previous eight years for going easy on selected
women's cases. Naming twenty-one lawyers, three bondsmen, and two detectives
who had bribed him, he estimated he had interfered in some six hundred cases
and freed about nine hundred women. In the event he might someday be called
to account for his actions, he had kept a meticulous record of the cases, though
without noting the bribes.[58]

Revelations about the vice squad followed. The squad was supposed to suppress "commercialized vice," such as gambling (including the illegal "policy" or
numbers rackets popular in Harlem), liquor and narcotics violations, and prostitution. As these businesses were a lucrative source of protection money, some
officers did more to keep them alive than to suppress them. The squad also used
stool pigeons to entrap women, extorting money from them that the officers then
split with bondsmen, lawyers, and court officials like Weston.

Chile Mapocha Acuna was one of the squad's most successful stool pigeons.
A Chilean immigrant, he found work as a waiter on Broadway. In 1927 he picked
up information about a killer and went to the police. Impressed with his language
skills, some detectives recruited him as an informer. Two years later a member of
the vice squad trained him to be a stool pigeon, a role that included the "comedy"
of being "slapped around" by arresting officers. The job earned him about $150
a week. Then a friend of an entrapped woman begged him to testify on her behalf. Knowing she was innocent, he agreed, but his testimony angered one of his
handlers, who got him arrested on an attempted extortion charge. After serving
a year in jail, he heard about the Seabury investigation. Worried his work as a
stool pigeon would be exposed and his former handlers might try to silence him,
he offered to tell the investigators what he knew in return for protection. His
public testimony in late November and early December made daily front-page
news. Here at last was proof of the illegal goings-on in the magistrates' courts that
women had been protesting since the mid-1910s. Ironically, Seabury considered
Acuna's testimony so "indelicate" that at first he cleared the courtroom of women
attendees, who of course already knew how a stool pigeon worked.

Acuna, soon mocked in the press as the "Human Spittoon-ah," provided the
names of thirteen stool pigeons and details on the scams:

> The policeman would give us $5 or $10 in marked bills. Then we would all
> set our watches together. We would arrange it so I would have just enough
> time to give the marked bills to a girl and watch where she put them, so
> the detectives could get the evidence. Then when the policemen entered

they would go through their little comedy with me. They would insult me and accuse me of everything they could imagine, and I would deny it all, insisting that the woman was my wife and that I had been there for days.

Then they would take me into another room and pound on the wall, to make it sound as though they were beating me, but it was just more of the comedy. Finally, I would give them a fictitious name and address and hurry back to the station house. They would always bring the girls in as prisoners. Then the next day when the case came up in court the officer would testify that the man in the case was unknown, that he had given a fictitious address and could not be found. I was always the unknown man.[59]

He said that sometimes the police would enter before he could get the "evidence." Telling the officers of his failure made no difference. They would make the arrest anyway. Harlem received the brunt of this treatment. When business was slack, headquarters demanded the vice squad maintain arrest averages. So they "swooped down upon the Negro section of Harlem, 'crashed flats' and made arrests at random."

Chief Counsel Kresel then called some forty or fifty police officers into the courtroom. Acuna went up to the glowering officers and identified each by name. One was John McHugh, who had arrested Emma Hammerstein and would later be charged with conspiracy. Five victims then testified. Mary Palmer, arrested with her cousin Elizabeth Wilson, paid $575 in bondsmen's and lawyer's fees. Winifred Grayson and Marjory Wharton were arrested, knocked downstairs, and loaded into an automobile that took a circuitous ride to the station; the officers sat the women on their laps, "telling us if we'd give them a break, they would give us a break." Betty Smith, twenty-two and an orphan, was in her one-room apartment on West Seventy-Third Street when Acuna knocked on the door. When she opened it, others followed. She saw a plainclothes policeman plant $15 in marked bills under her pillow and then empty her purse of cash. Unable to pay for lenient treatment, she ended up in the House of the Good Shepherd for ten months. Acuna's testimony confirmed the charge that plainclothes officers had arrested Icie Sands, a young black woman, without any evidence of wrongdoing. Seabury charged that some 150 "respectable" women had been victims of trumped-up charges.[60]

Mayor Walker fought back. He called accusations of police dishonesty libelous to the entire force. He also downplayed the framing charges, which he called exaggerated. He stuck to this position even after Police Commissioner Mulrooney returned all of his current vice squad officers to uniformed duty. Walker later called an emergency meeting for December 23 of civic and welfare organizations, including over a dozen headed by women, to discuss the resulting decline in police morale and the need to continue to fight vice. One administration critic, municipal reformer William H. Allen, derided Walker for his "executive helplessness" in asking civic leaders "to stop vice that flourishes openly only with police protection."[61]

Chief Counsel Kresel next targeted bondsmen and lawyers. Keeping offices across the street from police stations and courthouses, these men charged far in excess of the legal rate. They then promised victims exoneration but kept raising the amounts required. All denied the allegations, but after aligning bank account transactions with arraignments and court appearances, Seabury's staff confirmed the scams. Out of the hearings came the first mentions of a "tin box"—a safe-deposit box rented under family members' names, or a box secreted under beds or in trunks at home. The "tin boxes" that mysteriously, if not magically, filled themselves up with cash became a running public joke worthy, Polly Adler said, of a Marx Brothers movie.[62]

The women's court hearings progressed beyond the New Year. One big news story covered Kresel's charge that magistrates (including Jean Norris) had illegally sent seventy-seven "girls" to Bedford Reformatory. By mid-January, Kresel was focusing on the magistrates themselves. To avoid testifying, three simply resigned, claiming illness. Jean Norris did not take that exit. While questions had come up about some of her convictions, no one had accused her of buying her seat, socializing with gangsters, taking bribes, or allowing politics to influence her rulings. Thus, when invited to testify at the end of January, she came willingly, first for private, then public, examinations. Her testimony continued on and off over the next six months.[63]

Close scrutiny of the magistracy's sole female judge was probably inevitable. Norris had convicted more women on vice charges than any other magistrate, a fact that amazed her when Kresel revealed it. Kresel also noted that she had based most of her convictions on the sole testimony of one witness, the arresting policeman. When asked to justify her rulings, Norris replied she was confident that sworn officers of the law would tell the truth. Judge Seabury took her to task for committing minors to Bedford without hearings. One particularly egregious case from 1928 concerned a twenty-year-old Miss Bodmer. After spying on Bodmer, a church deaconess told a policewoman that the young woman was living in "meretricious relations" with a married man. Seabury pointed out, first, that such relations were not illegal in the state, and second, that Norris never advised Bodmer of her rights or gave her a chance to obtain counsel.

Seabury's staff soon dug out more of Norris's faults. From 1929 to 1930 Norris held a small number of stocks in a surety company with which her court did business, a clear conflict of interest. Seabury also chastised her for accepting $1,000 in 1927 for posing, in her judicial robes no less, in a testimonial for the digestive benefits of Fleischmann's yeast. Most damaging, in two vagrancy cases she changed the stenographic record to make her own conduct look more fair. In one case, she removed evidence that she had refused the woman's counsel's request to depose favorable witnesses and then had judged her guilty. Confronted with the case's original transcript against the final, which showed Norris's handwritten changes, Norris at first denied having done anything more than correct errors in grammar or construction. Later, she apologized.[64]

As the days passed, Norris lost patience. Seabury wanted her to be on hand whenever a case relevant to any of her decisions came up. Her attorney said she would not appear unless told the questions a day in advance. Seabury refused this request and issued a subpoena, the first time he compelled a magistrate to appear. On May 28, he released a sixty-five-page report to the appellate division recommending Norris be removed from the bench. He cited five grounds: her failure to question the word of any vice squad policeman; her "callous disregard" of defendants' rights; her altering of an official court record and then "exercising a woman's prerogative" to change her explanation of this act; her purchase of stock in a company with which the courts did business; and finally, her exploitation of her judicial standing to profit from advertising a commercial product. This last act, he said, "discloses a willingness to cheapen and vulgarize the judicial office and in my opinion demonstrates a shocking lack of appreciation of the proprieties attaching to judicial office."[65]

In early June Norris sent a written defense to the appellate division. She said that her altering of the stenographic notes was only for accuracy and did not prejudice the defendant's case; she never convicted defendants solely to maintain a high conviction rate; her sentences of one hundred days were standard for women found to be "diseased"; her stock ownership in the bail-bond company was minute and in no way affected the discharge of her duties; and, while her Fleischmann's testimonial may have been "unwise," it in no way compromised her honesty or efficiency. She also went on at length about her educational qualifications for the magistracy; charitable work; many memberships in political, quasi-official, legal, and women's organizations; and work in probation court and family court, no aspect of which had been criticized. Her record was, in fact, far more impressive than that of many of her colleagues.

The appellate division took up her case on June 22. Seabury, who led the cross-examination, tore relentlessly into her every self-justification. There were a few redeeming moments. Seventeen character witnesses testified on her behalf, including two women who worked with "wayward girls" who said Norris was "most maternal" and "extremely sisterly" toward defendants. Attorney Bertha Rembaugh, who in 1919 had failed to win election as the city's first woman judge, said that Norris had the reputation of being "uninfluenceable." Frances Perkins, then state industrial commissioner, told the court she and Norris had served on many civic and organizational boards together and that her reputation was excellent. Unmoved, on June 25 the five justices of the appellate division voted unanimously to remove her. According to the press, on hearing the judgment she "reddened and swayed." Though she left the court by a side door to avoid the press, someone spotted her and alerted a crowd, which booed her as she fled.[66]

Many in the public regarded Norris, the city's first female magistrate, as representing women in general, a burden many first women appointees carried. When Florence Knapp, the state's first female secretary of state (elected from upstate in 1924), was charged with forgery and grand larceny, the public reacted with snide remarks about the purity women were supposed to bring to politics.[67] A similar reaction followed Norris's removal. Some women attorneys called her unyielding and lacking in judicial temperament. While not leaping to defend her, attorney Lena Madesin Philips, president of the International Business and Professional Women's Clubs, was an exception. She pointed out that when four other magistrates had been removed no one cried out "that men are unfit to sit on the bench."[68]

Had Norris delivered excessively lax rulings, her male colleagues would surely have chastised her. The Fleischmann's yeast testimonial was in poor taste, but not unethical. For good reason, the American Medical Association had forbidden its members from endorsing health products (doctors from abroad had no such restrictions), but a judge—even one allowing herself to be photographed in her robes—would not necessarily have seen a conflict. Norris may also have believed the fee for her endorsement justly compensated her two-week use of the product, described by a *Fortune Magazine* reporter as having the "texture of a deteriorated ink blotter, and a taste that defies description except as a mild blend of wet horse-hair and acetylene."[69] In any case, her endorsement pales against the corrupt behavior of some of her colleagues, whose qualifications for office were nowhere near as high as hers.

Neither Seabury nor Kresel had been disposed to give her any sympathy. Seabury's failure to include any women attorneys on his staff indicated a lack of confidence in women professionals. He had bristled at Norris's refusal to remain constantly available to testify. That he had included in his formal charges her exercise of "a woman's prerogative" of changing her mind revealed he believed in age-old stereotypes of a woman's presumed inconstancy.

Kresel held similarly biased views. In a 1929 speech to a group of Jewish women in Brooklyn, he said women "have made great progress," and "in some lines of business, such as dressmaking, stenography, telephone switchboard operation, you are no longer a problem but a necessity. But in many respects you are not fitted to lead in what we call the professions. A woman lawyer, for instance, is a misfit in a courtroom." His audience of professional women ridiculed him. Saying Kresel was "suffering from an inferiority complex which makes him imagine himself superior to women," physician Sophia P. Harned recommended psychoanalysis. Dr. L. Adele Cuinet said he "belongs to the last century." Attorney Sarah Stephenson thought that perhaps he had once been beaten in court by a woman lawyer and had not forgiven her. Successful real estate operator and political activist Rebecca Talbot-Perkins said he was one of those men who howl when they see "a woman sitting at a desk and drawing a big salary." In another speech, Kresel said women were "not fitted to discharge the duties of high political office or to cope with the great political and economic questions which our law-making bodies are called upon to settle." He advised women who had won the vote to take "a little rest and try to digest the food you have bitten off rather than try to bite off any more right now. Each sex must occupy the sphere in which it can accomplish most." Talbot-Perkins riposted, "That is where such men would like to see us women."[70]

As soon as Seabury had charged Norris with malfeasance, the New York City women's political community assumed her career was over. Pauline Mandigo, a journalist who had reported on politics and legislation for Albany newspapers during the suffrage campaign and then launched a successful career as a promoter of women's employment and political leadership, knew Norris's removal would mark a sad day for women in politics. In a letter to the *Times*, she called on Mayor Walker to "prove his faith in women" as officeholders by asking the county and city bar associations to appoint in Norris's place "a woman lawyer of fine judicial qualifications and a real understanding of the functions of a city magistrate." Pointing to the 190 qualified and distinguished women members of the county bar association (the city association still excluded women), she assured the mayor that he would have ample ranks from which to choose. She said further that having Florence Knapp and now Jean Norris represent women in office was unfortunate, but Walker's appointment of a woman would encourage women's future engagement in public service.[71]

Tammany women also alerted Mayor Walker and Tammany boss John F. Curry that vindicating their sex by replacing Norris with a woman mattered to them. They offered several names, including Rose Rothenberg, Clarice M. Baright, Anna Moscowitz Kross, and Ruth Lewinson. The press named several Republican women, including Olive Stott Gabriel and Bertha Rembaugh. By mid-July, some twenty women were contending for the post. Curry reported he was unsure if a woman should be on the bench at all. Walker was said to be looking for a nonpolitical appointment. Unconcerned about the reaction of women in politics, the mayor appointed a "highly qualified" man whom he had long wished to promote. A month later he swore in five new magistrates. All were men.[72]

In 1933, Jean Norris filed suit against the authors and producers of a Broadway melodrama, *Four O'Clock*, saying its dialogue libeled her. Based on elements of the Seabury investigations, the play gave a "crooked woman judge" in a vice case "false, scandalous and defamatory" dialogue, including such lines as: "It will cost them plenty"; "she framed me"; "she got enough graft to help you"; "she is a good fixer"; and "she said you have been accepting bribes. I said, 'why talk shop.'" At first the authors denied the play was about Norris and said they would not change a line. The suit was settled amicably when the authors agreed to make the judge male.[73] Though this change may have saved Norris further embarrassment, it was also ironic: even on stage, a man once again replaced New York City's first woman judge.

# 5 FALLOUT

The Seabury investigations kept New Yorkers enthralled for more than two years. The press published daily front-page reports of accusations, denials, dismissals, resignations, and convictions. Writers, composers, and comedians fixed these events into popular culture. Jokes circulated about a "little tin box," the new symbol for "boodle" or graft. "But the tin that got you all in trouble, was the tin in your old tin box" was only one of many lines from satirical songs city political reporters performed at their annual Inner Circle dinner in March 1931. Stanley Walker, city editor of the *Herald-Tribune*, composed the limerick that immortalized stool pigeon Chile Acuna as the Human Spittoon-ah. "Judge Crater, call your office!" was a popular punch line. Paramount Studio rushed into production two ripped-from-the-headlines motion pictures: *The Vice Squad*, based on former *World* reporter Oliver H. P. Garrett's story of a man forced by a crooked cop into framing innocent women, and *Night Court*, about a crooked judge who framed a young mother as a prostitute because she had accidently seen his bankbook, proof of his villainy. In a parody of his own Pulitzer Prize–winning *Of Thee I Sing*, the first Broadway musical to satirize politics, playwright George S. Kaufman depicted a mayor tap-dancing his way out of a tough interrogation, singing

Fee, fi, fo, fum!
Whoops-a-daisy, and ho hum! . . .
Where do you get your questions from?
Hey, diddle, doodle!
The cash and the boodle—
    It's ten to one they'll win again!
So what do I care
If you give me the air—
    They'll only vote me in again!

Mayor Jimmy Walker insisted there was nothing wrong with New York City, saying it was all "just so much politics." But in fact, "they" would not vote him in again.[1]

Seabury ran three separate but overlapping investigations. The first was as the appellate division's referee to examine alleged corruption in the city's lower criminal courts. The second was as Governor Roosevelt's commissioner to respond to a City Club petition to remove New York's district attorney for "incompetence." The third was as counsel to a joint legislative committee authorized to investigate corruption in various departments of the city's administration. The first and third had the gravest consequences. Some police officers went to jail; others were demoted or dismissed. Judges lost their seats. Governor Roosevelt removed the county sheriff for graft. Citing Seabury's discoveries about Mayor Walker's bottomless well of cash, Roosevelt subjected him to a public trial that forced him to resign. Since the exposed malfeasants were all affiliated with Tammany Hall, the organization emerged deeply wounded.

All of these events interested women as much as they did men. New York City women civic activists followed them avidly, attending the hearings, discussing the revelations at their meetings, and passing resolutions for reform, which they then presented to local and state authorities. Some traveled to Albany to confront legislators and urge the governor to take action, such as pardoning women now revealed to have been falsely accused of sex crimes and expanding the investigations to the outer boroughs. When the investigations' focus turned from the women's court to city governance, women were on the front lines of discussions of the city's future and then helped bring a reform administration into power under the leadership of independent Republican Fiorello La Guardia. In short, women were engaged in not only the specifics of the corruption Samuel Seabury exposed but also the consequences of that exposure for New York City's future.

Philosopher John Dewey, a Seabury admirer and municipal reformer, described New York City's government as combining two kinds of power, official and unofficial. The power of the unofficial—Tammany's "sachems" or bosses— exceeded that of the official, the regularly elected. Some machine leaders took city jobs; most did not need to. According to Dewey, "incidental rewards" kept their tin boxes full.[2]

The board of standards and appeals, the agency that modified or waived building and zoning codes, generated many such rewards. Dr. William F. "Horse Doctor" Doyle, once a fire department veterinarian, put together a lucrative practice helping builders win variances. Seabury's staff uncovered proof of his graft and of the influence of politics on the board. The most egregious example implicated William J. Flynn, the Bronx's commissioner of public works. After winning board approval to build a garage, Flynn got the board to deny a

competitor, Louis H. Willard, permission to build a similar facility on his property across the street. The banks foreclosed on Willard's property and home; both
he and his wife later committed suicide.[3]

Other tragedies that especially disturbed the city's women activists came from
police complicity in "vice." In February 1931, thirty-two-year-old Vivian Gordon
volunteered to tell Seabury's staff how, eight years earlier, her ex-husband and a
policeman had framed her as a prostitute. After she gave preliminary testimony in
private, the staff asked her to bring in corroborating evidence. Before she could do
so she was abducted and strangled to death, her body dumped in Van Cortlandt
Park in the Bronx. Her sixteen-year-old daughter later killed herself.[4] Gordon's
murderer was never found.

Seabury's hearings brought other sensational moments. To nail down details
on "fixing," Seabury subpoenaed the city's most notorious madam, Polly Adler.
Born in 1900 in a Belorussian village, Adler had immigrated to the Golden Land
of America at age thirteen. Living with relatives, she earned her keep in sweatshops
until she was raped by a foreman, had an abortion, and was thrown out by her
relatives. She soon fell in with a fast crowd of showgirls and drug addicts. In 1920
a bootlegger rented an apartment for his assignations and asked her to take care
of it. Soon she was supplying his friends with women she met in dance halls and
speakeasies. Later she attracted gamblers, racketeers, and well-heeled clients, including cops and politicians. Moe, of the crack prohibition team Moe Smith and
Izzy Einstein, who sometimes dressed in drag to trap miscreants, was one of her
customers. Polly's became the city's most famous house of ill repute—a "combination club and speakeasy with a harem conveniently handy," as she described
it. Even the city's literati, including members of the Algonquin Hotel's famous
Roundtable, partied at Polly's.

Though she paid off the vice squad, occasionally they hauled her in to meet
their arrest quotas. This treatment made her welcome Seabury's hearings, which
she called a healthy "airing of soiled linen." When warned that Seabury wanted
to interrogate her, however, she fled out of state, terrified she would be murdered,
like Vivian Gordon, if she gave testimony. After the Gordon furor died down,
she thought she was safe, but as soon as she got home Seabury brought her in.
She denied knowing any of the men he asked her about. Although Seabury's staff
produced her canceled checks, she also denied having paid off policemen. Unable
to shake her silence, Seabury let her go relatively unscathed. She later said the
news coverage boosted her business.[5]

In addition to Seabury's interrogation of Adler, his pursuit of women's court
magistrates other than Jean Norris attracted wide public notice, especially from
women activists. Admitted to the bar in 1899 and active in Bronx Democratic
politics, in 1920 Jesse Silbermann won appointment to the magistracy. Seabury

suspected Silbermann of "fixing." He had let off so many women caught shop-lifting at Samuel H. Klein's self-service department store that Klein had stopped bothering to get them arrested. Silbermann also issued diametrically opposite verdicts in identical "vagrancy" cases. Finally, he had ruled favorably on women defended by a lawyer who had bribed prosecutor John Weston and admitted that a Tammany boss had interceded on three or four dozen cases. In June 1931, Seabury formally charged Silbermann with allowing "considerations outside of the record" to enter into his decisions. On July 2 the appellate division unani-mously found Silbermann guilty of "fixing." Striking his fist on a table, a stone-faced Silbermann uttered only one word: "Out." Twenty minutes later, he and his family left in an automobile, taunted by a hooting crowd.

One-fifth of the total number of Manhattan and Bronx magistrates were now "out."[6] Seabury's staff sifted charges against others—notably John McHugh, the arresting officer in the Emma Hammerstein case, and Earl Smith, who had ignored police perjury and found her guilty. Defending his pursuit of these and other wrongdoers linked to the criminal justice system, Seabury said, "A trinity of three dominating powers existed in Women's Court": representing the bar was the lawyer who paid bribes to get women off; the man representing the district attorney's office was a "confessed bribe taker"; and on the bench sat a judge "aware of police perjury for years" yet who did nothing. He called on the public to "make the magistrates' courts . . . true temples of justice in which the bench is the altar and not the bargain counter of crooked attorneys and political brokers."[7]

Seabury's suspicions fell upon many other Tammany-affiliated officeholders. Three stand out: District Attorney Thomas C. T. Crain, Sheriff Thomas M. Farley, and Mayor James J. Walker. Women civic activists followed the cases against these men with avid interest: Crain because of his ineptitude, especially in regard to the Vivian Gordon murder; Farley for his blatant corruption; and Walker for his cav-alier disregard of women's treatment in the criminal justice system.

In early March 1931, the City Club petitioned Governor Roosevelt to expand the court inquiries into city government and to remove Crain for his "incom-petent, inefficient, and futile" pursuit of criminality. Crain, a former New York Supreme Court judge whom Tammany's boss Curry had handpicked to run for district attorney in 1929, had promised to solve the Rothstein murder within fifteen days of taking office, but had not done so. In February, forty witnesses essential to his pursuit of vice squad perjuries suddenly "could not be located." Vivian Gordon's murder was the last straw. After Seabury declared him incompe-tent but not criminal, Crain kept his post, but the detailed catalog of his failures intensified reformers' zeal to uproot the machine that had put him there.[8]

By the time of the next big scandal—revelations about Sheriff Farley's "tin box"—the Republican-dominated legislature had finally won Governor

Roosevelt's approval of a joint committee "To Investigate the Affairs of New York City." Manhattan state senator Samuel H. Hofstadter chaired the committee; Seabury was appointed counsel. Roosevelt was now eyeing the presidency and realized he could not keep saying no to an expanded inquiry. For him, a handwritten letter sent on March 1 by Charles C. Burlingham, the "dean" of New York City lawyers and an old friend, may have been a tipping point. The letter reminded the governor that in his pre-election speeches he had promised to "act promptly and vigorously" in the event "something definite was pointed out. . . . Has not Seabury shown enough to justify your intervention?" Burlingham asked. "Is not this sinister coincidence of the murder of Vivian Gordon enough?" It was time, Burlingham asserted, for the governor to act.[9]

"Good government" groups reinforced Burlingham's message. On March 18, the city affairs committee filed formal corruption charges against Mayor Walker. On March 20, municipal reformer William Harvey Allen leveled lengthy public charges against Walker of "inefficiency" and failure "to do his duty as mayor to stop extensive crimes by police officers." On March 21, William Jay Schieffelin, chair of the Citizens Union, announced he had completed formation of the Committee of One Thousand to fight corruption in city government and defeat Tammany in the 1933 elections. "Men and women of all shades of political opinion are joining the movement," he said. By mid-April 1931 his committee had more than 1,200 members and a steering committee of 150 lawyers, who would sift complaints from the public and plan government reforms to prevent corruption in the future.[10]

Individual citizens, men and women alike, flooded the governor's office with letters and telegrams. Some correspondents defended Mayor Walker. Tammany assemblyman Louis Cuvillier called the mayor's critics "professional fault-finders," whose "reckless and irresponsible statements . . . would not stand legal test." Several writers launched anti-Semitic attacks against Rabbi Stephen Wise, cochair of the city affairs committee: "If Rabbi Wise would take care of his Hebrew Synagogue & mind his own business he would be better off," one wrote, asserting further that, if Walker were Jewish, Wise would not have gone after him. A cleric from Long Island admitted that the mayor's decision to take an extended Palm Springs vacation "for his health" when the uproar over Gordon's murder was at its height showed he lacked "moral courage." Still, he was sure the mayor was not himself corrupt.

The vast majority of correspondents said they were fed up with Walker and corruption. One thought many judges and prosecutors were probably honorable but admitted that most citizens believed justice unreachable without "adroitly placing something in itching palms." He blamed the mayor for neglecting his duties, "red-baiting" his critics, and "governing by wisecracking." If indeed the city "is victimized by a *plunderbund*" (political corruption), then the people were entitled to drive the plunderers out. A handwritten letter from an "old time Democrat" said that if the governor delays any longer "it would seem to many you did not want clean government . . . but were forced by clean people to order the investigation." Another writer blamed the "so-called reformers," such as the antiprostitution Committee of Fourteen, for having backed those who preyed on women, along with their "sneaks, magistrate intimidators and appointment endorsers."[11]

At the end of March the governor authorized $250,000 for Hofstadter's committee; he later doubled that amount. The committee's work, which began on April 8, 1931, lasted until the end of December 1932. While gathering evidence against Walker, Seabury went first after an easier target, Sheriff Farley, who over his six years in office had accumulated $360,000 more than his salary warranted. Cash had somehow "appeared" in a tin box he kept in a safe at home, he said. "Kind of a magic box?" Seabury prompted. The press had a field day with that. Seabury eventually laid eleven charges on Farley, including his lack of understanding of the duties of his office and his moving official funds to different banks to pocket extra interest. In early February 1932, Governor Roosevelt presided over hearings on the charges. When Farley could not make credible explanations, Roosevelt ordered his removal.[12]

Angered by what happened to Farley, Mayor Walker and his friends now went after Seabury, accusing him of bias, wasting public funds, and harming the city's reputation. Walker continued to deny any role in graft. As for corrupt policemen, Walker said they were few in number and easily cleaned out. If graft existed, it was only "petty," and those who said otherwise were "slanderers." Unmoved, Seabury's staff kept amassing proofs of benefits Walker earned from favoring friends' businesses. Though Walker's salary was $25,000, he lived high. "Beau James" always dressed in one of his seventy-five immaculately tailored suits, spats, and perfectly matched haberdashery. In addition to his night-clubbing (not for nothing was he called the "Night Mayor of New York"), he took frequent vacations not just to Palm Springs but also to the Riviera. Even New Yorkers who loved him had to wonder where he got his money.

Seabury would soon find out. His eye fell first on Walker's aid to a consortium of Ohio bus and tire manufacturers formed by his friend state senator John A. Hastings that sought a New York City bus franchise. Walker also helped a wealthy newspaper publisher who had invested in a company selling tiles to subway contractors and won approval for a board of taxicab control that limited the number of cabs, a ruling that favored cabs already on the streets. Seabury subpoenaed Walker's financial agent, Russell T. Sherwood, who promptly decamped for Mexico on his honeymoon. Since extradition did not cover recalcitrant witnesses, Seabury was powerless to get Sherwood, whose "honeymoon" lasted two years.

In the end, Seabury did not need Sherwood. Tipped off by a bank employee that they should look for Walker's letters of credit, Seabury's staff found a paper trail of payoffs. They also discovered that, between 1927 and 1929, Walker's publisher friend had set up a secret joint brokerage account with Walker that earned a quarter million dollars. Walker dismissed the earnings as mere "beneficences" given by caring friends worried about his financial welfare. At turns defiant and sarcastic, he rejected probes into his private affairs and branded the entire inquiry a "Red plot." Crowds of New Yorkers were with him, booing Seabury's arrival at hearings and cheering Walker's. When Walker left for the day a dozen young women flanked the doorway throwing roses. A few days later, a crowd of eighteen thousand cheered Walker at a Madison Square Garden police graduation ceremony. Told this, Seabury snarled that crowds had once also cheered Tammany's notorious past leader, Boss Tweed.

In June, a few weeks before the opening of the Democratic National Convention, Seabury laid out his case against Walker before Governor Roosevelt. In August, Roosevelt, the victorious nominee, began hearings into the case. Broadcast over the radio, with transcripts published in the papers, the hearings riveted the nation. Walker insisted that Republicans had designed the case to divert public attention from the failures of Herbert Hoover's Republican administration in the current economic crisis. He denied any of the monies he received compensated him for favors. For three weeks governor and mayor sparred, with Seabury providing evidence and Walker's lawyer challenging every detail.

Depressed and worn out, after attending the funeral of his brother on September 1, Walker resigned, effective immediately. Seabury called the act a confession of guilt. Walker did not agree. Denouncing his "mock trial," he vowed to run in the November special election called to choose someone to complete his term. With their eyes on the coming national election and worried about the Democratic Party's reputation, Tammany's sachems urged Walker not to run. Walker obeyed. Joseph V. McKee, president of the board of aldermen, became acting mayor and ran in the special election, but lost to John Patrick O'Brien, another Tammany acolyte. Formerly corporation counsel (the city's chief law officer) and for the previous ten years a New York County surrogate judge, O'Brien also beat Republican and Socialist candidates. Tammany may have been down, but it was hardly "out."[13]

In late 1930 and early 1931 the vice squad–stool pigeon–bondsman–lawyer "racket" had been top national news. By the end of Seabury's three investigations in late 1932, the public eye had shifted to incompetence (Crain), graft (Farley), and payoffs (Walker). Like the male-led "good government" forces, including the city and county bar associations, the City Club, and the Citizens Union, as well as ad hoc groups such as the city affairs committee and the Committee of One Thousand, women civic activists would eventually focus on how to change the city's government to prevent future corruption. But before anyone raised governance issues, more than any other group women focused on the women's court and the treatment of women in morals cases. In addition, their organizations demanded an expansion of the court inquiries into the outer boroughs and an end to the double standard of morality that jailed women while letting men go free.

Catherine Parker Clivette's Society for the Prevention of Unjust Convictions (SPUC) led the charge. Yet another framing case, which arose between Emma Hammerstein's conviction at the end of May 1930, the Mary Crow case from early June, and the opening of Seabury's public hearings at the end of November, fueled the group's outrage. In August, one Minnie Miller, a Brooklyn mother of three, was charged with vagrancy. When the magistrate saw conflicts in the arresting officers' testimony and discovered that one officer was reading from a blank arrest record, he acquitted her. By late September, when Clivette found out that Police Commissioner Edward P. Mulrooney had done nothing to punish the arresting officers for their perjury, she and the group's counsel, Brooklyn lawyer Michael Gold, led eighteen members over to Mulrooney's office to demand action. Mulrooney listened respectfully, assigned the case to a deputy for investigation, and eventually suspended and then dismissed the officers. Later that fall, Mulrooney was still insisting his department never used stool pigeons, a claim he would soon have to retract.[14]

As 1930 drew to a close, the New York Federation of Women's Clubs' committee of three lawyers—Anna Hochfelder, Ruth Lewinson, and Olive Stott Gabriel, working with former policewoman Mary E. Hamilton—began pressing officials, including Governor Roosevelt, to grant pardons to women arrested on perjured testimony. After consulting with Seabury, Roosevelt learned that he could pardon only the six still serving sentences. The pardons annoyed Catherine Clivette, who said, "The Governor should have apologized to those women instead of pardoning them. They have done nothing for which to be pardoned."[15] She had a point, but surely the six were thrilled.

Hochfelder's committee continued to agitate for more changes, meeting with Chief Justice Corrigan, District Attorney Crain, Commissioner Mulrooney, Judge Seabury, and presiding appellate division justice Frederic Kernochan. They also offered to help the mayor with his efforts on crime prevention. Walker did not respond until the following February, when he appointed eleven representatives (only four of whom were women) from social agencies to a committee on the coordination of agencies for crime prevention. He asked this group to work with the police department's new crime prevention bureau on future steps to prevent crime, especially among juveniles. Establishing this committee allowed Walker to show he was responding to women's concerns, but he did not provide concrete follow-up. He stayed only briefly at its first meeting, making clear he was more interested in having his city "look clean" than in getting to the bottom of framing. He then left on a month-long Palm Springs vacation.[16]

At the same time, Catherine Clivette was launching a campaign to start a Seabury-type investigation in the outer boroughs. Speaking for the SPUC, Michael Gold cited two Brooklyn cases of concern: those of Jacob Cohen, whose case a police officer offered to "fix" for $250, and Bertha Padnos, who was putting her six-month-old baby to bed when a "plumber" gained entry, followed by officers who arrested her. Vice squad framing in Brooklyn "has been going on for years," Gold charged. "The mere separation of the boroughs by the East River certainly does not isolate the deplorable conditions disclosed in . . . Manhattan." Clivette put it more baldly, charging, "The Brooklyn court is just as rotten as the Manhattan court."

Roosevelt took the SPUC's request seriously, asking Edward Lazansky, presiding appellate division justice for the outer boroughs, to respond. Asserting that no substantiated complaints against Brooklyn magistrates existed, Lazansky declined to act. Then, in January 1931, W. Kingsland Macy, newly elected Republican state chair, relaunched his party's quest for an extended legislative investigation. Clivette opposed this move, arguing that an investigation by the legislature would be "politically minded and controlled." Instead, she called for an investigation along the same lines as Seabury's in Manhattan and the Bronx. She even volunteered to raise its $25,000 budget herself so as to spare taxpayers. Her collection of a thousand signatures from Brooklyn residents in support of an extended inquiry convinced Roosevelt to approach Lazansky again, in part to clear the air but also to preempt a Republican probe. "Better late than never," Clivette snapped, saying she fully expected Lazansky to take "full cognizance of the growing evils in our courts." He did not. At the end of February Lazansky reported that by a vote of four to two his appellate division colleagues still found no reason to hold an inquiry. Though Roosevelt was not pleased, he dropped the matter, and Clivette's proposal died.[17]

Meanwhile, Clivette was also campaigning to end the double standard in morals cases. In early January 1931, speaking to Dr. L. Adele Cuinet's Brooklyn Women's Hoover-Curtis Constitutional Committee, she complained that the criminal code makes men and women equally guilty, but the authorities prosecute only women. She lambasted Chief Magistrate Corrigan for justifying this inequity by publicly declaring that "men are only casual offenders while women are habitual offenders." Her charges escalated. She insisted that justice in the city was unavailable without "paying a fixer." Doctors were using unsterile instruments to draw blood from women arrestees. Prison doctors were keeping such poor records that negative test results became positive. In response to the Vivian Gordon murder, by early March she was planning a rally of a thousand women to demand of Commissioner Mulrooney a woman's right to carry a pistol. On March 1 she told a reporter from the *Herald Tribune*,

> I have known for years that there was a crying need for reform, but it was never possible to turn the light of publicity on these cases, because the women victims were terrified at the thought. The case of Mrs. Hammerstein, however, aroused the wrath of many women who never before had thought about these things, and a large and energetic group followed every step of that trial with its eventual reversal of the decree by the Appellate Division.[18]

She claimed that her Society for the Prevention of Unjust Convictions now had more than two thousand members and had turned over to investigators many letters from unjustly imprisoned women. She reminded the reporter that the Seabury investigations began to uncover whether magistrates had bought their seats, but "it took its present turn because we women called Mr. Seabury's attention to some other evils existing in the courts."[19]

Many representatives of other city women's organizations, including the Women's City Club, the League of Women Voters, the National Women Lawyers Association, and the New York branch of the National Woman's Party, had all been following the Seabury investigations closely. At the February annual convention of the city's Federation of Women's Clubs, Anna Hochfelder's committee asked that antiprostitution laws be applied equally to men and women and that magistrates throw out all cases that fail to produce the "unknown man" as a witness. They also demanded that the courts appoint (and if necessary fund) counsel for all women arrested for prostitution, that judges give no more weight to the arresting policeman's testimony than to that of other witnesses, and that the "stool pigeon" system be abolished. The convention's 850 attendees unanimously approved these proposals. The federation's resolutions added weight to Clivette's demands for a single standard of morality in the treatment of women brought before the women's court.[20]

On March 12, 1931, Police Commissioner Mulrooney held a two-hour conference of city officials to address police department "evils." The previous October he had resisted any change in procedure, but now he made a startling announcement: from now on cases in which a vice squad witness implicates an "unknown man" would be disallowed; either the man must appear or the magistrate must throw the case out. On April 11 Mulrooney formally announced new antivice policies. He was abolishing the current vice squad and returning its 300 officers to uniformed duty. Reassuring the public that the police were not giving up their pursuit of commercialized vice, he began assigning 245 new officers to a "revamped" squad, which would not draw "hasty conclusions of guilt or innocence" or resort to entrapment.[21] Mulrooney never admitted he was acting because of the demands of women's organizations. But the leaders of those organizations could only have been gratified.

By spring 1931, some women activists had begun to pay more attention to the issue of official corruption—the "cash" and the "boodle" and the "magical" tin boxes. One woman politician's response shocked her good-government friends. Tammany's Nineteenth Assembly District (AD) coleader, Annie Mathews, the county register whose 1921 electoral victory suffragists had celebrated, had just completed her second term. In a speech to the League of Women Voters on April 15, 1931, she surprised her audience by justifying the payment of "gratuities" to some politicians. Despite all the hard work party leaders do—raising money and managing campaigns—"no political party ever pays its district leaders a salary," she noted. "Is it reasonable to expect them to do all this work for nothing, just for love of country?" She gave the following example:

> A vacancy arises for a judge's position. The district leader gets a chance to recommend a man for the position at $25,000 per year for 14 years. If he is a Democrat here or a Republican in Philadelphia he is sure of reelection, so he practically has the position until he retires for age. If somebody offered you a thing like that, would you just say "Thank you" and not offer that person a present? Would you really be such a rotter?[22]

Distinguishing a "present" (a thank you for an appointment) from a bribe (paid in advance), she explained she would never condone the latter. What she wanted, she said, was for politics to be run like a business, with bosses paid actual salaries.

Some members of the public praised Mathews for her frankness; others expressed horror. Tammany's female coleaders said they had never heard of such a thing as a present. The *Times* described Tammany as "the best organized business" in the city, with its "regular system of assignments, appointments, promotions, rewards, and also punishments": it never failed to get paid in some form, whether in political services or votes. In response, Mathews observed that every political party organizes itself similarly and called for frank recognition that political workers need to be openly paid. This would, she thought, free the winning party from having to "reward those who have worked hard to achieve victory." Finally, she praised Tammany for having favored "every worth-while piece of constructive and human legislation, which has been wrung out of a reluctant and reactionary majority."[23]

Mathews was right about Tammany's support for progressive legislation, especially when it was popular with voters. Moreover, her argument for paying party workers favored modernization: instead of giving volunteers secret deposits, the parties would treat them as professionals. While some women political activists said they were appalled, others recognized that properly paid political workers might find bribes less tempting. At least at some levels of political life, this would be the way of the future.

At about the same time as Annie Mathews was making her case for modernization, the Seabury investigations were moving toward probing New York City's administration. Accordingly, the interests of women activists now focused less on the courts and more on governance. Writing in March 1931 to the *Times*, social settlement leader Mary Simkhovitch praised the "wave of indignation and demand for political change," but warned that cries to "turn the rascals out" would not be enough. What the city needed was continuing self-criticism. "Denunciation and excitement will never take the place of knowledge, patience and the constructive development of one aspect after another of our city's life," she counseled.[24] Citizens will now have to ask: Could the city reconstruct itself? If so, how? These would become the great questions of the next few years, and for the first time in the city's history women would be involved in both framing the discussion and finding answers.

At least 150 women joined William Jay Schieffelin's Committee of One Thousand. Attorney Dorothy Kenyon headed its health division. Other women members included Caroline Lexow of the League of Women Voters, Republican Party activist Rosalie Loew Whitney, and former social settlement worker Augusta Salik Dublin. The sole woman on the committee's executive committee, Dublin headed its "neighborhood cooperation" division to examine issues of concern in the city's congested areas.

In his speech at the committee's first town hall meeting on April 16, the idealistic William Jay Schieffelin disparaged Annie Mathews's support for political workers' salaries. In his view, "self-interest, financial or otherwise" should not be a motive for entering politics. He also said it was time to end the city's historic pattern of Tammany dominance alternating with ineffectual reform. To bring about a more permanent solution, he proposed abolishing the ward-based board of aldermen and electing a city council by proportional representation, or PR, as the voting system was called. He would retain the board of estimate to make appropriations but put a city manager in charge of spending.[25]

Judge Seabury favored this plan. His first priority was to take the courts out of the political spoils system. He wanted the appellate division, instead of the

mayor, to appoint magistrates and justices. He also argued for the consolidation of the lower courts into a single, new, court of special sessions that would
be housed in a central building instead of spread across the city's boroughs. He
wanted all court personnel brought under the civil service, bail bond and probation bureaus centralized, and lawyers defending the indigent to be paid from the
public treasury. While Seabury recognized that minority representation in a legislative body was no panacea, like Schieffelin he wanted one-party rule to end. He
agreed that to achieve this result the city must abolish the board of aldermen (a
"total waste of money") and board of estimate (a mere "rubber stamp"), replacing
them with a single, twenty-five-member chamber elected by PR. For Seabury, the
use of PR as a voting system for New York City's legislature would mean "all the
difference between a sustained good government year in and year out, such as
Cincinnati and some other cities have enjoyed, and a spasm of reform once in a
generation, such as has characterized our experience in New York."[26]

The clubs that had first criticized the poor organization of the city's judicial
work were pleased with Seabury's ideas on court consolidation. Hochfelder had
made a similar proposal for the centralization of the magistrates' courts, and also
called for the establishment of a special group to monitor them. Women's groups
were especially intrigued by the city manager idea, which several hundred cities
had already tried. In April 1929, long before the court scandals and the ensuing
investigations, several speakers had addressed the idea at the closing dinner of the
Women's City Club and League of Women Voters second annual two-day conference on public affairs. Murray Seasongood, a law professor and former mayor
of Cincinnati, had won a city manager for his city, convincing city elites that such
a manager would run the city like a business and get rid of boss rule. Richard
S. Childs, then head of the City Club, argued that a manager plan was appropriate for New York. Mayor Walker did not agree. As civic activist Genevieve
Beavers Earle would later recall, Walker made wisecracks,

> shot his cuffs, and rolled his eyes. There wasn't a laugh in the audience.
> They didn't come to be entertained. They wanted the Mayor of the City of
> New York to explore the whole possibility of the city manager plan as ap-
> plied to New York City.... He was pretty nettled when he left the room. It
> was reported that he remarked angrily that that was the last time he would
> ever be the guest of the League of Women Voters.[27]

Little affection remained between the league and this mayor.

Despite Walker's seeming dismissal of at least this particular group's political
concerns, many Tammany women still supported him. The Woman's Democratic
Club of New York City worked hard to re-elect him in 1929. Bessye Bearden,

unofficial head of Democratic women in Harlem, praised his support for "colored owned" businesses and a children's health center. Republican, independent Democratic, and Socialist women attacked him relentlessly. In 1929, from her vantage point of three years' service on the board of aldermen and years of leadership of Republican Party women, Ruth Baker Pratt assailed the graft, scandals, and lack of thrift in his administration. She cited his patronage of dubious businesses, the failure to convict Rothstein's murderer, delays on traffic relief until a few months before the election, graft in sewer construction in Queens—her list went on. On the opposite side of the political spectrum, Juliet Stuart Poyntz of the United Council of Working Women represented striking cafeteria workers who also censured Walker for doing nothing about "Tammany graft and corruption."[28]

By early 1931, women political activists had become even more negative toward Walker. Now, however, the issue was his dismissiveness toward framing. In March, in response to warnings from Seabury that more revelations were coming, Walker met in open conference with the eleven members he had appointed to his committee on the coordination of agencies for crime prevention, several members of the crime prevention bureau and state crime commission, and Chief Magistrate Corrigan. Opening the meeting, Walker confessed, "I have been more or less shocked by the reports of the framing of innocent women. While the reports are revolting, I am at a loss to understand why organizations like yours, why our great newspapers with reporters in every court, did not discover the situation until it broke out in headlines."[29] Of course many others—from Anna Moscowitz in the 1910s, to newspaper editors and social workers in 1920s Harlem, to Catherine Clivette and the city's Federation of Women's Clubs in 1930—had been protesting framing for years, and officials, including Walker, had either not responded or denied its existence.

Popular journalist Heywood Campbell Broun Jr. wrote a stinging rebuke of Walker's nonchalance. Homing in on "the duel between 'less' and 'more,'" he asserted the former had "won the day." While he had no doubt that Walker truly needed the California vacation he now took, he thought the city's health was also "precarious." Suppose only one woman had been framed, Broun continued. Suppose that "lone case had concerned a notorious harlot." The public would still "expect from the Mayor something much stronger than 'more' or 'less.'"[30] When it came time for the first open duels between Seabury and Walker in the May 1932 hearings before the Hofstadter committee, the city's women political activists would be following closely.

Women activists thus reacted vigorously to the issues raised in the Seabury investigations—from police and magistrate malfeasance to official graft and corruption. The investigations of the early 1930s into New York City's lower criminal court system brought to a head their frustrations of the previous decade in trying to win the public policies they favored and the positions of public authority to bring them about. Despite their repeated requests for more women on the bench, not to mention the presence of hundreds of well-trained women lawyers in the city, only one, Jean Norris, had received a full-term appointment as a magistrate. Women were still excluded from juries. Sheppard-Towner had lost its funding. Legislators continued to block laws against the exploitation and endangerment of women workers. The court investigations re-energized progressive feminists' commitment to public policy and government reform. They would spend the rest of the decade pursuing the quest they had begun after winning the vote: a modern, unbossed city government.

Two early 1930s government appointments of women—social worker Henrietta Silvis Additon to head the crime prevention bureau (CPB) and attorney Anna Moscowitz Kross to the magistrate's bench—signaled significant advances for the city's progressive feminists. Although neither would have called herself a modernizer, both women expressed commitments to modern ideas and methods of criminal justice. They were both professionals who understood the varied causes of crime and who had the expertise to develop nonpunitive, creative approaches to its prevention and treatment.

From a career perspective, Kross fared better than Additon. Though Kross rose through loyalty to Tammany, she flourished under Mayor La Guardia, a nominal Republican. Policy and tactical disagreements often tested Kross's relationship with La Guardia (they both had pugnacious and outspoken temperaments), but they had been friends since law school (she called him "Florrie") and their relationship was one of respect and affection. Additon was a different story. Her career had advanced under Mayor Walker, which to La Guardia meant she was tainted. Worse, she could never convince La Guardia that the crime prevention program she ran was worth funding. As a result, her city career was cut short and she never received credit for her groundbreaking work.

Rates of juvenile delinquency had risen sharply in the 1920s. Most city officials responded with a tough line: more cops, stiffer sentences, larger prisons. Social workers and penal reformers countered that "brass buttons" and "nightsticks" would never work with kids. Children are not born criminals, they argued, but turn to crime because of poverty, disease, and family dysfunction. Addressing these conditions is costly, they continued, but expanding law enforcement costs more.[31]

In 1928 Governor Smith's state crime commission had urged the police to engage directly in preventive work instead of relying on social workers. In response, Police Commissioner Grover Whalen had formed an advisory committee on crime prevention, which convinced him that police departments could both apprehend criminals *and* prevent crime. In January 1930 he hired social worker Virginia Murray, a delinquency expert, to design a crime prevention bureau to work with social welfare agencies. The bureau she organized for New York City hired twenty-five civil service investigators, three of whom were African American women assigned to Harlem, where rates of juvenile delinquency were said to be rising.[32]

The crime prevention bureau boasted some early successes. By mid-May it had handled 1,878 complaints and arrested only 142 juveniles. Then, rumors of Whalen's impending resignation brought fears that his successor might cut or cancel the bureau's budget.[33] Civic, legal, and other welfare agencies rushed to pass a city charter amendment making the CPB permanent and its director a deputy police commissioner. Whalen's successor, career policeman Edward P. Mulrooney, endorsed the amendment and authorized a search in which Henrietta Additon emerged on top. On June 22, 1931, Mulrooney swore her in as the city's sixth deputy police commissioner.[34]

Born in 1887, Additon grew up in northeast Georgia, where her favorite pastime was playing baseball with an older brother. At age fifteen she umpired her father's furniture-store team's games; at nineteen, she won over some difficult sixth graders with "baseball talk." After graduating in 1907 from Piedmont College, in 1911 she earned a master's degree in history and sociology from the University of Pennsylvania and won a doctoral fellowship. As a result of her volunteer work with a local boys' club, Jane Deeter Rippin, chief probation officer for the Philadelphia juvenile court, drew her away from academics with a job offer, and then during World War I moved Additon to Washington, DC, to assist her in directing the Women and Girls' Section of the War Department Commission on Training Camp Activities. Additon returned to Philadelphia as executive secretary of the Big Sisters, in 1928 publishing a monograph, *City Planning for Girls*, which laid out a comprehensive approach to female delinquency.[35] By the time Additon accepted the directorship of the New York Police Department Crime Prevention Bureau, she was a nationally known corrections professional.

"The true prevention of delinquency," Additon told the *Times*, "challenges every condition in society—family life, school and church, community and neighborhood conditions, industry, courts, and all the works of social welfare." "It is no easy task," she continued,

> to secure satisfactory personality adjustments or to succeed in bringing about a change in behavior through the development of wholesome interests and the establishment of new habits of thought. Many people, troubled because of the existence of misery and crime, have put their faith in bricks and mortar. A belief in the miraculous reformative power of

institutional care has been so strong that institutions have been created by the hundreds. Their promoters . . . have not stopped to look into the results of the efforts already made to provide similar care. They have had little appreciation of the cost of really effective institutional care, and they have seldom remembered that the inmates needed to be fitted for life outside of institution walls.[36]

Preferring social treatment over institutionalization for juveniles labeled "delinquent," Additon hoped to make as few arrests as possible. She told her staff to observe, report on, and help eradicate "breeding spots of delinquency," such as unsupervised dance and pool halls, movie houses, gambling centers, and places displaying obscene literature or pictures.

In its efforts to turn children into good citizens, the bureau tried to break up gangs, increase the number of public recreational resources, resolve family rifts, mediate between offenders and victims, found boys' clubs, separate accused juveniles from older criminals, and help patrolmen develop friendly relations with city youth. Additon hoped children would come to see the police department "as a protective rather than a merely repressive agency." While she could never prove that the bureau prevented specific crimes, she could attest to fewer juveniles landing in court. She recognized that voters might ask, in tough economic times, whether a community could afford crime prevention. Her answer was simple: unchecked crime costs more. Still, in 1933 funding challenges plagued the CPB. Concerned about the safety of children playing on city streets, Additon asked for more money for playgrounds, but of course did not get it.[37]

Testifying to a US Senate subcommittee investigating "rackets," she justified police involvement in prevention by detailing the bureau's results. She spoke of the individual boy who gains respect for the police "in a manner that doesn't harden him," of parents who come to the police department seeking help with their "wayward" children, and of school officials referring children who extort "2 cents a week for protection from the younger children in the schoolyard" or threaten store owners with broken windows if refused free sandwiches and apples. The bureau handled a wide variety of problems, from boys gambling in candy stores to employment agencies luring young girls with fake jobs. Most important, she had convinced Babe Ruth to help enroll seven thousand boys in baseball teams, her favorite constructive work. "We called them the Junior Police Athletic League and had P.A.L. on their shirts," she said, because its purpose was "not only to keep the boys busy" but also to show them "the police were their friends." Putting the police on the front line of preventive work was a new idea, she said, but it was not "a little fad that is tucked on from the outside. It is a real responsibility." Additon's congressional testimony revealed a person who was caring and knowledgeable with a sense of humor. When a senator asked, "Don't you think those boys who were levying a tribute of 2 cents probably learned that from the banks?" she replied, to the audience's amusement, "No," if they had "they would have levied six."[38]

While Mayor La Guardia liked the idea of prevention, he needed concrete answers to immediate problems, such as street accidents with small boys. Shortly after coming into office in January 1934, he asked his police commissioner, John F. O'Ryan, to justify the CPB's budget, which had grown from $100,000 to $600,000. Without waiting for an answer, in February La Guardia released a stinging letter to O'Ryan that complained about the bureau's "personnel, its methods, policies and for what, to date, it has failed to accomplish." He told O'Ryan to "spruce it up, pep it up, put some vision into it and see that it obtains results." He complained that the bureau had failed to stop small boys from hitchhiking on the backs of moving vehicles. He wanted work on streets, in schools, and in homes to stop these "stunts," not "speeches about it at 5 o'clock tea parties," a slap at Additon's outreach to women's groups.

La Guardia went further. He told Ryan he wanted daily reports of accidents caused by automobiles and trucks involving children. Dismissing Additon's concern about janitors objecting, he demanded off-hour recreational activities in school buildings. Despite his past views on labor contract sanctity, he asked, "Since when has the school janitor the last word on such an important civic and social welfare activity? . . . I know of nothing more pathetic than seeing youngsters trying to climb over a high fence in order to get into their own school yards" on weekends and holidays, he said. Finally, he demanded that Additon's investigators not sit in police departments but in schools, social centers, and settlement houses, and insisted on meeting all twenty-five investigators, three at a time, daily at 4 o'clock, until he had met them all.[39]

Police statistics at the time showed youth crime had actually fallen. In June 1933 La Guardia's predecessor, Mayor O'Brien, credited this drop in part to the CPB's citizenship work. The *Times* reported that during the previous decade child deaths from street accidents had declined by half. Additon had met with board of education representatives about opening school property to children after hours but needed qualified supervisors to keep from violating custodial contracts or damaging property. Funds for these were unavailable.[40]

A few days after La Guardia's letter appeared, rumors flew of the CPB's imminent demise. Needing to cut $30 million from the budget, La Guardia saw the bureau as an easy target. Women leaders affiliated with "child saving" through the Women's City Club and Big Sisters persuaded him not to close it. The League of Women Voters was already on record protesting threats against it. Rachel Hopper Powell, president of the Women's Prison Association, praised the bureau, noting that out of its 1,983 cases in the previous year only 67 had gone to court. Writer Fannie Hurst, who knew La Guardia well, begged him to get to know Additon better. She assured him that Additon was not a Tammanyite, but "feels precisely as you or I would along those lines, and she is guiltless of the politician's technique." Hurst hoped La Guardia would not "antagonize citizens who are important to you and who think as you do, which is to say, intelligently."[41]

La Guardia was unmoved. At the end of September O'Ryan resigned, saying he was tired of the mayor interfering in his department. La Guardia replaced him with Lewis J. Valentine, a tough-on-crime career policeman. This was Additon's signal to go. Valentine promised to retain the CPB but would rethink its mission.[42]

Additon did not go quietly. She accused La Guardia of having but a "superficial knowledge" of the bureau's work and harboring a "distinct animus" against it. Many agencies and organizations had supported the bureau, as well as her leadership of it, including the state crime commission, women's civic groups, and the welfare council, founded in 1925 as a loose federation of the city's voluntary social welfare, charitable, and health organizations. Additon decried La Guardia's summoning of her staff to his office and deplored his public release of his attack on the bureau before O'Ryan had seen it. She explained that the bureau had neither personnel nor authority to supervise activities in schools and dance halls, and that the mayor had refused to fill key vacancies while demanding the bureau do more. Worse, despite repeated requests, he had "rudely" declined to see her. These "devastating conditions," she said, had forced her to resign. As a parting shot, she echoed Fannie Hurst by wondering whether "an informed and articulate citizenry has any part to play in the administration."[43]

Saying nothing about Additon's departure, Valentine reduced the CPB's personnel and budget. Early the next month, the welfare council spearheaded a protest by seventy social agencies urging him to consult them before making further "drastic changes" and pleaded with the mayor to preserve the bureau's budget. "It is painful to have to record the retirement of so faithful a public servant as Miss Henrietta Additon," the *New York Times* editorialized. It went on to describe her as a "social worker of vision and intelligence . . . [who] labored earnestly to translate ideals into reality." The editorial concluded with the assertion that her services to the city should be publicly recognized.[44]

Additon never received credit for her contributions to crime prevention in the city. In fact, they were erased, including her invention of the Police Athletic League and her coining of the term "PAL." Rebecca Rankin, municipal librarian and chronicler of La Guardia's administrative achievements, would later mock the CPB as "principally engaged in accumulating case records" while putting little effort into preventing delinquency.[45] Neither Grover Whalen nor Lewis Valentine mention Additon in their memoirs. In lamenting the high cost of prisons, Valentine repeated Additon's oft-reiterated point, as if it was his own, that prevention is less expensive. He then illustrated the point by quoting not her but a noted New York judge, who said: "I remember going to the laying of the cornerstone of the New Tombs Building in New York. That building cost 19 million dollars, yet you can't even get $19,000 for keeping those kids out of there." Valentine omitted Additon as the inventor of PAL, instead praising one of her successors, James B. Nolan, as the one who had built PAL into a national model. He boasted that preventive work was now as much a part of police science as laboratory work and a bureau for youth as important as one for detectives. He credited neither Additon nor any of her colleagues with having fought for decades to make this concept a reality.[46]

Additon's career survived. She maintained her connections to the city's reform community, which had believed in and honored her. In 1940, the Women's City Club helped persuade Governor Lehman to appoint her superintendent of Westfield State Farm, a post that put her in charge of almost six hundred women and girls in the Bedford Hills Reformatory. In the general praise following this appointment, the *Times* noted her past breach with Mayor La Guardia but said it had been repaired. In 1942, however, La Guardia's wartime budget eliminated the New York Police Department Juvenile Aid Bureau, its renamed crime prevention program.[47]

Years later, only after Additon retired, her ideas about how to address juvenile delinquency received belated validation. In 1957, the New York Police Department (NYPD) created a youth division; in 1963 it appointed police-woman Theresa M. Melchionne, the first woman since Additon to hold the rank of deputy commissioner, to run it. Melchionne supervised the work of five hundred men and women, plus eighty-one patrolmen assigned to each city stationhouse to recruit youth into the Police Athletic League. The NYPD finally accepted Additon's theories about the importance of community policing and police-sponsored youth programs.[48]

Unlike Henrietta Additon, Anna Moscowitz Kross held on to her city posts for close to forty years. As the city's first female assistant corporation counsel from 1918 to 1923, she had focused on family and union issues. She surveyed children's and family courts in four major cities and then argued for New York combining its family and children's courts into a domestic relations court, a change that finally took place ten years later. Over her twenty years on the magistrate's bench she published scholarly works on judicial organization and created innovative specialized courts to address some of the city's enduring criminal justice problems. In 1954, Mayor Robert Wagner Jr. appointed her commissioner of corrections, a title she retained for twelve years. She was only the second woman in the city's history to hold this post.

Still, Kross never reached the career heights she dreamed of: a seat on the state supreme court at the very least, better yet on the federal bench. Nor did she achieve one of her lifelong passions: what she called a "socio-medical" approach to prostitution. Nonetheless, her career as a political activist, judicial innovator, and corrections administrator surpassed those of most women lawyers of her time. Some of her admirers called her "a mighty outraged woman." A number of passions lay behind that outrage—for the rights of workers and unions, women's advancement, and above all an approach to crime that considered its underlying causes. These very passions, and her penchant for speaking her mind about them, most likely capped her further rise in the judiciary.[49]

Kross was New York City's third woman magistrate. The ill-fated Jean Norris was the first. The second was Jeanette Goodman Brill, a 1908 Brooklyn Law School graduate and specialist in women's, children's, and family issues. After suffrage, Brill co-led the Eighteenth AD Democratic organization and worked in Al Smith's election campaigns. In 1923 she became the state's first woman deputy attorney general, assigned to labor and compensation issues. In 1929 Mayor Walker appointed her to fill an unexpired term on the Brooklyn bench and in 1931 to a full ten-year term. When Brill's term expired in 1941, La Guardia did not renew her appointment, instead giving her seat to Frances W. Lehrich, a Barnard College and Yale Law School graduate who in 1938 had succeeded Pearl Bernstein as board of estimate secretary.[50]

Kross's ascent to the magistracy was Tammany based. Mayor O'Brien appointed her on December 30, 1933, the eve of his last day in office. O'Brien had become her boss when Mayor Hylan appointed him corporation counsel in 1920. Two years later, Tammany's boss Murphy nominated O'Brien for surrogate of New York County, a post he won. In a "first" for women attorneys, Anna Kross, along with Ruth Lewinson, spoke at the January 1923 ceremonies inaugurating new judges, including O'Brien. In August 1924, O'Brien entrusted Kross with the job of protecting the interests of financier J. Pierpont Morgan's minor heirs. Throughout the 1920s Tammany women's meetings and campaign events featured her as a speaker. In 1925 she served as secretary of Joseph McKee's campaign for president of the board of aldermen, a post he won. When O'Brien ran for mayor in fall 1932, Kross headed his women's campaign. Described in the press as "an able student of politics" and a "seasoned campaigner who can run the ranch and also step onto a platform and make a speech with the best of them," she promised a "great women's vote" for her former boss. Two hundred women worked under her direction. They were "not pink tea workers," she said, using a current derogatory term applied to clubwomen, but serious about politics and willing to "stay on the job until early every morning." O'Brien won.[51]

O'Brien's appointment of Kross to the bench thus made sense: he both trusted and owed her. Years later she put it another way, calling herself "just an ordinary run of the mill judge who was appointed in the ordinary run of the mill way—I knew the right politicians at the right time." While this was true, her appointment went beyond party spoils. Her qualifications were outstanding. On April 12, 1923, she had resigned from the city's legal office to assist attorney Jonah J. Goldstein, a well-known activist in Lower East Side and Jewish affairs, in his defense of thirty-six plasterers' union executives indicted for technical conspiracy. Her work so impressed them that by July the union had made her an honorary member and the building and allied trades compensation service bureau had hired her as general counsel, winning the job over many male applicants.[52]

The job entailed educating thousands of workers about their rights and responsibilities under workers' compensation, informing leaders about changes in labor laws, and even listening to their domestic cares. Thomas J. Curtis, the manager of the compensation bureau who hired her, said she could talk to the men "in a way they understand," as well as make them feel "as if she were one of them." The men had confidence in her honesty, her legal training and experience, and her personal reputation. Although most of her clients were men, a few women carpet sewers were among them, along with widows of men killed in workplace accidents.[53]

Kross believed women attorneys were especially suited for labor work. Today's worker, she elaborated, is entitled to know "as much about the laws which govern his job as do the lawyers or the organization which employs him." A woman will explain things to him "straight, . . . without personal axes to grind or ulterior ambitions to foster." She thought that women were also "more single-purposed and conscientious than men and much, much more willing to attend to detail." She also thought women's personal approach meant they would fight harder in courts of law.

> Say an ironworker is hit on the head with a brick and incapacitated for three months. The woman lawyer will instantly picture that man's wife putting the clothes to soak while she runs to the hospital to visit Pat; walking blocks to buy vegetables for the children's dinner a few cents cheaper in order to stretch Pat's maximum compensation; paring down expenses to save the rent money.[54]

Kross believed these stereotypes justified her winning the job.

For the same reasons—women's honesty, attention to detail, and passion for justice—Kross thought herself uniquely qualified for a judgeship. In 1919, she had lost out to Jean Norris. In 1922, when a vacancy opened on the children's court, her name came up along with Bronx lawyer Agnes L. Craig and Norris as possible candidates (for Norris, the post would have been a promotion). Women lawyers argued that a female appointee was not only appropriate but also their "due," now that they were voters. Kross's activism in Al Smith's gubernatorial re-election campaigns put her in a strong position to win the coveted appointment, but neither Kross nor any other woman got it. Kross kept to her labor practice and continued to give loyal service to Tammany. Belle and Henry Moskowitz, who were close friends of the Krosses, were not happy with Anna's attachments to "all the petty politicians" of Tammany Hall and told her younger sister Henriette Voorsanger to suggest Anna detach herself from them. Anna's response was, "Belle is sitting pretty. She started at the top [with Al Smith] so she didn't have to work her way up." Anna did.[55]

In September 1933, reminding Mayor O'Brien of the importance of having a woman on the city's new domestic relations court, Kross renewed her campaign for a judgeship. The delinquent girl, in particular, she said, needs a judge who can take the place of a mother. One court vacancy after another came and went without a woman appointee. Then, as O'Brien's term came to an end, the wives of both O'Brien and Tammany's boss John Curry, who socialized often with the Krosses, pressured the mayor to appoint her. In the middle of the afternoon of his penultimate day in office, he called her up, told her to grab her husband, hail a taxi, and get to city hall. Come in the side entrance, he added; do not say a word to anyone. "Every leader in the city is waiting outside with his candidate," he said, in words she later relayed to her sister, "but my last official act will be to swear you in as Magistrate."[56]

City leaders, both male and female, had indeed been waiting. A male assistant district attorney of Italian ancestry, who had been told to expect a judgeship, had sat in city hall for eight hours, surrounded by supporters, only to be humiliated when Kross's name came through and not his. Supporters of Rose Rothenberg, former assistant district attorney in the women's court and Tammany coleader of the Seventeenth AD, had also been waiting. Italian Americans, who had worked for O'Brien's mayoral rival, Fiorello La Guardia, were more than disap-pointed: they were furious at not being warned. "Someone would pay for the slight," they muttered.[57]

Members of Kross's circle worried about the political cloud over her appoint-ment. In her memoir, Zelda Popkin, a journalist and friend, remembered that some people called Kross "O'Brien's last breath," thereby linking her to Tammany's decline. Feminist journalist Isabelle Keating reported that a male colleague had told Kross she would have a "lot to live down." Still, Kross's sister remembered that important people were on Kross's side, including former governor Al Smith and Governor Herbert Lehman. On her first day on the bench these two men sent flowers to the courtroom she had been assigned—ironically, the old Jefferson Market women's court she had so much wanted abolished. Anna Rosenberg, who had assisted Kross on the Tammany speakers bureau and would soon be a rising star in the New Deal bureaucracy, arranged a reception. After drawing an affectionate picture of Kross, Governor Smith said that the lower court "is one of the most important courts of the land." He counseled, "Don't ever be afraid, Anna, to see anyone who wishes an audience with you. Whether he be banker or politician, wealthy or poor, see him."[58]

Despite the shadow over her appointment, Kross told Keating she was proud of her previous twenty years in the law. She never disclaimed her association with Tammany, although she always objected to the corrupting influence of the "big business men" who used the machine for profit. Yet as a lifelong Democrat, she knew the importance of machine loyalty. If getting something accomplished meant occasionally stomaching some less-than-palatable political associations, she seemed ready to pay that price.[59]

Kross's interests ranged widely—from court reform to the social causes of crime to racial and gender justice and politics. At the top of her list was changing the way society treated prostitutes, a topic that intersected with all of these interests. "We don't need night courts," she told Isabelle Keating. "We need play courts." To her, prostitution was evil, but using the police to end it was futile. Most of her contemporaries were conflicted over the topic. They believed society should neither condone nor tolerate prostitution: it was morally repugnant, spread venereal disease to innocent families, and brought irreparable harm to its practitioners.

Most progressives agreed on these points but disagreed on the causes of prostitution and how government might curb, or better yet, abolish it. Many thought the causes were economic, and if society could only provide prostitutes with "wholesome" work they would leave the profession. Programs to accomplish this rarely succeeded, as prostitutes could earn more and at a faster rate through sex work, even though they could not keep it up for long. Others believed abolition was impossible but government should not allow prostitution to be a public nuisance. Some suggested the state could control it with segregated red-light districts, licensed brothels, and mandatory medical exams. In Kross's era, most Americans rejected these ideas.

Feminist lawyers' campaigns against the women's court brought attention to all of these issues. While the campaigners did not approve of sex work, they were unanimously appalled by the state's repressive approach. Assigned (unhappily) to the women's court, Kross told Popkin that stepping into that old courtroom made her feel "like Rip Van Winkle," wondering "whether I had been asleep for twenty years." The setup was exactly as before the war. There was the same crowd of bondsmen, shyster lawyers, dealers in vice, defendants out on bail, looking the judge over, and well-dressed visitors drawn by curiosity. I heard the droning voice of the clerk, reading the familiar charge, the girl denying, the plainclothes men affirming, the old familiar debate over who spoke first—the woman or the officer—on the decision of which justice hangs in this court. I saw the same kind of tawdrily dressed girls and women—a little younger perhaps, a little thinner, than those of twenty years ago, but still obviously the failures, even at this profession—a drab parade of the stupid, diseased, poor and unsuccessful.[60]

The laws of ancient Greece and Rome, Kross added, left the "glamorous courtesan" alone but went after "the woman who must make the streets her marketplace." To her, the same old story prevailed in New York City's women's court.[61]

After she gave newly inaugurated Mayor La Guardia an earful on the issue, he asked her to make a formal report. Kross recruited Popkin to help. The two women wrote to chiefs of police in other cities to see how they handle prostitution. Many described the same situation as in New York. Kross called the criminal justice system's treatment of prostitutes a "merry-go-round. . . . We drag them in off the streets, convict them, rest them up in jail, send them out again." Kross knew she could not reform prostitutes. What she wanted was to prevent women from becoming prostitutes in the first place and treat prostitutes with therapy if prevention failed. Above all, she was not interested either in teaching morality or in punishment.[62]

Completed in March 1935, Kross's report declared prostitution not a police but a social problem. It required "a new technique" to solve it. She called for well-paid medical workers empowered to "apprehend all persons engaged in the practice of prostitution and, therefore, liable to have contracted a venereal disease." Instead of filing a technical legal complaint, these professionals would conduct a full medical, physical, and mental exam and take a social and environmental history that would then be presented to an informal tribunal of a doctor, a psychiatrist, and a lawyer. She also wanted a "liberal, modern, scientific, social health code, applicable to both men and women," that would empower this tribunal to "apprehend and detain." Instead of a sentence, the tribunal would prescribe an individualized treatment plan, utilizing all of the community's resources to cure, reform, and train the patient until rehabilitation is achieved. There was more: reformatories needed to focus on rehabilitation and "intelligent sex and mental hygiene guidance," especially but not exclusively for the young.[63] A thorough plan, advanced for its time, it would influence the thinking of corrections professionals for more than a generation.

"Everybody knows that houses of prostitution in New York are rife," Kross told a reporter who interviewed her about the report. When the La Guardia administration ramped up an antivice crusade, she called it silly and futile. She disdained such efforts, including the Seabury investigations. They brought "nothing new to the surface," except for a few new faces and names, she said. As for the prostitutes, they "never get a square deal." She opposed "disorderly houses," as they were nuisances; nor did she approve of licensed houses of prostitution. The best plan was to have free social clinics treating venereal diseases on a medical basis. Pointing to the recent seizure of Polly Adler's "little black book," rumored to contain the names of two hundred financiers, lawyers, bondsmen, and procurers, she declared that nothing had changed in the "whole sordid panorama" of commercialized vice in the city. She told the *New York Times* that, since prostitution is a social problem, not a crime, it does not belong in the courts. In her view, the police and the courts have been proceeding only against the victims of prostitution and leaving commercialized vice unscathed. "Every vice investigation from Page to Seabury has told the same story," she said. "But it is time now that the community did something more than express its indignation and feed its pornographic imagination upon details of wire-tapped conversation. A vice investigation is of value to the community only if it stirs the community into constructive action."[64]

The Women's City Club concurred. A year after she sent her report to the mayor, attorney Caroline Simon assigned five women to visit the magistrates' courts. They reported that while most of the courts conducted themselves in a businesslike, dignified manner, in the women's court "a flippant familiarity" prevailed that was out of place. Worse, the way the police get evidence against prostitutes was "disgraceful." For plainclothesmen to allow themselves to be solicited and then tell the whole story in court, including descriptions of the woman's naked body, seemed "unwise and degrading," the club's report proclaimed. Catching a few individuals this way never included the more "serious offenders" who run the houses of prostitution. Echoing Kross's call for a new approach, the club asked that prostitution be removed from the criminal code and treated as a social and public health problem.[65]

Members of the medical community concurred. Dr. Harry J. Benjamin, consulting endocrinologist at City College and noted sexologist, found her recommendations progressive and echoed her call to end the government's interest in prostitution. While advising voluntary health measures to curb the spread of venereal diseases, he thought that prostitution, engaged in voluntarily, should be tolerated. "Fornication for pleasure" is not against the law, he said; "fornication for a monetary consideration should likewise be a purely private affair of the individual." On the other hand, social harm from prostitution required legal action. This included cases of exploitation, coercion, fraud, and seduction, especially of minors and the "feeble-minded," and violations of "public decency" or deliberate infection of someone with disease. He proposed that a publicly funded board of sanitary control offer medical, educational, and economic assistance to those prostitutes who ask for such services.[66]

City officials were unlikely to adopt either Benjamin's or Kross's ideas. Kross herself said that her suggestion had "a long road to travel before it reaches consummation." She asked the mayor to approve some immediate changes to remedy the "more glaring injustices and iniquities" of the women's court. First, she asked for a small conference of social welfare experts to consider a fundamental approach to the problem of prostitution in the city. Second, harkening back to her days as chair of the legal committee of the Church of the Ascension, she called for a committee of "volunteer defenders" for the women arraigned in the court. Serving without pay, these volunteers would "eliminate the shyster lawyer evil and break the alliances between bondsmen and lawyers." Finally, she asked for physical changes to the court, whose benches merely invite spectators to observe an "unending, degrading, public spectacle of vice on parade." She advised splitting the courtroom into two smaller rooms, with one for the probation department, which did not have enough space for its work.[67]

Zelda Popkin described what followed. Mayor La Guardia acknowledged the report. It received respectful attention on newspaper front pages and in editorial columns. The mayor appointed a committee to study it. The committee met. The committee studied it. Nothing happened. After the major antivice raids of 1936, which ended with the jailing of prostitution kingpin "Lucky" Luciano, gangsters who at that time were "in rompers when Luciano went to jail, grew up to try to establish another vice empire."[68]

Unable to shut down the women's court, Kross did what she could to improve it. In 1936 she established a social work–based court docket to deal with female minors up to age twenty-one. Two years later she tried to get herself out of the city magistracy by running for an opening on the state supreme court, a race she lost. By then, she had refused to sit in the women's court anymore and convinced the chief magistrate to assign her elsewhere. In 1940, when her magistrate's term was up, La Guardia delayed reappointing her. At 10:00 a.m. on June 30, the last day of her term, she showed up at his office to find out why. His assistant said the mayor was too busy to see her. She sent word that her family was outside in the car waiting to go on vacation and she would give him fifteen minutes. When La Guardia finally called her in, she asked him why he was mad at her. A "torrent of angry words" poured out, she told her sister. When he said she was the only one of "my forty-nine magistrates" who had defied him, she countered, "What do you mean by *my* magistrates?" Her oath of office was to the people of the city of

New York, and if he did not like what she was doing he could prefer charges with the appellate division. "And you talk about Tammany Hall and its methods," she went on:

> Let me tell you something. The fact that you have forty-eight mice instead of men whom you can dictate to, isn't going to change this woman magistrate one iota. . . . I wonder how you will feel when word gets around, as it inevitably will, that La Guardia doesn't reappoint Magistrate Kross because she won't take orders from City Hall.

Buzzing for his assistant, he told him to bring in Kross's family to witness him swear her in.[69]

Kross never learned why La Guardia had become so angry with her. According to her sister, in later years he taunted Kross about her Tammany district leader, Jimmy Hines, notorious for his ties to gangsters such as Dutch Schultz and others in the "policy" racket. La Guardia implied that Hines had been one of Kross's mentors, but she reminded him that Hines had supported another candidate when Mayor O'Brien made her a magistrate and that Tammany refused to endorse her when she ran for the supreme court.[70]

Anna Kross spent her next decade as a magistrate developing experimental, specialized courts to solve particular social problems. Her home term court, which dealt with domestic violence, and her social court for men, which helped recidivist alcoholics stay out of jail, became internationally renowned. She was good at persuading philanthropists and professionals to support multiple social work projects associated with her magistrate duties. The Magistrates Courts Social Service Bureau, which helped families in distress connect with social services, functioned for four years until Henry Curran, then chief magistrate, and Mayor La Guardia abolished it in 1942, saying its resources needed to go elsewhere.[71]

Kross was ahead of her time. While she could not get La Guardia to act on the women's court, his successors were more receptive to her ideas. Her views on the treatment of prostitutes are not what later feminist welfare activists would necessarily follow, but her campaigns against a punitive system provoked new thinking and ultimately led to change. In 1951, when shortly after becoming chief magistrate John M. Murtagh spoke to the state's association of chiefs of police, he appropriated almost word for word Kross's call for the abolition of the women's court. He called instead for a noncriminal, informal court that would operate on a "socio-medical" basis. Noting that prostitution was not a police problem, he echoed Kross's and the Women's City Club's view that sending young male patrolmen to induce women into sexual situations was degrading. His 1957 study of prostitution, *Cast the First Stone*, borrowed freely, often without attribution, from Kross's pioneering work.[72]

It would be gratifying to say the Seabury investigations led to a permanent end to corruption in New York City's governmental affairs. Changes did occur, many of them positive, and Tammany's power declined. But its power was far from eliminated. The judiciary remained political plums. In April 1931, when the legislature expanded the number of supreme court judges in the state, the two parties split the new seats between them. Neither county nor city bar associations could stop this division of the spoils. Consolidation and streamlining occurred, but not—as was clear from Mayor O'Brien's last-minute picks—the removal of judgeships from politics.

Nor were as many malfeasants punished as Judge Seabury would have liked. Prosecutor John Weston had named twenty-one lawyers as bribers. Since Weston was only an accomplice, in the absence of corroborative testimony a judge dismissed cases against all but two, who were disbarred; one other was only reprimanded. Two magistrates resigned immediately, three others pending their public hearings. The appellate division removed two more. Six policemen received criminal convictions; thirteen others lost their jobs or resigned. For the thousands of pages of testimony Seabury and his staff collected, this was a meager result.

Polly Adler had a different take. In her memoir she said the investigations "turned New York into a wide open town." The "guardians of the law" were so busy answering questions that the "law-breakers" (herself included) "had a holiday." Her own life got easier.

> The police no longer were a headache; there was no more kowtowing to double crossing Vice Squad men, no more hundred-dollar handshakes, no more phony raids to up the month's quota. In fact, thanks to Judge Seabury and his not-very-merry men, I was able to operate for three years without breaking a lease.[73]

Moreover, in the past, all a policeman had to do was stage a raid, bring in the girl, write up on a green sheet whatever he wanted, and change the charge if a bribe had softened him up. Now, she said, this abuse was no longer tolerated. This perhaps desirable result hardly constituted "what the reformers and citizens' committees and legislators had hoped to accomplish."[74]

In 1935, thanks to new appeals to smash the racketeers and clean up the city, stories about the women's court again blared across front pages. The police arrested Adler and three of her "inmates" for keeping a disorderly house in an eleven-room East Side apartment. They also seized Adler's black book of patrons, news that sent "shivers of apprehension" along Park and Fifth Avenues. Moreover, in a closet they found indecent movies and a projector. When rumors spread that magistrates would view the films in open court to determine their decency, spectators jamming the women's court convinced the judge to cancel a public showing.

Then still presiding in women's court, Magistrate Kross imposed a $2,500 bail on Adler and $500 on each of her three inmates. Possession of the films took Adler to a different court, where a magistrate imposed a further $1,000. In response to her lawyer's protests against such high bail for a person never convicted of a crime, the magistrate cited her ten prior arrests and notoriety. Described in the press as "short, stocky, with heavily rouged lips and cheeks and brightly tinted finger nails" and wearing an expensive fur coat, Adler, the proverbial "painted woman," "kicked and shouted torrid words at photographers who tried to take her picture as she was led into court." After many postponements and plea changes, Adler eventually pleaded guilty. She got a thirty-day sentence and a $500 fine; her inmates' sentences were suspended, but two infected with a "social disease" were mandatorily hospitalized.[75]

The 1935 raids had several purposes. One was to eliminate the higher-ups running Harlem's policy rackets; another was to rout out taxicab drivers, called steerers, who took men to Harlem brothels and then tipped off gunmen of the men's whereabouts to facilitate robberies. The goal that most interested the city's women was to identify and arrest the ringleaders in the city's "commercialized vice" system. Magistrate Kross had noted that only two male lawyers (one white, one black) were representing 80 percent of the women arraigned before her. When she asked the women about the men, they admitted they had neither retained nor knew them, but had relied on higher-ups to see to bail. These conditions convinced Kross that a highly organized vice ring was operating in the city. Using the raids to publicize anew her plea to abolish the very court over which she was presiding, as proof of the rings she laid before a grand jury a briefcase full of records with the names of lawyers, bondsmen, women, and houses of prostitution figuring in the cases that had come before her.[76]

Government pursuits of racketeers the following year once again put a spotlight on Anna Kross and the women's court. Thomas E. Dewey, whom Governor Lehman had appointed an antirackets special prosecutor, launched a massive raid against New York City's vice rings. Dewey's prosecutions pleased the public, as they ended in the successful conviction of Lucky Luciano and eight codefendants for prostitution. Keeping her eye on the women affected, Kross called Dewey's raids a "futile and costly scavenging expedition" with no effect "upon the absurdity, ineffectuality and injustice of New York City's treatment of the problem of prostitution." She compared vice crusades to the raids on bootleggers during

Prohibition, observing that "by making prostitution contraband we create the vice exploiter, the shady lawyer and bondsman, the corrupt policeman and official, just as liquor prohibition created the bootlegger and those who protected him." Finally, she pointed out the irony of paying millions of dollars for "politically inspired crusades and investigations" while no money goes to help prostitutes lead better lives. Dewey dismissed her comments as "an amusing attempt to get publicity." The *Eagle* reported that, while most people agreed with Kross on the futility of police raids and show trials, they disapproved of her denigration of Dewey, a "progressive" Republican whose popularity would later bring him three terms as governor and two presidential runs.[77]

The Manhattan women's court continued to be a source of complaint and controversy. Not all critics agreed on what to do. In 1934, La Guardia merged the Brooklyn women's court with Manhattan's as an experimental economy measure. The Brooklyn Women's Court Alliance, which for years had campaigned for better quarters for Brooklyn's women's court, now worked hard to convince La Guardia to reverse the decision. Counseled by attorney Helen P. McCormick, the alliance argued that the merger had ended Brooklyn's social clinic plan. Put into effect in October 1933, this plan focused on getting prostitutes to leave "the life," whereas Kross's plan, McCormick said, accepted prostitution as inevitable and as a result had turned the Manhattan women's court into a revolving door. Second, conditions in Manhattan's Women's House of Detention were deplorable. Overcrowding worsened after the vice raids of the mid-1930s. With a capacity of 430, the house was soon using kitchens and community rooms as dormitories for a population of 571. Equally bad, all rehabilitative work had stopped. Third, poor Brooklyn families now had the extra burden of having to travel to Manhattan for court business. As one Brooklyn magistrate put it, if Manhattan's court was suddenly transferred to Brooklyn, "universal protest" would erupt from those living on the other side of the river. McCormick's sudden death in February 1937 took the breath out of the alliance's campaign and Brooklyn never got its women's court back.[78]

In the meantime, some improvements took place in Manhattan's women's court. Thanks to pressure from the city's organized women, framing and stool pigeons were no longer issues. Mayor La Guardia had followed up on Kross's suggested physical changes in the courtroom, later taking credit for eliminating sessions "held for the benefit of spectators' sordid curiosity." On September 1, 1936, he publicized the changes by presiding over a women's court hearing himself. Flanked by Magistrates Kross and Brill (brought over from Brooklyn), he was able to conduct the proceedings discreetly, in a low voice and sitting below the dais to find two prostitutes guilty. Jonah J. Goldstein, Kross's colleague in the 1920s and now a magistrate, brought other changes. When he presided over the women's court, he required medical exams of all male customers caught up in vice sweeps.[79]

This did not lead to the prosecution of customers. Indeed, when the city's first African American magistrate, Myles A. Paige, sat in Harlem court, he sent three women to the women's court but merely lectured fifteen arrested white men before letting them go. He added, however, "If this thing keeps up in Harlem, I'm going to send all the men to jail. Harlem must be cleaned up. You ought to thank the cops who raided the joint. They may have saved you from the fate of these women. If you men didn't go there, these women could not remain in business."[80]

Magistrate Goldstein agreed with Paige, blaming much of the city's vice problem on white men going to Harlem "in their shiny, flashy roadsters, backed up with bankrolls and looking for trouble or entertainment." Customer legislation (so-called john laws) would not pass judicial muster in New York State for several more decades.

Even so, women had had an impact on the Seabury investigations and their aftermath. Members of the Society for the Prevention of Unjust Convictions deserve a good part of the credit. Without the fuss they had made about Emma Hammerstein and framing, stool pigeon Chile Mapocha Acuna might never have come forward to expose the ring he worked for, and because of his testimony, investigations of buying judgeships turned overnight to the entrapment and fleecing of women. Once Acuna's testimony was corroborated and publicized, women's special concerns took center stage, at least for a while.

Women's political gains from the investigations were not, in the short run, huge. But they could see signs of improvement, even if subtle. As Magistrate Kross, county justice Agnes Craig, and now deputy commissioner of licenses Rosalie Loew Whitney noted when the New York League of Business and Professional Women honored them at a luncheon in 1935, women lawyers were no longer curiosities. "Eighteen years ago," Craig said, when she had just begun to practice, "there was curiosity about any woman who went into law." Today, she continued, there is less curiosity, but if a woman is able, she will reflect credit on herself and her profession. Kross concurred, gesturing toward the prominent women attorneys at the speakers' table as her evidence. Women can be judges, she said, "not merely by the sufferance of men, but because of the vote of both men and women." She referred with pride to the recent elevation of Judge Florence Allen of Ohio to the US Circuit Court of Appeals and praised President Roosevelt's "courage" in appointing her. Whitney pointed to the thousands of women across the country serving in appointive government positions and assured the audience that the woman lawyer's "outstanding ability would carry its possessor on to distinction without the necessity for organized action."[81]

More gains were on the way. By the time discussions about the future shape of city government had peaked, Fiorello La Guardia would be using his mayoral bully pulpit to revise the city's charter. Moreover, he would have appointed women in record numbers to make the new charter work. As a result, the city's women activists would begin to see themselves closer to the center of the city's political affairs than they had ever been before. Without women's strong reactions to the Seabury inquiries, this development might never have taken place.

Harriot Stanton Blatch and Rose Schneiderman speak at a rally for the Equality League of Self-Supporting Women. As the renamed Women's Political Union, it focused on recruiting working-class women into the suffrage movement, organized New York City's great suffrage parades, and encouraged direct political action. *Tamiment Library & Robert F. Wagner Labor Archives, Photos.010*

New York City suffrage leader Mary Garrett Hay shows partisan affiliation with her "elephant" pendant, a symbol of the Republican Party since the late nineteenth century. *New York Public Library, MSSCol1363*

# Women Serve Tea in Old-Time Saloon
## To Elect Bertha Rembaugh a Judge in
## The Old Battery Dan Finn District

In 1919, attorney Bertha Rembaugh became the first New York City woman to run for a municipal judgeship. *Evening World* cartoonist Ferdinand G. Long found it amusing that her all-female campaign committee (which included Fiorello La Guardia's wife, Marie) served only tea at her campaign headquarters, a former saloon. *Evening World, October 22, 1919*

# Women Who Took Part in Free for All Debate
## Over the Issues and Candidates of the Campaign

The 1921 city election, the first mayoral contest in which women could vote, prompted the city's first all-female partisan political debate. The participants were all well-known partisan political activists. Cartoonist Ferdinand G. Long captured this moment for New York's *Evening World* magazine. *Evening World, October 28, 1921*

Eleanor Roosevelt, Caroline O'Day, Marion Dickerman (standing, left to right), and Nancy Cook (seated) edit the *Women's Democratic News*. Launched in May 1925, the monthly newspaper was the New York State Democratic Committee Women's Division's effort to publicize the party's agendas and unite Democrats across the state. *Franklin D. Roosevelt Presidential Library and Museum, Hyde Park, New York, 63-488*

Belle Moskowitz, seated behind Eleanor Roosevelt and across from Louis Howe (Franklin Roosevelt's campaign manager), works on plans for Democratic governor Alfred E. Smith's 1924 re-election campaign. Among these plans was a tour of the state in an automobile topped with a canvas mock-up of a "Singing Teapot" to call attention to challenger Theodore Roosevelt Jr.'s involvement in the Teapot Dome scandal. *Franklin D. Roosevelt Presidential Library and Museum, Hyde Park, New York, NPx 58-348*

The Committee on Legislation of the Women's City Club of New York, a civic action group, kept track of municipal and state legislation and then represented the club's positions on proposed laws to government officials. Eleanor Roosevelt (center, first row) served as its chair from 1927 to 1928 and on the club's board of directors. *Archives & Special Collections, Hunter College Libraries, Hunter College of the City University of New York, Subseries 7.1, Box 49, Folder 8/14*

Ruth Baker Pratt, a Republican, was the first woman to win a seat on the city's board of aldermen (1925) and the state's first woman to serve in the US House of Representatives (1928). Though re-elected in 1930, she lost her seat in the Democratic Party sweep of 1932. *Collection of the US House of Representatives, 2010.142.000*

# P R O P O R T I O N A L   R E P R E S E N T A T I O N

The City is NOT divided into districts. The citizens
of each borough vote for all candidates from that
borough.  You vote your first, second, third choice,
and so on.

### A PAPER BALLOT LOOKS LIKE THIS

When you receive it                     When you put it in
                                        the ballot box.

| | | | | |
|---|---|---|---|---|
| JOHN WHITE | | | JOHN WHITE | 4 |
| ADAM BROWN | | | ADAM BROWN | 1 |
| JOSEPH GREEN | | | JOSEPH GREEN | |
| THOMAS HALL | | | THOMAS HALL | 2 |
| MARY JONES | | | MARY JONES | 5 |
| ANN ROSS | | | ANN ROSS | |
| HARRY SMALL | | | HARRY SMALL | 3 |

if your first choice is beaten, your second choice vote
will be counted; if your second choice loses, your third
choice vote will be counted. OR if your first choice has
enough votes to be elected without yours, your vote will
be counted for your second choice, and so on.

There is a new kind of VOTING MACHINE which can be used
for P. R.  Or, if a paper ballot is used, there will be
a central, well-supervised count.

### Y O U R   V O T E   A L W A Y S   C O U N T S

In 1936 the Women's City Club of New York published a primer on the proposed proportional representation voting system for the new city council. This sample ballot included the names of two women but did not make them winners. *Archives & Special Collections, Hunter College Libraries, Hunter College of the City University of New York, Subseries 11.3, Box 188, Folder 6*

# 2 Women Force Vote
# To Put Sex on Juries

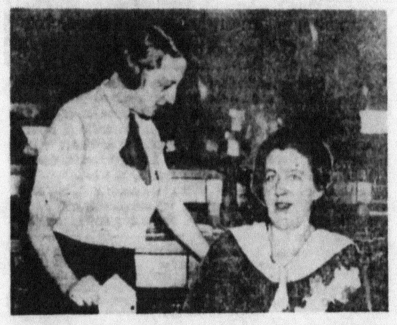

Doris I. Byrne of the Bronx (left) and Jane Todd of Westchester.

## Fifteen-Year Fight Finally Won in Assembly as Doris Byrne and Jane Todd Whip Veteran Opponents to the Tune of 103–33

New York State Assembly members Doris Byrne (Democrat) and Jane Todd (Republican) led the legislative campaign to permit women to serve on juries. Although they won the assembly vote in 1935, they lost in the state senate, and a bill allowing women to volunteer for jury service would not pass for another two years. © 1935 Brooklyn Eagle, *March 27, 1935*

A cartoonist for the *Durham Morning Herald* depicted a destitute Emma Swift Hammerstein, widow of theatrical entrepreneur Oscar Hammerstein, and her collie, Teddy, "On a Park Bench Listening for the Stars That Sing No More." In 1930, her arrest as a prostitute prompted an outcry against the framing of women for sex crimes and led to the investigation of the city's women's court. *Durham Morning Herald, November 5, 1922*

An artist's rendering of the city's women's court captures its churchlike structure and the all-male personnel who would question women brought up on charges of "vagrancy" and other petty crimes. *New York Tribune, November 30, 1919*

Representing the New York City Federation of Women's Clubs, in December 1930, former policewoman Mary Hamilton and attorneys Ann Hochfelder and Ruth Lewinson (left to right) arrived in Albany to demand pardons for young women falsely accused and imprisoned for sex crimes. *Author's collection*

Catherine Clivette (right) stands with her husband, Merton, and daughter, Juanita. Clivette led the first protests of middle-class white New York City women against the framing of women for sex crimes and the double standard of morality applied to them in the women's court. *Courtesy of the Merton Clivette Estate*

As a New York City magistrate, Anna Kross testified before Congress on February 15, 1938, in favor of an appropriation to fight syphilis. Later that summer she would announce her run for the New York State Supreme Court. *Photo by Bill Wallace/NY Daily News via Getty Images*

Mayor La Guardia administers the oath of office in January 1937 to Genevieve Earle, the sole woman elected to the new city council. She was the only new member whose swearing in attracted press attention. *La Guardia and Wagner Archives, La Guardia Community College/The City University of New York, 01.001.1281*

The "Women of the La Guardia Administration" attend a dinner they organized on December 6, 1937, honoring the re-election of Mayor La Guardia (seated at center back) and election of Genevieve B. Earle (seated to the mayor's right) to the new city council. Dorothy Kenyon is on the lower right. *La Guardia and Wagner Archives, La Guardia Community College/The City University of New York, 01.001.2103*

In this cartoon from the *New York World Telegram*, chaos reigns on the city council in January 1938. Only Genevieve B. Earle is seated (quietly) in the center, doing her work. *New York World Telegram, January 24, 1938*

Frances Perkins investigates industrial working conditions for the New York State Factory Investigating Commission, established in response to the 1911 Triangle Shirtwaist Factory fire. Thirty years later, Perkins would become US secretary of labor and the first woman in a presidential cabinet. *Rare Book & Manuscript Library, Columbia University, MS#0989*

On July 22, 1939, Mayor La Guardia administers the oath of office to Jane M. Bolin to serve as a judge on the court of domestic relations. Her husband, Ralph Mizelle, is at her side. Bolin was the nation's first African American female judge. *Photo by Bill Wallace/NY Daily News via Getty Images*

Elinore M. Herrick, New York regional director of the National Labor Relations Board, testifies in February 1938 before a joint hearing of the Senate Labor and Commerce Committee on threats from "communist agitators" against the settlement of a maritime strike. *Library of Congress, LC-DIG-hec-24012*

Mary Kingsbury Simkhovitch, vice chair of the New York City Housing Authority, speaks at the dedication of the Queensbridge Community Building on May 4, 1940. *La Guardia and Wagner Archives, La Guardia Community College/The City University of New York, 02.002.01477*

Anna Rosenberg, New York regional director of the Social Security Administration, often served as an informal labor adviser to Mayor La Guardia. Wearing one of her famously elaborate hats, she leans over La Guardia's shoulder as he signs a press release announcing a labor agreement in 1941. *Kheel Center, Cornell University, 5780PB12F30C*

**WHAT A GAL!**

Meet Caroline Simon, a terrific fireball; Republican candidate for *President of the City Council*. She has already racked up enough "firsts" to make history. Now she is racking up one more — the first woman ever nominated for City-wide office by a major political party. Here's why:

CAROLINE SIMON has been a *fighter* against juvenile delinquency as a member of the New York State Youth Commission; a *leader* in New York's anti-bias campaign as one of the drafters of the Anti-bias Law and as a member of the State Commission Against Discrimination; a *champion* of fair play as a member of the Workmen's Compensation Board, establishing fair compensation awards for injured workers; a *crusader* in many other fields, including parole and probation; law reform; employment and guidance service; legal aid; community interests of women.

CAROLINE SIMON, while a wife, mother and grandmother, has the training and background of a dynamic civic leader; educated in public schools; NYU law degree; a practicing lawyer since 1925; active with leading bar associations, women's groups, and many civic and philanthropic organizations including: Community Council of New York, League of Women Voters, National Probation and Parole Association, Women's City Club, Metropolitan Council of Jewish Welfare Board, National Council of Jewish Women (former Exec. Dir. New York Section), Jewish Board of Guardians (Trustee), UJA, American Jewish Committee, National Women's Committee for Brandeis University.

CAROLINE SIMON has (1) Administrative know-how for the City's local legislative body; (2) Ability and experience to bring sound judgment to bills before the City Council and the Board of Estimate; (3) A woman's point of view to provide guidance in matters affecting education, health, sanitation, welfare, air pollution, traffic and parks.

*What a gal!*

**ELECT CAROLINE SIMON**
**A REAL CITY COUNCIL PRESIDENT**

Citizens Committee for election of
CAROLINE K. SIMON
51 Vanderbilt Avenue, New York

PULL LEVER **3A**

Caroline Klein Simon's campaign flyer for her run for city council president in 1957 emphasized her clean-up of the city, a theme then deemed appropriate for female political candidates. *Schlesinger Library, Radcliffe Institute, Harvard University*

# THE WOMEN OF THE ADMINISTRATION

On December 6, 1937, at New York City's Hotel Brevoort, the self-named "Women of the La Guardia Administration" gave a dinner to honor newly re-elected Mayor La Guardia and his wife. Genevieve Beavers Earle, who sat at the mayor's right hand, was also honored. The sole woman on La Guardia's Charter Revision Commission of 1935, Earle was the only woman elected to the new city council. Instead of ending the event with the usual after-dinner speakers, the evening's hosts presented a skit that spoofed La Guardia's first term and set out a vision for his second. They called it "Fifty Women and One Man, A Play in Three Scenes and One Axe."[1]

The play opens with the mayor rushing into his office and hurling his famously oversized black sombrero into a corner. He calls for his commissioners. Mitzi, his secretary, reports that Valentine (Police) is down in Houston, "reorganizing the police department"; Goodman (Water Supply) has a sore thumb from "stopping the leak in the Croton Dam"; Moses (Parks) is "hanging gardens in Babylon"; Rice (Health) is administering "pre-marital Wassermans" (blood tests) at Yale for junior prom week; Goldwater (Hospitals) has sailed for Russia to put Soviet hospitals on a five-year plan. No one is in. The mayor is livid.

The phone rings. It's President Roosevelt, who commands the mayor to fly down to Washington to "determine with certitude/The degree of moral turpitude/Between Magda and Senor Mussolini."[2] As he dashes off, the mayor asks Mitzi to tell Deputy Mayor Curran to "get after those Commissioners." Since Curran is also not in, Scene II opens with the "Acting" deputy mayor, who is knitting. "The Mayor's away to a star-gazing conference[3]," she says, "and since the Commissioners are gone too, now let's see what the women can do." She asks her secretary to "call up the girls," the "Acting Commissioners." As they file in to give their reports, she uses her axe as a gavel.

The acting police commissioner brags about current "shake-ups." Instead of being "stuck in Juvenile Aid" (Henrietta Additon's former crime prevention bureau), she has set cops to catching "thugs" in

Central Park. She has raised their pensions and replaced the "fat, moth-eaten matrons" with civil service "babies/Who certainly know their duties."[4] After complaining she has "never seen such ramification/In a single matter of classification," the acting civil service commissioner has repaired the list. She wishes the commissioner would become a judge so that she could make more reforms. Delivering her report with a Yiddish accent, the acting commissioner of public markets depicts her boss as a "big fish man," but not the kind who smells of herring. She reports on enclosing the Orchard Street pushcarts and getting rid of cheating on weights and measures. She declares she too enjoyed her day being in charge, so much so that she hopes her boss will go away again.[5]

The acting health commissioner's list of successes includes popularizing premarital blood tests for syphilis, even among "socialites." As for "street-walkers," while government cannot save them from "perdition," "We medicate them thoroughly/So they 'walk' in good condition." The acting budget director, who sets her report to "Sing a Song of Sixpence," begins by complaining of lax budgeteers and high judicial salaries:

And really ma'am the Budget Office
Is just a bit too fickle
When my hard-working steno
Isn't even raised a nickel!

She ends by referring to women's reputation as "the world's wise spenders," but then notes that as there is no female budget examiner she is instituting "a new examination/Opened to men and women/Without sex discrimination!"

After castigating the city's "rulers" for sending their own children to private school, the president of the board of education explains they do so because teenagers today are squeezed into classrooms like sardines and schools have such "antique sanitation/That the stench has even reached/The Board of Education." Putting custodians to work day and night, the board now has schools where everyone, young and old alike, can play, and where a woman custodian has made even filthy washrooms smell sweet. She complains, however, that only two of forty-six high school principals are women.[6]

The president of the council gives the longest report. She describes the "crash of cymbals—a burst of song" that accompanied Genevieve Earle's almost royal entrance to her first council meeting. After listing Earle's legislative successes (as if they had actually happened) and reporting on the council's work on pensions, relief, and culture, she reveals that some "lazy guy" got up to say: "We've worked an hour—enough for today!" But the women are not done, and so she concludes:

If the Mayor would show more inclination
To add women to the administration,
And if our luck were a little stronger
So the Commissioners' junkets would last longer,
We could continue, with innate ability,
To beautify and administer the City.

Four more commissioners wrap up. Welfare boasts of doing away with munic-ipal lodging houses ("Where an attendant grabs a guest/And officially him delouses") and then praises Camp La Guardia, which restores homeless men's health and morale. Parks (delivered in a southern accent) mocks Robert Moses's ruthless methods by shouting, "I am the Czar of the Parkway! Nothing stands in *my* way!" Housing delivers a parody of the "Night before Christmas" and Water Supply announces plans for "cheaper electrification," "universal meterization," and a Coney Island "high-pressure pumping station most adequate to quench the severest conflagration."[7]

The mayor returns for Scene III. He ties up his plane at the "mooring mast" of the Empire State Building, his temporary quarters while city hall was being renovated, and looks through the telescope reserved for "star-gazing." He is astounded by what he sees: new parkways, a dirt-free Coney Island, a hundred new cops in Central Park, no pushcarts on Orchard Street, "rosy-cheeked babies" with healthy mothers, a new housing project, a new water supply! "Great Scott," he says, "you women put me on the spot/You did it as well as I. I used to fire my commissioners for cause—now I'll fire them for good cause. Girls, raise your right hands. I'm going to swear you all in as commissioners." And so he does.

When the skit was over, the mayor rose to say thank you and to invite them to "visit him regularly and offer advice like they gave him in the show." One par-ticipant responded, "We'd be afraid you would think we were nagging." "I get no nagging at home," he replied, "so I can take it in public life."[8] Whether that was true remains unknown, but it shows the mayor recognized the serious agenda embedded in "Fifty Women and One Man." The skit told him that the women of his administration would be integral to his policy goals. Moreover, it distilled the feminist and social justice ideals they had been espousing since suffrage: an end to sex discrimination, an expansion of measures to benefit human welfare, and the achievement of pay equity and more career opportunities for women. It advised him that, as his appointees, they would carry out his modernizing agendas as well as, if not better than, the men he had appointed commissioners. The reforms they dreamed of having made during their one day of fantasied em-powerment conveyed a clear message: this is what women can do, Mr. Mayor. Now they demanded a chance to do even more.

Five minutes past midnight on New Year's Day, 1934, Fiorello Henry La Guardia took his first mayoral oath of office in the home of Judge Seabury. Only a handful of witnesses were on hand. They included Charles Culp Burlingham, who had been instrumental in urging Governor Roosevelt to widen Seabury's inquiries and then, as chair of a harmony committee of political fusionists, had helped rival factions settle on La Guardia as their best hope for 1933.[9] Having gotten through the Seabury investigations, the repeal of Prohibition, and now the start of FDR's New Deal, New Yorkers were eager for a "little new deal." They would get it, and a growing number of the city's women activists would be on the front lines to help make it happen.

Though La Guardia was born in Greenwich Village in 1882, he did not set down roots in the city until almost twenty-five years later. His father, a lapsed Catholic from Italy, and his mother, a Jew from Trieste, had immigrated in 1880. After Fiorello's birth his father joined the army and took the family to the Southwest, where he worked as a band leader. In 1898, when he became gravely ill from tainted meat and was discharged, the family moved back to Trieste, where Fiorello found work in the American consular service. In 1906 he returned to New York as a translator on Ellis Island. He took night courses at New York University Law School, earning his degree in 1910 and becoming involved in local Republican politics. In 1914 he ran for Congress from Lower Manhattan. Though he lost to the Tammany candidate, the state Republican victory that year won him a post in the state attorney general's New York City office. He soon got into trouble with Republicans and Democrats alike. He angered Republican governor Charles Whitman by pursuing New Jersey corporations, whose fumes were drifting over to Manhattan, and he irked Democratic state senator Jimmy Walker by supporting the Housewives League's complaints against meat packers who "shorted" weights. In 1916 he ran for Congress again—and won.

When the United States entered the war in 1917, La Guardia took a leave from Congress and joined the Aviation Service of the Army Signal Corps. Discharged in 1918 as a major, he returned to New York, married former garment worker Thea Almerigotti, and entered municipal politics. In 1919 he ran for president of the board of aldermen, campaigning for the five-cent transit fare and against firetraps and rising food prices. The Citizens Union and much of the press endorsed him, and he won, though narrowly. Again, he made enemies on all sides. He clashed with Tammany officials over finances but developed a personal friendship with Tammany mayor John Hylan. He angered Republicans when he denounced them for refusing to seat the five duly elected Socialist assemblymen. In spring 1921 tragedy struck. His baby daughter died of spinal meningitis, his wife of tuberculosis. At the end of his aldermanic term in December, his political career seemed over.

La Guardia rebounded and ran for Congress again, this time from an uptown district with a predominantly Jewish and Italian population. His Democratic opponent, Henry Frank, tried to appeal to Jews by calling La Guardia a "pronounced anti-Semite and Jew-hater." La Guardia challenged Frank to a debate—in Yiddish. He won again, though barely, but remained in the House for the next ten years, where he supported veterans' bonuses and attacked "special privilege," immigration restriction, the Supreme Court's voiding of welfare legislation, corporation lawyers' use of injunctions to break strikes, and motion picture censorship. He argued that Prohibition not only was unenforceable but also hurt poor urban workers while letting the wealthy drink at will. He was a major force in winning government control of power projects on the Tennessee and Colorado Rivers. In 1924, having given up formal affiliation with the GOP, he won re-election as the candidate of the American Labor Party, a mixture of Socialists, single taxers, and trade unionists. In 1929 he ran for mayor of New York against Jimmy Walker. Though he lost, his accusations against a Tammany judge's links to gangsters started the drive that brought down Mayor Walker. La Guardia's 1933 mayoral campaign succeeded, as did his campaigns of 1937 and 1941.[10]

Ever since the passage of woman suffrage, women voters had been vital to La Guardia's campaigns. In 1919, when he announced his run for president of the board of aldermen, former suffragists sprang into action. Women Republicans and independent Democrats put together a La Guardia Greater New York women's campaign committee headed by Frances Parsons, a successful suffrage district captain. Applying suffrage house-to-house canvassing techniques, Parsons pledged to get votes "wherever women get together—in department stores, factories, settlement houses and drawing rooms." She praised La Guardia's pledges against government "extravagance" and New Yorkers' high cost of living, and complimented his challenging of the bureaucratic incompetence that had "defrauded" soldiers and sailors naturalized overseas of their voting rights. As Parsons put it, "it is time to beat Tammany in this town."[11]

Journalist Denis Tilden Lynch believed that Tammany boss Charles F. Murphy's failure to endorse two well-regarded judges in order to appoint his favorites caused women to flock to La Guardia. They wanted an "unbossed judiciary," he wrote, and thus came in the hundreds, representing all walks of life—lawyers, doctors, writers, artists, businesswomen, wage workers, and homemakers. Former suffragist Mary Garrett Hay and the wives of prominent Progressives such as Jacob Riis and William Jay Schieffelin joined Parsons's committee. The wives of wealthy Republicans such as Andrew Carnegie, John Pratt (Ruth Pratt would become the city's first female alderman in 1925), John D. Rockefeller Jr., former governor Charles Whitman, and Columbia University president Nicholas Murray Butler were among La Guardia's many contributors. These women visited voters, wrote to thousands of them, and telephoned many more. On Election Day Parsons assigned six hundred women to poll watching while others got out the vote. Years later La Guardia would still recall women's support for him in 1919, saying that while Republican leaders had seen no hope for his candidacy, it was women who had put him over.[12]

Shortly after becoming board of aldermen president, La Guardia took a first step toward repaying this debt by naming Charlotte Delafield his executive secretary. A wealthy socialite, former Women's Political Union suffragist, and now a League of Women Voters leader, Delafield had been Parsons's vice chair. She had headed the La Guardia Noonday Meetings Committee that revved up street corner crowds in preparation for the candidate's arrival. As a Republican Party captain in a district where the outcome was doubtful, she got out the vote on Election Day. "Miss Delafield is an expert on municipal matters," La Guardia said when asked about the appointment. "I have asked her to look up some pressing school matters and conditions in the Department of Correction that were brought to my attention. She is a hard worker and has devoted much time to the study of conditions in New York."[13]

When a reporter asked Delafield whether a woman of wealth should hold a job that could have gone to someone who needed the income, she retorted that reporters never ask men such a question. "Men are appointed to office because of their qualifications, not because of their poverty," she said.

> Why should it not be that way with women, too? There is nothing inherent in a poor man that makes him a good public servant—in fact, you never consider a man's financial rating at all when you offer him a position. . . . We should do the work for which we are fitted and which we enjoy, regardless of the salary attached.[14]

Despite this espousal of feminist principles, after only a year Delafield quit to get married. Still, added to the naming of another suffragist, Harriett Porritt, as secretary to the commissioner of public works, Delafield's appointment opened the door for city officials to begin appointing women to office.[15]

La Guardia campaigned for mayor in 1921. He called on Republican women to support city charter reform and protect the direct primary, telling them "the women of America are the hope of American politics." Declaring that "the men whom Theodore Roosevelt drove out of politics" are now back in Albany, he warned, "If you don't come in and help us out, I don't know what will happen." But neither Republican nor anti-Tammany women's ranks were uniformly for him. Anti-Tammany women formed a coalition that gave its support to Henry Curran, then Manhattan borough president. Rumors that La Guardia tended to lose his temper deterred some women from supporting him, even though one leader who had watched him before the board of estimate thought newspapers exaggerated on this point. A number of Republican women leaders stuck with him. Brooklyn's Elizabeth Brownell Collier, a Hunter College professor already persona non grata among "regular" Republicans for having opposed US senator James W. Wadsworth Jr., resigned from the coalition to found a pro–La Guardia New York Republican league. Staten Island activist Grace Hurd Gaines followed her example, publicly accusing coalitionists of showing an ethnic prejudice against La Guardia. By summer's end, each borough had "women for La Guardia" committees.[16]

La Guardia lost the primary against Curran (who later lost to incumbent mayor Hylan). He tried again for mayor in 1929 against the popular Jimmy Walker. La Guardia's women supporters criticized Walker's lax Prohibition enforcement, his profligate sartorial style, and Tammany's lock on municipal offices. An early boom for Congresswoman Ruth Pratt to be mayor almost derailed La Guardia's nomination, but when she failed to get a unanimous vote she withdrew and La Guardia's way was cleared.

May M. Gooderson, Republican coleader of the Eleventh Assembly District (AD) and a dramatic speaker, led the pro–La Guardia women's campaign. She hoped La Guardia, as a former board of alderman president, would provide inside information about Walker's failings. Saying that women were "tired of an orgy of spending," Gooderson contrasted La Guardia's wartime service with Mayor Walker's European pleasure trips. She painted La Guardia as fearless, sincere, "boyish," and "one who has the courage to fight for his convictions." She praised his "emotionalism" and "vitriolic tongue," qualities that others criticized but which she considered necessary to keep Tammany from continuing to swallow up her party. She flayed Tammany for twelve years of maladministration and interference with the judiciary. To her, La Guardia represented "the future progressive party of the country" and a "spirit of the real soldier . . . for which women should love him alone." La Guardia spoke at campaign events in Gooderson's race for register. In response to critics who opposed her "solely because she is a woman," he said voters should back her "not only because she is a woman . . ., but because she is as capable of filling the office of Register as any candidate."[17]

La Guardia used food prices to court women's support. When the Housewives' League, an organization founded in 1911 to fight against "shorting" on weights and violations of food safety rules, he attacked Mayor Walker for allowing prices for bread to rise higher than in any other eastern city and for failing to provide adequate terminal markets to reduce costs. What was a penny or two to "the habitués of the Park Casino and the Ritz?" he asked, answering: "The Mayor will call it 'penny-snatching.' I call it highway robbery." His positions on civil rights and race prejudice won him support from women on the Harlem Citizens' Welfare Committee. On October 22, the committee officially endorsed him for his well-known stands on the "Negro and social justice." As congressman, La Guardia had resisted reduced appropriations for Howard University, demanded the removal of a judge from the Brooklyn federal bench for displaying racial prejudice, and urged a memorial to the 369th Infantry Regiment, the troop of African Americans known as the Harlem Hell Fighters.

Republican women were divided about La Guardia. Whereas Gooderson admired his pugilism, others found it off-putting. Republican Genevieve Earle, head of Brooklyn's League of Women Voters and only later a La Guardia loyalist, announced she was joining Socialist candidate Norman Thomas's campaign. Gooderson reacted sharply, charging Earle with doing the city "an irreparable wrong." "Norman Thomas is a dreamer of dreams, a reader of books. He has not a practical idea in his head as [to] the proper government. He is only full of theories," she said. A temperance rival also drew women's support. Two hundred fifty members of the Brooklyn Women's Hoover-Curtis Committee had been for La Guardia, but when he backed down on promising to enforce the law on Prohibition, the group rallied around former state senator and temperance advocate William Bennett, who "would do everything in his power to uphold the Constitution, particularly in regard to Prohibition." Speaking for the Brooklyn women's division of the Constitutional Campaign Committee, former state legislator Ida B. Sammis Woodruff said Bennett was the right man.[18]

La Guardia lost this race. By November the crash of the stock market caused Democrats to swamp the city's Republicans, including May Gooderson. Norman Thomas won almost 175,000 votes, the largest vote for any city Socialist. Walker racked up close to a 500,000-vote plurality.

Four years later, the Seabury investigations had shifted the balance. Two related issues were now at stake: how to end Tammany's grip on city offices and restructure the government to make permanent changes. Seabury and other municipal reformers called for major charter reform. Former governor Smith, once a staunch Tammany loyalist, entered the discussion on December 1, 1932, when he presented his ideas to the Hofstadter Committee. His template was the state government reorganization plan developed ten years earlier by Robert Moses, chief of staff of Belle Moskowitz's reconstruction commission. He argued first for increasing the executive power of the mayor while removing extraneous positions, including county and borough government posts, which Tammany had long used to reward its loyalists. Further, the mayor should appoint judges instead of having them elected. Finally, a small bicameral legislature should replace the Tammany-controlled board of aldermen.

Many commentators were ecstatic about Smith's ideas. Still smarting from his defeat by Roosevelt for the presidential nomination the previous summer, Smith was back. The *Herald Tribune* praised his "simple and obvious modernizations" and suggested he run for mayor. Calling him the "best possible Mayor of New York," the *Evening Post* said no one could produce a better new city charter than Smith, whose sketch had been "masterly." The *Times* wanted the city to just give itself to the "son of whom it has the right to be so proud." On December 5, a nonpartisan citizens committee to draft Al Smith for reorganization mayor issued a statement declaring that Smith, though a Tammany product, was the man to break Tammany's grip. A political comeback seemed within his grasp. Then Belle Moskowitz unexpectedly died on January 2. Unable to face another electoral contest without her aid, Smith withdrew from politics for the rest of the year.[19]

With Smith out of the picture, after much debate anti-Tammany forces finally settled on La Guardia as the candidate of a new City Fusion Party. Women were involved in making this choice. May Gooderson, Rosalie Loew Whitney, and Lillian A. Garing served on a committee of ten Republicans who conferred with a "harmony" committee to agree on the candidate best able to defeat Tammany's choice, the current incumbent, John P. O'Brien. On the Democratic side, O'Brien faced Joseph McKee. A Recovery Party candidate backed by Bronx Tammanyites, McKee won support from New Dealers. The Socialists ran Charles Solomon, one of the assemblymen elected in 1919 and refused a seat on the ground of alleged disloyalty.[20]

Despite Anna Kross's long friendship with "Florrie," out of loyalty to O'Brien she chaired his women's committee. By then, O'Brien's popularity had dipped. A summer 1933 *New Yorker* profile predicted he would soon "eclipse the fame of Dogberry and Malaprop." Speaking to a Jewish audience, he referred to "that scientist of scientists, Albert Weinstein." He told a Harlem audience, "I may be white but my heart is as black as yours." More significantly, the profile noted that the city's financial problems, a result of both the Depression and the failings of previous Tammany administrations, had put O'Brien in an impossible bind: by instituting "real economy" he avoided taxpayer revolt, but budget cuts angered Tammany contractors, officeholders, and city wage earners.[21]

Women worked for La Guardia's election in at least five different ways: through the City Fusion Party women's division, the Kings County GOP executive committee, a Republican 1933 mayoralty committee, the Republican state committee, and the Women's National Republican Club. In Harlem, oldline African American Democrats at first favored McKee, but when La Guardia won endorsements from W. E. B. DuBois, editor of the National Association for the Advancement of Colored People's (NAACP's) *Crisis* magazine, and Illinois

congressman Oscar De Priest, to whom La Guardia had offered the office next
to his when a southern US representative refused him that courtesy, black voters
shifted to La Guardia as a "friend of the Negro." Maria Lawton, indefatigable
leader of black women's clubs and Brooklyn Republicans, gave critical support,
organizing eighteen African American women to work in registration campaigns.
One of these, Florence Springer, only recently a prominent Democrat, now
"bolted" to join the fusionists.[22]

The women's campaign for La Guardia opened over the summer on Long
Island, where Eugenie May Davie, finance chair for the Republican state
committee, hosted an event for society women. She read a letter from Judge
Seabury urging them to help get Tammany out lest it "be fastened upon the city
for many years to come." Davie chided her own class for playing golf on Election
Day and refusing to enter politics because it is "dirty." "If politics are dirty, it's our
own fault," she declared. In early October, Pauline Sabin, prime mover behind repeal, put together a group of women fusionists. What attracted her to La Guardia
was his independence (he was "not controlled by anybody"), his deep knowledge
of the city, and his role in inspiring the Seabury investigations. A brilliant organizer, Sabin attracted to the City Fusion Party women's division dozens of her
repeal colleagues and over fifty progressive feminists. These included settlement
leader Lillian Wald, who praised La Guardia's lack of "shackles." "Those of us who
feel strongly, almost passionately, upon the importance of men in public office
who are free from controlling influences, see in Mr. LaGuardia a significant encouragement," Wald said. Settlement leader Mary Simkhovitch, Barnard's dean
Virginia Gildersleeve, muckraking journalist Ida Tarbell, and social investigator
Pauline Goldmark also joined Sabin's campaign. With repeal almost won (the
Twenty-First Amendment would be ratified on December 5), Sabin's followers
were ready to get La Guardia elected mayor.[23]

A hundred women in Brooklyn launched a vigorous telephone, automobile,
and doorbell-ringing crusade to register women voters. Later, they held a series
of events, including bridge and tea parties, for fusion candidate appearances.
Leading their work was an executive committee of women picked not just
for their political experience but also their ties to different city communities,
such as May Gooderson (Kings County Republicans), Maria Lawton (Empire
State Federation of Colored Women's Clubs), Mrs. Harry H. Tracey (Jewish
philanthropies), Marie Frugone (Italian women), and Mabel C. McCurrach
(business and professional women). Pauline Sabin adopted a similar strategy,
assigning specific workers to naturalized women, nurses, hotel workers, and
saleswomen. Lillian Wald and Mary Simkhovitch enlisted supporters from social
and health workers' communities.

While the campaign never centered on feminist issues, they were part of the rhetoric. When McKee opened his campaign on October 12, he pledged to appoint only those fit for office, but as an indication of the growing importance of women to city politics he also promised to ask the "women of high ideals and ability and experience" to accept important places in city government. In a remark unlikely to endear him to feminists, he called women "mighty good housekeepers" who could be of service on economic questions. Two days later, La Guardia pointed to McKee's record as a "flat contradiction," noting that in a 1915 article McKee had written, "It is not expedient that woman should vote, for she has little to gain and may lose much with the gaining of the vote. It is not necessary for the welfare of the State.... Woman's greatest work consists not in policing public morals but by her influence in the home."[24] Ione Page Nicoll, vice chair of Sabin's women's division, a long-time Republican Party and repeal activist, and wife of a former state senator, pointed out that La Guardia had espoused woman suffrage since 1910 and worked for the Nineteenth Amendment. McKee retorted by saying that the words La Guardia quoted came from an article in the *Catholic World* that predated his "conversion" to woman suffrage, and that he had then voted for suffrage when he was in the state legislature.[25]

When fusion women held their final rally, Raymond V. Ingersoll, candidate for president of the borough of Brooklyn, singled them out for praise. He cited the "crushing burden of taxation" that weighs on the home and women's interest in playgrounds and good schools. Pointing to their dissatisfaction with bossism, he said he hardly knew how to express his appreciation for their "splendid help." At La Guardia's final, huge rally in Madison Square Garden, the League of Women Voters' Caroline Slade spoke of the need to free the city from machine control and Ione Nicoll emphasized hopes for a new charter and the reorganization of city government. La Guardia won the mayoralty by more than a quarter of a million votes over McKee, his closest rival. Fusion candidates won a majority on the board of estimate.[26]

The newly elected mayor soon found concrete ways to express his appreciation to his women supporters. Shortly after his inauguration his administration already boasted seventeen women. Some—like Henrietta Additon and Anna Kross—were already there; Additon would not last the year. Others—like Rosalie Loew Whitney and Justine Wise Tulin—would start out as deputies and rise to judgeships. Yet others—including Genevieve Earle, Ruth Shoup, and Jane Bolin—were not yet on the horizon, but soon would be. Each would make her own mark on the city's history. After La Guardia's election, someone sent him a new broom, a gift symbolizing his plan for a "clean sweep" of city offices. Perhaps appointing more women to city offices was part of that plan, but no fusion candidate gave more than lip service to the idea, and only when speaking to predominantly female audiences. Appointing women was not high on the agendas of male fusionist leaders. Charles Culp Burlingham, for example, who had done so much to achieve La Guardia's nomination, was in the thick of suggesting appointees but recommended only men. He was supportive of women's careers, and when asked his opinion of a woman professional, such as Rosalie Loew Whitney or Dorothy Kenyon, he always had good things to say. But women's names were never at the top of his lists.[27]

The top posts all went to men: Professor A. A. Berle Jr., as city chamberlain (a title that meant little but gave this New Deal "brain truster" great access), Paul Windels as corporation counsel, and Paul Blanshard as commissioner of accounts—all well-known Tammany foes. The women La Guardia appointed were all assistants, deputies, or secretaries. That did not mean they lacked power. Their responsibilities were significant as gatekeepers, planners, litigators, and policymakers, and as "Fifty Women and One Man" made clear, when the bosses were away they were often in charge. Moreover, their presence made the sight of high-level professional women in city hall no longer a novelty.

The city's organized women took note. On March 20, 1934, two months after La Guardia's inauguration, the Women's City Club, League of Women Voters, and Exposition of Women's Arts and Industries arranged a dinner to honor the administration's women appointees. Mary Van Lear Findlay Allen of the Women's City Club, the event's chair, allowed each appointee only two minutes to introduce herself and her work, sounding a gong when the speaker's time was up. "For years," Rosalie Loew Whitney, newly appointed first deputy commissioner of licenses, said, "women have been talking about what they would do if they had but the opportunity to improve municipal government. Now, with 17 important city positions held by women we are putting our theories into practice and can already report progress that is substantiated by definite accomplishment in all departments." One woman administrator soon attracted wide support from the city's women. La Guardia had appointed Frances Foley Gannon deputy markets commissioner, a post he created. Gannon's morning radio "food service" reports were so popular with women that, when Bronx borough president James Lyons moved to eliminate her post from the budget, city women mounted a huge protest.[28]

By the end of 1935, the number of women holding leadership municipal posts had risen to thirty. "Women holding important political places are no longer novelties," journalist Alice Cogan commented in an article praising the many women of the accomplishment of now holding administrative posts. When Rosalie Loew Whitney was later elevated to the judiciary, Cogan began by describing her as a grandmother of six but then quickly acknowledged her distinguished public service as a lawyer. This service included her highly publicized pro bono directorship in 1930 of a neighborhood laundry owners' association to end a protection racket in Brooklyn's large "wet-wash" laundries. Though her crusade ultimately failed, incidents of intimidation in the laundry industry declined and Whitney's reputation as a crime fighter grew. When Whitney's husband Travis suddenly died shortly after La Guardia took office, the mayor appointed her deputy license commissioner, a post in which she counseled the commissioner on legal matters and did the department's litigation. A year and a half later he made her a justice on the court of domestic relations.[29]

Justine Wise Tulin (later, Polier), the first woman appointed to a position higher than magistrate in the state judicial system, had preceded Whitney on that court. The daughter of Rabbi Stephen S. Wise, an avid labor activist, and Yale Law graduate, Tulin joined the city's law department on January 1, 1934. Her report on Tammany's gouging of the workmen's compensation system to benefit a clique of Tammany physicians—a practice revealed during the Seabury investigations but never addressed—led Mayor La Guardia to reform the entire system. Her subsequent work on unemployment relief led him in July 1935 to offer her the judgeship, at first only on a thirty-day appointment. Angry at her public critique of the city's New Deal relief program, he almost reneged on a promise of a full term, telling Charles Culp Burlingham, "I have got to have discipline in the judiciary." Tulin recalled that, when they heard this, Burlingham and Felix Frankfurter "hit the ceiling." The next day, the mayor sent for her, charging her with being "just like her father," saying things "without caring for consequences." Even so, he confirmed her to a ten-year term. Intending to stay only a short time on the court of domestic relations, Tulin found the work so important she served thirty-seven years.

Tulin did not self-identify as a feminist. Responding to journalist Dorothy Kilgallen about whether the domestic relations court "needed" women judges, she replied, "No, not especially. I think there is a tremendous need for good people on the bench, but not women necessarily. I'm not a very good feminist, I'm afraid. I don't think that if there are six men judges there should be six women, too."[30] She rejected the idea of "some feminist groups" that women are better fitted in certain professions than men. Like many of her feminist colleagues on the bench, however, she stressed the importance of delving into family life to get at the root of the social problems that came before her.

Though Tulin may not have thought of herself as a "good feminist," the press included her in their lists of La Guardia's women appointees and assumed she shared their distinct identity. According to journalist Alice Cogan, the appointees had formed an organization that met for dinner once a month to discuss civic problems. They visited the courts, arose at dawn to tour the markets, and were equally diligent about inspecting other city departments, such as hospitals and playgrounds. The "fusion girls," as Cogan called them, also had their "lighter moments." At a dinner honoring Whitney when she became a justice (La Guardia was, as usual at these sorts of events, the sole man present), they performed a skit with parodies of popular songs, poking fun at themselves. They presented both the mayor and Whitney with dime-store gifts "in keeping with the Mayor's edict against expensive presents." Whitney received a flat iron "to iron out difficulties in the Domestic Relations Court" and a "bagatelle game, which symbolized the brilliant campaign she waged against the pin ball game in the Licenses Department."[31]

Newly installed in government posts, many of these women professionals were still involved in their women's voluntary associations, such as the League of Women Voters and Women's City Club. They still carried on their old nonpartisan activities of monitoring government institutions on their own time, or at least that was the impression they gave Cogan. They also continued, as they had for years, to honor each other's achievements and put on little entertainments for themselves and their bosses, just as the "Fifty Women" would do after La Guardia's re-election in 1937. As time passed, such activities waned. Women in government posts in the 1940s would have less time for them. The women of La Guardia's administration (at least of his first two terms) represented a transitional era: they had moved from volunteer to professional to government officeholder but were still juggling all three identities at once.

Pearl Bernstein is a case in point. When La Guardia appointed her to administer the board of estimate she did not yet have credentials as a professional administrator, but even after she took that job and later became administrator for the city colleges, she maintained active memberships in the League of Women Voters and Women's City Club. Her job as board of estimate secretary required her to learn fast. She and her staff prepared the board's weekly calendar. As La Guardia's commissioners passed along budgetary requests to him for approval, the mayor controlled the bulk of those requests. The borough presidents also submitted requests, as did various study groups. Her job was to prioritize and do "traffic control." She was also in charge of the city's employees' retirement system, then the fourth-largest insurance system in the state. She found it just as chaotic as the board's processes. Each fund—for policemen, firemen, sanitation workers, teachers, staff members of various boards—had different rules. The mayor asked her to rationalize the system, but when she suggested that, as an economy measure, policemen and firemen should no longer be allowed to retire after twenty years, he refused, explaining that such a change would doom his re-election. His refusal brought her face to face with "the facts of life," she recalled: it was harder to remove a benefit than to resist it from the start.[32]

Her job occasionally gave rise to conflicts. When La Guardia objected to budgetary items proposed by others, she had to remind him that board rules prohibited his interference until the item came to the floor for discussion. Though he raised the roof with her, she said that she held firm. He became angry with her over other issues. Once, when she refused to fire a staff member he accused of lying in a court case against the city, he did not speak to her for at least a month or two. She also clashed with Parks Commissioner Robert Moses, who would not take no for an answer. When one of his requests failed to appear on the calendar he charged her with incompetence. They later reconciled. As for running for office herself, she never thought of it. In her estimation, public officials were under too much pressure to solve every problem, and if they did not they were "out."[33]

Attorney Dorothy Kenyon also juggled multiple identities and loyalties, but the short time she spent in La Guardia's administration indicates she was less successful at this than Bernstein or Whitney. When Whitney was elevated to the judiciary in December 1935, La Guardia appointed Kenyon in Whitney's place as deputy license commissioner. Too busy now for major voluntary assignments, Kenyon still spoke out on feminist topics, such as the legal status of women, jury service, and married women's right to keep their jobs.[34] Like Anna Kross, she did not see eye to eye with La Guardia on prostitution. Referring to the conviction of "Lucky" Luciano, as a spokesperson for the welfare council, the League of Women Voters, and the Women's City Club she argued for the "regular prosecution of the brokers, agents and bail bond shysters who reduce our existing Women's Court procedure to a mere farce." She explained:

> These, the exploiters, are the only real criminal offenders in any prostitution case. That they can and should be arrested and sentenced, Prosecutor Dewey has proved. But the girls whom Lucania exploited by offering them protection from the endless round of arrest, trial and penalty meted out to unorganized prostitutes at the Women's Court, are at this minute seeking new protectors.[35]

Kenyon suggested that a sympathetic social (as opposed to punitive) treatment would lead to thousands of vice racketeers losing their livelihoods. While she found the women's court ineffective in getting at prostitutes who are protected, she insisted that punishing them is equally inadequate in changing their way of life. What the "girls" need, she concluded, is "shelter, food, guidance and vocational training . . . and to be led to a better way of life." For Kenyon, the logical next step was to decriminalize and license prostitutes. La Guardia made it quite clear he would never condone such an approach.[36]

Kenyon and La Guardia came into open conflict over a related topic, the city's burlesque shows. Burlesque was a form of vaudeville consisting of striptease acts and comedy skits heavy on sexual innuendo. It attracted audiences primarily of men and boys. In summer 1936, La Guardia, who wanted the shows gone, sent Kenyon to observe them incognito. As she would write in August 1936 in an occasionally hilarious six-page report, departmental rules about "decency" were more "honored in the breach, and *only* in the breach, and once not even there." As for the clothing worn by chorus and striptease artists, "It was undressmaking made into a fine art . . . more skimpy and suggestive" than she had supposed possible. The city's rule about covering the lower part of the torso was obeyed with a "bit of brilliant green satin cut into an exaggerated triangle" that concealed nothing and served only to call attention to the very part of the body it was designed to conceal. To her mind, this showed the futility of such rules and turned the rule makers (i.e., the bureaucrats) into "laughing stock."

She waxed almost poetic about an audience filled with the men whose daytime work she licensed—ice men, truck drivers, laundry agents, pool parlor and pawn shop operators, car salesmen, and stand keepers. "All the little people of the city, drab men with drab wives at home, here they came for the kind of release from drab lives that a fairy story or a moving picture of Hollywood life is supposed to give." She asked, Do the shows prompt these men to "rape little girls"? Or were they mere "blood-lettings which sent them back to their monotonous lives (and wives) happier and healthier than before"? She did not know but concluded that burlesque is "not beautiful [as] it cheapens sex." She did not care about its effect on adults, but worried that it was a source of real danger to adolescents. She recommended the enforcement of current city laws to keep out young boys under eighteen. As for her department's rules about proper clothing, she thought them foolish. Since obscenity could not be defined, she abhorred the idea of giving the commissioner of licenses censorship power. Best let the penal code and due process do their work, she advised: the police should see the shows and make their arrests, and a judge and jury should try the cases. In the meantime, "the show goes on."[37]

La Guardia did not find Kenyon persuasive. His campaign for a "cleaner city" required concrete action. A report of masturbation and homosexuality in the back rows of the houses convinced him they should be shut down. He was aware that such a step would throw thousands out of work, but when the houses began giving away twofers to youth he had had enough. The sole action his license commissioner could legally take was to refuse to renew the houses' licenses. As these expired on May 1, 1937, the following day a wholesale revocation took place. By then Kenyon had resigned to return to private practice, a step she said she regretted, as she was fond of La Guardia and considered him a friend. But given her personal anticensorship views, staying in his administration was not tenable.[38]

Genevieve Beavers Earle was a third example of a woman juggling multiple identities in this era. Among La Guardia's female appointees, she was destined for even greater contemporary prominence than Whitney, Bernstein, or Kenyon. In January 1935, when La Guardia named her a member of his City Charter Revision Commission, she became this body's sole female among eight distinguished men. The commission's chair was Thomas D. Thacher, a former US district judge and US solicitor general. The other members were S. John Block, lawyer and middle-of-the-road Socialist; Frederick L. Hackenburg, a justice of the court of special sessions; Charles E. Hughes Jr., former US solicitor general; Joseph D. McGoldrick, former city comptroller; Charles D. Meyer, real estate developer; Thomas I. Parkinson, president of the state chamber of commerce; and Joseph M. Proskauer, a judge of the appellate division of the supreme court.[39] Earle had been active in city affairs for some thirty years. She lacked the public stature of her charter commission colleagues, but her roots in social work, government research, suffrage, and women's voluntary associations gave the mayor confidence she was up to the task.

A resident of Brooklyn Heights, Genevieve Beavers was born in 1883 and attended Adelphi College, where she was editor-in-chief of the yearbook and president of the student association. An Adelphi sociology professor, Annie M. McLean, introduced her to trade unionism, woman suffrage, social settlements, modern philanthropy, housing reform, and socialism. After graduating in 1907 she assisted McClean in a national YWCA study of working women, and then got a job with the Bureau of Municipal Research (BMR), an organization then at the forefront of applying scientific methods to urban administration. Over the next five years she wrote reports and publicity on BMR research projects. She later said the work made her an enthusiastic progressive.[40]

After Beavers married businessman William Pitman Earle Jr. in 1913, she became a civic and political volunteer and raised two children. She served as an investigator for the Curran Committee, established after the 1912 murder of gambler Herman Rosenthal, who was gunned down on the street the night before he was to give evidence on police corruption. She studied entry-level policemen's salaries, concluding that their low $800 a year made them susceptible to corruption. She claimed her report led to an increase in their salaries to $1,200.[41]

Earle was an avid supporter of nonpartisan city government, in 1913 campaigning for John Purroy Mitchel, who won the mayoralty backed by an earlier fusion campaign of independent Democrats, Progressives, and progressive Republicans. In 1917, in an effort to re-elect him, she formed and chaired the Women's Committee of One Hundred for Non-Partisan City Government.

Her effort failed; Mitchel lost. Then serving on the city's board of child welfare, Earle was unable to work with Mitchel's successor, Tammany's John F. Hylan, and soon resigned. In 1921 she supported another losing mayoral candidate, Henry H. Curran, and in the latter part of the decade campaigned for government re-organization under Governor Smith. She tried to work with Mayor Walker's committee on plan and survey but declared it "useless, too big," issuing reports that then lay dormant. She also found Walker to be indifferent to women's views.[42]

During the 1920s she volunteered with several New York women's civic or-ganizations, chairing conferences on city affairs and studying the school budget. In 1930 she served as secretary of Governor Roosevelt's Commission for the Stabilization of Industry to Prevent Unemployment, and in 1933 headed a cit-izens committee for the election of Raymond V. Ingersoll as president of the borough of Brooklyn. She then took a paid position as executive secretary of the Women's City Club. It was in this role that she first met Mayor La Guardia. She had invited him to speak and they had a pleasant talk. He must have been impressed, for soon after he invited her to city hall to offer her a seat on the Charter Revision Commission. This work, she said, was "the most important thing that I was ever associated with, except possibly the Council," to which she would later be elected.[43]

Charter revision, initiated in the aftermath of the Seabury investigations, had gotten off to a rocky start. This was due in part to a key but controversial pro-vision in some reformers' plans, most notably Samuel Seabury's, to replace the board of aldermen with a city council elected by proportional representation (PR). An idea that originated as an eighteenth-century corrective to the tyranny of a majority, PR gave voters representation in proportion to the number of votes cast. Reformers thought it perfect for New York City, where minority candidates for alderman rarely won enough votes to carry wards that Tammany dominated.[44] In May 1934, as a follow-up to the Seabury investigations, the state legislature ap-pointed former governor Smith and Judge Seabury as cochairs of a twenty-eight-member bipartisan city charter commission. When its members clashed over PR and other divisive issues, such as borough government and the role of county offices, Smith and others resigned. Governor Lehman soon ended the commis-sion and got the legislature to authorize La Guardia to appoint a new one.[45]

Reformers had been promoting PR for New York City since the mid-1890s. Few observers took the idea seriously until Judge Seabury said he thought it was the best way to undercut Tammany Hall. The nonpartisan Citizens Union seconded the idea, pointing out the absurdity of electing 94 percent of the city's board of aldermen by a party that received only 65 percent of the vote. The city's Republicans, Socialists, and African Americans also supported PR, hoping it would give them representation even if they failed to win pluralities in the wards.[46]

Though it is not clear that PR alone would have helped women win more electoral offices, in the 1930s some women activists thought it might. The contemporary literature either for or against PR was, however, silent on this point. When the merchants association explained why New Yorkers should vote for PR, it argued that the system would reapportion seats more in line with outlying boroughs' burgeoning populations, end gerrymandering, raise the caliber of candidates to include "our ablest men," save money by eliminating primaries, and, most important, help end machine domination. The mock ballots they used to explain the method did not list any women's names. The ballots included Socialist Norman Thomas, but also lacked any male candidates of color.[47]

The prospect of electing more women was absent not only from the literature produced by male-dominated civic organizations but also from the pro-PR literature women put out. Genevieve Earle oversaw the contributions of the Women's City Club, which since 1932 had been holding mock PR elections to learn how the voting method worked. In 1936 the club issued a primer on PR, a pamphlet written in simple language, with stick characters (none wore skirts) and other graphics to illustrate its points. The primer argued that, under the current system, if one party wins a plurality, then most of the Republican votes, all of the Socialist votes, and all other minority votes are wasted. The primer's second argument was that PR would give proper representation to the outlying boroughs, especially Queens and the Bronx, which had grown substantially since the world war.[48]

The club's primer gave only a token nod to women as possible candidates. Women's names appeared on a page that showed a sample ballot of seven names, two of which were female. But when examples of votes for the seven were shown, one woman received the lowest number, the other zero. In the 1930s, the Women's City Club boasted a membership of the city's most politically involved and well-connected women. Still, even this group held back on PR's potential for increasing women's representation. This potential had certainly occurred to them, but, perhaps fearing the idea would arouse opposition from opponents of women being active in politics, they had decided to avoid mentioning it. Instead, they emphasized only PR's potential for encouraging "distinguished citizens" to run for office.[49]

At least Genevieve Earle, as a member of the Charter Revision Commission, was able to promote the idea. In contrast to the Smith-Seabury commission, which in Earle's view had been too large and filled with "strong political people" deeply divided over PR and county government reorganization, the Thacher commission was so small that it could work as a committee of the whole. Since Earle was its only woman member, everyone knew her name from day one (they called her "Gen") and seemed to accept her without a fuss. She organized the commission's research work, gathering government documents relevant to the commission's needs from Rebecca Rankin, director of the Municipal Reference Library. She persuaded another Women's City Club member, Mildred Blout Goetz, to volunteer her services. A long-time Democratic Party activist, Goetz was married to Norman S. Goetz, a lawyer in the firm of commission member Joseph Proskauer. A Barnard College graduate, she had headed the correspondence bureau during Alfred E. Smith's 1928 presidential campaign and, during Smith's ill-fated attempt to win renomination in 1932, managed Smith's Chicago headquarters. As "volunteer assistant secretary" to the Charter Revision Commission, she organized the office staff, arranged meetings and hearings, issued reports and memoranda, took part in the study of city government, and campaigned for PR to pass—all work for which she was later honored.[50]

In the debates over charter revision that took place in the mid-1930s, both the League of Women Voters and Women's City Club favored PR. While Earle agreed with the goal of an "unbossed" city government, she did not rubberstamp everything these organizations said. For example, the league wanted a city manager for New York instead of a mayor. Agreeing instead with her commission colleagues, Earle preferred to strengthen the role of an elected mayor. Also, in a nod to historical considerations, she favored keeping the borough government system.

In the end the commission took away the boroughs' legislative powers and abolished the board of aldermen. It also consolidated departments with overlapping duties and, for the first time, created a planning commission to plan for the city's growth. It gave the mayor a deputy mayor to take care of daily business, decided against breaking up the Sanitation Department (Earle said she submitted a successful memorandum on this topic), and chose to keep the housing and building departments together. The new charter also retained the board of estimate's control over the city's budget. The commission was conflicted over PR. In addition to Earle, Socialist John Block made the strongest case for it. Professor McGoldrick, Judge Hackenburg, and Charles Hughes also favored it. Despite the opposition of Judge Proskauer and businessman Thomas Parkinson, the new voting method passed. Earle then devoted herself to win voter support.[51]

Even before New York voters had a chance to vote on PR, its opponents mounted constitutional challenges. One suit claimed that the legislature had no authority to establish the Charter Revision Commission at all. A state supreme court judge accepted this argument, but the court of appeals reversed him, saying that home rule authorized a new charter. A second constitutional challenge came from a woman who argued that PR violated the right of the elector to vote unqualifiedly for a candidate, and that the method wastes funds. The court replied that the voters should decide this issue.[52] Other opponents of PR included Democratic Party followers of former governor Alfred E. Smith. On October 31,

1936, shortly before the vote on the measure, Smith called PR a "complicated and freakish device." He complained that it does away with traditional city districts and predicted that half the voters will not know how to mark their ballots. Even the head of the Republican Party said PR was too complicated, although some Republicans, notably Nicholas Murray Butler, president of Columbia University, favored the idea.[53]

In the 1936 election, PR won, but not impressively; the vote was 923,186 to 555,217. As the state chamber of commerce later pointed out, "less than half of the voters participating in the election [were] sufficiently interested to vote 'for' or 'against'" either PR *or* the new charter. Despite this lack of voter enthusiasm, many of the city's women political activists were elated. One who was not was Martha Byrne, then Manhattan's register and a Democratic Party women's county leader. Calling PR a "horror," she warned, "It will cost more than a million dollars to the taxpayer." Whoever is responsible for it should be "strung up on a rail."[54] For the next ten years, the question of whether to retain or repeal PR would dominate many local political debates.

Rebecca Rankin, librarian. Eunice Hunton Carter, prosecutor. Jane Bolin, judge. Elinore Herrick, industrial pacifist. Anna Rosenberg, "manpower" expert. In the New York City of the mid-1930s, anyone following political affairs would have heard of these five women. Most of them self-identified as feminists and modernizers. All of them had a direct relationship either with Mayor La Guardia's administration or his policies, programs, or causes. All contributed to La Guardia's success as mayor.

The least likely to play such a role was the librarian. Rebecca Browning Rankin, director of the Municipal Reference Library of the City of New York, was one of La Guardia's most valued resources. Calling her "a human index of city affairs," he turned repeatedly to her for facts, sometimes only a few minutes before he needed them for a speech or statement. She would then drop whatever she was doing and rush to get him what he wanted. But this was not the only reason she was important to him. Two years into his first term she began to compile, edit, and publish books that publicized all he had done to modernize city government. La Guardia came to rely on her so much that he called the reference library "my library" and Rankin "my commissioner," a title she of course never officially held.[55]

Born in 1887, Rankin attended the University of Michigan and earned a library degree from Simmons College in Boston. After directing the Washington State Normal School Library, in 1918 she went to New York to help her sister take care of their mother. When she heard that the director of the New York Public Library (NYPL) was seeking an assistant, she applied. Ordinarily, he would have held out for a man, but this was wartime and so he hired her. Soon he assigned her to work with the director of the Municipal Reference Library, then still part of the NYPL. When its director resigned in February 1920, Rankin won his place.[56]

Her relationship with La Guardia began when, in search of new revenue for unemployment relief, he asked her to document other cities' experiences with special taxes on gross business receipts. She and her staff found that, when cities exempted food and medicines from the taxes, citizens accepted them. In November 1934 Republican alderman Morton Baum introduced an emergency tax bill that made those exemptions; La Guardia signed it into law. While Baum got all the credit for the bill (over the next few years it generated almost $50 million annually), Rankin felt her staff deserved it more.[57]

During his first hundred days, La Guardia had Rankin document the licensing fees departments had collected during the 1920s. Since many departments did not publish annual reports, she had to dig through departmental files to find the data. Urging better record-keeping in the future, she suggested reviving the municipal yearbook, which had ceased publication. La Guardia endorsed the idea and asked her to make it dramatic, putting in stories, graphics, and photographs. The result was her 1936 edition of *New York Advancing: A Scientific Approach to Municipal Government*.

The book was a major achievement. More than 350 pages long and weighing over two pounds, it provided a comprehensive portrait of La Guardia's stewardship. Its ninety-one photographs and charts gave vivid evidence of his progress. For helping her make the book "dramatic," Rankin gave credit to seven assistants, almost all female, including Pearl Bernstein (board of estimate secretary) and Dorothy Kenyon (deputy license commissioner). "Women," Rankin told a *Times* reporter, "have the 'feel' of the tie-up between the man in the street and his government" and thus knew how to make the book accessible. La Guardia was supposed to write the first chapter. Despairing of ever getting it, Rankin sent him the message that all he had to do was dictate his main points and she would do the rest. A month before the book was due at the printer's, La Guardia finally went down to Rankin's office to deliver his points. Rankin and Bernstein transformed them into an essay in the mayor's voice.[58]

The book's theme was modernization. Each chapter highlighted how the mayor, unlike his predecessors, had applied "scientific method" to government. La Guardia's chapter gave the specifics. He had replaced political appointees with "the best qualified persons" and followed the merit system "as never before." By getting politics out of law enforcement, he had made the city "unsafe and uncomfortable for racketeers and gangsters." The courts were "no longer the rendezvous of politicians and fixers"; the corporation counsel's office now contained lawyers chosen solely on "record and ability." Thanks to the Works Progress Administration (WPA), he had been able to raze "unsanitary, dangerous, fire-trap tenements" and erect "low-rent sanitary apartments." The New Deal had facilitated new hospitals, a public health laboratory, ten health centers, and ten baby health stations. "Gangsters" and "political wardens" were no longer running city correctional facilities. The administration had pioneered in arts education, performance, and exhibition and founded a high school of music and art; it also professionalized other quality-of-life areas, such as traffic, sewage disposal, street cleaning, and firefighting.

He had not won on all points. The state legislature's refusal to grant the city home rule meant he could not cut "useless jobs" and consolidate offices. This meant he had to raise taxes on public utilities and gross business and professional receipts, dedicating the funds to aid the poor and complete parks and playground projects. "Much remains to be done!" La Guardia concluded. He promised more "transit unification, charter revision, low-rent housing, a municipally operated power plant, and a municipal art center, including an opera house, symphonic concert hall, and city auditorium."[59]

Rankin crowded into the book's main body a wealth of data so valuable that historians still use it as their chief primary source on La Guardia's administration. She made much of this material readable. The author of the section on small claims court provided dramatic examples of how claims may be small but loom large to those who press them. The author of the section on the Department of Licenses (probably Dorothy Kenyon) described the people coming into the hearing room as "frequently poor and confused, smarting under a sense of injustice and knowing only that they want their rights." The Department of Public Markets report asked readers to imagine what would happen if a calamity destroyed the city's bridges, tunnels, and railroads. "Within three days New York's teeming millions would be on the brink of starvation!" The author then told of a butcher, now in jail, who increased poultry weights with lead shot embedded in fat, and "racketeers," such as Joseph "Socks" Lanza, who had controlled the Fulton Fish Market. The section on the Department of Correction began with "An eventful day!"—a reference to a January 24, 1934, raid on the old Welfare Island penitentiary that had revealed "scandalous conditions." The last prisoner from this "ancient institution with its long history of human misery" had now departed.[60] Rankin had done what La Guardia had asked: made potentially dry material dramatic.

Graphics added to the book's appeal. There were before-and-after photographs of building restorations, new markets, bridges and highways, testing laboratories, clerks (all male) collecting taxes, citizens (mostly women) lining up to pay them, firemen in training or putting out fires, a policeman taking a lost toddler home, health clinics and hospitals, prisons and reformatories, street cleaning and snow removal, dumps and incinerators, subway cars and stations, and New Deal agencies at work. Further enlivening the text were shots of La Guardia in action—racing to a fire in the middle of the night or smashing slot machines with a sledgehammer.

In constructing this portrait of La Guardia as both modernizer and progressive, Rankin performed a unique service. She alone could have collected and edited material from across the city's bureaucracy. Most of the text was positive, with the book blaming failures on recalcitrant citizens or unsympathetic legislators. It avoided anything negative, such as the 1935 Harlem riot and its unsatisfactory aftermath, or La Guardia's loss of Republican approval because of his support for the New Deal. Yet the book was no mere puff piece. Though uncritical of him, it was a well-documented monument to his achievements.[61]

The book was popular. Costing only fifty cents in paper (a buckram-bound version sold for one dollar and twenty-five cents), the first printing of ten thousand sold out in a few months. Rankin orchestrated an elaborate book launch on the steps of the New York Public Library at which the mayor spoke. For the book's second edition in 1937, she staged a launch at R. H. Macy's department store. The mayor worked a large crowd, signing copies, answering questions, even making change for buyers. He joked that *he* was responsible for the "nice things" that had been written about him. The book aided in his decisive re-election victory that fall.[62]

At the same time as Rankin was preparing the various editions of *New York Advancing*, she handled other political tasks. She helped the Charter Revision Commission almost daily, working closely with Genevieve Earle to compile information on departmental rules and regulations, county government, and charters of cities around the state. She promoted proportional representation in radio talks and, when it passed, noted that the new system had both worked and brought in a "higher type of city councilmen." Her boss, NYPL director Harry M. Lydenberg, referred to her as "commissioner-in-chief, high admiral of the fleet, field marshal and everything else."[63]

Rankin never held these titles or anything close to them. Like many other mid-twentieth-century women in politics, she did not make the story about herself. At her first book launch she turned down an invitation to lunch with the mayor and the head of the NYPL, saying, "the Harvard Club is a better lunching place for you men alone." Since La Guardia's name appeared on both the spine and title page of *New York Advancing*, a reader might have assumed he had written the book himself. In March 1936, thanks to Earle's intervention, the Women's City Club showed that its members knew otherwise. In honoring her for her "distinguished service to the city government," they said they regretted how little public recognition she had received for all she had done.

After La Guardia retired, Rankin continued to work on modernizing the city's information systems. Her founding of a municipal archive made a lasting contribution to the city. At her suggestion La Guardia had ordered department heads not to destroy records without checking with her first and persuaded the board of estimate to fund a building for an archive. Suspended during the war, the archives project revived under La Guardia's successor, William O'Dwyer, who put Rankin in charge of it. When she retired, the *Times* editorialized that she was a " 'Rock of Gibralter' in the reference field. 'Everybody downtown depended on Becky' ... Mr. La Guardia expected her to know everything and was seldom disappointed."[64] Rankin never thought of herself as a politician. But as she had helped create the public opinion that won La Guardia two more terms, she was just as much a critical aide to La Guardia as Belle Moskowitz had been to Al Smith.

Eunice Hunton Carter was important to Mayor La Guardia on a totally different front. When he appointed her a member of his commission to determine the cause of the March 1935 Harlem riot, she was already a well-known political figure. One of the city's first African American female law school graduates, she had lost a race for the state assembly the previous year but won many admirers for the high quality of her campaign. Her work on La Guardia's commission brought her into even wider public consciousness and led to a prestigious appointment later that year.

The Harlem riot began on the afternoon of March 19 after Lino Rivera, a sixteen-year-old boy, tried to steal a cheap penknife from a five-and-ten-cent store on 125th Street. Two employees caught him, but even though the boy bit them the store's owner told police to let him go. To avoid a growing crowd of shoppers concerned about the boy's fate, the police took him down to the basement, where they planned to let him out the store's rear door. One woman, sure the boy was going to be beaten, became hysterical and was arrested. Medics arrived to tend to the injured employees, but when they drove away in an empty ambulance some onlookers concluded the boy was dead. Then, in an unhappy coincidence, a man intending to visit a relative who worked in the store drove up in a hearse. When the crowd gathered outside the store demanded the police produce the boy, the police merely told them to go home. Someone threw a stone that broke a store window. By evening, two youth groups, the Young Liberators and Young Communist League, were distributing leaflets that screamed, "Child Brutally Beaten—Woman Attacked by Boss and Cops—Child near DEATH!" Crowds surged, spreading east and west along 125th Street, smashing windows and looting. By the next evening, after newspapers published a picture of a smiling Rivera standing between two plainclothes policemen, all was calm. Three black citizens were dead and nearly sixty injured. The police had arrested seventy-five, most of them African Americans. Property damage was extensive.[65]

La Guardia quickly appointed a commission to look into the riot's cause and suggest action. Its membership consisted of a mix of civil rights activists, including A. Philip Randolph (president of the Brotherhood of Sleeping Car Porters), municipal court justice Charles E. Toney (one of the city's first African American judges), poet Countee Cullen, William Jay Schieffelin (then a trustee of the Tuskegee Institute), publisher of *The Nation* Oswald Garrison Villard, and Eunice Hunton Carter. As she was the commission's sole woman member, her colleagues elected her secretary.[66]

Born in Atlanta in 1899, Eunice Hunton was the third child of a distinguished couple: William Alphaeus Hunton, a national YMCA executive, and Addie Waites Hunton, nationally known social worker and clubwoman. The family had moved to New York City after the 1906 Atlanta race riots. Eunice studied in Strasbourg (Alsace-Lorraine) for two years while her mother traveled in Europe on peace missions. On her return she went to Smith College, graduating in 1921 with both bachelor's and master's degrees. After working in family service agencies, in 1924 she married dentist Lisle Carter, with whom she had a son. According to a childhood friend, at eight years old Eunice said she was going to "be a lawyer so she could help people and see that all the wicked were punished." In 1927, she enrolled in Fordham University Law School night classes. She also supervised Harlem relief fund agencies and traveled to Albany to lobby for housing reform. She earned a law degree in 1932 and passed the bar in 1934.[67]

That year marked her only foray into electoral politics. Hoping to unseat four-term Democrat James E. Stephens, the county committee of the Central Republican Club nominated her for the state assembly from the Nineteenth AD. In September women formed a Eunice Carter nonpartisan league to work for her election. Journalist Thelma Berlack-Boozer publicized her campaign in her *Amsterdam News* column, "The Feminist Viewpoint," and after endorsing her, the paper gave Carter, whom it called a "militant, intelligent young attorney," an even chance to win. The Citizens Union endorsed her, as did the *World-Telegram* and *New York Age*. Mayor La Guardia and two of his cabinet members, Comptroller Joseph D. McGoldrick and Housing Commissioner Langdon W. Post, spoke at a final rally held at the Mother AME Zion Church for Harlem candidates, including Eunice Carter.

Carter's platform addressed issues of Depression-era Harlem. She would reduce the age limit on pensions and lessen the paperwork required to qualify. She favored immediate action on slum clearance and compliance with tenement laws. She wanted an end to race discrimination in public works employment. Finally, she argued for stricter regulation of utilities, laws to curb creditors from unjustly confiscating wages and furniture, and reapportionment to ensure the election of a Negro to Congress. Her opponent retained his seat in the Democratic sweep that year, but Carter did well, attracting national interest in her campaign and winning a total of 5,987 votes against Stephens's 7,636. Even a better candidate could not have beaten Stephens, Harlem newspapers mourned.[68]

Though Carter's political career failed, it should not be dismissed. In the larger picture of women's politics—and especially of black women's politics—it was significant both to her and to the city's women's community. Here was a woman of superior qualifications who ran ahead of other Republicans on the district's ticket, garnering 45 percent of the vote. Her candidacy had appealed to a wide range of Manhattan supporters, especially women, whom she complimented by saying a "woman would have a keener insight into the needs of the community." White suffragist journalist Rheta Childe Dorr had boosted her candidacy, along with many politically active black women such as Sarah Pelham Speaks, a lawyer and lifelong Republican who herself would later run for the assembly. In a different political climate—when Republican candidates had a better chance in the city—Carter might have won, thereby becoming the first African American woman in the nation to win a state legislative seat.[69]

Moreover, Carter's race advanced her career. Organizations called on her to speak, and when Mayor La Guardia was looking for a woman to serve on his Harlem riot commission she was a clear choice. Many citizens found her inspiring. In an open letter, Thelma Berlack-Boozer warned Assemblyman Stephens not to construe his victory as "conclusive evidence that you are the best person" to serve the district. She noted that Carter had lost by "a mere 1,600 votes," which indicated his "days were numbered." And so they were. Stephens lost the primary in 1935 and never won another nomination. As for Carter, her plate would soon be too full to permit her to run for office again.[70]

When the Harlem Commission divided up its responsibilities, it assigned Carter to investigate the "outburst" (it avoided the term "riot"). Schieffelin, Justice Toney, and attorney Arthur Garfield Hayes worked closely with her. As secretary, Carter received all communications from citizens offering information. Thus, while the secretary post might seem to be a typical female assignment, in this context it was powerful: she served as the filter through which community feedback reached the commission. Still, complaints abounded about the commission's make-up—it was insufficiently representative of those suffering from conditions in Harlem, did not include a Harlem minister, and despite Carter's presence lacked "college women." And why was a poet (Countee Cullen) on it? Resentment brewed over making Communists scapegoats. The commission concluded that, while the riot's immediate cause was rumor, the deeper cause was "pent-up feelings of resentment and insecurity" rooted in employment discrimination, police aggression, racial segregation, and institutional neglect. The commission warned of a potential recurrence.[71]

In August 1935, a new and even more visible appointment came to Carter when Thomas E. Dewey, recently appointed special prosecutor to investigate racketeering, hired her for his team. This made her the nation's first female of color appointed a deputy assistant district attorney. Only one of Dewey's twenty assistants, she came to play a pivotal role. She turned Dewey's attention to the rise of prostitution rings that had surfaced after the Seabury investigations. Not wanting to look like a moral crusader, Dewey was skeptical about taking on this issue, but Carter persuaded him otherwise. Earlier that year she had volunteered in women's court, where both she and Judge Anna Kross had observed the same bondsmen and lawyers showing up to get cases "fixed." She convinced Dewey he should pursue the "big business" of prostitution. She assigned detectives to follow the "fixers" and put wiretaps into brothels to record conversations among bondsmen and lawyers, many of whom had been disbarred.

In late January 1936 Dewey conducted a raid that rounded up twenty-nine major suspects—gunmen, drug peddlers, and pimps—and then in February raided houses of prostitution. The police netted hundreds of prostitutes, madams, and customers, all as witnesses for a larger prosecution. Eventually, Dewey's team flushed out "Lucky" Luciano as the ring's head, a success that rested on Carter's scrupulous preparation. Citing Carter's "devotion and hard work," Dewey said words were inadequate to express his gratitude to her. When in January 1938 he took office as New York district attorney, he kept Carter on, raising her salary and putting her in charge of women's court and special sessions cases. Still the only woman on his staff, she stayed on until 1945, when she returned to private practice.[72]

Carter remained close to Dewey. When she campaigned for him for governor in 1938 she humanized him for other women. By then Smith College had awarded her an honorary doctorate for distinguished public service. The national black press put her on the same level as Crystal Bird Fauset, the nation's first African American female state legislator (elected in Pennsylvania in 1938), Mary McCleod Bethune of the US Federal Youth Administration, and contralto Marian Anderson.[73]

Mayor La Guardia advanced another African American New York City woman lawyer into prominence. On July 22, 1939, he summoned Jane Bolin, assistant corporation counsel, to come to his summer office in the New York City Building at the World's Fair in Flushing Meadows. He told her to bring her husband, attorney Ralph E. Mizelle, with her. When the mayor heard the couple had arrived he breezed past Bolin and took Mizelle into his office. Bolin, since 1937 the first African American female in his law department, was sure he was going to give her a hard time about something. To her surprise, when the two men came back they were both smiling. Still without explaining, the mayor asked an assistant to bring in photographers. At last he turned to Bolin. "I'm going to make you a judge on the Court of Domestic Relations," he said. "Raise your right hand." Stunned, Bolin complied. With that, the thirty-one-year-old Jane Matilda Bolin became the nation's first African American female judge.[74]

Mayor La Guardia made national news with this appointment, which won him credit among African Americans across the country. From a feminist perspective, the way he treated Bolin that day was, however, reprehensible. His keeping her in the dark and informing her husband first may have amused him, but it was disrespectful of her. Contrast it to Mayor O'Brien's appointment of Anna Kross to the magistracy at the end of 1933. O'Brien let Kross know in advance and told her to come with her husband (family was always invited to such ceremonies) to his office through a side door so as to avoid competing office seekers. In contrast, La Guardia put Bolin on the defensive and made her think, in a stereotypically female fashion, that she had done something wrong. He never would have treated a man this way, letting the man's wife in on the secret while leaving the man clueless. La Guardia may have appointed more women into government posts than any previous city executive, but he did not do so out of a feminist sensibility.

Like Eunice Carter, Bolin came from a professional family background. Her father, Gaius Bolin, was the first African American to practice law in Poughkeepsie, New York; her mother, a Northern Irish immigrant, died when Jane was eight. In 1924, when Jane was ready at sixteen for college, Poughkeepsie's Vassar College did not accept black students, but Wellesley did. Wellesley also accepted one other African American girl, who was assigned as Bolin's roommate despite their dislike of one another. When she graduated, Bolin was honored as one of twenty Wellesley Scholars. Though a counselor told her there was no room in the world for a black woman lawyer, she had quietly applied to Yale Law and been admitted. Her father opposed her going, saying that a woman lawyer would have to hear "dirty" things. She insisted, and in the end he gave her his support. At Yale she was one of only four women and the only African American. Her experiences were isolating. Either she felt "invisible" or was subjected to slights (men allowed doors to slam in her face, southern professors never called on her in class). Her only positive social experience was meeting Ralph Mizelle at the home of an African American dentist. Fifteen years her senior, Mizelle practiced law in New York City. They married in 1933 and eight years later had a son.

After passing the bar Bolin at first practiced with her father and brother, and later with Mizelle. Like Eunice Carter, she entered politics briefly, running in 1936 as a Republican for the same state assembly seat Carter had sought. That year she was the only woman on a major party ticket in the city. The Citizens Union endorsed her but also called her opponent, incumbent Democrat Robert W. Justice, qualified. The Women's Department of the Republican State

Committee Colored Voters Division came out in force for her in Harlem, rallying around the Democratic Party's segregationist policies. The department's codirector, Dr. Julia Coleman Robinson, decried the waste, extravagance, and increased taxes of the New Deal. But by then Harlem had moved decisively toward President Roosevelt and returned Democrats to office in a landslide. Bolin was crushed. She won only 4,600 votes to more than 20,000 for her opponent. Though she lost, like Carter, she earned political credit from the race.[75]

The following year, she applied for a post in La Guardia's Law Department. Although a clerk told her there were no openings, Paul Windels, one of La Guardia's closest advisers and then corporation counsel, hired her, perhaps with an eye to winning favor in Harlem. He assigned her to work as trial counsel with the new court of domestic relations.[76] The court's two divisions, family court and children's court, were coping with a rise in cases involving African American families. A study commissioned by the court's presiding justice in 1934 showed that over the previous thirteen years crime among black youth had increased by more than 240 percent. Moreover, in Manhattan, 25 percent of juveniles arraigned in children's court were African American and more than 25 percent of nonsupport cases involved black families. The Depression had hit Harlem hard, with the area suffering from unemployment, poor public services, and heavy-handed policing. Bolin's appointment to the Law Department helped the mayor show he was responding.[77]

Working with the domestic relations court, Bolin got to know Rosalie Loew Whitney, whom La Guardia had recently appointed a judge on that court. They became good friends, and Whitney may have recommended Bolin when La Guardia was looking to add a judge. Other women who supported Bolin's career at critical junctures included Eleanor Roosevelt, who intervened with Democratic mayor William O'Dwyer, who Bolin had heard was not going to reappoint her to another ten-year term. Family court judge Justine Wise Polier joined forces with Bolin in her campaign to have cases assigned to probation and publicly funded child-care agency officers regardless of an offender's race or religion. "They used to put a big N or PR on the front of every petition, to indicate if the family was black or Puerto Rican," she told *Times* writer Judy Klemesrud. In 1942 Polier and Judge Hubert T. Delaney, one of the city's first African American judges, worked closely with her to enact a city charter amendment prohibiting racial segregation in all city facilities, including hospitals and maternity facilities. In 1943, she challenged newspapers to stop identifying the name and race of children below age sixteen arrested for crimes. After 1950, she lobbied for desegregated housing, supporting a bill proposed by Councilmen Earl Brown and Stanley Isaacs to bar discrimination in all publicly assisted housing. By 1954, their bill outlawed discrimination in all future private multiple dwellings built with government-guaranteed mortgages. Bolin played a key role in this initiative.[78]

Bolin would remain the only African American woman judge for two decades. Widowed in 1943, in 1950 she married Walter P. Offutt Jr., a Baptist minister and later special assistant to the commissioner of the state division of human rights. He died in 1974, four years before Bolin retired.[79] When that retirement came, Constance Baker Motley, the nation's first African American federal judge, called her one of her role models:

> There is a great deal to be said for role model influence. I thought you would like to know that you provided a role model for me at a time when there were very few, if any, black women in the law. I also recall hearing nothing but praise with respect to your legal ability when I first came to New York in 1941. When I thereafter met you, I then knew how a lady judge should deport herself. I want to thank you for that.[80]

Bolin turned down an offer to be nominated for a federal judgeship, saying she felt she could render the greatest service by remaining in family court. She was devoted to children. Her granddaughter Natascha Mizelle recalled that she once asked Bolin why she always left her judicial robes in her chambers instead of wearing them in court. "Then the children will be afraid of me," her grandmother replied. For her, court was not to be a place of punishment. Its purpose was to find solutions.[81]

The field of labor relations brought Elinore Morehouse Herrick into La Guardia's circle of advisers. Her prominence began in September 1934, when Senator Robert F. Wagner Sr. asked her to come see him. He wanted her to serve as "volunteer chair" of a regional board set up to implement Section 7(a) of the 1933 National Industrial Recovery Act (NIRA), which unions interpreted as giving employees the right to bargain collectively. The board would oversee industries in portions of New York, New Jersey, and Connecticut. In response to Wagner's request, Herrick made three points: the region contains a quarter of all American industry, chairing the region's board is a full-time job, and she had two boys to support. Wagner conceded, replying he would pay her a salary and make her executive vice chairman, but she should pick her own unsalaried chairman, "someone who won't interfere with what you are doing." Cleverly, Herrick picked Wagner's own former law partner, Judge Jeremiah T. Mahoney, "an association which worked out most happily all around," she later wrote.[82] Once again, as the women of the La Guardia administration were learning, the man got the title and the woman did the heavy lifting. While accepting this reality, at least Herrick got paid.

Herrick's career had revolved around working for industrial peace and improving women's status in the workplace. Born in New York City in 1895, she grew up in Springfield, Massachusetts, where her father, Daniel Webster Morehouse, a Unitarian minister, moved the family for his health. Her mother, Martha Adelaide Bird, had been registrar at Brooklyn's Pratt Institute. Elinore studied economics and journalism at Barnard College. She took courses with famed historian Charles A. Beard and heard lectures by muckraker Lincoln Steffens and unionist Rose Schneiderman. At the Beards' home, she met other radicals—writer Max Eastman and his sister Crystal, an attorney; famed lawyer Clarence Darrow; and Freda Kirchwey, who would go on to edit *The Nation*.

In 1916 Elinore dropped out of Barnard to marry Horace Terhune Herrick, a chemical engineer. They moved to Buffalo, where Elinore bore two boys. After the marriage foundered, Elinore fell on hard times. She worked first in a home for delinquent girls and then ran a friend's home, caring for the friend's three children and her own. When they started school, her widowed mother came to live with her while she took factory jobs. First she made paper boxes, then machine belting and shoe polish. In this last job she had to stand for nine hours "dipping hot shoe-polish into little tins." Before it hardened into a flat cake, the polish burned her hands; the smell nauseated her; the rough-edged tins cut her fingers. Anxious to make good on her first day, she worked so fast that the girl across the bench whispered harshly: "Hey sister, what are you trying to do? Kill the job?" An angry group enlightened her at lunch: if they work too fast they show up coworkers or, worse, deplete the shoe polish supply so the bosses send them home and dock their pay. Herrick would later cite this experience as her first lesson in industrial labor relations.[83]

Soon she was tending spooling machines at a DuPont rayon factory for twenty-eight cents an hour. Advancing to supervisor, in 1923 she moved to Old Hickory, Tennessee, as a textile division production manager in a new DuPont plant. When it became clear her employers would not advance her any further, in 1927 she took her family to Antioch College in Ohio to finish her education. To support herself, she lectured on industrial problems, assisted the college's president, and helped her mother run a boarding house. She earned a bachelor's degree in labor economics in 1929 and moved to New York City just before the Depression hit. Weighing multiple job offers, she accepted the one with the least security: executive secretary of the New York Consumers' League (NYCL). This job—both "a challenge and socially useful"—lay the foundation for the rest of her career.[84]

At the NYCL, she worked closely with labor reformers Rose Schneiderman, Molly Dewson, and Harvard law professor Felix Frankfurter on a new state minimum wage law for women and minors. A 1923 US Supreme Court decision had invalidated an earlier version. Appalled by what she called the Depression's "cata-strophic" breakdown of labor standards and determined to relaunch a minimum wage campaign, early in 1933 she went to Albany to lobby for a new bill from the New York Consumers' League (NYCL). Dewson, Frankfurter, and Frances Perkins went with her. Newly inaugurated governor Herbert H. Lehman invited the group to spend the night at the executive mansion. At dinner with the gov-ernor; his wife, Edith; and his counsel, Charles Poletti, Herrick heard Lehman say he favored a minimum wage but was unsure about making it mandatory or, as in Massachusetts, voluntary, enforceable only by publicity. After Frankfurter bit-ingly described Boston's "conscienceless employers," whose business orders went up from the free publicity they got when they violated the law, he won over both Lehman and Poletti to a law with teeth. The group ended up planning strategy until early morning.[85]

Following the governor's message to legislators that the league's bill was a "must," the NCL released a statewide study showing factory wages had been cut by two-thirds or more. Canneries, in particular, were paying as little as eight cents an hour. In early January 1933 the NCL brought together fifty organiza-tions to push for their bill and later placed their pamphlet, *Cut-Rate Wages*, on every legislator's desk. Herrick pressured a senate leader especially hard, refusing to accept amendments limiting the bill's coverage to only first- and second-class cities. In the end the bill went through the senate as written. When she reported this to the governor, Charlie Poletti "threw his arms around me and whirled me round and round the big reception room of the Governor's office," to Lehman's "vast amusement."

"It was an exciting battle," she wrote, one that continued in the assembly. A bitter opponent snarled at her, "I've never voted for a labor measure yet, not even when drunk, and I never will." Fortunately, his Albany hotel mate was a former student of Frankfurter's, who tipped off Herrick to a planned Republican Party caucus against the bill. She forestalled it with articles in smaller upstate newspapers. The caucus collapsed.

There were some light moments. Senators on their way home from Albany teased her on the train, telling colleagues to stay away from her or "she'll flood you with so much mail . . . you'll have to hire another secretary out of your own pocket." To continue to look fresh, Herrick adopted a uniform of black and white onto which she buttoned fresh white collars and cuffs, a trick that amazed her home-stay hostess. The day before the bill came to the assembly floor the bill's floor leader asked her to supply him with all the arguments to meet every possible legal, economic, and social objection. "I had never done such a job before," she recalled. Since there was no time to call in her experts—social investigators Pauline and Josephine Goldmark, Dewson, and Frankfurter—she called on the Department of Labor Statistics and her host's secretary to help her. She then stayed up all night, drinking multiple cups of black coffee as she typed up the brief.

The NCL's bill passed, but so did two others, including a bill sponsored by the National Woman's Party (NWP), which demanded a minimum wage for men too, a bill that Herrick was sure would be held unconstitutional. Both opponents and proponents packed the chamber at the governor's special hearing on the bills. "The suspense was awful," she wrote. Which bill would the governor sign? All she could do was put her feet up on a desk to rest them "from that horrible marble in the Capitol," which had made her feet hurt as she tramped from office to office. She read and reread a letter Frankfurter had sent her, which said that bills such as the one passed "do not just happen. They are the product of skill, unflagging alertness and devotion in the strategy and tactics of legislation. I happen to know how much of the great achievement will be due to your unusual effectiveness." The letter made her proud.

And then came the call. An operator said, "Mrs. Herrick, someone who says he is the Governor is calling from Albany. May I put him on?" When the governor began with an apology, Herrick was sure he was telling her he had signed the other bill. But what he was apologizing for was having forgotten to arrange a ceremony when he signed "your bill." He had signed it that evening.

The minimum wage fight was far from over. The US Supreme Court reversed the law, but its later approval of a similar Ohio law in 1937 legalized New York's. In the aftermath, Herrick wrote that a million women had already begun to feel the law's benefits. "Minimum wage orders in the laundry industry guarantee $14 a week for 40 hours and beauty parlor women are assured $16.50 for 45 hours work," she later wrote. "Employers should not growl too much at such modest sums." Reiterating the "entering wedge" argument, she predicted that men would soon have similar benefits.

Herrick went on from this success to lobby for other protective labor laws, including a forty-eight-hour workweek, unemployment insurance, and improved workers' compensation. At one point she found herself spontaneously settling a strike, an experience that led her to leave the league in 1934 to become a mediator as executive vice chairman of the regional board of the National Recovery Administration (NRA). After Mayor La Guardia appointed her a labor adviser, she helped him avoid or settle strikes in the taxi, laundry, hotel, bakery, restaurant, markets, knit goods, building services, and transit industries. Her national visibility peaked when the Wagner Act of 1935 established the National Labor Relations Board (NLRB) and Secretary of Labor Frances Perkins got President Roosevelt to appoint her director of the board's District Two (the same district she had handled for the NRA). This was one of its eleven regional boards and now the only one led by a woman. She later said that her office handled a fifth of all cases brought under the Wagner Act and had the highest percentage of voluntary compliance of any region in the nation.[86]

Herrick's chief goal as NLRB regional director was to help labor and business cooperate, an approach nurtured by her years with the New York Consumers' League. To that end, she tried to get employers to come to the negotiating table without their lawyers, and when they refused to sit down with unionists she shamed them for being thin-skinned. At the same time, she would not allow unions to pursue unsubstantiated claims. In her dealings with the recalcitrant on both sides, she never hesitated to use colorful language. In a long profile for *Harper's Magazine*, journalist Dorothy Dunbar Bromley wrote that Herrick could "swear without sacrificing her dignity," using language that could deflate "any stuffed shirt." "The hell you will," Herrick said, when an employer threatened to bring in the army to get aviation workers to do his bidding. When he said he would report her to President Roosevelt for promoting a strike, she snapped that she could get to the president more easily than he could. "If I yielded to threats from either employers or unions," she told Bromley, "and I have had plenty of them—I should be a jellyfish by this time."[87]

After 1936, Herrick became involved in partisan politics. Labor leader Sidney Hillman, founder and president of the Amalgamated Clothing Workers of America, asked her to join the American Labor Party (ALP) to re-elect President Roosevelt and Governor Lehman. When he agreed to pay her the same salary she was earning at the NLRB, she took a three-month leave from her federal post to work as the party's campaign director. She was thrilled when the party polled a decisive three hundred thousand votes under its own emblem. In high demand as a speaker, she helped the ALP for several more years as a promoter of proportional representation, specific bills, and candidates.[88]

She had a strong late career. During her seven years as a regional director of the NLRB, employer-labor antagonisms and rivalries between the two largest federated unions—the Congress of Industrial Organizations (CIO) and American Federation of Labor—hampered her initiatives to maintain industrial peace. In early 1940, when she protested the NLRB's red tape and delaying tactics that she believed were encouraging strikes, the NLRB investigated her. The CIO accused her of colluding with employers in a union election, threatened her with picketing, and demanded her removal from office. She grew increasingly impatient with unions dominated by Communists who rejected her conciliatory approach.[89]

She held on, resigning only in August 1942, when the huge Todd Shipyards Corporation hired her to integrate women and minorities into its workforce. At Todd she insisted that women workers receive proper training, enjoy nonexploitative conditions, and not be treated as cheap labor or used to lower men's wages. In October she joined an eighteen-woman group appointed by New York State industrial commissioner Frieda Miller to help draft new state laws to assist the growing number of women in war work. The group wanted to influence policy on wage discrimination, protect women from chemicals and radium, standardize work hours, and provide child care and communal meals for factory families. By the following August, in protest against state officials ignoring them, the entire group resigned. After the war Herrick campaigned for women's freedom to keep their industrial jobs. She joined the *Herald-Tribune* as director of personnel and labor relations and as a member of its editorial board.[90]

During Herrick's career in politics and administration, she was often in the thick of contemporary debates over women's social, economic, and political roles. She urged women to ally themselves with an organization or party as an entry to government work, and then once in government to fight to make public policy. Speaking from her own experience, she told them to develop "thick skins" so that they can "take all sorts of knocks." She certainly had had her share.[91]

Like Herrick, Anna Rosenberg also made her name in the labor field, but less as a negotiator than as an organizer and administrator of what was then called "manpower." Her career in politics began early. In 1915, when she was fourteen, she enrolled in Wadleigh High School for Girls at Seventh Avenue and 114th Street in Manhattan. New York suffragists were sure they would be voting come fall. In response, Anna started a political club she called the Coming Voters League. She was still the club's leader when, two years later, some boys at neighboring De Witt Clinton High School threatened to go on strike to protest compulsory military drills, which were lengthening their school day. Speaking at a meeting at the school, Lederer pledged Wadleigh's support to their cause but asked them not to strike. "We will stick with you to the end but for God's sake don't queer things by striking," she pleaded. She brought down the house. Later she led a delegation to the board of aldermen asking for a shorter school day to relieve overcrowded classrooms.[92]

Thus began Anna Rosenberg's career in local politics. She was the second daughter born to Albert Lederer, a furniture manufacturer in Budapest, Hungary, and Charlotte Bacskai, a writer and illustrator of juvenile fiction. After Albert's business failed in 1912, the family immigrated to New York. Anna left school at seventeen to volunteer in the war effort, nursing at a debarkation hospital and then selling Thrift Stamps and Liberty Bonds on a street corner. When the war ended she went back to Budapest to further her education but never took a formal degree. On her return to the United States, in fall 1919 she married Julius Rosenberg, a wholesale rug merchant, with whom she had a son in 1920.[93]

Rosenberg was already involved in party politics. She joined Tammany Hall, where she assisted Anna Kross, then chair of the Women Speakers Bureau (people would later refer to them as "the two Annas"). In the early 1920s she spoke at a meeting of the Seventh AD's Amsterdam Democratic Club about women's political concerns, and when its leader, James J. Hagan, showed no interest, she cried out, "With that attitude it's no wonder you can't carry your district!" Impressed, Hagan made her his protégé. In the early 1920s she managed four local and state political campaigns, work that brought her to the attention of Belle Moskowitz, who asked her to organize a concert to raise funds for charity. "I thought it was a voluntary job and returned the check she sent me," Rosenberg said later. "It came back again with a note saying, 'If your time is worth nothing to you, it's worth nothing to others.'" Acting on this advice, Rosenberg opened a public relations office modeled on Moskowitz's. She arranged events for Jewish philanthropies and managed public relations for firms with southern factories. In a few years, she had an established reputation as an expert in assessing a company's "manpower" and winning labor management cooperation. Years later, this expertise would lead to federal assignments.

A series of political and administrative credits led to that outcome. After running three more local political campaigns, she began climbing the ladder of New Deal agencies in the New York region. She worked first coordinating the Works Progress Administration and then as Nathan Straus Jr.'s chief administrative officer when he became regional director of the National Recovery Administration. Setting up offices in New York, Buffalo, and Albany, she organized the drafting of the state's NRA codes and directed code compliance. When Straus resigned in 1934, she succeeded him as director, becoming the only female regional director in the entire NRA system. At first her staff of four hundred lawyers, investigators, clerks, and stenographers won cooperation between business and labor, but when mediation failed she turned to legal enforcement. Then the Supreme Court struck the NRA down. Businesses ignored her pleas not to abandon fair wage and hour standards. On May 29, 1935, she announced she no longer had the authority to enforce the codes and suspended action on thousands of pending cases.[94]

A succession of government posts followed, so many that she became known as Seven-Job Anna. In 1936 she became regional director of the social security board—again, like Herrick, the only woman to head a regional federal board. She implemented the Social Security Act, interpreted it to the public, and calmed fears about how it worked. One woman was afraid her husband would find out she had lied about her age. A factory worker worried that his boss would learn he had lopped off a few years from his "under forty" job application. A young woman stenographer feared her boss would see she was married and fire her to comply with the 1932 Economy Act, which discouraged hiring government workers' spouses.[95] Rosenberg's staff fielded thousands of similar inquiries an hour. She promised the anxious, "Give your true age and circumstances, and Uncle Sam and I will keep your secret." By 1939, her staff had enrolled close to six million New Yorkers and were maintaining twenty-two field offices.[96]

Rosenberg also accepted assignments from La Guardia, not as an administrator but as adviser. In 1937, he appointed her one of three impartial negotiators for his industrial labor board and named her to his business advisory committee. In 1940 she helped him put off a transit strike, acting as a go-between for La Guardia and John L. Lewis, president of the Congress of Industrial Unions. In 1938, President Roosevelt also enlisted her services. He sent her abroad as one of a nine-member committee to report on employer-employee relations in England and Sweden. When the United States declared war in 1941 he appointed her regional director of the Office of Defense Health and Welfare Services, a post she held for two years as, once again, the only woman among eleven regional directors. He consulted with her frequently, bringing her down to Washington for discussions of public opinion and manpower issues and to help mediate disputes. She became one of his confidants. Telling television journalist Diane Sawyer about her frequent working dinners with FDR, she confessed that, unable to handle the liquor he insisted she drink, she poured it into a rubber plant. Eleanor Roosevelt complained she was ruining her plants.[97]

Rosenberg always had to reconcile her career with her own and others' gender expectations. In a 1935 *New York Times* profile, she said:

> I want to be regarded as a public official. The fact that I am a woman plays no part. The other day some girl interviewer asked me my favorite color, my favorite recipe and a lot of similar foolish questions which had nothing to do with my work. I know my house is run just as efficiently as it would be if I were at home all the time. My boy of 14 is away all day at school, so he is not deprived of much of my time. Moreover, I don't play bridge.[98]

She regretted only that she could not get to movies, theaters, art exhibitions, and concerts and that she had to order her clothes and hats over the phone. The reporter described her as a "slip of a woman" (she was barely over five feet and weighed 115 pounds). He also noted her democratic, friendly manner to all, yet said she could be forceful when necessary and tell a labor man "where to get off."

The rest of Rosenberg's career was at the federal level. Between 1942 and the end of the war Rosenberg directed the War Manpower Commission for the New York region—like Herrick, the only woman among eleven regional directors. In this job she placed agricultural workers on farms, organized child care, found employment for the disabled, and fought union prejudice against black workers. Her most celebrated wartime job was as chief manpower recruiter for the Manhattan Project, which constructed the atomic bomb. Appealing to men "who aren't afraid to do a real man's work," she hired thousands of workers—from electricians, carpenters, and bricklayers to chemists, engineers, and physicists.

During the war President Roosevelt frequently employed her as his emissary, at one point sending her to Europe to ask soldiers what they wanted after the war. She reported on their fears of being so far behind when they got home they would be unable to catch up. According to her, the president said, "Go see Sam Rosenman" (his counsel and speechwriter) and "devise the bill." She claimed that out of that conversation came the GI Bill of Rights, Congress's most important postwar legislation. Providing veterans with educational and financial benefits, the officially titled Servicemen's Readjustment Act of 1944 had actually been long in the works, but Rosenberg's report may have encouraged Roosevelt to advocate for it. After his death she helped President Truman lobby for its passage.[99]

In 1950, George C. Marshall, then Truman's secretary of defense, named Rosenberg an assistant secretary of defense, a first for a woman in that department. Red-baiting marred her confirmation hearing. US senator Herbert Lehman, a close friend who attended the hearings, wept when an accuser stood up, pointed his finger at her, and said he had seen her at Communist meetings. Though exonerated (it was a case of mistaken identity), she found the experience draining. She later said that Marshall insisted she tell him the moment her appointment was confirmed, and when she did he said, "Now go get yourself a facial, you look like hell!"[100] Ever conscious that as a woman in the public eye she had to look her best, she obeyed. Charged with issues of procurement and policymaking in military manpower, Rosenberg remained at the Pentagon for three years. She did not have an easy time there. Calling her Madame Bangles, the brass objected to her "vigorous personal approach," fancy hats, and clanking gold bracelets. She defended her fashion choices as part of her plan to avoid reminding men of some of the "annoying traits of their wives." Financier Bernard Baruch, in his letter of introduction for her to Winston Churchill, wrote, "She has the mind of a man but the warm, brown eyes, and the heart of a woman." He meant it as a compliment, she said, without having any idea of the "male prejudice" it showed.[101]

Rosenberg's career spanned almost the entire twentieth century: from woman suffrage to local New York City politics and a successful public relations business, to a national administrative profile during the New Deal and World War II. Generally forgotten today, in the 1940s and 1950s, next to Eleanor Roosevelt she was the nation's most prominent woman in government and world affairs. She counted herself a feminist and a part of the supportive women's community that had come up through postsuffrage politics and the La Guardia era: both Belle Moskowitz and Anna Kross had mentored her when she was young.

The cliché "a woman in a man's world" is more aptly applied to Anna Rosenberg than to many others among La Guardia's circle of women supporters. She did not spend much time with them. Until Franklin's death, Eleanor Roosevelt was not a close friend. In some ways they competed with one another for the president's attention. Rosenberg told Diane Sawyer that Eleanor "bothered" Franklin with her own agendas. He would be exhausted from working all day and she would come in with some need or story: "Now Franklin, there's a boy. . . ." In contrast, Rosenberg made herself "useful to him." He told her not to go on trips with Eleanor, Caroline O'Day, and the "other women." "You just work with me," he said.[102] And so she had.

How much was the success of these five women—Rankin, Carter, Bolin, Herrick, and Rosenberg—dependent on Mayor La Guardia's patronage? He had promised his supporters to free the city from all the party "men" named to offices regardless of qualifications. His turning to the one group of potential appointees who stood outside that tradition—the city's rising number of experienced, professional women—set him on a path to fulfill that promise. Moreover, a number of these women had helped him win, and later hold on to, his office, and some of them had hoped to be recognized, if not rewarded, for having done so. He was ready to reward them, but only if they demonstrated a level of competence no one could question. Yet he went only so far, withholding from them the top posts many of them knew they deserved. At least he had made a start, one that thrilled the city's women politicians and activists and made them think that more women would advance in the future.

Their advancement did not rest solely on the favor of one man, however. They had made themselves, doggedly pursuing their educations through challenging apprenticeships and taking their knocks along the way. They worked hard, harder than many men had to work to lead similar careers. While differing in upbringing, ethnicity, and life experience, none of these women believed they were entitled to opportunities. They had earned them.

The first election that used proportional representation (PR) to choose the new city council was a mess. Earning ten dollars a day, 1,680 "bi-partisan canvassers" counted the votes in armories across the five boroughs. After three weeks, the counts for the Bronx, Brooklyn, and Queens were still not done. Mayor La Guardia added an hour to the canvassers' daily seven. Using loudspeakers, supervisors urged them to speed up. Some canvassers got fired for arriving late, loafing, or taking bribes. Costs mounted. La Guardia quipped that after the 1939 election "we'll use the world series system. The players get the receipts of the first four days and after that it all goes to the management." No matter how long the job took, canvassers would get only a flat fee.[1]

Two hundred eleven candidates competed for the council's twenty-five seats. Fourteen were women, a number that seems small but contrasted sharply with past elections. In the run-up to the referendum on PR, city women activists had avoided even hinting that the new voting method might improve their chances, but as the nomination deadline neared, more women explored running, indicating a belief that it would. Women with business, professional, voluntary, or political party experience had little difficulty collecting the two thousand signatures from their boroughs required by the nomination process. In the end, five women each from Manhattan and Brooklyn, one from the Bronx, and three from Queens (none entered from Staten Island) made the deadline. A big question remained: could a woman candidate count on women voting for them? They would soon find out, as candidate Genevieve Earle would later comment: "Women do not vote specifically for another woman."[2]

Over the summer of 1937, a few newspapers reported sparingly on women's progress. In naming some women already being talked about as possible candidates, Brooklyn fusionist Marie Frugone said that if women's voluntary associations picked a representative mother, teacher, and businesswoman, the city would have "a mother to guide it, a teacher to teach it, and a business woman to help finance it." Frugone later talked up Margaret Doyle—an employment agency executive, Catholic welfare group activist, and First Assembly District (AD) Women's Democratic Organization vice president. Doyle exemplified the type of woman who ran in 1937—one combining professionalism with voluntary and partisan activism.[3]

In August, Manhattan writer Anabel Parker McCann reported that women's organizations that had worked hard to pass PR were now pressing party leaders to consider eligible women. She highlighted two top possibilities: Amy Wren, Brooklyn Republican and equal rights lawyer, and Helen Knopping, League of Women Voters (LWV) official and Bay Ridge civic worker. She named dozens more with distinguished political résumés. In the fall, columnist Dorothy Dunham Bromley criticized the "liberal" American Labor Party (ALP) for throwing only "a few crumbs" to women. "It was big of the Labor party," she wrote, to nominate three women out of more than sixty nominees for the upcoming constitutional convention. One of the three ALP nominees, Rose Schneiderman, defended her party, writing Bromley that most women, dreading the rigors of a campaign, had declined to put themselves forward. Women would still work hard for a cause, she said, but not for themselves.[4]

A citizens nonpartisan committee chaired by Judge Seabury endorsed only three women: settlement leader and vice president of the city housing authority Mary K. Simkhovitch; Charter Revision Commission member Genevieve B. Earle; and Rachel Nichols Williams, a New York League of Women Voters board member. The Citizens Union and City Affairs Committee endorsed two others—Frances Deutsch, widow of late aldermanic president Bernard S. Deutsch, and attorney Ruth Lewinson, active in women's court reform. Harlem's *New York Age* endorsed Simkhovitch, citing her support for desegregation and the recently opened Harlem River Houses.[5]

As Election Day neared, the press gave women candidates more coverage, but mostly on back pages. Emphasizing their "female qualities" of generosity to others, a *Times* article called Simkhovitch and Earle "ideal types for the job"; it praised them "not only for the keenness of their grasp of municipal problems, but for their altruistic effort on behalf of their constituents, with little regard for conservation of their own time and energy." The city's leading families credited "Mrs. Sim" for advances in middle- and low-income housing, a goal she fostered when few others were interested. Earle's service on the Charter Revision Commission and thirty years of work on public issues received effusive tribute.[6] The article gave thorough coverage, describing every woman who was running, but it appeared on page thirty-nine.

Dorothy Bromley promoted Simkhovitch's candidacy in her column in the *World-Telegram*, writing, "Here in Manhattan I shall vote with special pleasure for Mary K. Simkhovitch, well-known and well-loved head of Greenwich House, whose motto is, 'It is not enough to believe in democracy—you have to live it.'" No one was surprised, Bromley remarked, that Mayor La Guardia and the Seabury nonpartisan committee drafted Simkhovitch, a tireless worker for public housing, to run for the council. "If we can have her and Mrs. Earle," Bromley concluded, "our sex will be ably represented." The *Herald-Tribune* frequently covered feminist issues, thanks to its publisher Helen Rogers Reid, a Women's City Club charter member. The paper publicized the Kings County Republican Committee's formal support for Amy Wren (the only woman the party endorsed) and reviewed her advocacy for women subway workers. In a long piece about women candidates, journalist Emma Bugbee cited PR as encouraging feminists to "dare the ballot." She noted PR's "rosy promises" of increasing the chances of independents (not necessarily women), who though unelectable in a close aldermanic race might win enough votes across a borough to win.[7]

When, at the end of November, the tallies were done, no woman had come near the 75,000 votes required to be declared automatic winners. Genevieve Earle came closest, earning 65,474 votes to win one of Brooklyn's nine seats. Her victory came after canvassers transferred 15,000 votes from fusionist Benjamin F. Butler Jr., a popular African American florist, who had been eliminated near the end. Butler and Earle seemed to have harbored no bad feelings over this outcome. When he ran again in 1939, Earle led an interracial women's nonpartisan committee that worked hard (though in vain) to elect him. As for whether women would vote for women, Earle cautioned her friends not to count on it. No "women's vote" had helped her win, she maintained. Had there been such a vote, "I would have been elected on the first ballot instead of barely getting in."[8]

The 1937 city council election yielded Democrats a slim majority of two, enough to block any legislation. Still, *Times* journalist Warren Moscow thought PR a success: the council now included a "higher class citizen" than had ever been on the old board of aldermen, a greater cross-section of voters now had representation, and PR recognized the growing outer-borough populations. PR supporters were generally pleased. Before 1937, Tammany Democrats had won sixty-two of sixty-five aldermanic seats, often by only a handful of votes. This time, laborites had elected five of their seven pro–New Deal candidates, and fusionists and Republicans gained eight seats and put Republican Newbold Morris in as council president (the body's twenty-sixth member). A few African Americans and one self-identified Communist ran in 1937, but none won. By the time that changed, so had the political climate, and the prospects for PR remaining the council's voting system dimmed.[9]

"Everyone" was surprised she had won, Genevieve Earle claimed. In retrospect, she was the only woman who could have won. Her three decades in suffrage, municipal reform, state government reorganization, and philanthropy, especially giving aid to child polio victims, had solidified her reputation as a generous and capable civic activist. During the Depression she organized Brooklyn women block by block to help at least one unemployed neighbor and raised over $100,000 for the Brooklyn Emergency Unemployment Relief Commission. Many news articles elaborated on this long record of service.

In January 1937 the Downtown Brooklyn Association awarded Earle a gold medal for her civic work, the first it had ever given to a woman. Its citation began with general praise for "her trained ability, her initiative, her sanity of mind, her courage and forcefulness." It continued:

> It was particularly fortunate, upon her appointment by the Mayor to serve upon the Charter Revision Committee of the City of New York, that her entry into this work found her solidly qualified by study, active and practical experience and qualities both of temperament and of mind which enable her to make a most important contribution to the work of that Commission.... [She] brought to the discussions an understanding of the people's needs and aspirations which was invaluable.... She showed that rare quality of judgment which, striving for the highest objectives in the public interest, could, nevertheless with infinite common sense and understanding quickly grasp the difficulties of each problem and objectively reach a sound conclusion after sympathetic hearing and consideration of the views of others.[10]

Earle gave a gracious response, in which she said the award affirmed women's roles in community life and then invited women to "take a walk from the kitchen and nursery to the public forum" where they can contribute to the solution of the problems facing the city. Brooklyn borough president Raymond V. Ingersoll recognized her service to Kings County by calling her "Queen of Kings." Though he had been ill, Mayor La Guardia surprised Earle by attending the award ceremony. In his speech he spoke positively of working not only with her but also with women in general. "Women are valuable workers," he avowed, invoking the stereotypes that women were "less selfish, less ambitious and will always respect a confidence." The mayor's encomium permanently endeared him to her.[11]

After this ceremony, the press covered her advocacy of women's jury service, PR, the federal child labor amendment, La Guardia's re-election, and government support for welfare and culture. She received more attention when La Guardia appointed her to the committee on city planning, which under the new charter would become the city planning commission.[12] Many of the other thirteen women running for the council in 1937 had constructed impressive résumés, but Earle's stood out.

Some unconventional aspects of her lifestyle also made her stand out. Of medium height, with a high forehead, broad jaw, and muscular figure, she often referred to herself as "older than the Brooklyn Bridge and in much better condition." She spoke in a low-pitched, "cultivated" voice, which many found soothing. As fashionable as the city's first alderwoman Ruth Baker Pratt had been, Genevieve Earle was the opposite. She wore only comfortable clothes, favoring a slouch hat and low heels. Pastels? Hated them. She disliked the label "politician," preferring "sportswoman." From youth onward, she had loved tennis, swimming, and golf. For recreation, she and her husband fished, sailed, and tramped over fields flushing pheasants (without guns). They owned two eighteen-foot sailboats and, on a whim, when they needed to get their daughter and her friends to the beach, bought an old thirty-foot oyster "lugger" they called "Gen's Wild Oat." The press (and her neighbors around their summer home in Bellport, Long Island) loved this story, as she had paid too much for it and was a terrible sailor. The Earles had also endured tragedy. On November 29, 1935, the day their son turned nineteen, he was struck and killed by an automobile at an unlit Manhattan intersection.[13]

Earle was ambivalent about partisan politics. As late as January 1937, months before she declared for the council, she told a reporter that, unlike other suffragists, she had never joined a political club nor sought a political job; furthermore, she did not want one. She had run because people she respected had pressured her. Ray Ingersoll was the first. In the summer he called her up in Bellport. "Gen,"— nobody ever called her "Genevieve," she said—"[y]ou worked hard for P.R. You believe in it. You ought to go out now and take some of your own medicine that you prescribed for this city and show that you think it's good." She answered, "Raymond, I wouldn't think of it. I *never* would think of running for public office. I'm not interested." Ingersoll persisted, offering to drive the seventy miles out to Bellport to press his case. Not wanting to impose such a trip on a busy official, she drove to his office, where he told her not only Mayor La Guardia but also the charter revision commissioners wanted her to run. "They wanted the new Charter in the hands of its friends," Ingersoll said. In the end she accepted the challenge, interested to see what a woman and an independent could do under the new system.[14]

Looking back on her political career years later, Earle said that without PR she would not have won. For her, politics was not a career opportunity. She saw city government not as a locus of personal power but as "our greatest social service organization." Only someone grounded in social welfare activism would have held such a view, a point made by a *Post* columnist, who noticed that many politicians running in 1937 had backgrounds in social or settlement work. Including both Earle and Simkhovitch in his list, he attributed the phenomenon to the Depression, which had made these candidates see they were merely dressing wounds instead of going to the "source of the infection."[15]

Earle's political principles were rooted in progressive feminism. Before La Guardia's election in 1933, she had decried the elimination of women's and children's social services that had taken decades to build. Why, she asked, cut summer playground supervisors while leaving eleven board of estimate sergeants-at-arms at $22,000 a year? She charged that our leaders, "with blind, wife-beating anger, strike out at the defenseless, forward-looking services of government." It is as if they are crying, "Women and children first! They can't strike back!" When asked to comment on recent attempts to remove married women from the job force, she replied,

> Just as I believe that democracy is incomplete without women voting, so I believe that married women are people and should have a right to work for wages without any qualification whatever. The desire to limit work to single women . . . would turn back the progress of women for which both men and women have worked for hundreds of years.[16]

When she ran for re-election in 1939, she stated, "I am not primarily working from a woman's point of view, though I do believe there is such a thing in politics, and that it is useful." She pointed out that a woman is more aware than anyone of the declining value of the dollar. When she ran for re-election in 1941, she promised more services for women consumers.[17]

When reporters asked if she felt disadvantaged as the sole woman among men on political bodies, she confessed that the status got her publicity that even the most distinguished men could not. As a result, she never had to raise a large campaign fund. Moreover, she boasted, she was the only new council member photographed being sworn in by Mayor La Guardia. She was, however, tired of the title of sole woman and was amazed at how, after her victory, the press wanted to know only about her domestic skills. Once in office, she insisted on being called "Councilman," saying, "there was no question of sex" in her work. When told the proper dress for councilmen marching in the Saint Patrick's Day Parade was a cutaway coat with striped pants and a high silk hat (spats optional), she went along, though spats were the only part of the costume she owned. She worried about doing something that reflected badly on women in general. La Guardia had rubbed the point in. "Now remember, Genevieve," she recalled him saying to her. "Women are new in politics, and they have to learn to take it on the chin. When one woman fails, all women fail. Their success will be measured by your success. So watch your step."[18] She took his advice seriously, in her early time on the council making sure she was carefully briefed on everything she said.

Over time she became more self-confident, but at the start of her political career she felt burdened by having to represent her sex, a dilemma common to women tokens of public visibility.

Though Earle had not always supported La Guardia (in 1929 she had voted for Socialist Norman Thomas), by 1937 she was an avid fan. She admired, first, his appointments of dozens of women into important government posts and judgeships. Suggesting voters go to Rebecca Rankin's book *New York Advancing* to find documentation of the many reasons to re-elect him, she cited his record of "non-partisan, non-plunder administration," which for the first time in years had given good government to New York City. As a person she found him "incorruptible, vigorous, and humane . . . tender-hearted toward the weak and unfortunate . . . while hard-hearted toward the wrong-doer and grafter."[19] As the years passed she became more critical of him, but at this point she was unquestioningly loyal.

As her 1937 campaign progressed, she announced her policy goals. The need to reform the city's pension system was originally at the top of her list. She would not get any further on that score than her friend Pearl Bernstein, board of estimate secretary, had. County reorganization was, in her view, an even more urgent goal, as paying the salaries of "obsolete" county sinecures cost taxpayers money they could ill afford. Some of her other causes came out of consumer issues often associated with a woman's perspective: improving the grading of meats, regulating the weight of bread, and winning food and drug protections. In the interests of city beautification, she agreed with Parks Commissioner Robert Moses on limiting the number of "disfiguring billboards," and she hoped to modify the city's traffic rules, a cause linked to her son's untimely death in a Manhattan intersection.

Brooklyn women fusionists persuaded Earle to take up another cause: preventing the harassment of women and children on subways. Writer Oliver R. Pilat reacted derisively to this initiative, publishing a piece about a "score of petticoat-politicos" listening to Brooklyn fusion cochair Ellen Agnes Olson propose such an ordinance and asking women to tell their husbands to vote for whomever they want for first choice as long as they voted for Earle for second. Then Pilat joked about how "sexual degeneracy on the subways" was women's top issue. Earle soon realized she had to support the initiative, and though it never became one of her top causes in 1949, she urged the city to double the number of transit police to address rising rates of subway sex crimes and muggings.[20]

Women flocked to support Earle. Recalling her work for suffrage and her "many good causes," long-time Republican Party worker Rebecca C. Talbot-Perkins spoke up for her, even though her party had not endorsed her. Writing in the *World-Telegram*, Dorothy Bromley said she wished she lived in Brooklyn so she could vote for Earle. Earle always took an objective approach to good government, Bromley wrote. She wanted the job not because she liked to feel important but because she wanted to help implement the charter she helped prepare and "save it from the Tammany boys who would change it."[21]

The campaign exhausted Earle. She took all speaking opportunities, attending meetings of ten or five hundred. She covered the borough in a battered Ford, mostly alone, though at night her husband went too. She worked harder for her own campaign than she ever had for anything except the charter, in part to disprove Rose Schneiderman's claim that women "never went into a thing for their own selves as hard as they went in for other causes." No other woman candidate worked as hard as she did, she thought, and most of them lacked knowledge of either the charter or city government (a charge she applied to some men too).[22]

She got through the campaign because, she said, "I was a strong, vigorous person" who had never been ill and "could bounce up in the morning feeling fine." As the 1937 count dragged on, she got tired of visiting the armory every day and went down to Virginia, to visit friends and play golf and tennis. The night before the count was completed her husband called her recommending that she rush home, as she was going to win. She hurried back. Reporters greeted her on her front stoop, wanting to know all about her home life. "Can you sew?" "I can't sew at all," she answered. "Can you cook?" "Not a lick." To satisfy them, she retrieved a damask napkin from the dining room and took them into her library, where she pretended to dust the top of a book.[23]

At a Women's City Club luncheon honoring her election, Earle promised to remain an independent. She prepared hard for the job, rereading the new city charter, as well as old board of aldermen minutes. Explaining why she got to city hall early every day, she told journalist Bromley, "You've got to be forewarned and armed. [T]here's sniping and sharp-shooting at every session." Earle promised to keep at this punishing schedule, but confessed it exhausted her.[24]

She proved her resilience by shouldering leadership in the fight for county government reform. Long a central issue for municipal reformers, including the League of Women Voters, county reorganization had passed in a 1935 state constitutional amendment by a three-to-one margin. The amendment eliminated the posts of sheriff, register, commissioner of records, public administrator, and commissioner of jurors, but left the implementation to the board of aldermen, which ignored the mandate. Party men objected to the loss of posts central to their revenue streams and patronage. Over the next two years Mayor La Guardia's efforts to force the board to act got nowhere.[25]

The council's first meetings in January 1938 addressed the issue anew. Earle put herself into a toxic vortex by proposing cutting the five county posts, claiming the cuts would save the city $2.4 million in salaries. Disputing this figure, the Democratic leadership kept her bills locked in committee for the rest of the year.

In early December, Mayor La Guardia chastised the council for inaction. He told them that not only constitutional duty but also current economic conditions required action. A few days later, Earle rebuked her colleagues for accomplishing so little. During their first year they had passed ninety-eight bills, sixty-one of which were street name changes at a cost of $5,000 each. "The mountain has labored and brought forth a lot of little mice," she remarked.[26]

Her bills finally came up for debate on December 20. The council brawled for almost twenty hours overnight before defeating them seventeen to nine. The press made much of Earle's absorption in the fray—so much that she forgot to phone her husband to tell him she would not be home. Worried about her, at 5:00 a.m. he called the police. "If a man stays out all night, no one is concerned," Earle remarked; "if a woman . . . then it's 'news.'" Her frantic mate spoke admiringly of his wife's ability to stay up all night, predicting, "She'll probably stay up until Christmas Eve."[27]

As the fight went on, Earle remained at its forefront. In 1940 the council's minority of two Republicans, one fusionist, and two American Labor Party members took advantage of her absence to elect her minority leader, a post she called "thankless." Still, being elected to it made her a rare (if not unique) woman to hold such a rank in any legislative body. It also gave her a bully pulpit for promoting county reorganization. Backing off from cutting five posts, now she focused only on those of sheriff, register, and commissioner of records, all "obsolescent" and, if eliminated, saving the city $501,929. When the chair of the council's Committee on General Welfare pressed her to prove this claim, she produced a thirty-two-page memorandum she released to the press. "At no other time in the history of this nation," her memo concluded, referring to the present world crisis, has it been so important to assure "our fellow citizens that their government units are being . . . operated at a maximum degree of efficiency and with a minimum waste of public funds." The council's response was to file a counter bill that, under the guise of reorganization, essentially preserved the posts she was trying to abolish. La Guardia said he would not sign it.[28]

Despairing of council action, Earle eventually helped form a citizens nonpartisan committee to campaign for a referendum to implement county reorganization. Headed by Thomas D. Thacher, former chair of the Charter Revision Commission, the committee collected eighty thousand signatures on the necessary petitions (Mayor La Guardia signed the first one). The committee then mounted a publicity campaign to get it passed, putting out a flyer with political cartoons that showed how the money saved would fund medical care and housing. Paul Blanshard of the city affairs committee targeted the sheriff's post with a jingle:

The Sheriff is a man with feet
Who sits upon the county seat.
If we should take his desk away,
His feet would have no place to stay.

Former governor Smith, who had once held the post, derided it as "finished." If it had not been for the war, he admitted, "I would have had nothing to do." Calling county government archaic, Governor Lehman said it forces taxpayers "to bear an unjustified burden." In November, the referendum passed overwhelmingly, which the press credited to Earle's perseverance.[29]

Procedural and eligibility issues dominated the council's early months. Members debated endlessly where they would sit and how. Earle did not want the members to sit according to party label; she lost on this point. Questions about the legal residencies of three councilmen led to a "long-winded, grotesque investigation. It was really like a musical comedy of the roughest kind," she recalled. For a while council sessions were broadcast over the city's radio station, WNYC. She remembered the speeches were interminable but they kept the public informed.

The women of the city had people in their homes for coffee at two o'clock on Tuesdays. They'd bring their knitting and their sewing, and spend the afternoons in each other's houses, listening to the radio. The Democrats didn't like that because, you see, the general public got the idea that they were pushing us around—which they were.[30]

Franklin Pierce Adams, writing in his *Post* column "The Conning Tower," said that Earle sent him the following quatrain written by a young Brooklyn woman in response to the broadcasts:

The gentlemen of Tammany
Would make me blush to be a he;
But Mrs. Genevieve B. Earle
Fills me with pride that I'm a girl.

At the bottom, Earle had penned her own response:

Let each Tammany he in the Council
Use his Brain instead of his tounsil.[31]

In the fall of 1939 a poll revealed that approximately a million listeners liked the minority more than the majority. Some citizens found the proceedings so amusing they went down to city hall to watch. This was too much for the Democrats. In early 1940 the majority leader argued that the broadcasts should end, as in these "critical times" (a reference to the European war) some council member might say something offensive to our European friends or embarrassing to the US government. Though she found this argument ludicrous, Earle was powerless to stop the majority leader from ordering the radio station to take the microphones out. "It was a great loss to the city," Earle said.[32]

She often despaired about the council's conduct of its business. She told a writer for the *Christian Science Monitor* that in 1939 the majority set aside important consumer protection bills to pass a bill requiring standardized whiskey glasses at bars "for the protection of drinkers." At the last meeting in October, shortly after the start of a new European-wide war, they left fifty or more important bills undiscussed. They did pass three resolutions: asking the board of estimate to erect a child health station in Brooklyn, requesting all city buildings to display an American flag, and congratulating the Boy Rangers of America on their activities. Earle reported that this last resolution crushed her spirit.

Free speech and academic freedom were two other issues that concerned Earle. In the spring of 1940 the City College of New York invited the British philosopher Bertrand Russell, who had been teaching in California, to be a visiting professor. Members of the clergy exploded, calling Russell's approval of premarital sex and adultery "morally bankrupt" and demanding the appointment be canceled. Ordway Tead, president of the board of higher education, asked Earle and her colleague Robert K. Straus to seek La Guardia's support, but the mayor, loath to anger the city's clergy, declined. An unpleasant debate ensued. Earle appealed to council members to guard academic freedom as zealously as freedom of speech, religion, and assembly, and said the council had no right to pass upon academic questions. Her argument failed. The council voted sixteen to five to rescind Russell's appointment, a vote then affirmed by a state supreme court judge. Despite widespread student and faculty protests, the mayor cut the position from the department's budget and Russell never taught at City College.[33] He did teach that fall at Harvard and went on to a distinguished career that culminated in the Nobel Prize for Literature in 1950.

Earle would go on to win four more council elections (until 1945, terms were only two years). She served a total of twelve years, and in general got along with her council colleagues. Though she voted for Democrats Roosevelt, Lehman, and Smith, she acted with total independence. She told Democrats she abhorred their record of corruption and told Republicans they were weak. She considered most minority members, including those of the American Labor Party, ignorant about government. More interested in improving labor conditions, ALP members wanted good government but had no idea how to get it. Floor debates, she recalled, were meaningless. Everything was settled in committee beforehand, and even had she been eloquent (which, she said, she was not), her speeches would not have changed minds.

According to Earle, by 1940 the council had become the "most disorderly and undignified legislative body in the country." She tried to mediate, a role she felt suited her as a woman. While the men riled one another with sarcasm, she used a quiet voice to make everyone lean forward to hear her. She tried to make her remarks constructive. In her view, one reason the council worked so poorly was its functional reliance on Albany; another was the conflict among a central city government, five borough governments, and five county governments. This conflict had motivated her to fight for county reorganization, but not even the full minority had supported her.[34]

As minority leader, Earle hired a bright young African American woman, Emily V. Gibbs, as her secretary, an appointment that gave her credit in the city's black community. She herself paid for the services of attorney Amelia Lewis as her legislative assistant. Lewis researched every proposed law to determine its need, enforceability, and cost. The minority usually sat down together to work out a common strategy, but in 1941 the council's first Communist, Brooklyn's Peter Cacchione, won election, and after that two or three "reactionary Republicans," as she termed them, refused to sit in the same room with him. At that point, she recalled, "The Minority jumped on horseback and went off in all directions!" When the second Communist, Harlem's Benjamin Davis, came in, both he and Cacchione cooperated with her, but whenever they disagreed with anyone they called them Fascists, just as Democrats and Republicans called anyone they disagreed with Communists. She gave up introducing bills and instead did her best to improve the quality of the bills proposed by the majority.[35]

In late December 1943, when fusionists were becoming increasingly impatient with La Guardia's dictatorial and inattentive governing style, Earle defended him, taking exception to Brooklyn Democrat Walter R. Hart's investigation of alleged ethical lapses in the sanitation department. She maintained friendly relations with La Guardia, although at times she found him difficult. "He was quick, too quick for me. His mind circled around mine. . . . He assumed I knew about things on which he had all the information. I'd get these *ex-cathedra* statements from him and I'd have to rush back to my office, not wanting to stand there all day arguing with him."

Like everyone else, she wasted time waiting for appointments with him, as he was so busy. Above all she admired his boundless energy and broad abilities. "He had his faults," she recalled, "but he was a dynamo. He interfered with the heads of his departments. He played every instrument in the band." She remained loyal to him to the end.[36]

Earle also remained loyal to PR. She believed it brought distinguished members to the council, including people associated with nonpartisan, nonreligious community causes. She thought the Democrats who had been on the old board of aldermen were the best of that body, as they had political experience. The newer members were more loyal to party than to fairness. They would introduce resolutions and bills they had no hope of passing, merely to get attention. Throughout, everyone was nice to her. On her wedding anniversary, the men from both sides got up to congratulate her. She told them she wished they would skip the flowery language and instead send her a few good votes. They never did.

In July 1940 Earle's husband died after a short illness. Though she subsequently suffered from neuritis, a condition that severely depressed this woman who once said she had never been ill, she ran for re-election and served as minority leader until the defeat of PR in 1947. At that point, convinced her chances of re-election were nil, she retired. She died in 1956 in a fire in her Bellport bedroom, caused by smoking in bed, a heart attack, or both. She was seventy-two.[37]

When Earle looked back on her legislative career, she said she did not feel she had done much. The Democratic majority had seen to that. But this was a self-assessment typical of many women in public life during this era, including, for example, Belle Moskowitz, who subordinated her own importance to the man whose career she had served, Al Smith. As a role model for how women in civic life might contribute to the community's well-being, however, there is no doubt that Earle had made an impact. Her mere presence on the council—her political independence, outspokenness, and conscientious preparation—advanced the interests of all women then seeking public roles. In congratulating her on her gold medal from the Brooklyn Downtown Association, Cleveland Rodgers, editor of the *Eagle*, had told her she underestimated her influence on others, including his college-aged daughter who he knew would be inspired by her story. Columnist John A. Heffernan called her "Fusion Joan of Arc." Distinguished attorney Charles Culp Burlingham called her a veritable "Gibralter." "You have stood so firm and strong for the right and the sensible amid the wild waves of the Council," he wrote her.[38]

Her death brought many more encomia. The *Times* singled out for praise her efforts to improve parks, playgrounds, schools, and housing, and bring about comprehensive child-care programs, meat grading and standard loaves of bread, rent control, and racial cooperation. Citing the clarity and humanitarianism of her philosophy of government, the *Herald Tribune* mourned the loss of "one of its most valued civic leaders." In response, three women wrote a joint letter saying that Earle had inspired many women in the 1930s to take personal responsibility for civic action. Declaring they owed much to her "vigor and imagination" and citing her devotion to progressive goals, they named her a pioneer of twentieth-century women's political effectiveness. A year after Earle's death, Brooklyn civic and club leader Seth S. Faison called for a return to proportional representation, in part because the system had given the city good legislators, like Genevieve Earle, "a most forceful and effective legislator, a lady of such courage and integrity that she was both feared and admired by her opponents." Joining Faison in a call for a return to PR in 1958, Stanley Isaacs, who had succeeded Earle as minority leader, called her the council's "most distinguished member."[39] Despite her own self-denigration, then, Earle had left a strong legacy.

Genevieve Earle never thought of herself as having (or wanting) a political career. Not so Anna Kross. Convinced she would rise both politically and professionally, after suffrage she joined Tammany Hall where she headed its Women Speakers Bureau. A year later she became the city's first female assistant corporation counsel, a post she held for five years before going into private practice. On the last day of 1933, Tammany mayor John P. O'Brien appointed her the city's third woman magistrate.

For Kross, this was not enough. In 1938, after four years on the bench, she announced a run for a vacancy on the state supreme court, where no woman had yet sat. To win, she had to hazard her first electoral campaign. As a nod from Tammany was tantamount to election, she courted the machine first, but by the late 1930s her ties to it were stale. She had undertaken her crusade against the women's court without getting the consent of Tammany's boss Charles Francis Murphy, an error for which she lost her headship of the Women Speakers Bureau. Moreover, as a magistrate she had had to stop her partisan political activity. Finally, she was female and Jewish. As her campaign developed, she came to believe that those two identities limited her electoral prospects.[40]

Kross began her campaign in the summer by turning first to her women's network. One member was writer Zelda Popkin, with whom she had worked on women's court reform. She asked Popkin if she would prepare radio scripts for her and whether she would recommend Pauline Sabin, the formidable head of the repeal movement and a Republican leader, to chair a woman's committee "if one can get her." Her campaign theme would be "the challenge to American womanhood to utilize their suffrage for the preservation and protection of democracy." She would also argue that in a time when Fascism and anti–New Deal reactions were on the rise, the presence of professionally trained women in high official positions, especially elective ones, was critical. To her, the most important of these were judicial posts, as they can interpret and preserve a liberal viewpoint toward the law.[41] It seems doubtful Tammany's sachems would have found such a nonpartisan and female-centered approach a reason to support her.

Kross formally launched her candidacy at the end of August. Helen Rogers Reid of the *Herald-Tribune* helped with an editorial that named Kross as an obvious possibility for the supreme court, saying she was well known

> for the intelligence and energy with which she has addressed herself to the basic problems of the legal treatment of vice, and for the considerable improvements which, in conjunction with Mayor La Guardia, she has helped to effect in the Women's Court procedure.[42]

Reid assigned political writer Denis Tilden Lynch to compose a long follow-up. He began by noting the New York Women's Bar Association's resolution that the state should follow other states' lead and put women on supreme courts. Although the association did not name a particular candidate, Lynch reported that Kross's advocates—who included former suffragists, court and slum reformers, and trade unionists—were urging Tammany to nominate her. Lynch went on to cite Kross's accomplishments, both political and legal, highlighting her fifteen years as vice chair of the speakers bureau and service in the lower courts. In thanking Reid for her personal interest in her candidacy, Kross called her "a shining example of what women can do for one another and for a cause in which they both believe."[43]

In September Kross's friends formed a thousand-person sponsoring committee. Kross opened her first headquarters at the Hotel Commodore on September 10. Two weeks later, before a hundred Harlem men and women leaders in welfare, professional, religious, and civic life, she opened a second at 2260 Seventh Avenue. Harlem welfare workers admired Kross's rehabilitation work with African American prostitutes. Maud Smith, writing Kross on behalf of Nineteenth AD coleader Jeanne Wells, told her that Harlem women were elated over the news of her candidacy and that thousands of men and women believed her record would easily elevate her to the court seat she sought. Assembly candidate Eugene McIntosh, a Democrat who had bolted from Tammany over its segregationist policies, also offered a hand, praising Kross for her understanding of social problems. Many Harlem ministers, including Father Divine, the controversial Harlem religious and civil rights leader, invited her to address their congregations. To a query from Harlem Baptist minister Daniel L. Reed about giving "a square deal" to the Negro, she replied: "Bigotry and race prejudice have no place in either my public or private life. Moreover, I have consistently worked for the improvement of economic and social conditions in Harlem, and in this work have enjoyed the splendid cooperation of members of your race." She assured him that "the colored people know me as a sincere friend."[44]

The *National Negro News* cited another reason to support Kross: her desire to break through prejudice against women in higher judicial office. "The people of Harlem know what prejudice is," the *News* editorialized. "They know it from bitter experience. The prejudice against the Negro people not only here, but else-where in the United States, has been of all, the ugliest blot on American democracy." Her sympathetic treatment of card players arrested for gambling also won Harlem's appreciation. In one case in 1936, she denounced "snooping" policemen for raiding private card games, telling them to track down "real criminals" and discharging the defendants. In another she rebuked police for raiding a private apartment without a warrant and arresting eleven women for "maintaining a gambling establishment." "Since when is it a crime to play poker?" she asked. "I don't know the game, but I do know that it is no crime to play it." In yet another case, card players arrested at their club told the "flatfeet" they were law-abiding members just having a friendly game. "Now I ain't a man what puts much faith in women," one of the defendants said about coming before Judge Kross in the morning. "They're liable to be too prissy in matters like these. And I didn't feel no better by a long sight when she listens very quietly to these cops' lies about public gambling and all that junk." After listening, however, Kross said, "Officer, when you get around to raiding the Union League Club downtown or any of those clubs where rich men hang out and haul them into court, I'll consider pun-ishing these boys. Case dismissed." The alleged gamblers were now reported to be working for her election.[45]

Women's organizations were unsure about endorsing Kross. Citing the entry of other women into the race for the supreme court, they argued that endorsing Kross would divide the woman's vote. Still, the Democratic Junior League (Eleanor Roosevelt, Edith Lehman, Caroline O'Day, and Frances Perkins were members), the New York Women's Bar Association, and the National Association of Women Lawyers (Kross had been a founder) endorsed her. Other women's groups held back. Lena Madesin Phillips, president of the International Federation of Business and Professional Women, declined on the ground that she had heard that another federation member planned to run. The American Woman's Association refused Kross's request to use its facilities, saying it did not want to give the impression of an endorsement. "I fully understand your posi-tion," an angry Kross snapped, "although, very frankly, I think the American Woman's Association ought to be the logical forum for women of all groups and it is high time that *women* stop eschewing politics."[46]

When Tammany district leaders endorsed two other women attorneys for the supreme court—Ruth Lewinson and Julia M. van Dernoot, both with long records of professional and civic accomplishment—Kross was not worried. She told Constance Sporborg, club leader and long-time friend, "the more women who are in the race now the better my chances. That's what I stated in the begin-ning and the more that appear the more encouraged I feel because my idea of a woman has finally permeated." Still, she thought her qualifications set her ahead of any other woman. She wrote Sporborg, "candidly, what we want to impress is not that I am a woman but I have the qualifications that entitle me to consideration" by all political parties. Ironically, a few days later Kross wrote to former license commissioner Dorothy Kenyon thanking her for her "gracious" gesture in declining the American Labor Party's nomination for the Supreme Court. "I have been informed that you did this because you were aware that I planned to campaign . . . as an independent candidate, sponsored by the Women of New York City, and you did not wish to see two women opposed to one another for this office." Apparently seeing no inconsistency, she heaped praise on Kenyon for her unselfish devotion to "progress and good government."[47]

As Kross honed her platform she emphasized two points: that the judiciary should be divorced from politics, and only the candidate's qualifications, "irrespective of political affiliations, race, color or sex, should be the criterion." When Kross used the term "race" she sometimes meant the Jewish "race." As her campaign progressed, the rise of anti-Semitism and the myth of Nordic-Aryan superiority worried her more than gender prejudice. She came to believe that her being Jewish led to her difficulty getting editorial comment. She wrote writer Janet Mabie, whom she asked to help her contact editors, that some newspaper publishers were "anti-semites of the worst order." To run as an independent, she told Mabie, she would have to rely on women to support her.

Women, though, were another worry. She wondered if women could be roused from their lethargy and be interested enough in suffrage to exercise it. She continued to send appeals to former suffrage colleagues, writing to one that "I am trying somehow to find the formula to reawaken the enthusiasm and spirit of those early days." The task was hard, but she was continuing in the spirit of Mary Garrett Hay and Anna Shaw, New York and national woman suffrage leaders, and hoped "to be daunted by nothing but *carry on*. That spirit brought success. Maybe I too would succeed."

The endorsements she received came from varied sources. A Republican county committeeman from Larchmont, William Harvey Smith, tried to get his committee to endorse her. He wrote that he had never seen such "a combination of intelligence, regard for legal precedent, and sound common sense . . . on the Magistrate's Bench, and all too infrequently on the Supreme Court Bench," adding in a personal note that she was "exquisitely feminine and lovely" too. Eventually the American Labor Party and the City Progressive Party endorsed her (neither party had nominated her, however), and she ran under their labels.

When the Association of the Bar of the City of New York declined to endorse her, Professor I. Maurice Wormser of Fordham University Law School deplored the "narrow-mindedness, chauvinism and pettiness of viewpoint which deny such judicial position to a woman." Alfred A. Cook, chairman of the bar association's judiciary committee, had said to Kross's face that he opposed both women lawyers and women judges. She hit back, calling his views as more than "a repudiation of an individual. It is a complete public revelation of antediluvian prejudice against women in public office." Cook's statement goaded Carrie Chapman Catt and other Democratic, Republican, and independent women leaders to say they were ready to fight for woman suffrage all over again. It also led Mayor La Guardia to endorse Kross and make public appearances on her behalf, actions he rarely undertook for candidates. Calling on New Yorkers to work for her election, he noted that she "has not crawled and cringed and begged for a nomination" and praised her "vision and courage."[48] Though La Guardia and Kross had disagreed on some issues, he remained in her camp.

As her race neared its end, Kross pressed hard to get more energetic support from women. In late October she appealed to the New York City Federation of Women's Clubs to recognize the relationship of her campaign to suffrage. "What originally was a candidacy of an individual woman for recognition in this office, has now become a crusade on the part of many women who fought vigorously for Suffrage and recognition for women," she wrote the president. She complained that both city and county bar associations had said that, while she had demonstrated ability in her work, she lacked the necessary legal training. "It is obvious that this statement is a subterfuge concealing the last ditch prejudice against women on the bench," she told National Woman's Party activist and president of the National Association of Women Lawyers Laura Berrien, whom she asked to get statements from other women judges who had faced similar jibes. Mary O'Toole, a former Washington, DC-area judge, recalled a male judge of the DC Supreme Court saying to her that "having a petticoat on any Bench made their positions ridiculous."[49]

In the final days of the campaign, Kross's supporters pulled out all the stops. On November 3 they mounted a motorcade for her with banners and a band. It started at First Avenue and 42nd Street, went down to the Lower East Side, up to Park Avenue and 42nd, over to Broadway, up to 181st (where it met up with a Bronx motorcade), and then through the Bronx.

A few days later a two-page illustrated spread on Kross by Emma Bugbee appeared in the *Herald-Tribune Sunday Magazine*. Bugbee's piece noted that Kross was sometimes called an "East Side Cinderella." "No fairy godmother waved a wand for her," Bugbee corrected. "No fabulous prince placed her on a throne. No clock striking twelve found her wasting time at a royal ball. She was always studying at midnight." Bugbee went on with stories from Kross's career, emphasizing how her lifelong defense of women offenders had gotten her into trouble with Tammany, which had never regarded her as a thoroughly regular

Democrat and sometimes had criticized her for not being sufficiently loyal to the organization. Bugbee portrayed Kross as fighting bias against women lawyers and judges and running to keep "the feminist torch aflame." After reminding readers of one of Kross's favorite sayings—that women in public life must be "one hundred per cent better than their colleagues and satisfied with fifty per cent of the credit," she ended with Kross's view that, because women's experiences often differed from men's, the future of the judicial system in a democracy required their perspectives.[50]

Neither motorcade nor press coverage helped. Tammany's two male candidates (Kross called one of them a "hack") won handily. Kross came in fifth of six candidates, with 229,784 votes. She had never been ashamed of her relationship to Tammany. Many of her closest male politician friends—Al Smith, Robert Wagner Sr., and Herbert Lehman—had all reckoned with Tammany at some point in their careers, and so had she. She now thought Tammany was no longer what it once was, as "big business men" had corrupted it, a theme she had emphasized since she first went on the bench in 1934.[51]

Kross received many notes of sympathy for her loss. The ones from women were the most moving, as they showed what her attempt had meant to them. Fay S. Paul wrote that, "as a result of my association with you," she planned "to be more attentive to governmental problems, particularly where women are affected." Others praised her "noble effort" and brilliant showing in the face of organized party machines. Most important, they said she had encouraged other women to enter races in the future. Kross told Judge O'Toole, "all my friends are unanimously of the opinion that I have made the first dent and that the possibilities for a woman on our New York State Supreme Court bench are not remote. We are going to continue the fight and it is comforting to know that the women have finally realized that they must fight to obtain recognition." She continued her letter to O'Toole by commenting that men with blatant biases against women in the law, such as Alfred Cook, "may have the satisfaction of having helped to keep a woman from the Supreme Court [but] I am confident that he will derive very little satisfaction from the results of the election since he helped to elect a male he knew wasn't fit to be on the bench."[52]

Perhaps to console herself, Kross put her defeat into the even larger context of its meaning for democracy. She mourned the "general defeat of progressive and liberal thought all over the world," calling it "a most discomforting and disquieting situation." The remarks of Ohio judge Florence Allen, the first woman elected to a state supreme court, kept coming back to her—that civilization is about to "sink in the morass of darkness." Once again, in Kross's view, women were her only hope. To writer Fannie Hurst, one of her keenest supporters, she said,

The world needs them so badly today. . . . Individually they are so grand and so willing. Is there no way? The whole picture is so dark today that it is frightening. . . . In my mind, the future of civilization today lies in the hands of women. That is why I feel we must seek and keep on seeking the way and manner in which they can be made to cooperate and be effective."[53]

In December 1938, the New York Women's Bar Association (of which Anna Kross had been a founder) urged Governor Lehman to appoint a woman to the state supreme court to occupy the seat being vacated by Charles Poletti, then lieutenant governor-elect. Such an appointment was not forthcoming. Almost twenty years passed before a woman, Birdie Amsterdam, won a seat on that court. Amsterdam, like Kross, was a former suffragist, a women's rights champion, and Jewish. Unlike Kross, as a Tammany district coleader she was "all organization." Growing up on Manhattan's Lower East Side as one of six children in an Austrian Jewish immigrant family, she had gone to public schools and then, while working, studied at New York University Law School at night. She earned her degree in 1922. Her arguments before local, state, and federal courts won her a stellar reputation, especially for her pro bono work. "There is a look in the eyes of people I have been able to help that has paid me more than any money possibly could," she said, defining her work in both law and politics as a social service. In 1939 she ran under Tammany's banner for justice of the municipal court and won easily, the first woman to do so in Manhattan (Agnes Craig had won in 1935 in the Bronx). In 1957, Tammany nominated her for the state supreme court and she won.[54]

Why did Amsterdam succeed where Kross had failed? By the late 1950s, some of the "anti-petticoat" biases so prevalent in the legal community when Kross launched her crusade had softened. Moreover, though Amsterdam was as female and Jewish as Kross, she had been a Tammany loyalist and a Tammany nomination was still tantamount to election.

The year 1937 had been a banner year for New York City women activists. After a twenty-year campaign, advocates of women's jury service were finally able to celebrate the passage of a bill in March that authorized women to serve. Even though their service was still optional, the women who had fought for it felt that it greatly enhanced their potential for active citizenship.

Though the next victory was small, it was huge for the city's women attorneys. They won admission to the city's most prestigious organization for their profession, the Association of the Bar of the City of New York. Perhaps because of the recent passage of women's jury service, the question of women's admission came up at the association's annual meeting in May. Alfred Cook, whose opposition to

Anna Kross's candidacy for the state supreme court would so outrage her, tried to put off a decision until October. Only 78 of 230 members present supported him. Though in the end a majority of the association's members approved women's admission, the arguments they used in favor of it reveal persistent blind spots. One member noted that when the association was formed in 1869, there were no women lawyers. This point failed to note the association's continued rejection of applications from the many women lawyers who had passed the bar since then, starting with Rosalie Loew Whitney, who had first applied in 1903. Another member argued that the pronoun "he," the presence of which in the by-laws had justified rejecting women's admission, had in other contexts included women. Again, no one asked why the association had taken so long to recognize that custom. Finally, association members cited expedient arguments, such as that the association might lose its tax exemption "so long as it excluded half of the eligible electorate from membership."[55] One member admitted that accepting women might persuade the Women's City Club and League of Women Voters to support its reform proposals. None of these arguments acknowledged the simple injustice of the group's long-lived ban. Women lawyers had found the ban especially irksome as it barred them from the association's library, said to be one of the finest in the country.

After voting to admit women, however, the association did not elect its first women members until October, and then chose only twelve, all of them white. Jane Bolin did not gain entry until 1943, immediately after the association adopted a resolution to investigate reports that the American Bar Association did not admit "Negro lawyers," a fact that, if true, it deplored.

Other feminist causes did advance during the summer of 1937. At its annual meeting in July in Atlantic City, attended by representatives of the sixty-five-thousand-member National Federation of Business and Professional Women (BPW), an event occurred that inspired an impromptu celebration. The US Senate unanimously repealed Section 213 of the 1933 National Economy Act. The BPW had argued that requiring the dismissal of spouses of government employees discriminated on the ground of marital status and potentially harmed women. The BPW and many other national women's organizations, including the National Woman's Party, League of Women Voters, and Democratic and Republican women's clubs, had worked together to bring about repeal. New York activists, including Assemblywoman Jane Todd, Congresswoman-at-Large Caroline O'Day, and First Lady Eleanor Roosevelt, had been among the many leaders of the repeal campaign. When the federation conventioneers heard the news, they snatched up banners and poured out onto the boardwalk. They fashioned signs saying, "Good-bye, 213" and "Thank You, McKellar and Celler," referring to the repeal's cosponsors, Tennessee senator Kenneth Douglas

McKellar and New York congressman Emanuel Celler. Marching to trumpet and accordion music, they sang the World War I marching song "Pack All Your Troubles in Your Old Kit Bag."

Lena Madesin Phillips saw the campaign's success as encouraging average women "to take an even more active part in righting wrongs against their sex." By fall, however, some of the elation had passed. Because reinstatement was discretionary, only 154 employees out of almost 2,000 had gotten their jobs back. Still, organized women took their united action against "213" as a good sign.[56]

Other political news that cheered New York City activists in 1937 included Secretary of State Edward J. Flynn's promotion in May of Assemblywoman Doris Byrne to the post of executive deputy secretary of state. Women celebrated La Guardia's re-election in the fall, because of not only his policies but also his growing list of women's appointments to government posts. In addition to Genevieve Earle's election to the city council, for the first time in the state's history women would be delegates to the constitutional convention the following April. Only six won election, a meager number when set against a total of 168 delegates, but since women had been trying to win delegate status since 1915 this small victory felt like big progress.[57]

Also in the fall election, two African American women entered the electoral path to office first paved by Eunice Hunton Carter and Jane Bolin. They made little headway, however. Ruth Whitehead Whaley, the first black woman to earn a law degree from Fordham University (1924) and practice law in New York, entered the race for an assembly seat as a Democrat but, lacking support from either Tammany Hall or Harlem constituents, lost. Attorney Sara Pelham Speaks, a Harlem Republican and fusionist and experienced campaigner for Republican candidates, accepted the nomination for a different assembly seat from the Square Deal Republican Club. Though PR did not apply to her race, she hoped the current quest for greater diversity among legislators might help her. It did not. Her rival in the primary fought her candidacy saying she had not lived long enough in the district, a charge that led to a court case, which she won. She went on to beat him in the primary but then faced a popular black male Tammany incumbent, who circulated a rumor that Speaks was a white woman trying to "fool the Negro voters of the district." Harlem women still flocked to support her. Even so, she lost the general election, though by fewer than three hundred votes.[58]

In a year-end retrospective, *Times* writer Anne Petersen admitted that these few markers of progress might appear insignificant when compared to women's larger goals or the time and effort put into reaching each of them. She thought, however, that "a glance at the recessions felt in the status of women in countries abroad" would spur them to refocus their energies in the coming year. For its part, the New York City League of Women Voters, which in May merged with

Brooklyn's league, was leading a national campaign to oppose Senator McKellar's bill to remove postmasters from civil service requirements. They also launched a statewide campaign on issues slated for discussion at the 1938 constitutional convention, including the fate of PR.[59]

In the coming years, a few more women won seats on the city council, but the numbers were unimpressive. In 1939 six women ran, a big drop from the fourteen in 1937, and only one woman ran from Manhattan: Marion E. Rooney, who campaigned as an independent from a wheelchair, which she had used for twenty-eight years after contracting polio. Again, Brooklyn's Genevieve Earle was the only victor. Two years later three of five women running were victorious: Bronx Socialist Gertrude Weil Klein, who had been seeking elective office since 1918, when she ran unsuccessfully for the state assembly; Rita Casey, a teacher, Catholic charities worker, and Brooklyn Democrat; and Earle. In 1943, the number of women candidates jumped to ten and included Layle Lane of Harlem, the first African American woman to make the attempt. Both Earle and Klein were re-elected, but all the others lost. The last council election under PR took place in 1945, an election that increased council terms from two to four years. The number of women running returned to fourteen and included three African Americans: two from Harlem, attorney Ruth Whitehead Whaley and a young garment worker named Louise Simpson, and from Brooklyn, civic activist Maude B. Richardson. The only successful candidates were Earle and Bronx attorney Bertha Schwartz, a Democrat who left a job in the Office of Price Administration to run. Schwartz won again in 1949 but left the council in 1953 to become a justice on the municipal court. Gertrude Klein was not re-elected.[60]

Despite these disappointing numbers, most women civic activists held on to their hopes for PR. If they had not experienced many victories themselves, then at least some independents had. Even so, election after election, the Tammany machine retained its majority.

Many New Yorkers condemned PR for having allowed the election of two Communists. The first was Peter Vincent Cacchione, a former railroad worker and committed unionist. Coming to New York broke and jobless in 1932 at the age of thirty-five, he was soon protesting flophouse conditions on the Bowery and agitating for soldiers' bonuses. In 1936 he became head of the Bronx County Communist Party and the next year led the party in Brooklyn. He had admired the work of civic reformers like Samuel Seabury but targeted the social system for facilitating corruption. He also criticized labor (as had Earle) for lacking the know-how to achieve efficient and clean government. Cacchione entered politics in the hope of bridging this gap.

In 1937, though Cacchione wanted to go abroad to fight the Nazis, his party persuaded him that the PR voting system gave him such an unprecedented chance to achieve office that he had to run. He urged his supporters to give their second-, third-, and fourth-choice votes to two American Labor Party candidates and then to Genevieve Earle, advice that led to a cordial relationship between the two in later years and even to Communist Party endorsements of Earle's campaigns. Though Cacchione did not win in 1937, he came close. Some thought votes were "stolen" from him, as he had been running far ahead of Republican Abner Surpless, until Surpless surged ahead near the end to win by 367 votes. Cacchione wanted, but could not afford, a recount. His supporters punned, "We Marxists long ago learned about surplus value. Now the old parties have learned the value of Surpless."[61]

Cacchione kept at it, running again in 1939, but the board of elections cited a technicality to invalidate his ten thousand signatures. His supporters organized a write-in campaign that netted a substantial number of votes but not enough to win. When in June 1941 Germany's attack on the Soviet Union aroused loud calls for a united front against the Nazis, anti-Communist fervor calmed. Cacchione finally won election, the same year Manhattan elected its first black councilman, Adam Clayton Powell Jr. Cacchione's success appalled all of the city's newspapers except the *Post*. Councilman Hugh Quinn, a Queens Democrat, wanted to challenge Cacchione's election on the ground that the Communist Party was not legal. Quinn's attempt went nowhere, but Cacchione's legislative career never took off. With support from only the small council minority, his proposals died in committee or were appropriated by others and watered down.[62]

In 1943, Benjamin J. Davis, an African American Communist from Harlem, ran for the council. Davis grew up in a middle-class, intellectual family in Georgia; went to Morehouse College and then Amherst; and earned a law degree from Harvard. He became a Communist while acting as volunteer counsel to Angelo Herndon, whose work trying to unite black and white unemployed workers in Atlanta during the Depression had led to a charge of inciting insurrection. Later, in New York, Davis became an editor of the *Daily Worker*. In 1942, when he learned that Adam Clayton Powell planned to run for Congress, he sought Powell's council seat. His platform included the banning of racial segregation in Stuyvesant Town, a massive housing project financed by the Metropolitan Life Insurance Company; an African American on the board of education; a public market for Harlem; an end to police brutality; rent and price controls; and the outlawing of all forms of racial discrimination, including anti-Semitism. Davis won, and ran again in 1945, this time opposed by Tammany's nominee, attorney Ruth Whitehead Whaley. Davis scoffed that her "only qualification was that she had won some elocution prizes many years before." He won easily.[63]

Cacchione and Davis worked together closely, but their conjoined presence on the council enflamed the mounting opposition to PR. Both men had received widespread support not just from the Left but also from the city's African Americans, shopkeepers, and Jews for their strong anti-Nazi and antidiscrimination stands. Tammany continued to blame PR for their presence on the council. Genevieve Earle thought the election of the two Communists "was the emphatic but false issue that killed proportional representation." Anti-Communism was on the rise. In June 1947 Congress passed the Taft-Hartley Act, which not only reduced the power of labor unions but also banned Communists from holding union office. Mayor La Guardia was no longer present to defend PR, of which he approved in general while deploring its failure to elect a fusion majority. In any event, he had declined to run for a fourth term in 1945 and died a month before the 1947 election.[64]

Critics of PR cited an ever-growing list of reasons to reject it. They claimed it had led Adolf Hitler to become Germany's chancellor and thus was an anti-American system that favored totalitarianism, including Communism. Defenders of PR pointed out that Europeans used a "party list" voting system, which led to splinter parties, whereas the method used in New York and other American cities was the "single transferable vote," which gave votes to individuals, not parties. Still, in the view of the Young Democrats of New York, PR was a "crackpot method of election" that increased public apathy and gave a "lion's roar to irresponsible fleas." Even the system's defenders, such as Robert K. Straus, who had won election because of PR, had decided that government works better under "party discipline" and that smooth government was more important than the representation of every minority. Many of the city's high-circulation pro-PR newspapers now turned against it. These included the *Eagle*, which said the system was unnecessarily complicated, deprived voters of citizenship rights, and allowed minorities (such as Communists) to create blocs all out of proportion to their numbers. "Complicated, trying the voters' patience, tiresomely long and costly to count, apt to play straight into the hands of alert and sinister Communist-led minorities," the *World-Telegram* editorialized, "it also makes straightforward Council legislation much more difficult than under the old two-party, majority-and-minority system." The *Times* cited the election of "un-American" legislators and left it at that.[65]

Other critics of PR cited its enduring practical problems. The costs of verifying nominations and paying canvassers were high. No voting machine had been invented to speed the long manual count. Voters remained confused: election after election canvassers threw out thousands of incorrectly marked ballots. Voters lacked the patience to wade through long lists of nominees to rank them. Even women's organizations, such as the Women's International League for Peace and Freedom (WILPF), which had been eager to use PR in their own elections, had given it up. On the eve of the election that would determine the fate of PR for the city, the New York City Federation of Women's Clubs voted three to one against retaining the system, saying they no longer had faith in an "un-American" system.

PR supporters had known for a long time it was in danger. Their campaigns to defend it began as early as 1939. Attorney Caroline Simon urged her colleagues in the League of Women Voters to get out the vote because PR was "on trial." She called it a "system which is naturally against the interest of machine politicians," adding, "We want to see it vindicated." The New York section of the Council of Jewish Women, the Brooklyn Women's Civic League, and the Women's City Club joined in PR's defense. Juliet M. Bartlett, Women's City Club vice president, had worked as a canvasser in 1939. After the election, she defended PR by pointing out that its purpose was not to achieve or eliminate any party's majority. "It is merely the most accurate system yet devised for securing the representation of every important group in proportion to its voting strength," she said.

Genevieve Earle devoted considerable energy to saving PR. "Everything that has happened since I came to the Council has convinced me of its worth," she told the *Post* in May 1947. "An effective minority is one of the safeguards of democracy. I will do everything in my power with other alert citizens of all parties to help defeat any move for its repeal." Throughout the year she spoke to hundreds of groups, mostly of women, in an effort to convince them to keep the system. Mixing her metaphors, she argued that voting it out to get rid of two Communists was like burning down a house to roast a pig. She thought that PR's opponents were using Communist representation as a "smoke screen" to make possible a return to "an unchecked one-party steam roller." On Election Day eve, she debated Eugenie May Davie, now chair of the Women's Auxiliary of the New York County Republican Committee, on the system's merits. Davie accused PR of favoring "splinter parties" that led to chaos and dictatorship; Earle countered that, on the council, splinter parties had not been obstructionist and 80 percent of all legislation was passed unanimously.[66]

Earle's powers of persuasion were not enough. The vote for repealing PR in 1947—935,222 to 586,170—was almost the inverse of the vote in favor of it in 1936. Less than a week later, Cacchione suffered a fatal heart attack. Davis lost re-election in 1949 and then was tried and convicted for "conspiring to teach or advocate the violent overthrow of the government," a violation of the Smith Act. Convinced that without PR she could not possibly win re-election, Earle retired in 1949. For nonpartisan reformers, laborites, and radicals, repeal meant the end of their elected representation in the nation's largest city. No woman won a seat on the city council again until 1965, when Aileen B. Ryan, a Democratic state assemblywoman, was elected councilman-at-large from the Bronx.[67]

# PART III LOOKING FORWARD

# 8 LEGACY

In her 1942 novel *Lonely Parade*, Fannie Hurst based one of her main characters on Elisabeth Marbury—literary agent, publicist, Broadway producer, and in 1928 New York State's female representative on the Democratic National Committee. Calling the character Charlotte (or the Charlottenburg, after Berlin's largest palace), Hurst paints her as a large, brutally honest, and funny woman. At the height of Charlotte's commercial success as a theatrical impresario and producer, a delegation from the "Merger party" (a thinly veiled reference to the Fusion Party) asks her to run for mayor. Charlotte laughs. A woman candidate would "be chiefly a comic strip," she says, "not necessarily because she's comic, and not because she probably wouldn't do a good job, and perhaps better, than the average stuffed shirt," but because the "timing is bad." She likes the idea of being mayor, "to prove that city government can get free of dirty politics. I'd like to run this city in a big clean way. I'd like like hell to revolutionize city management. Maybe it will take a woman to do it," she concludes. "But not yet."[1]

In the early 1940s, when Hurst wrote this novel, her friends in the New York City women's political community would have said that since winning the vote women's political prospects had not advanced by much. Even a decade or so later the obstacles to women's advancement seemed as high as ever. As one of Hurst's friends, attorney Caroline Klein Simon, would say when she addressed audiences in the 1950s and 1960s, "A woman must look like a girl, act like a lady, think like a man and work like a dog," adding that "more of skill and more of function is expected of a woman in the same post than of a man doing precisely the same work."[2] No matter how hard women worked, what today is called the "glass ceiling" always blocked their climb.

Hurst had had political ambitions of her own. She did not want to be a politician but hoped to use her celebrity as a popular writer to boost the social justice campaigns of her friends, who included Eleanor Roosevelt, Anna Moscowitz Kross, Mary Simkhovitch, and Fiorello La Guardia. Calling La Guardia a "prophet . . . of fearless leadership," after his 1933 victory she told him she was ready to help and awaited his "command." A month later, when she got wind he was appointing women to office, she made a case for Cyd Bettelheim, an activist in Jewish charities. He snapped, "I expect better advice from you. I will not appoint Cyd to any office." Though he thought Bettelheim able, in his view she had too big a heart to keep things under control. The next year, Hurst urged La Guardia to look more favorably on the work of Deputy Police Commissioner Henrietta Additon. He ignored that advice too.[3]

Their exchanges continued, with La Guardia complaining in 1943 that she always turned him down whenever he asked her to do something. This was not true, she answered, writing further that in the previous six years

> you have only asked me trivialities; window-dressing, etc., which would scarcely warrant a negative reply. I feel that I could have been of value to you in some of the organic departments of city government. With no partisan axe to grind; a concern for the social and civic stamina of this unparalleled city; and a deeply rooted desire to see it become the industrial, cultural Colossus it should, and must be, I flatter myself that I could have been constructively helpful.
>
> Well, you've never liked my way. Perhaps it is because you knew me "when," and continue to regard me as the gal from back there. Or perhaps alas, it is because you just had not the interest nor the evaluation that would give you the impulse to permit me to cooperate more vitally with you.[4]

She signed off bitterly, ""Faithfully and for Auld Lang Syne," and told him not to bother to reply.

He continued to call on her, however, but not in ways she wanted. She envisioned a "constructive role in the civic set-up of our town," in education or radio, but then he asked her to make a speech to the Boy Scouts. She tried to get him to appoint other women to office, including Caroline Simon, who had wide political experience to offer—but again La Guardia ignored her. Still, the next year Hurst defended him at a meeting of the Teachers Guild, which had denounced him. While admitting he was headstrong, she assured the teachers he was "talented, social-minded and on the side of the angels." As he grew more irascible and his opponents increased in number, she expressed concern about "the mounting prejudices that are crowding in upon you" and advised him to hold back on his "treat 'em rough" behavior to regain his former disciples. In her last letter, which she wrote by hand, she praised his recent performance at a luncheon and graced him with a paean to his enduringly lovable character. "Really, Fiorello, when you are good, you are so very, very good, that when you are bad, you are 'horrider' than you would be, if you weren't so very, very good when you are good. Play this over on your piano."[5] She was still his friend and would mourn his death deeply, but her failure to win from him the role she wanted must have entrenched her pessimism about women's political prospects.

Hurst may have been pessimistic, but other observers of women in politics after suffrage saw more progress than she did. *Times* reporter Kathleen McLaughlin observed in the fall of 1938 that the proportion of women to men delegates in state conventions was becoming more gratifying. "Skippers of each crew still are masculine, but the feminine corps can muster some capable 'first mates' in party service," she wrote. Chief among them were Democratic congresswoman-at-large Caroline O'Day and Republican assemblywoman Jane Todd. Helen Z. M. Rodgers of Buffalo, who during the recent state constitutional convention had been the first and only woman to chair a session, was the favorite among three Republican women challenging O'Day for her seat. The League of Women Voters was pressing hard to win approval of the federal child labor amendment and support for the civil service merit system. The election of the first woman secretary of the state party convention, Katherine Kennedy, a Brooklyn Republican, cheered her party's women. Although her position was largely organizational, her election publicized women's aptitude for higher-level party work.[6]

As the fall campaign neared, to demonstrate how many capable women were available for public posts the New York League of Business and Professional Women held a mock contest to nominate women for office. Among the winners were Eleanor Roosevelt for governor (typically, she declined the nomination but won anyway); Congresswoman Caroline O'Day and state senator Rhoda Fox Graves for US Congress; Assemblywoman Jane Todd and political activist Virginia Murray Bacon (widow of Robert Low Bacon, Nassau County Republican congressman) for US Senate; Frieda Miller for commissioner of labor; Genevieve Earle for commissioner of agriculture and markets; Virginia Gildersleeve (dean, Barnard College) for commissioner of education; settlement leader Mary Simkhovitch for chair of the state board of social welfare; and Anne Morgan (president, American Women's Association) for superintendent of banks.[7] By publicizing the executive ability of so many of the state's women, the league's contest disproved the canard that the state lacked women qualified for government posts.

Progress was, however, far from linear. In the 1938 campaign, apart from Anna Kross, then running for the state supreme court, the city's women mostly kept to their traditional political roles. Democrat Mary Van Lear Findlay Allen and Republican Caroline Simon, who had once worked in concert to re-elect District Attorney Thomas E. Dewey, now led opposing "feminine divisions" on behalf of gubernatorial opponents, incumbent governor Lehman and challenger Dewey. The women spent weeks organizing telephone brigades in apartment buildings and sending "flying squadrons" of canvassers into faltering districts. Lehman's victory brought reappointments for Frieda Miller as industrial commissioner, Rose Schneiderman as state department of labor secretary, Dorothy Straus to the state planning board, and Mabel Leslie to the state board of mediation. Except for Miller's, none of these were top posts.[8]

In 1940 McLaughlin summarized women's accomplishments since suffrage. She bemoaned young American girls' lack of knowledge of the movement, writing that the "vote, to them, is merely a contemporary blessing on a par with telephones, air mail—or capsule vitamins." Meeting over three days in late November, the Woman's Centennial Congress, conceived by octogenarian suffrage and peace movement leader Carrie Chapman Catt, met to celebrate a hundred years of female achievement. The congress, attended by more than three hundred women, focused on four fields—religion, economic and social problems, government and politics, and peace. When it was over Catt protested that its final "declaration of purposes" was too conservative.[9] As the world war increasingly absorbed women's attention, memory of the congress's action plans faded.

Another indication of a declining interest in feminist activism was the failure of historian and activist Mary Ritter Beard's effort, ongoing since 1935, to establish the World Center for Women's Archives, a clearinghouse for the collection and storage of historical materials related to women. By 1940 the project had collapsed, weakened by financial problems, apathetic women leaders, and disagreements over racial inclusion.[10] Though women's political opportunities expanded during the war, feminism as a source of future action, though not dead, appeared stalled.

On a more positive note, McLaughlin reminded her readers that since suffrage twenty-five million women had gone to the polls and the number of women entering state legislatures was on the rise. No woman's voting bloc had emerged, but 65 percent of New York State's new voters were female. In addition, women were no longer voting as their husbands instructed, but just as men do, as individuals and for as many kinds of reasons: economic, social, or personal concerns and biases. Though McLaughlin saw these developments as good omens, New York women had already learned that women do not necessarily vote for women and that prejudices against women as politicians remained strong.

At a Women's City Club debate in fall 1940, for example, *New York World* journalist and Democrat Herbert Bayard Swope denigrated the current women in Congress as "thorough-going ward heelers who take orders from their bosses." His debate opponent, Republican diplomat, lawyer, and civic leader Francis T. P. Plimpton, declared women in politics "an almost total failure." A few years later, at a meet-the-candidates luncheon held by the New York section of the National Council of Jewish Women, a rabbi's wife introduced the contenders by noting that because interest in women in politics was growing, she foresaw a woman candidate for mayor. She admitted later she was just being facetious to please her mostly female audience. In 1946 *Times* writer Page H. Dougherty asserted that politics was still "a man's game" and women had to learn how to play it. She cited a political leader who told her that women would go further in politics if they would tell party chiefs they wanted to run for office, just like men. "Women make the mistake of expecting us to seek them out for office," he continued, "more or less in the same manner that they expect a man to ask their hand in marriage." Finally, she quoted the well-known public official Anna Rosenberg, who said that women must be assertive or risk falling into "the natural error of organizing themselves as a pressure group," a strategy Rosenberg herself had long since abandoned.[11]

The pattern of women having better luck with appointive than elective office continued. In January 1940 Birdie Amsterdam became the first woman to take a seat on the New York County Municipal Court. In 1941 Mayor La Guardia appointed his law secretary, Florence Perlow Shientag, to a temporary seat on the domestic relations court; two years later she won appointment as the first woman assistant US attorney in the Southern District of New York. In 1942, when Governor Lehman sought a replacement for a member of the New York City council on military duty, he appointed former assemblywoman Doris I. Byrne, then executive deputy secretary of state, to serve out the remainder of the term. Mayor William O'Dwyer appointed her a city magistrate in 1948, the year she also began to serve as vice chair of the New York Democratic State Committee, and in 1950 O'Dwyer elevated her to the court of special sessions, a seat she held for ten years before retiring in 1965. She was the first woman ever to serve in this court. On the Republican side, in another first, attorney Mary Donlon became resolutions vice chair for the GOP national convention in 1944.[12]

One indisputable indicator of political advances for postwar New York women was the number of women attorneys holding public office in 1953. New York's tally of eighty-four (the most of any state) included many from New York City: Birdie Amsterdam, Jane Bolin, Mary Donlon, Anna Kross, Justine Wise Polier, Bertha Schwartz, Caroline Simon, and Ruth Whitehead Whaley.[13] Not all of these women identified as feminists, but all had found support from their nonpartisan and partisan women's networks.

Success at the polls still proved elusive. In some cases, the reason was purely political: running as a Republican, an independent Democrat, or a third-party candidate remained a disadvantage. Attorney Caroline Simon's experience was illustrative. Encouraged by the rising numbers of women voters (in the 1952 national election, they had outnumbered men), in 1957 she undertook her first run for elective office. In doing so she joined a record number of New York State women running for office that year—some two hundred Republicans and more than forty Democrats, the *Herald-Tribune* reported.[14] During the previous decade Simon's state appointments—to the industrial board, workmen's compensation board, and the Commission against Discrimination—had established her bona fides as a public servant. Setting her sights on the presidency of the city council, she won nomination from a mainstream political party for citywide office, the first woman to do so. Her chief problem was that the nomination came from the Republicans, not Tammany Hall.

Convinced that the large registration of the city's women, which now outnumbered men by more than fifty-four thousand, was a "portent of victory," Simon appealed to women voters with a campaign flyer topped by a cartoon of herself wielding a mop, broom, and dustpan. Her speeches targeted increases in crime, the lack of care for juvenile drug addicts and alcoholics, and the need for more housing for the elderly. The press was not always kind to her. The *New York Age* referred to her (and to Florence V. Lucas, an African American running for the city council that year) as "lady candidates"; the *Times* noted how often she changed her hat and gloves and, despite her five-foot-nine-inch height, wore heels; the *Herald-Tribune* emphasized she was "tough" but then hinted she used "feminine wiles" to please her audiences. She lost.[15]

Newly elected Republican governor Nelson Rockefeller thought well enough of her—she had polled 684,172 votes, a hundred thousand over the Republican mayoral candidate—to ask her to be his secretary of state. She declined at first, telling him, "I want to do anything I can to make your term a superb one, but I promised myself, I promised my family, I promised my law associates that I never would go back into public service again." But after she learned more about the job, she decided it interested her, asked her family and associates to release her from her pledge, and accepted the post. Much publicity surrounded her appointment, the first of a woman since Florence Knapp's disastrous tenure in the office in the mid-1920s. In 1963 she received an even higher prize: appointment to the court of claims.[16]

Like Simon, Anna Kross, who also lost her only electoral race, found greater opportunity in appointive office. After twenty years as a city magistrate, in 1954 Mayor Robert F. Wagner Jr. appointed her commissioner of corrections, making her one of only two women to hold this rank. A tireless reformer and agitator for decent treatment of the incarcerated, Kross held the post for twelve years. At Rikers Island and the Women's House of Detention, she worked to modernize both these antiquated institutions, introducing a beauty salon, language programs, and vocational training for the women and new educational facilities and an adolescent remand center for the men. She improved staff training and hired more medical and psychiatric personnel. She lobbied constantly for measures to end prison overcrowding, which in her view arose from arresting people who "are not criminals in any rational sense of the word," such as drug addicts and alcoholics, the senile and mentally ill, and vagrants. Kross had no easy answers for this enduring problem. She pleaded for more coordination among the various agencies concerned with correction, such as education, welfare, police, parole, and probation. She also begged taxpayers to understand that her department could never supply the accommodations and services they demanded without an appropriate budget, which she felt she never got.[17]

She did have the satisfaction of seeing changes to the court system for which she had worked her entire career. In 1962 a restructuring of the city's courts that integrated them into a statewide "unified court system" abolished the magistrates' courts and replaced them with a city-wide criminal court system. In 1965, revisions of the state's penal laws allowed prostitutes' customers to be prosecuted and reduced the maximum penalty for all prostitution-related offenses from a year in jail to fifteen days. After her retirement in 1966, in mid-September 1967, the women's court, which she had wanted to be shut down since her years as a volunteer lawyer at the court in the 1910s, was quietly closed. The first arrests under "Operation John," promoted by Mayor John Lindsey as a way of dealing with midtown "fleshpots," did not take place until 1972. Ironically, at that time the New York Civil Liberties Union opposed the use of women police decoys to "entrap" men, just as Kross and her feminist colleagues in the Women Lawyers' Association had protested male police decoys entrapping women.[18]

Cold War politics affected the careers of some La Guardia–era women. The same year Anna Rosenberg was accused during her congressional confirmation hearing of being a Communist, US senator Joseph McCarthy targeted Dorothy Kenyon in his pursuit of Communists in government. Since leaving La Guardia's administration, Kenyon's political profile had grown. In 1938 she became the first female and only American to serve on a League of Nations committee to study the international status of women. The following year La Guardia appointed her to a vacancy on the municipal court. When she ran for a full term, despite concerted efforts by women lawyers on her behalf and endorsements from both the Republican and American Labor Parties, like so many other non-Tammany candidates she lost to a Democrat. In 1946 the State Department named her a delegate to the United Nations Commission on the Status of Women, where for two years she championed women's equal wage, property, and political rights. Because of that nominal connection to the State Department, in 1950 McCarthy charged her with being a Communist. On the advice of her friend Senator Lehman, she volunteered to testify before the Senate subcommittee investigating the charges, and like Rosenberg was exonerated. Many of the so-called Communist fronts she had joined were anti-Fascist groups that included many distinguished American politicians and scientists.

Kenyon's career in politics was over, however. Clients and speaking engagements fell away and she never again held government office. She continued to pursue causes of free speech and the rights of women, consumers, and the poor. In the 1960s, she and attorney Pauli Murray convinced the American Civil Liberties Union (ACLU) that women should base their claims to equality on the Fourteenth Amendment. In 1971, future US Supreme Court justice Ruth Bader Ginsburg acknowledged her intellectual debt to these two New York City lawyers by putting both of their names on the title page of her brief before the US Supreme Court (*Reed v. Reed*), in which she argued that sex discrimination is an unconstitutional denial of equal protection. In her final years Kenyon was immersed in local New York City reform politics, creating legal services for low-income Manhattan residents. She also wrote briefs for the National Association for the Advancement of Colored People (NAACP) and the ACLU and marched in Memphis with striking sanitation workers. In 1968, Senators Robert Kennedy and Paul Douglas chaired her eightieth birthday party, an event attended by more than 350 admirers.[19]

The city's African American women had equally frustrating political experiences in their quests for office. Though few had attempted, or were even given a chance, to run, ever since suffrage they had used their political clubs to address issues of discrimination in housing, jobs, health care, and education. They also worked hard in men's political campaigns. In contrast to Eunice Hunton Carter and Jane Bolin, who ran in 1934 and 1936 as Republicans, in 1937 Ruth Whitehead Whaley entered a primary race for an assembly seat as a Democrat. Unable to get the attention of Tammany Hall, she lost. Sara Pelham Speaks, a lifelong Republican, won her primary bid but only after a recount; in the general election she lost to a Tammany man, also African American, who spread a rumor that she was a white woman trying to fool the black voters of her district. In 1944 Speaks tried again, this time against a formidable opponent, Adam Clayton Powell Jr., pastor of Harlem's Abyssinian Baptist Church and winner of a council seat in 1941. In 1944 Tammany and labor supported him for Congress. Speaks challenged him, presenting herself, especially to women, as the more reliable and trustworthy candidate. More than two hundred women organized a nonpartisan committee to support her, and the *Amsterdam News* endorsed her. Still, Powell won easily.[20]

After the war a rising number of New York City black women developed political profiles. The Depression and World War II had given college-educated African American women job opportunities in New Deal and home front agencies and then in electoral politics. Ada Jackson and Maude Richardson were migrants from the South who became activists in Brooklyn's Bedford-Stuyvesant neighborhood. Jackson, daughter of a former slave, worked to improve race relations, job opportunities, housing, and city services. Her electoral races were all unsuccessful, however. In 1944 she ran in the Republican and American Labor Party primaries for the state assembly and refused to drop out when warned that her candidacy would divide the African American vote. The press emphasized her maternal abilities and responsibilities; critics suggested she was neglecting her family. She ran again for the city council in 1947 and as a Progressive Party candidate for Congress in 1948. She ran her last race—for Brooklyn borough president on the American Labor Party ticket—in 1949. Despite winning nearly eighty thousand votes, she came nowhere close to either of the mainstream party candidates, who garnered hundreds of thousands of votes (the incumbent Democrat won). Maude Richardson attempted to win a seat on the city council during the 1946 election, the last under proportional representation. She sought an assembly seat the following year, facing the more left-wing and labor-oriented Ada Jackson in the primaries. Jackson eventually offered to endorse Richardson, but it was too late to get off the ballot herself. Richardson lost by seventy-seven votes to the incumbent, a white male Democrat.[21]

Anna Arnold Hedgeman, an executive in the YWCA, worked in the La Guardia administration as a supervisor in the Emergency Relief Bureau, the forerunner of the city's Department of Welfare. During the war Crystal Bird Fauset and Eleanor Roosevelt sponsored her for an appointment in the Office of Civil Defense. In 1953 Hedgeman's friends urged her to run for Manhattan borough president, but when Tammany's Harlem leader responded with "That's no job for a woman!" she declined. Calling Mayor-Elect Wagner's attention to the lack of African Americans holding city policymaking offices, leading Democrats urged him to appoint Hedgeman as commissioner of welfare. When he offered her the deputy post, she turned it down, eventually accepting a vaguely defined post of assistant to the mayor. Gradually her portfolio evolved: welfare, civil service, libraries, museums, and air pollution, all with a focus on race. Before leaving city hall in 1958, frustrated by Wagner's caution and by black male political leaders' lack of support, she joined Judge Jane Bolin in advocating the city's antidiscrimination housing bill and then spoke for the bill before the state legislature. Hedgeman ran for office three times, all without success: for Congress in 1960 (nominated by the East Bronx Committee for Democratic Reform), city council president in 1965, and the state assembly in 1968. In her electoral races the press focused more on traditional female qualities (her dress, soft voice, and "sparkling" home) than her long years as a civil rights worker. Later a founder (and vice president) of the National Organization for Women, she thought her greatest handicap in politics had been her sex, not her race.[22]

Hedgeman was a mentor to many young black women, one of whom was Pauli Murray. Inspired by her friend and labor organizer Maida Springer's run for the New York State Assembly, in 1949 Murray ran on the Liberal Party ticket for one of Brooklyn's seats on the city council. Both the Citizens Union and Americans for Democratic Action lauded Murray's reformist vision and wide experience in public affairs. Though it described her as pert, and a "youthful Portia," the press took her seriously, publicizing her civil disobedience against racial segregation in interstate travel and sex discrimination in graduate school admissions. When Murray came in third, Caroline Ware, her former Howard University history professor, attributed the loss to proportional representation's downfall, which had deepened Tammany's entrenchment.[23]

On the positive side, after Ruth Whaley campaigned hard to elect Vincent Impellitteri mayor in 1951, he appointed her secretary of the board of estimate, a post that made her the highest-ranking African American city officeholder. In 1952, seven black women ran for state office, but all on doomed third-party tickets. In 1953 civil rights campaigner Ella Baker, then the first female president of the New York City NAACP, took a brief hiatus from activism to run on the Liberal Party ticket for the city council; her fate was the same as Pauli Murray's: a Tammany man won. After supporting Herbert Lehman's race for the US Senate in a 1949 special election, Bessie A. Buchanan, a former musical comedy performer, threw herself into Harlem's Democratic Party politics. When she won election to the New York State Assembly in 1955, she became the first successful black woman political candidate in New York. After serving eight years as a Democrat, upon leaving the assembly she switched to the Republican Party.[24]

Greater political success for New York City African American women did not come until 1964, when attorney Constance Baker Motley became the first black woman to win a seat in the state senate, and Shirley Chisholm, a teacher and administrator in early childhood education, went to the state assembly.[25] Both of these women were born in the early 1920s into large families of working-class Caribbean immigrants, but in other respects they could not have been more different. After graduating from Columbia University Law School in 1946, Motley earned a national reputation assisting Thurgood Marshall, then chief counsel of the NAACP's Legal Defense and Educational Fund and future US Supreme Court justice, in a series of successful civil rights cases, including before the Supreme Court. She had no plans to enter electoral politics until in 1963 two women members of Manhattan's Riverside Democratic Club, both Motley's former classmates at Columbia, persuaded her to run for a state senate vacancy. She won both a special election the following spring and a full term in the fall.

In contrast, Chisholm came to politics in a more traditional way, starting with debating as a Brooklyn College undergraduate, being mentored by political science professors, and working her way up in Brooklyn Democratic Party clubs. In 1964, tired of organizing women's activities and canvassing for male candidates, she defied her male club leaders by announcing she would compete for a seat in the state assembly. She not only won but went on to win re-election three times.

Motley did not stay a state senator for long. In spring 1965 Tammany's first African American "boss," J. Raymond Jones (aka "the Harlem Fox"), who hoped Motley would be the city's first black female mayor, convinced her to accept nomination for the newly vacant Manhattan borough presidency.[26] Endorsed by Jones and Wagner, she won a full term that fall. Then, early in 1966, President Lyndon B. Johnson nominated her for a seat on the US District Court for the Southern District of New York, the nation's largest federal trial court and one that had never seated a woman or member of a minority. Motley, always more drawn to the intellectual challenges of the law than to politics, won confirmation and left electoral politics for good. In 1968 Chisholm again defied her party's leadership by declaring for Congress. Her stunning victory (she won more than twice as many votes as her opponent, former Congress of Racial Equality head James L. Farmer Jr.), made her the nation's first African American female US representative. Four years later she immortalized her reputation for fierce independence by seeking the Democratic Party's presidential nomination.

A cross-race coalition of prominent New York City women in politics supported Motley, most notably Dorothy Height of the National Council of Negro Women, philanthropist Brooke Astor, Corrections Commissioner Anna Kross, and attorney Dorothy Kenyon, and when she looked back on her life Motley acknowledged them and her African American predecessors in the law, Jane Bolin and Eunice Carter. Women supported Chisholm too, but instead of taking cues or mentorship from her local political predecessors, such as Jackson, Richardson, Hedgeman, and Buchanan, she carved out her own path. As borough president, Motley pursued issues of racial and social class justice but found the process of analyzing and modernizing governmental processes of greater interest than being at the center of governing herself. In contrast, Chisholm unabashedly pursued power in her quest for progressive laws benefiting racial and ethnic minorities, women, and the poor. She astonished her party's male political hierarchies with her ability to outmaneuver them (until she could not). "Unbought and unbossed" (as she would famously shout from her campaign posters), in the end she did not get what she wanted, but she never stood aside.

In the decades going forward, New York City women in politics took similarly varied paths to power. The accidental death of Edna Flannery Kelly's husband, a city magistrate, propelled her into political activism. After reviving the moribund women's auxiliary of Brooklyn's Madison Democratic Club, she joined the county executive committee and then for seven years was the party's research director for the state legislature in Albany. In 1949, when a death created a congressional vacancy, the committee nominated her. She campaigned to support Truman, fight for child care, and investigate milk prices "as ardently" as she had worked for the Fair Employment Practices Act, Social Security, and health and welfare measures. She advocated equity in women's pay, credit, and tax policies, including deductions for child care. Running from the Tenth Congressional District, she defeated two men (a Liberal and a Republican), a win that made her the first New York City Democrat and the first woman since Ruth Baker Pratt to enter Congress. Re-elected nine times, she served until 1968, rising to third in rank on the House Committee on Foreign Affairs. When changing demographics altered the racial make-up of her Brooklyn district, she challenged Emanuel Celler in his district but lost to him in the primary.[27]

Many of these New York City political pioneers deserve books of their own, and some have gotten them. The same can be said of some of their successors. Like their La Guardia–era predecessors, they developed careers marked by uphill battles with partisan forces and enduring commitments to feminist progressive reform and modernization agendas.

A few stand out. In the 1960s, attorney Bella Savitzky Abzug, who had gone to law school with Constance Baker Motley, cofounded Women Strike for Peace, went to Congress in 1970, and despite redistricting and intraparty challenges won two more elections. She gave up her seat in 1976 to run for the US Senate, but lost to Daniel Patrick Moynihan. Attorney Elizabeth Holtzman served in John Lindsay's administration and then became a Democratic Party activist. In 1972 she ran in the primary against fifty-year congressional incumbent Emanuel Celler, defeating him and going on to become, at age thirty-two, the youngest woman ever elected to the House of Representatives. She was a highly visible participant in the Watergate hearings that investigated President Nixon's White House cover-up of illegal campaign activities. She campaigned for the Equal Rights Amendment and the barring of sex discrimination in federally funded employment programs. Her 1980 bid for the senate failed, but the next year she won election as the first woman to be district attorney in Kings County and in 1990 New York City's comptroller. For Holtzman, the changes that made a political career possible for her began with Susan B. Anthony's hopeful phrase, "Failure is impossible." "Anthony didn't live to see the changes she fostered," Holtzman wrote in her memoir, "but the changes happened because of her."[28]

Elected a state senator in 1973, in fall 1977 attorney Carol Bellamy succeeded in a race many women before her had sought in vain, the presidency of the New York City Council. Her bids for higher office failed, but she then had a distinguished career as director of the Peace Corps and executive director of the United Nations Children's Fund (UNICEF). Teacher and social worker Ruth Messinger tried for the state assembly in 1976 and lost, but the next year won a seat on the New York City Council. Elected Manhattan borough president in 1990, she supported gay rights, affordable housing, and public school funding. In 1997, she secured the Democratic Party nomination for New York City mayor (another women's first) but lost to incumbent Rudolph Giuliani. In 1977 Miriam Bockman, a Hunter College graduate who worked in Edward Koch's mayoral campaign, became the first woman to head Tammany Hall, since the 1960s in decline but still the chief organization of New York County Democrats. Geraldine Ferraro graduated in 1960 from Fordham University Law School and in 1978 ran in a three-way contest for an open congressional seat, a race she won. Benefiting from Speaker "Tip" O'Neill's mentorship, in 1984, as chair of the Democratic National Convention's platform committee and vigorously sponsored by feminist Democrats, she became presidential candidate Walter Mondale's vice presidential running mate. The Mondale-Ferraro ticket lost, but Ferraro's attempt inspired many women to reach for high political office. In the 1990s, Ferraro lost two more bids for the US Senate. Her connection to feminist political traditions, dating back to suffrage, stayed with her. When she voted for Hillary Rodham Clinton in the presidential primary of 2008, she said she could feel Susan B. Anthony and Elizabeth Cady Stanton standing beside her.[29]

Other women who emerged from New York City's mid-twentieth-century women's political world never ran for office. Few today now remember their names. But their federal policymaking appointments permanently changed American culture, empowered consumers, and advanced feminist causes. Brooklyn Law School graduate Frieda B. Hennock, for example, was named in 1948 by President Truman as the first woman on the Federal Communications Commission (FCC). At a time when all television was commercial, Hennock defied the networks and won approval of publicly funded educational TV, leaving a precious legacy to the nation. In 1951, fifteen years before Constance Baker Motley rose to the federal bench, Truman nominated Hennock for a federal judgeship in New York. It was not to be. The New York City and American Bar Associations pronounced her "unqualified." The Senate Judiciary Committee heard rumors she had had an affair with a married New York judge. When confronted, she insisted she had merely helped the judge in his political campaigns and they were just friends. Despite vociferous support from women's bar associations, women judges, and her FCC colleagues, charges of "personal misconduct" forced her to withdraw. President Eisenhower did not renew her appointment to the FCC. In the late 1960s feminists used the term "sexism" to explain why Hennock was denied a judgeship.[30]

Mary Gardiner Jones, the first woman appointee to the Federal Trade Commission (FTC), had been inspired by her aunt, Rosalie Gardiner Jones, who after organizing spectacular publicity stunts for suffrage went on to earn a doctorate in civil law. Despite her family warning her, "Don't be like your Aunt Rosalie," Mary, born in 1920, went on to a stellar career at Wellesley and Yale Law School. After many unsuccessful attempts to get a job in a law firm, she landed a post in the New York field office of the Antitrust Division of the US Department of Justice, an appointment that led in 1964 to her post on the FTC. As a commissioner, Jones followed in the women's consumer reform tradition by introducing the three-day "cooling off" period that allowed buyers to change their minds after signing an installment-loan contract and supported an end to on-air tobacco advertising and deceptive marketing. In one way she did not emulate her Aunt Rosalie. She wrote in her memoir that she accepted "the male view of women and rarely questioned why there were so few women in key leadership positions," adding that she never critiqued the annoying compliment that a successful woman had "a mind like a man." She called herself "a woman in conflict," one keenly aware of sex discrimination but unlike Rosalie never seeing herself as a pioneer. "I wanted to be treated as an equal but it never occurred to me to challenge the customs or attitudes in the predominantly male world where I worked. I just wanted to be let in," she wrote.[31] It would take another generation for women like Mary Gardiner Jones to begin to resolve that conflict.

A third federal appointee of the era with early connections to the New York City women's political community, Esther Peterson, had less of a conflict with feminism. After graduating from Brigham Young University in 1927 with a degree in physical education, she moved to New York, where she earned a master's degree and, with her husband, Oliver, was swept up in social reform and labor movements throughout the Northeast. From 1939 to 1944 she worked with New York labor leader Bessie Abramowitz Hillman at the Amalgamated Clothing Workers of America (ACWA), organizing new locals and leading integration efforts in garment shops. Later, she worked in Washington, DC, as a lobbyist for the minimum wage, unemployment compensation and insurance, and social security for the American Federation of Labor-Congress of Industrial Organizations. During Senator John F. Kennedy's 1960 presidential campaign she held the "labor desk," and after his victory was named director of the Women's Bureau in the US Department of Labor. This appointment made her the highest-ranking woman in the Kennedy administration.

Peterson's post put her in a strategic position to confront women's loss of millions of high-skilled industrial jobs after World War II, a painful development that had plagued working women after World War I. She convinced Kennedy to establish a presidential commission to collect reliable national data on women's earnings, address discriminatory hiring and unequal pay, and resolve the decades-long deadlock over the Equal Rights Amendment (ERA). Though Eleanor Roosevelt served as its chair (her last public post), as its executive vice chair Peterson did all the commission's organizational work. She focused chiefly on equal pay legislation, which finally was passed in March 1963, a victory that many observers credited to Peterson's many twelve-hour days. Later, as President Johnson's special assistant for consumer affairs, she won lower credit card interest rates and curbs on misleading advertising and deceptive packaging. She got care instructions sewn into every garment and helped pass the Fair Packaging and Labeling Act of 1966. She also laid the groundwork for changes not institutionalized until the 1970s, such as truth in lending laws, the requirement that advertisers submit proofs of claims, and the elimination of higher rates for minorities. Her work attracted the ire of advertisers, who labeled her a "scoutmistress leading the first hike of spring," a woman who engaged in the "politics of the pantry," and even "the most dangerous thing since Genghis Khan." Working in the private sector in the 1970s, she led the modernization of the retail food industry by winning sell-by dates on perishables, nutritional information on labels, and other reforms. In 1981, she received the nation's highest civilian award, the Presidential Medal of Freedom. For a woman wont to describe herself as "just a gym teacher," this was no mean achievement.[32]

In 1944, two years after the appearance of Fannie Hurst's novel, New York City writer Eve Garrette published *A Political Handbook for Women*. College political science courses adopted the book and, for a few years at least, Garrette received invitations to lecture on the suddenly popular topic of women in politics. Most of her handbook outlines how government and political parties work. The last chapter, "Politics—Career for Women," was different: it was an outright plea to women to see politics as "*the* coming career," a natural for women's skills and talents.

She opened the chapter with a *New Yorker* story about a nine-year-old girl, who when asked what she intended to be when she grew up replied: "When I was young, I wanted to be an actress. But now I've decided to go into politics." Garrette, who loved this story, used it to urge women to follow this little girl's example. Decades before the modern women's movement of the 1960s and 1970s began to make substantial breakthroughs into the country's mainstream political parties, she was sending the message that it was now acceptable for a woman to be and act political. Times seemed to be changing.

But not by much. When Garrette spelled out why women should do as she said, her reasons were not all that different from journalist Esther Coster's in 1921. Garrette's list of women's qualifications for office included their realistic approach to solving life's problems, knowledge of human nature, moral courage, intuition, tact, and efficiency. In fact, she confided, the modern housewife is the nation's greatest "efficiency expert." When she ended her handbook with practical steps a woman should take to enter politics—start at the bottom by registering to vote, join a political club, and get elected to a county, state, and eventually national party committee—she never suggested that women could or should aspire higher. And while she cited a few New York women who had won elective public office (New York's Ruth Pratt was her prime example) and noted that thousands of women nationwide had won county offices, state legislative seats, posts as secretary of state, and even governorships (Nellie Tayloe Ross and Miriam A. Ferguson had briefly succeeded their husbands in office), nowhere did she make a case that women should seek higher goals and demand opportunities to achieve them.[33]

Many members of New York women's postsuffrage political community were making such a case from the moment they won the vote. Despite persistent barriers against their rise in partisan circles, they were able to win policy victories that permanently changed the ways our society works, plays, and thinks. These victories comprise a substantial part of their legacy. On the local level of the city's politics, because of their powerful reaction to the revelations of the Seabury investigations, they were able to win better treatment of women in the criminal courts and play important roles in the investigations' political aftermath. Without their activism at the state level, acceptance of federal monies under the Sheppard-Towner Act, women's jury service, protective labor laws, and the expansion of women's reproductive rights and the civil rights of minorities, not to mention the growing roster of appointments of women to office, might never have come to pass.

Although women's quest for power in the early postsuffrage era remained unfulfilled, their story was not all disappointment. Contrary to the stereotypes about woman suffrage—that too few women voted to make a difference, that women voted just as their husbands did, or that women failed to win political office (as if it was their fault)—New York women gradually increased their voting numbers, voted independently from the men in their lives, and often chose sides with women's policy agendas in mind. Despite enduring biases against their holding office, hundreds of them entered partisan political arenas again and again, drawing strength, example, and tactics from their suffrage-era networks. Though they certainly disagreed with one another on important issues, they nonetheless used both partisan and nonpartisan networks for support and formed strategic coalitions across racial, class, and ideological lines to achieve specific goals.

Given the broad spectrum of biases against women exercising political power in the postsuffrage era, a smooth and seamless transition of women into positions of political equality with men after centuries of male dominance was probably not possible. Gender equity in New York City politics still requires work, especially in the realm of electoral politics. In 2017, the city council, the body women fought so hard to penetrate in the 1930s and 1940s, had fewer women members (thirteen) than ran for seats in this body in 1937 (fourteen).[34] Growing pains continue. Still, women who persist might take some lessons, if not inspiration, from the example of the New York City women of the early postsuffrage era. In any event, the story of how the government scandals of the early 1930s opened previously unimaginable opportunities for them in La Guardia's and subsequent administrations deserves a prominent place in the mainstream of their city's history.

# APPENDIX

## "FIFTY WOMEN AND ONE MAN": A PLAY IN THREE SCENES AND ONE AXE

Presented by the Women of the Administration, December 6, 1937[1]
Hotel Brevoort, New York City
The characters in this play are purely officious and impurely fictitious.
The authors are anonymous and not all synonymous with

### THE CHARACTERS IN THE PLAY

| | |
|---|---|
| Mayor | Mrs. [Pearl Bernstein] Max |
| Secretary | Mrs. [Mitzi] Somach |
| President Roosevelt | Mrs. Oliver |
| Deputy Mayor | Mrs. [Sophie] Olmsted |
| Acting Police Commissioner | Mrs. [Frances Foley] Gannon |
| Civil Service Commissioner | Mrs. [Sybil Stearns?] Madigan |
| Acting Markets Commissioner | Mrs. [Rose] Miller |
| Acting Health Commissioner | Mrs. Goldstein |
| Acting Director of the Budget | Mrs. [Lucile L.] Kraft |
| Acting President of the Council | Mrs. [Sophia L. C.] |
| Battistella President Board of Education | Mrs. [Ruth (Mrs. Carl)] Shoup |
| Acting Welfare Commissioner | Mrs. [Charles F.] Murphy |
| Acting Park Commissioner | Miss Baikie (?) |
| Housing Authority | Miss [Dorothy] Kenyon |
| Acting Commissioner of Water Supply, G. & E | Mrs. [Frances] Lehrich |

## SCENE I

Mayor's Office
Empire State Building
Room 2210

Mayor comes into the office quickly; hurls his large black hat into the corner of the room, speaks hurriedly:

MAYOR: Mitzi—Where is that girl? Mitzi, Get Commissioner Valentine.

MITZI: (Telephones) – Commissioner Valentine is out of town.

MAYOR: Where *is* he?

MITZI: He's down in Houston, Texas, reorganizing the police department.

MAYOR: Tell him that shake-ups begin at home. Tell Goodman I want to see him right away.

MITZI: (Telephones) – Commissioner Goodman is not in.

MAYOR: Where the hell is *he*?

MITZI: He's got a sore thumb. He's up in the water shed, stopping the leak in the Croton Dam.

MAYOR: Serves him right. What a bum job that was! Well, let's tackle the mail. Maybe there's some good news instead of headaches for a change. Here's a good one from Commissioner Moses—my pal! He only wants $162,000,000 for 75 parks and 100 playgrounds. He must think I'm the Director of the Mint. Get him on the phone. I'll have some fun with him. (Hurls crushed cigar into the air and catches it.)

MITZI: (Telephones) – Commissioner Moses is not in.

MAYOR: What? Moses too? What's the matter with *him*?

MITZI: His secretary says he's hanging gardens in Babylon.

MAYOR: Tell him to hang himself too. What about the other commissioners I asked you to call this morning?

MITZI: Commissioner Forbes resigned. He's just been made City Manager of Newark.

MAYOR: This looks like a frame-up of all my commissioners. How about Rice?

MITZI: This is Junior Prom week at Yale, and Rice went to New Haven to give pre-marital Wassermans.

MAYOR: And Goldwater? Is Goldwater helping him too?

MITZI: Goldwater just sailed for Russia to put the Soviet hospitals on a five year plan.

MAYOR: What the devil . . . . (Telephone rings) MITZI: Mayor, President Roosevelt is calling.

MAYOR: Hello, Mr. President.

PRESIDENT: Congratulations, F. H. I see we Communists won again. Now that you have won the election, F. H., I wonder if you could help me out. Hop on a plane at Bennett Field and fly right down to Washington.

I would like you to determine with certitude
The degree of moral turpitude
Between Magda and Senor Mussolini.

MAYOR: Of course, Mr. President. I'll be right down. I always did believe in a career
service for women. Goodbye.

Mitzi, tell Ryan I'm taking the next plane down to Washington.
Tell Curran to get after those Commissioners.

My darn commissioners are never around
Those darn commissioners can't be found,
The hell with them, they're a vagrant lot
It makes no difference if they're here or not.


SCENE II

Office of the Deputy Mayor

[ASSISTANT] DEPUTY MAYOR (knitting):

I am the Deputy Mayor,
For self-oblivion I've a flair,
I view with equanimity
My position for anonymity.

My manner's exquisite,
My diction correct.
I'm Fiorello's perfect foil,
In every respect.

(Takes out rubber blanket from knitting bag.)

On my shoulder I wear a blanket of rubber,
For the cranks with tzoros discreetly to blubber,
Even when Taxpayer Goldsmith hollers,
After a talk with me he feels like a million dollars.

By virtue ex-officio,
To 30 boards for the Mayor I go,
And when His Honor wants to duck an issue,
I'm the sap,
Who takes the rap.
(Yawns)
Well, the Mayor's away,
The town's mine today.

The woman's place is in the home,
The Mayor's is in the city,
But when they begin to roam,
Some say it is a pity.

The Mayor's away to a star-gazing conference, and since the Commissioners are
gone too, now let's see what the women can do.

It's almost time for my Cabinet to assemble. Betty, call up the girls but first get
me the Acting Police Commissioner.

BETTY: The First Deputy Police Commissioner is away.
The Second Deputy Police Commissioner is away.
The Third Deputy Police Commissioner is away.
The Fourth Deputy Police Commissioner is away.
The Fifth Deputy Police Commissioner is away but the Sixth Deputy Police
Commissioner is here.

DEPUTY MAYOR: Gannon, that's a fine name for a Police Commissioner. Even though
she isn't a "Latin from Manhattan," Gannon is a good name and she comes from the
right Borough.

Acting Police Commissioner Gannon comes in and makes her report. While she
is talking all the other Acting Commissioners come in. They report to the Deputy
Mayor in the following order: Police, Civil Service, Markets, Health, Budget, Council,
Education, Welfare, Parks, Housing, Water Supply. (Throughout proceedings Deputy
Mayor uses axe as a gavel.)

In each case, where apropos, the Deputy Mayor says: How are the children
(any grandchildren yet?), How's the dog, how's the cat? And by the way, how's your
husband?

DEPUTY MAYOR: That's splendid, Girls. You women deputies have accomplished more
in twenty-four hours than the men Commissioners have been able to do in the previous four years. The meeting stands adjourned. (Bangs axe.)

## REPORT OF THE POLICE DEPARTMENT

As Commissioner of Police
To headlines I aspire;
You can quote that the shake-ups
Daily reach ever higher.
At sixty-three cops retire
By a new ruling just been made;

Alas, all New York's finest
Were stuck in Juvenile Aid.
But I found both too expensive
As you, too, will aver,
So I gave this job to Moses' boys
At eighteen hundred per.
And I put the cops to work,
No longer do they lark;
Now they patrol their beats;
Catch thugs in Central Park.
From two per cent to five,
I raised the pension rate,
A solvent to the Pension Fund,
Formerly so scanty,
The fat, moth-eaten matrons,
War relics and no beauties,
We've replaced with Civil Service babies,
Who certainly know their duties.
The guys who got low car numbers,
And thought they were so smart;
Now are specially looked for
By my men in Traffic Part.


REPORT OF CIVIL SERVICE COMMISSION

Cabinet Ladies—shall I say?
Allow me to report on yesterday.
I've never seen such ramification
In a single matter of classification!

They've assistant clerks and deputy clerks
And deputy assistants and other quirks!
But do you think their duties are the same?
There's not the remotest connection twixt the job and the name!
You'll think I'm telling a Leacock story
When I tell you what all falls in one category!
The guy who makes change in a subway station
Is dubbed "Private Secretary, Board of Transportation."

In Sanitation they have sweepers
Who bear the title of "Bookkeepers,"
And truck-drivers—gentlemen of the road –
Are called "stenographers" in the Budget Code.

So-o-o, the Commission worked a solid day
Rearranging the list in such a way
That even a babe need not suspicion
A scrub woman to be a statistician.
The Mayor sure will be surprised to see
That a title is just what it seems to be!

*Next*, I changed the methods of examination
So they'll really help in a determination
Of the best fitted candidate for a given task
Their political affiliation we won't even ask!
For, if a cleaner know the sweeping art,
Who cares which Leader is nearest her heart?

I've arranged for training, in service and out,
So an appointee knows what the job is about,
Without having to pay exorbitant fees
For a cramming course at Delehanty's.
The cops teach police dogs the tricks of the game,
We propose to include the species humane!

In an I.Q. for firemen recently,
The candidates flunked indecently.
The Aldermen in chorus wailed!
A professor would have failed
A test with questions so roundabout
That only Einstein could dope them out!
Firemen are men of glory,
They're to rescue from the fifteenth story
A dashing blond, a blue-eyed child,
What difference who wrote the "Call of the Wild"?

To soothe the Aldermen's ruffled poise,
The same test was given to twelve year old boys,
Who found it right within their pale,
Catch the moral of this tale?

There are more reforms I'd like to make!
*If* the Commissioner should get a break
And become a judge (as I am wishin')
What *I* would do with this Commission!

## DEPARTMENT OF PUBLIC MARKETS

(To be said with Yiddish accent)
My Boss—he's a big fish man.
By this, I ain't in mind
That he stands behind the counter
And sells fish from every kind.
Naw! He is a Social Register,
And boy! Does he look swell,
From the best kind of herring
He doesn't begin to smell.
He flits from lower Park Avenue
Like the man on "The Trapeze,"
To the upper Park Avenue Market!
He ain't afraid of fleas;
And he no longer "flits" the peddlers,
He keeps them like hot-house roses
Behind glass what's full of sunshine,
So they don't freeze their noses.

He's got a brand new idea
What he talks about nights and days,
That it's time we took care
Of the people that pays.
I think he called them consumers
(It sounds like a disease)
But if they really pay money,
I think they should be pleased.
Anyhow—was I surprised
That they put me for a day
At the head of this whole business,
With only a dollar in pay.

So I rushed down to Orchard Street,
And did I make it swell!
I pushed out all the pushcarts
And got rid of all the smell.
The Department what weighs and measures,
I scrubbed it clean—you bet!
All the gips and chiselers

Don't know what happened yet.
I got together all their names
Into such a big list,
Done so careful and so good,
Not one of them was missed.

The Commissioner's wife,
She asked with her I should take tea,
Tea I can have in my kitchen –
But her home I wanted to see.
So I went in all my diamonds
And hoped to get lunch.
But no! Instead did I meet
A small elegant bunch
One look at Mrs. Commissioner
And believe me, I could see
That even if we didn't eat,
We wouldn't drink just tea.

Anyhow, I enjoyed my job
If only for one day,
And maybe, the Commissioner again
Will go away.


REPORT OF THE HEALTH COMMISSIONER

Our fair Police Commissioner
Has told you of ballistics.
My report shows health
And Mortality Statistics.

We deal with the body "beautiful,"
But we see little beauty
In the ailments and deformities
To treat which is our duty.

What diseases ravage
The poor human carcass!
T.B.—V.D.—D.T.
Also pneumococcus!

Halitosis, typhoid, scarlet,
Addison's Disease,
Tonsils, sinus, croup,
And water on the knees!

We concoct alleviates,
Medicaments and purges,
And segregate in a thousand tubes
The microbes of these scourges.

We use expert treatment
For each dastardly infection,
And secured tons of serum
For pneumonic injection.

We've made the Wassermans popular,
And things have gone so far
That they're begged for by the socialites
And the Dames of D. A. R.

Although we cannot wholly
Save street-walkers from perdition,
We medicate them thoroughly
So they "walk" in good condition.

We introduced a system,
Careful and persistent,
For treatment of dental troubles
Both future and existent.

On parisi-tology
We are experts all,
As the Mayor claimed to be
From his experience in City Hall.

He said at a recent luncheon,
He has time and incentive
To use his research data
On starting work preventive.

But we're way ahead of him!
In one day we were able
To make such progress in this field
That we have no mortality table.

I worry, if we continue
To progress as herein stated,
With no deaths and increased births —
We'll be overpopulated!!!

And then we'll look for colonies –
A vile fascistic vice!!!

So I better stop, and submit this
Report for Doctor Rice.


REPORT OF ACTING BUDGET DIRECTOR

Sing a song of sixpence
  Sing a song of tax
Methods of our budgeteers
  Are just a bit too lax!

For monies have been allocated
  To all the judges' courts
For just a lot of little pleas
  And many little torts!

The damn judicial salaries
  Were all restored, my dears
And what is more they went so far
  And paid up all arrears!

It is astonishing to find
  A General Sessions clerk
Who draws three legal salaries
  Without a stitch of work.

And really ma'am the Budget Office
  Is just a bit too fickle
When my hard-working steno
  Isn't even raised a nickel!

Expenditures as huge
  As a F. W. A. loan
Are all O.K.'d, but try and get
  An extra telephone!

Women held the purse-strings
  And are the world's wise spenders
And women know a thing or two
  About gyp money-lenders!

We cy-ni-cal-ly smile
  And give a loud horse-laugh
To find one female Examiner
  On the entire budget staff!

So in the one short day
    Of my reign o'er the City's money
My report to you, Ma'am, shows
    That I've really pulled a honey!

I've allowed no more transfers
    And called a new examination
Opened to men and women
    Without sex discrimination!

## REPORT OF PRESIDENT OF BOARD OF EDUCATION

I represent Board of Education,
    Both higher and lower
It's hard to tell who or what is sorer.
Here we are who the city rule
    And we send our children to private school.
          W H Y?
We disapprove of having
    Our children in their teens
Squeeze in high school classrooms
    Like canned sardines.

In grammar schools they have
    Such antique sanitation
That the stench has even reached
    The Board of Education.

Unwashed and unbrushed at home
    My and your white hope
In public schools don't get
    Either towel or soap.

We have so many officials
    Who in education tinker
(executives and administrators)
    But not a single thinker.

So when I found myself in power
    I wanted to go far
To reform the blasted system
    To bring it up to par.

Altman's mental cases,
    Who taught me and you
I had transferred at last to a ward
    In Goldwater's Bellevue.

I put all the custodians
    To work both night and day;
Now our schools are centers
    Where young and old can play.

Housekeeping is a woman's job
You've often been heard to say,
(Mr. Mayor) You'll be glad to learn

We now have a woman custodian
    In our pay
Who has the school kept clean
    And all the classrooms neat
Even once filthy washrooms
    Now have an odor sweet.

Of course, the teaching staff
    Is feminine through and through
So women principals in our high schools (46)
    Now number more than two.

This is one department, though
    You can't remake in a day;
So remember, Mr. Mayor
    There's a woman to be appointed
On the Ides of May!


## REPORT OF THE PRESIDENT OF THE COUNCIL

Madame Assistant Deputy Mayor,
(Or should the word "vice" be inserted there?)
And women colleagues of the City Staff:
I've come prepared to take the gaff
From His Honor: for who doesn't fall short
Of his expectations in any report?

But since he's astrally been called away,
I feel free to recite the events of the day.
It's hard to describe by word or code
Changes in the Aldermen's last abode.

In their age-old favorite places,
You find some really intelligent faces.
It looks as if twice ten Jack Horners
Cleaned Tammany cobwebs from the corners!

So many desks and seats are bare
We might put a housing project there!
But enough of comment, time is short,
So I submit the following official report:

The Council met in virgin session
Me, presiding with discretion.
I stared with ill-concealed delight
At each Fusionist and Laborite,
I might have stared for too long,
But for a crash of cymbals—a burst of song.

The standard's raised, the flags unfurl
And in walks Councilman Genevieve Earle!
The men bow low and chant and fuss:
"She made the Charter and the Charter made us."
Order is restored once more,
When Vladeck and Baldwin both want the floor!

It's strange to see in one political bed
Republicans pink, and Laborites red!
The clerk, from habit born of years,
Yells "Sixty-four to one"! 'mid boos and cheers,
But an actual roll call indicated
That Tammany's strength was vindicated.

What to do? How could I start,
Pushing through measures nearest my heart,
When I lacked two votes for acquiescence,
And I have *one* day! Time's of the essence!

So, ere Morris returns and intervenes,
I quickly talk turkey to the two guys from Queens.
We reach an understanding in a trice,
Of course,—non-political, and very nice.

So, with my vote to resolve the tie,
Business goes swimming along in high!
While the sun is shining, I make hay –
Lyons' Residence Bill is revoked in the fray,

And in the excitement born of this storm
We enact the half-dead County Reform.

At this point Chieffo considerately sends
Spittoons for the tears of our Tammany friends.
You'll admit it's tough, in the fell swoop
To lose registers, sheriffs and the rest of the troop!

Then up pops Kinsley—eye fixed afar,
And asks: "What the Hell is this P. R.?"
This made Genevieve very sore.
So she pipes up: "Let's work some more!
We've reforms to push!," and starts to list 'em.
First we consider the pension system.

We make pensioners pay more—the City less,
And on an actuarial basis close up the mess.
Next comes the pet, perennial woe –
Relief! We allot more and we pay as we go,
By devising means for local taxation
That delight the entire city population.

I've already got letters from every resident
Congratulating me for being a fine President.

Next, we get culture—declare it a pity
That music gets little support from the city.
So we enact an opera and symphony garrison.
(The Metropolitan's just a dog in comparison!)

Then some lazy guy gets up to say:
"We've worked an hour—enough for today!"
And I to postpone the countless bills
My office drew for the city's ills.

If the Mayor would show more inclination
To add women to the administration,
And if our luck were a little stronger
So the Commissioners' junkets would last longer,
We could continue, with innate ability,
To beautify and administer the City.

> With shortcomings admitted,
> This is respectfully submitted.

## REPORT OF THE DEPARTMENT OF PUBLIC WELFARE

In the City's Welfare work
    Of women such good care we take
That all I needed to do
    Was to give the men a break.

So we have done away with
    Municipal Lodging Houses
Where an attendant grabs a guest
    And officially him delouses

Then the guest must bathe
    And scrub himself quite clean
To get his small repast
    Of coffee and a bean.

We'll send all homeless men
    To the La Guardia camp
To restore their morale
    And their whole lives revamp.

At camp we'll make a special
    Comfortable reservation
For the homeless husbands of
    The Women in the Administration.

## REPORT OF THE PARK DEPARTMENT

(Say with Southern accent)
I am the Czar of the Parkway!
Nothing stands in *my* way!
I *never* step aside!
I *always* keep my pride!

No questions do I ask –
I just do my task!
I find it fun,
But believe me—it gets done!

Moses says: "Don't stop at rape
To cut the damn red tape."
But *I* use other methods,

And see what I have done!
Without giving offense
    To a soul under the sun.

While Moses' away,
    I made peace with W. P. A.,
And still am the boss,
    Right on my high horse!

And with the Mayor, too,
    I'm no longer in a stew,
Because he now *must* see
    He can't dictate to me!

In a word I'm sitting pretty,
Right in the heart of the City.

## REPORT OF HOUSING AUTHORITY

I've had a dream, a nightmare in short
Let me tell you about it as my report.

'Twas the night before Christmas,
When all through the house
Not a Vladeck was stirring, not even a Strauss.
The housing plans were hung by the chimney with care
In the hope that St. Franklin soon would be there.
Ma Simkhovitch in her blue prints, Pa Post with his maps,
Had both of them settled for well deserved naps.

When up on the roof there arose such clatter
We sprang to our feet to see what was the matter.
Down Stanley, whoa Mitzi, on Lester and Mary,
Whoa Goldwater, Moses, McKenzie and Carey!
In bursts the driver, so peppy and con brio
We know a moment it must be St. Fio.

The Authority pondered in spite of itself
Now why is *he* here, that queer little elf,
Filling our stockings with sneers on his lips
And cursing and swearing at stargazing trips.
We asked him for bread and he gave us a tone
So let him post haste out and leave us alone.

At this point we awoke; it was just a bad dream,
The slums had all gone, we had swept them quite clean.
In their stead were new houses, a beautiful sight,
So all's well that ends well, Happy Christmas, Good Night!


REPORT OF THE DEPARTMENT OF WATER SUPPLY

I'm proud of the smoothest department
    In the whole Administration,
Its spectacular accomplishments
    Deserve high commendation,
For serving the purest aqua
    Without taint or contamination,
To supply the endless demands
    Of our growing population.

To provide a most essential
    Additional deputization,
To insist upon the Utilities'
    More complete capitulation;
To build a Municipal Power plant
    For cheaper electrification –
The Departmental Budget alas
    Need a slight inflation;
To save impoverished realtors
    From additional taxation,
I've kept an increased water rate
    In active litigation.
I've ordered into effect
    For immediate operation
A plan for thrifty water use
    Through universal meterization.
To further squeeze water
    Out of every situation,
I have issued orders
    For stock dehydration.
I've built the Coney Island
    High-pressure pumping station,
Most adequate to quench
    The severest conflagration.

I've electrified my deputies
  Into such animation,
That now they dash about their work
  In one stream of perspiration,
Which may prove a reservoir,
  By a stretch of imagination,
In the event we should suffer
  More water defalcation.

Just one other item
  I report with exultation:
There are *no* further leaks
  In the Department's operation.
Stories of all these reforms
  In many a publication
Have served this modest Department
  From front-page annihilation.


SCENE III

Mayor returns in aeroplane (buzzing device). Ties up at mooring mast on Empire State
Building. Wears overcoat, black hat, and horn-rimmed glasses. Looks through telescope
usually reserved for star-gazing.

MAYOR: Hello Girls. How are all my deputy commissioners today?
  Well, well, there's the Empire State telescope. Let's see what's been happening to
    the City.
Look at those new parkways
  That one's a peach.
And there's Coney Island
  Without a speck of dirt on the beach.
What! Central Park with 100 new cops
  Actually patrolling their beats?

Don't tell me all the pushcarts
  Have been put off Orchard Street.

How clean the city looks
  In all the corners and nooks
See these rosy-cheeked babies
  And how well their mothers look.

Can that be a new housing project?
    And here a new water supply?
Great Scott, you women put me on the spot,
    You did it as well as I.
      I used to fire my commissioners for cause—now I'll fire them for good cause.
        Girls, raise your right hands. I'm going to swear you all in as commissioners.

MAYOR then mumbles regular oath "Do you solemnly swear to support the
    Constitution" (mumbles all the rest except "SO HELP *YOU* GOD," very loud).
GIRLS: We do. SO HELP *YOU* GOD!

THE END

# NOTES

| | |
|---|---|
| EMH-SL | Papers of Elinore Morehouse Herrick, Arthur & Elizabeth Schlesinger Library on the History of Women, Radcliffe College |
| ER | Eleanor Roosevelt Papers, FDR Library |
| ERA | Equal Rights Amendment |
| ESF | Empire State Federation of Colored Women's Clubs |
| FDR Library | Franklin D. Roosevelt Presidential Library, Hyde Park, NY |
| FIC | New York State Factory Investigating Commission |
| GBE-CCOH | Reminiscences of Genevieve Beavers Earle, 1950, Columbia Center for Oral History Archives, Rare Book & Manuscript Library, Columbia University |
| GBE-Col. | Genevieve Beavers Earle Papers, Rare Books and Manuscripts, Butler Library, Columbia University |
| GBE-NYCMA | Genevieve Beavers Earle Papers, Municipal Archives of the City of New York |
| *H-T* | *New York Herald-Tribune* |
| LaG-Archives | Fiorello La Guardia Papers, La Guardia-Wagner Archives, La Guardia Community College |
| LaG-NYCMA | Fiorello La Guardia Papers, Municipal Archives of the City of New York |
| MED-SL | Mary Elisabeth Dreier Papers, Arthur & Elizabeth Schlesinger Library on the History of Women, Radcliffe College |
| MKS-SL | Mary Kingsbury Simkhovitch Papers, Arthur & Elizabeth Schlesinger Library on the History of Women, Radcliffe College |
| NAACP | National Association for the Advancement of Colored People |
| NAM | National Association of Manufacturers |
| NAOWS | National Association Opposed to Woman Suffrage |
| NAWSA | National American Woman Suffrage Association |
| NCJW | National Council of Jewish Women |
| NCL | National Consumers' League |
| NCV | Narcissa Cox Vanderlip Papers [in the Frank A. Vanderlip Papers, Series I], Rare Books and Manuscripts, Butler Library, Columbia University |
| NLRB | National Labor Relations Board |
| NWP | National Woman's Party |
| NYCFWC | New York City Federation of Women's Clubs |
| NYCL | New York Consumers' League |
| NYCLWV | New York City League of Women Voters Papers, Rare Books and Manuscripts, Butler Library, Columbia University |
| NYCMA | New York City Municipal Archives |
| NYPD | New York Police Department |
| NYPL | New York Public Library |

| | |
|---|---|
| NYSLWV | New York State League of Women Voters Papers, Rare Books and Manuscripts, Butler Library, Columbia University |
| *NYT* | *New York Times* |
| NYWTUL | New York Women's Trade Union League |
| PB-AJC | Pearl Bernstein Max, American Jewish Committee Oral History Collection, NYPL |
| PB-WCC | Pearl Bernstein Max, Women's City Club Oral History Project, in author's possession |
| PR League | Proportional Representation League Records, 1900–65, Rare Books and Manuscripts, Butler Library, Columbia University |
| RNC | Republican National Committee |
| SL | Arthur and Elizabeth Schlesinger Library on the History of Women, Radcliffe College |
| SPUC | Society for the Prevention of Unjust Convictions |
| TWV | "The Woman Voter," *Brooklyn Daily Eagle* |
| UO | United Organizations for the Sheppard-Towner Maternity and Infancy Bill |
| WC | women's court |
| WCTU | Woman's Christian Temperance Union |
| *WDN* | *Women's Democratic News* |
| WEA | West End Woman's Republican Association |
| WILPF | Women's International League for Peace and Freedom |
| WJCC | Women's Joint Congressional Committee |
| WJLC | Women's Joint Legislative Conference |
| WLEO | Women's League for Equal Opportunity |
| WML | Woman's Municipal League |
| WNRC | Women's National Republican Club |
| WSP | Woman Suffrage Party |
| WTUL | Women's Trade Union League |
| YWCA | Young Women's Christian Association |

PREFACE

1. Reminiscences of Charles Poletti, Columbia Center for Oral History, Rare Books & Manuscripts, Butler Library, Columbia University (hereafter, CCOH), 1978, 288–89.
2. Elizabeth C. MacPhail, "Survey of Women Lawyers in Public Office," *Women Lawyers Journal* 40, no. 4 (Fall 1954): 26–30, and 41, no. 1 (Winter 1955): 22–24; for Greenberg's letter, see http://www.washingtonpost.com/archive/opinions/1993/07/04/first-generation-feminist-lawyers/1102f871-8917-407e-8389-4cd359b6fe36/?tid=ss_mail (accessed July 22, 2017).

3. *Papers of the Women's City Club of New York*, microfilm ed., University Publications of America, 1989–90.
4. See my "Critical Journey: From Belle Moskowitz to Women's History," in *The Challenge of Feminist Biography*, ed. Sara Alpern, Joyce Antler, Elisabeth I. Perry, and Ingrid Scobie (Urbana: University of Illinois Press, 1992), 79–96.

PROFILE

1. Bernstein gave two oral histories, one in 1984 to the American Jewish Committee (New York Public Library [hereafter, PB-AJC]), the other in 1988 for the Women's City Club Oral History Project (in my possession [hereafter, PB-WCC]). My thanks to Rebecca Edwards for sending me a copy of the former. PB-WCC includes a few more telling anecdotes but more errors of memory. For the story of her appointment, see PB-AJC, 23–26 and "LaGuardia to Keep Delaney to Direct Subway Projects," *New York Times*, Dec. 27, 1933. La Guardia appointed the highly respected Rufus McGahen of the Citizens Union as budget director: see "The New Budget Director" (editorial), *New York Times* (hereafter, *NYT*), Dec. 25, 1933.
2. Moley became one of President Franklin Roosevelt's "brain trusters"; McGoldrick was comptroller for nine years under Mayor La Guardia.
3. PB-AJC, 16. Married in 1929 to Louis W. Max, a PhD in psychology, Bernstein used her birth name professionally. Her concluding remarks in this paragraph are also from this volume.
4. PB-AJC, 26.
5. PB-AJC, 26.
6. PB-AJC, 36–37, 48ff. (on her thirty years with the Board of Higher Education). John R. Everett (later, president of the New School for Social Research) was CUNY's first official chancellor: see Ames Barron, "John Everett, CUNY Chancellor and New School Head, Dies at 73," *NYT*, Jan. 22, 1992.

CHAPTER I

1. I use the term "women's political culture" to denote the tactics, techniques, and networks women constructed to do their political work. Scholars offer other definitions, e.g., Kathryn Kish Sklar: "women's participation in public culture and the separate institutions women built to facilitate their participation" (*Florence Kelley and the Nation's Work: The Rise of Women's Political Culture, 1830–1900* [New Haven, CT: Yale University Press, 1995], xiii).
2. Declaration of Sentiments and Resolutions, Woman's Rights Convention, Held at Seneca Falls, 19–20 July 1848, Elizabeth Cady Stanton & Susan B. Anthony Papers Project, accessed Oct. 30, 2018, http://ecssba.rutgers.edu/docs/seneca.html.

3. Frances W. Graham and Georgeanna M. Remington Gardenier, *Two Decades: A History of the First Twenty Years' Work of the Woman's Christian Temperance Union of the State of New York*, 1894, 59, accessed Dec. 4, 2016, https://www.gutenberg.org/ebooks/20811.

4. The union won assurance that New York's exhibit at the 1893 Chicago World's Fair would be closed on Sundays (1891) and ban women tending bar (1892). Problems with school suffrage arose in defining who could vote and for whom.

5. Graham and Gardenier, *Two Decades*, 74–76.

6. The Wald quotation is from R. L. Duffus, *Lillian Wald: Neighbor and Crusader* (New York: Macmillan, 1938), as quoted in Doris Daniels, "Building a Winning Coalition: The Suffrage Fight in New York State," *New York History* 60, no. 1 (1979): 67–68. Simkhovitch's definition of a settlement is in "The Settlement's Relation to Religion," *Annals of the American Academy of Political and Social Science* 30, no. 3 (Nov. 1907): 62–67; her view of politics is in *Here Is God's Plenty: Reflections on American Social Advance* (New York: Harper & Bros., 1949), 136.

7. In the *NYT*: "The Growth of Women's Clubs," Dec. 12, 1897, and Ellen Scrimgeour's obituary, Mar. 22, 1903.

8. "Women Tell of Their Work for Jerome," *Herald*, Nov. 5, 1905; Lillian Wald, *Windows on Henry Street* (Boston: Little, Brown, 1934), 59f.

9. Mary Ritter Beard's *Woman's Work in Municipalities* (New York: D. Appleton, 1915) chronicles women's political work before suffrage.

10. "Clubwomen Celebrate Jefferson's Birthday," *NYT*, Apr. 3, 1906.

11. Villard, "Women in the New York Municipal Campaign of 1901," speech delivered to the National Suffrage Convention held in Washington, DC, February 14, 1902, accessed Dec. 25, 2014, http://hdl.loc.gov/loc.rbc/rbnawsa.n8366.

12. The African American press followed the careers of a few of these early leaders, but documentation is sparse. In 1905 Garnet and Dr. Verina Harris Morton-Jones, one of the nation's first African American physicians, a clubwoman and at the time president of Garnet's league, supported the Niagara Movement, a predecessor of the NAACP, on whose board Morton-Jones later sat. Keyser, "an important, but neglected figure of early twentieth-century America," was close to prominent African American activists, including writer Hubert Harrison, educator Mary MacLeod Bethune, and poet Lawrence Dunbar (*A Hubert Harrison Reader*, ed. Jeffrey B. Perry [Middletown, CT: Wesleyan University Press, 2001], 36). See also Susan Goodier and Karen Pastorello, *Women Will Vote: Winning Suffrage in New York State* (Ithaca, NY: Cornell University Press, 2017), chap. 4.

13. In the *NYT* of 1905: "Mrs. Mackay for Trustee: Announces Her Candidacy for Place on Roslyn School Board" (Apr. 22); "Mrs. Mackay in Politics: To Be a Member of Hempstead's Board of Education" (July 30). On Moorman, "Branch of Political Equality Association: New York Headquarters in Charge of Miss Irena L. Moorman," *Baltimore Afro-American*, Oct. 15, 1910. The following year, when

Belmont lost interest in the league's branches, Moorman moved her group into a "Woman's Progressive Political League" founded by Sarah Ruhlin. Wife of a retired prizefighter, Ruhlin organized boxing exhibitions to attract men to woman suffrage talks. See in the *NYT*: "Suffrage for Negresses" (Jan. 19, 1910); "Boxing Bouts to Aid Woman Suffrage" (Sept. 29, 1911); "Negro Vote for Mrs. Ruhlin" (Oct. 19, 1911); "Suffragists on Stage" (Jan. 27, 1914). On relations between Socialist women and suffrage, see "Women Socialists Rebuff Suffragists," *NYT*, Dec. 20, 1909.

14. Blatch and Alma Lutz, *Challenging Years: The Memoirs of Harriot Stanton Blatch* (New York: G. P. Putnam's Sons, 1940), 31, 35–42, 61–65, and 76–77. On Blatch's memoir, see Ellen Carol DuBois, *Harriot Stanton Blatch and the Winning of Woman Suffrage* (New Haven, CT: Yale University Press, 1997), chap. 9.

15. Blatch and Lutz, *Challenging Years*, 91–94, and Caroline Lexow Babcock, "The Women's Political Union: Its Organization, Achievements, and Termination," in Isabelle Keating Savell, *Ladies' Lib: How Rockland Women Got the Vote* (New City, NY: Historical Society of Rockland County, 1979), 51–53.

16. Blatch and Lutz, *Challenging Years*, 106–9.

17. Blatch and Lutz, *Challenging Years*, 114; Petrash, *Long Island and the Woman Suffrage Movement* (Charleston, SC: History Press, 2013), chap. 9.

18. The Levy Election Law of 1911 eliminated women as poll watchers (see *General Laws of the State of New York* [St. Paul, MN: West Publishing, 1912], Art. 14, par. 352), but they regained poll-watching rights for the woman suffrage referenda. See Blatch and Lutz, *Challenging Years*, 114, 116f.\

19. Blatch and Lutz, *Challenging Years*, 118–28.

20. Blatch and Lutz, *Challenging Years*, 118–28; DuBois, *Harriot Stanton Blatch and the Winning of Woman Suffrage*, 129–31. Lexow was the oldest daughter of state senator Clarence Lexow; see Savell, *Ladies' Lib*, 16ff.

21. Blatch and Lutz, *Challenging Years*, 129ff., 152, 212. For the women's campaign against Artemas Ward, see in the *NYT*: "Oppose Artemas Ward: The Woman Suffragists Hold a Meeting and Decide to Fight Him" (Oct. 23, 1910); "Women Make It Hot for Artemas Ward" (Nov. 6, 1910); an editorial praising the women's "aptitude for politics" (Nov. 7, 1910); and his obituary, "Artemas Ward Jr., Ex-Assemblyman" (Apr. 30, 1946). Also, "Cuvillier Wins; Suffragists Sad" (Nov. 8, 1911).

22. Blatch and Lutz, *Challenging Years*, chap. 3.

23. Jamie Schultz, "The Physical Is Political: Women's Suffrage, Pilgrim Hikes and the Public Sphere," *International Journal of the History of Sport* 27, no. 7 (May 2010): 1133–53; for press descriptions, see in the *NYT* for 1912: "Suffragists Plan Albany Pilgrimage" (Dec. 10); "Suffrage Host off for Albany To-Day" (Dec. 16). See also *History of Woman Suffrage*, vol. 6, ed. Ida Husted Harper (New York: National American Woman Suffrage Association, 1922), 451ff.; Petrash, *Long Island and the Woman Suffrage Movement*, chaps. 4, 6.

24. The *NYT* followed Jones's "hikes," e.g., "Here's Gen. Jones's General Order No. 1" (Jan. 21, 1913); "Gen. Jones Dodges the Color Question" (Feb. 20, 1913); "Suffrage Hikers Send Wilson a Flag" (Feb. 27, 1913).

25. Blatch and Lutz, *Challenging Years*, 198ff. In her oral history, Rebecca Hourwich Reyher gave this explanation for a woman on horseback leading the parades: "We were creating our own mythology of women on the march, women active, and dramatic," 124, accessed June 23, 2016, http://digitalassets.lib.berkeley.edu/rohoia/ucb/text/struggle4equalit00reyhrich.pdf.

26. Carrie Chapman Catt and Nettie Rogers Shuler, *Woman and Politics—The Inner Story of the Suffrage* (New York: Scribner & Sons, 1926), chap. XIX; Harper, ed., *History of Woman Suffrage*, vol. 6, 459–64.

27. Catt and Shuler, *Woman and Politics*, 283–87; and "Suffragists' Machine Perfected in All States under Mrs. Catt's Rule," *NYT Magazine*, Apr. 29, 1917.

28. [Harriet Burton Laidlaw], *Organizing to Win by the Political District Plan: A Handbook for Working Suffragists* (New York: National American Woman Suffrage Association, 1914). Also the source for quotations from pamphlet in following four paragraphs.; Petrash, *Long Island and the Woman Suffrage Movement*, chap. 8.

29. Harper, ed., *History of Woman Suffrage*, vol. 6, chap. XXXI (the volume's editor, Ida Husted Harper, credited Oreola Williams Haskell for this chapter). The heads of the party's departments included Leonora O'Reilly, industrial; Mrs. Thomas B. Wells, *The Woman Voter*; Mabel Russell, Speakers Bureau; Lillian Griffin, congressional; Anna Ross Weeks, the French; Catharine Dreier, the German; Oreola Williams Haskell, the press; and Mrs. John B. McCutcheon, ways and means. Assisting Hay were Margaret Chanler Aldrich, Mrs. Wells, Martha Wentworth Suffren, Mrs. Robert McGregor, Cornelia K. Hood, Marie Jenney Howe (later a leader in Heterodoxy, a radical feminist group), Mrs. Joseph Fitch, Mrs. A. J. Newbury, and borough chairs Harriet Laidlaw (Manhattan), Ethel Eyre Dreier (Brooklyn), Henriette Speke Seeley (Bronx), Mrs. Alfred J. Eno (Queens), and Mrs. William G. Willcox (Richmond).

30. Haskell, *Banner Bearers: Tales of the Suffrage Campaigns* (Geneva, NY: W. F. Humphrey, 1920), 292–99.

31. Blatch and Lutz, *Challenging Years*, chap. 5; in the *NYT* for 1915: "Women in Relay Crusade" (June 8); "Suffragist Torch Illumines Jersey" (Aug. 8).

32. In the *NYT* for 1916: "Plans All Ready for City's Fourth" (July 3); "Suffragists Silent in Park Gathering" (Sept. 24); for 1917: "Pacifists Quit Suffrage" (Feb. 16); "Suffragists See Victory" and "Suffragists March onto Albany Today" (Mar. 14); "Suffrage Fight Renewed" (Mar. 28). On picketing, see Mary Hay, letter, *Tribune*, June 23, 1917; and in the *NYT* for 1917: Harriet Lees Laidlaw, "Suffragists Opposed to Pickets Help Nation in War Work" (Aug. 19); "State Suffragists Condemn Picketing" (Aug. 31).

33. See in the *NY Age* for 1917: "Colored Suffragists to Argue Question" (Sept. 13); "Suffragists Drew No Line" (Sept. 20); and "Suffragists Choose Colored Vice Leader" (Sept. 27).

34. See in the *NYT* for 1917: "Suffragists' Machine Perfected in All States under Mrs. Catt's Rule" (Apr. 29); "500,990 Women Here Ask Right to Vote" (Aug. 28); "New Parade Idea" (Oct. 21); "20,000 March in Suffrage Line" (Oct. 28). Also, Eleanor Booth Simmons, "Novel Suffrage Stunts as Publicity Makers," *Herald*, Feb. 10, 1918.

35. "Women Confident of Winning Vote," *NY Age*, Nov. 6, 1917.

CHAPTER 2

1. *Philadelphia Tribune*, May 29, 1915. "Goodbye, My Honey, I'm Gone" was a popular song of the era. Just Gone's identity is unknown (V. P. Franklin, "'Voice of the Black Community': *The Philadelphia Tribune*, 1912–41," *Pennsylvania History* 51, no. 4 [Oct. 1984], note 18). Eleven states had granted woman suffrage before 1915; adding the Territory of Alaska, Alexander Keyssar, in *The Right to Vote: The Contested History of Democracy in the United States* (New York: Basic Books, rev. ed., 2009), lists twelve (Tables 17–20).

2. Frances Kellor, "Women in British and American Politics," *Current History* 17 (Feb. 1923): 834, and "Cloisters in American Politics," "rough draft" in fol. "Women in Politics," box 3, Ethel Eyre Dreier Papers, Sophia Smith Archives, Smith College (hereafter, EED-SSA).

3. "City Suffragists Keep Party Alive," *NYT*, Jan. 3, 1918.

4. Hay lifted her "ban" in April: "Suffragists Lift Ban on Old Parties," *NYT*, Apr. 2, 1918.

5. Upstate New York women also wanted more registration days so that more voters could favor "local option" on liquor. See in the *NYT* for 1918: "Suffragists Urge Haste" (Jan. 16); "Whitman to Call Special Elections" (Jan. 23); "Widen Vote for Women" (Jan. 28); "Bill to Pave Way for Women Voters" (Jan. 30); "To Enroll Women by Mail" (Feb. 7); "Women Voters to Register" (Feb. 19); "Women, Like Men, Tardy at Polls" (Feb. 23); "37,623, Not 131,216, Women Would Vote" (Feb. 24); "35,205 Women Can Vote" (Mar. 3). Also, "The Woman Voter" columns in the Brooklyn Daily Eagle (BDE) for 1918: Oct. 11, 12, and 14 (these columns began in July 1918 and continued for almost eleven years (hereafter cited as "TWV," *BDE*).

6. In the *NYT* for 1918: "Women Watchers to Serve at Polls" (Mar. 4); "Votes of Women Here Today May Change Congress" (Mar. 5); and "Democrats Sweep Every District" (Mar. 6). Also, Anna P. George, "Women as Voters in New York State," *Union Signal* (official organ of the National WCTU) 45–46 (Mar. 28, 1918): 7, where she notes that many women had not realized they could vote in this election (my thanks to Jill Norgren for this reference).

7. In the *NYT* for 1918: "Both Parties Urge Women to Enroll" (May 7); "284,114 Women Enroll in City; Many Stay Away" (May 26). For women's final enrollment figures, see "279,566 Women May Vote at Primaries" (June 16): officials threw out over 4,300 enrollment forms for errors and gave exact counts of women in each party—in round figures, Democrat over 160,000; Republican 96,000; Socialist 14,000; Prohibition 3,700. See also "679,618 Women Now on the Party Lists" (July 14), which gives statewide women's figures (Republican over 375,000; Democrat 247,000; Socialist almost 20,000; Prohibition almost 37,000).

8. In the *NYT* for 1918: "Women Can Elect Smith or Whitman as They See Fit" (Nov. 3); "Both Sides Predict Victory at Polls" (Nov. 5); "Women Cast Votes as Readily as Men" (Nov. 6); "City 258,544 for Smith" (Nov. 6). Also, "350,000 Women Cast Votes in New York State Today," *Evening World*, Nov. 5, 1918; and "TWV," *BDE* for 1918: July 24, Sept. 10.

9. Curran, *From Pillar to Post* (New York: Charles Scribner's Sons, 1941), 118–19.

10. "TWV," *BDE*, July 8, 1918.

11. McCooey's quote is in "TWV," *BDE*, July 13, 1918; "Tired of Waiting for Men, G.O.P. Women Go It Alone," *BDE*, July 18, 1918. Between July 1918 and on into 1921, "to separate or integrate" was the predominant topic in "The Woman Voter."

12. In the *NY Age* for 1918: "Harlem Women Form Non-Partisan League" (Mar. 23); "Women Voters Hold First Mass Meeting" (Apr. 27); "Women Voters Invite Leaders to Debate" (May 4); "Harlem Women Show Interest in Politics" (May 25); "Women Voters to Hold Big Meeting" (Nov. 2). Also, "TWV," *BDE*, Sept. 26, Oct. 10, 1918.

13. In "TWV," *BDE* for 1920: July 1, July 16, Aug. 12, Sept. 13. On the "Committee of Forty-Eight" (a reference to the forty-eight states), see "Radicals Plan for 'Political Revolt' in U.S.," *Tribune*, Mar. 21, 1919. On women's interracial campaigns for La Guardia, see chap. 6.

14. "TWV," *BDE*, Sept. 2, 7, 1918; "Were Ignored, Say Republican Women," *BDE*, Nov. 10, 1918.

15. "TWV," *BDE*, June 2, 1919.

16. "TWV," *BDE*, Feb. 25 and June 26, 1919.

17. The Woman Voter (Esther Coster), "Suffrage Victory Revives Demand for Woman's Party," Aug. 22, 1920.

18. "TWV," *BDE*, May 3, July 31, 1920. Also, in the *BDE* for 1920: C. C. Brainerd, "Democratic Women Delegates Exceed Republicans 4 to 1" (May 18) and The Woman Voter, "Women Want Plums Same as the Men" (Nov. 14).

19. After completing work for the "Pittsburgh Survey" (the Russell Sage Foundation's survey of industrial conditions), Eastman published *Work Accidents and the Law* (1910); she was the sole woman on the New York State Employer's Liability Commission.

20. Frances Perkins, Jan. 14, 1915, in State of New York, *Report by Laurence M. D. McGuire of the Factory Investigating Commission, Transmitted to the Legislature Mar. 4, 1915* (Albany, NY: J. B. Lyon, 1915).

21. Kristin Downey, *The Woman behind the New Deal: The Life of Frances Perkins, FDR's Secretary of Labor and His Moral Conscience* (New York: Nan A. Talese/Doubleday, 2009), 43.

22. See my *Belle Moskowitz: Feminine Politics and the Exercise of Power in the Age of Alfred E. Smith* (New York: Oxford University Press, 1987), chap. 3.

23. Perry, *Belle Moskowitz*, chap. 5.

24. Perry, *Belle Moskowitz*, 74, 111–12. See "Want Women Delegates," *NYT*, May 8, 1914, and "Suffrage Pro and Con," *BDE*, May 9, 1914. Many of the women in this campaign would figure in city politics over the next two decades: in addition to Wald, Ethel Dreier, Mary G. Hay, Carrie Chapman Catt, Frances Kellor, Frances Perkins, Helen Rogers Reid, Annie Rhodes, Pauline Goldmark, Vira Whitehouse, Olive Whitman, Cornelia Bryce (later Pinchot, wife of the future governor of Pennsylvania), and Dr. Katharine B. Davis.

25. Henry and his City College friends called their settlement the Downtown Ethical Society, and later, Madison House.

26. The twenty-two women included Perkins and Moskowitz, suffragist Harriot Blatch, National Democratic League leader Ella O'Gorman Stanton, FIC investigator Mary L. Chamberlain, settlement leader Mary Simkhovitch, literary agent and publicist Elisabeth Marbury, WTUL leader Maud Swartz, and Sarah A. Conboy, an officer of the United Textile Workers.

27. "Reminiscences of Frances Perkins," CCOH, II, 207–25. See Perry, *Belle Moskowitz*, chap. 7.

28. As her chief of staff on retrenchment, Moskowitz hired Robert Moses: see Robert Caro, *The Power Broker: Robert Moses and the Fall of New York* (New York: Knopf, 1974), chap. 6.

29. Moskowitz's salary was $4,000. A man was always Smith's "official" manager, but Moskowitz was the "go-to" person for access and strategy.

30. One observer of Smith's political career, Democratic Party activist Mary (Molly) Dewson, called Moskowitz his "tent pole": see Dewson, "An Aid to the End," unpublished memoir, Mary Dewson Papers, Franklin D. Roosevelt Library (hereafter, FDR Library). See also, Perry, *Belle Moskowitz*, introduction, chap. 10, and epilogue.

31. The *WDN* bore design similarities to Harriot Stanton Blatch's *Women's Political World*; the "Trooping" tours were modeled on suffragist tours. Mary Dewson credited Nan Cook with the idea ("Little Grains of Sand," Feb. 24, 1937, Speech file, box 9, Dewson Papers, FDR Library).

32. Eleanor Roosevelt, *Autobiography* (New York: Harper, 1961), 66.

33. Perkins, "Reminiscences," CCOH, III, 15–16.

34. Instead of herself she recommended John Frey (molders union) or Ed McGrady (legislative agent, American Federation of Labor), who are "really *first* class people and would be a help to you and keep you realistically closely aware of the fundamental needs and aspirations of the workers" (Perkins to F.D.R., Feb. 1, 1933: emphases are hers, handwritten letter, fol. 8 "P," Roosevelt Family Papers Donated by the Children of Franklin D. and Eleanor Roosevelt, FDR Library).

35. See Eleanor Booth Simmons, "Women Lacking in Patience in Politics," *Herald*, May 20, 1923; Virginia Swain, "Here's a Woman That Keep[s] a Secret; She's Social Service Advisor to Governor Smith," *Post-Crescent* (Appleton, Wisc.), Nov. 24, 1926; Anna Eleanor Roosevelt, *It's Up to the Women* (New York: Frederick A. Stokes, 1933), 200.

36. Roosevelt, *It's Up to the Women*, chap. XIV (exclamation point hers); Downey, *The Woman behind the New Deal*, 35.

37. Perry, *Belle Moskowitz*, 210.

38. See my "Defying the Party Whip: Mary Garrett Hay and the Republican Party, 1917–1920," in *We Have Come to Stay: American Women and Political Parties, 1880–1960,* ed. Melanie Gustafson, Kristie Miller, Elisabeth Perry (Albuquerque: University of New Mexico Press, 1999), 97–107; "Suffragists Plan Wadsworth Fight," *Sun and Herald*, June 24, 1920.

39. Grace Julian Clarke, "Says Club Women Are Equal to All Demands," *Indianapolis Star*, Sept. 19, 1920; Fay Stevenson, "New York League of Women Voters Pays High Tribute to Old Leader, Mary Garrett Hay, Who Retires," *Evening World*, Mar. 13, 1923; and "Miss Hay Tells of Experiences in Long Career," *Indianapolis Star*, June 2, 1925, all in Hay's Scrapbook, Mary Garrett Hay Papers, Rare Books & Manuscripts Division of the New York Public Library (hereafter, NYPL). See also Will Hays, *The Memoirs of Will H. Hays* (New York: Doubleday, 1955), 257–61.

40. "Republican State Convention May 1920, Statement of Mary Garrett Hay"; "Miss Hay Confers on Women Voters," *Chicago Tribune*, June 3, 1920; "Leader of GOP Women's Division to Leave Office after Convention," June 5, 1920, and "Morsels of Favor Passed Out by GOP Dissatisfying Women," June 10, 1920, both from the *Chicago Evening Mail*, all in Hay Scrapbook.

41. See "TWV," *BDE*, June 2, 1920. The *Tribune, Times*, and *World* all commented on Hay's demotions (July 24 and 27, 1920). For her views on men's treatment of women in the party, see her public statement (no title), June 1, 1920; articles from early June 1920 in the *Chicago News*; Gladys Denny Shultz article, *Des Moines Register*, July 16, 1920; and articles from the *Sun* and *Herald*, all in the Hay Scrapbook. On her early opposition to women running for office, see "She Wins Place, Beating Butler," *Globe*, July 18, 1918, and "Harding Wants Woman in Cabinet; Mary Garrett Hay Makes Conditions," *Evening Mail*, Dec. 16, 1920. On endorsing individuals, see "Present Responsibility of Women as Citizens," August 1920, Hay Scrapbook.

42. See "Miss Hay's Position," *Knickerbocker Press*, July 29, 1920. See also Emma H. De Zouche, "Fight to Defeat Wadsworth . . .," in EED-SSA, and "Women Delegates at Saratoga," *Evening Post*, Aug. 26, 1920. Antisuffragists also attacked Hay: "Watch the Woman Boss in Action," Hay Scrapbook.

43. In the *BDE*: "Crusading for Women Dr. Cuinet's Life Work" (Dec. 4, 1932) and "Dr. L. Adele Cuinet Dies; First Woman in Dentistry Here" (Nov. 21, 1933). The *NYT* carried her obituary on Nov. 22.

44. In the *BDE* for 1918: "Women's Civic League, New Society for Study of Non-Partisan Politics" (Feb. 6); "For 'Suff' Amendment" (June 12); "First A.D. Women Indorse [*sic*] Whitman" (June 21); "TWV" (Nov. 8); for 1919: "Mrs. Catt Champion of a World League" (Feb. 26); "TWV" (Apr. 10).

45. In the *BDE*: "Women Elected in First A.D. Club" (May 6, 1919); Esther A. Coster, "Party Loyalty Urged as Women Flay Wadsworth for Anti-Suffrage Vote" (Dec. 14, 1919); "Women Approve Primaries" (Aug. 20, 1920).

46. In the *BDE*: "TWV," Aug. 21 and Sept. 28, 1920.

47. Martin L. Fausold's *James W. Wadsworth, Jr.: The Gentleman from New York* (Syracuse, NY: Syracuse University Press, 1975) says only that "the senior senator was hurt by the charges of suffragists and prohibitionists" (133). Anti-Wadsworth slogans and verse are in "TWV," *BDE*, Oct. 20, 22, 1920.

48. "Revolt in League of Women Voters," *BDE*, Nov. 14, 1920. Also, Vira B. Whitehouse to Narcissa Cox Vanderlip, Feb. 10 [1920], box I-6, and Esther Lape to Narcissa Vanderlip, Mar. 1, 1923, box I-12, fol. "City-State-Nation, Corr.," Narcissa Cox Vanderlip Papers, Columbia University (hereafter, NCV). In "Cloisters in American Politics," Frances Kellor characterized suffrage leaders as "cynical through disillusion, and egotistical through use of power," a description that echoes complaints about Hay. Carrie Catt and Hay, who shared a house in New Rochelle, exchanged deeply affectionate and concerned letters, especially after Hay's ouster from the LWV. See *Carrie Chapman Catt Papers*, Library of Congress microfilm edition (hereafter, CCC), reel no. 3.

49. "TWV," *BDE*, Nov. 18, 1922.

50. Esther A. Coster, "Women Would Stop Being Neurotic if They Had Plenty to Do, Says Mrs. Charles H. Sabin," *BDE*, Jan. 18, 1925; "Longworth Wants Radicals Deported," *NYT*, Jan. 17, 1926. See chap. 3 for Sabin's repeal campaign.

51. In the *NYT* for 1926: "Women to Endorse Wadsworth Today" (Apr. 13); "Women Leaders Back Wadsworth" (Apr. 14); and "Mrs. Sabin Warns Republican Drys" (Oct. 5). "Wadsworth Strong Up-State, Women Say" (Oct. 28) lists women around the state working for Wadsworth.

52. This telegram is almost the only document in the folder "Senate campaign of 1926," James W. Wadsworth Jr. Papers, Library of Congress. Wadsworth used the word "fanatics" to describe his opponents ("Reminiscences of James W. Wadsworth, Jr.," CCOH, 344–56). Buffalo lawyer John Lord O'Brian said: "Wadsworth . . . had

always opposed woman suffrage . . . [and] that memory rankled with a great many of these women, particularly the professional women. . . . Then he was equally outspoken in opposition to prohibition. He had thus antagonized two groups of voters . . . and a number of the political leaders backed away from him . . . ." ("Reminiscences of John Lord O'Brian," CCOH, 325–27). Wadsworth later returned to Washington as a congressman.

53. Jessie Carney Smith, ed., *Notable Black Women* (Detroit: Gale Research, 1992–2003), *cv.* "Maria Coles Perkins Lawton (1864–1946)"; "The Delegates to Cleveland," *BDE*, Apr. 18, 1924; and Evelyn Brooks Higginbotham, "Black Women Leaders and Party Politics in the 1920s," in *Women, Politics, and Change*, ed. Louise A. Tilly and Patricia Gurin (New York: Russell Sage Foundation, 1990), 206.

54. M. C. Lawton to the Editor, *BDE*, Dec. 20, 1917, Oct. 14, 1920. Lawton's second letter responded to "The Negro Element in Ohio" (editorial, Sept. 29, 1920).

55. "Hearst Is Classed with Negroes' Foes by Preacher Here," *BDE*, May 23, 1922; "TWV," *BDE*, Apr. 18, 1924; "Mrs. M. C. Lawton Returns Home," *Amsterdam News*, Mar. 23, 1927; "Douglass Club to Hear Well Known Speaker Tuesday," *Times Herald (Olean, New York)*, Oct. 15, 1928; "Low's Brooklyn Strength," *BDE*, Sept. 26, 1897; "G.O.P. Women Organize New York State League," *Amsterdam News*, Nov. 27, 1929. For more on the National League of Republican Colored Women, see Higginbotham, "We Are in Politics to Stay"; Melanie S. Gustafson, *Women and the Republican Party, 1854–1924* (Urbana: University of Illinois Press, 2001), 192–93; Catherine E. Rymph, *Republican Women: Feminism and Conservatism from Suffrage through the Rise of the New Right* (Chapel Hill: University of North Carolina Press, 2006), 52–55; and Nikki Brown, *Private Politics and Public Voices: Black Women's Activism from World War I to the New Deal* (Bloomington: Indiana University Press, 2006), 153–54.

56. See Danielle Haas-Laursen, "Rosalie Loew Whitney: Lawyer, Crime Fighter, Judge, Political Activist, Suffragist," 2001, accessed Dec. 28, 2015, http://wlh-static.law.stanford.edu/papers/WhitneyR-HaasLaursen02.pdf.

57. See, in the *NYT*: "Bachelor of the Laws" (June 11, 1895); "Four More Women Lawyers" and " 'Our Learned Brother': Interviewed as to His Attitude Toward His Sister in Law" (June 16, 1895).

58. See, in the *NYT*: "First Time for Woman Lawyer" (May 7, 1896); "Women Lawyers' Club" (June 25, 1899); "Against Women Lawyers" (Sept. 27, 1903). See also Rosalie Loew, "Women of the New York Bar," *Metropolitan Magazine* (June 1896): 279–84; Barbara Babcock, *Woman Lawyer* (Redwood City, CA: Stanford University Press, 2011) 184–89; Jean H. Norris, "The Women Lawyers' Association," *Women Lawyers' Journal* 4, no. 4 (Jan. 1915): 28.

59. In the *NYT*: Rosalie Loew, "The Legal Aid Society" (Apr. 1, 1900); "Resigns Legal Aid Work" (Oct. 19, 1904); "Suffragists Thank Men of All Parties" (Dec. 4, 1917); "Not a Rubber Stamp, Mrs. Whitney Asserts" (July 17, 1918). Rosalie usually used

"Loew" for her legal and "Whitney" for her political work. For the debate over married women's names, see in the *BDE* for 1921: "Woman in Politics Drops Her Husband's Name as She Rises" (Jan. 17) and "Brooklyn Women Disapprove 'Woman Pays Club' Doctrine" (Feb. 3). See "Travis H. Whitney Dies in Hospital," *NYT*, Jan. 9, 1934, and subsequent articles praising his public service.

60. In the *BDE* for 1918: "Rosalie L. Whitney Scores Wadsworth" (July 23); "Should Women Be Put in Public Office?" (Sept. 29); "Legislation Urged to Protect Girls with Jobs in Peril" (Nov. 25); for 1919: "Republican Women for Miss Perkins" (Jan. 31); "TWV" (Feb. 2, Mar. 6, Nov. 4); "Educators Differ Over Plan to Raise School Age to 16" (Nov. 9); for 1920: "TWV" (Mar. 4, July 24); "Women Voters Lining Up in Fight on Bills at Albany" (Mar. 7); "Bill for a Women's Bureau in Department of Labor Urged by the Republicans" (Apr. 25).

61. In the *BDE* for 1920: "TWV" (Oct. 8, 17, 27, Nov. 9); "Mrs. Miller Guest of G.O.P. Women" (Oct. 26). Vanamee ran for register in 1929 (see "Grace D. Vanamee, Leader of Women," *NYT*, Dec. 11, 1946).

62. In the *NYT* for 1921: "Signs Industrial Bill" (Mar. 11); "H.D. Sayer Chosen New State Labor Head" (Apr. 5); and "Favors Republican Ticket" (June 21); in the *BDE* for 1921: "Dedicate G. O. P. Women's New Club" (Feb. 18); "TWV" (Feb. 19, May 6, 16, 25, June 4); "Women Work for Bill" (Apr. 15); "No Hope for Hylan, Says Prendergast, if Women Do Duty" (May 15).

63. See Curran, *Pillar to Post*, chap. 17.

64. Most of my information on Kross comes from the Anna M. Kross Papers at the American Jewish Archives, Hebrew Union College, Cincinnati, Ohio (hereafter, AMK-AJA). As they were not well processed when I read them, my citations may not match current organization; also, box and folder titles did not always match contents. I also consulted a small Kross collection at Smith College's Sophia Smith Archives (hereafter, AMK-SSA Papers).

65. For Kross's characterization of her family life, see "An Army Raised against Our System," *Bar Bulletin of the New York County Lawyers Association* 13, no. 1 (May 1955): 20, and citation when awarded an LLD from NYU, box 1, fol. 3, "Citations" (AMK-SSA). In the early 1950s, Kross's younger sister Henriette M. Voorsanger wrote a biography of Anna, "Everybody's Judge: Anna Moscowitz Kross" (type-script, property of Mae Quinn, who kindly lent it to me).

66. Joyce Antler, *The Journey Home: How Jewish Women Shaped Modern America* (New York: Schocken, 1997), 189. For her own comments on her early career, see Anna M. Kross to Bernard Trencher, Oct. 13, 1938, box 79, New York Supreme Court, First Judicial District, Correspondence; Reports, 1938, AMK-AJA. Also, "Woman Attorney Aids Plasterers," *Evening Post*, Apr. 14, 1923; "70,000 Work People Clients for Woman," *NYT*, July 22, 1923, in which she describes judges' biases against women lawyers.

67. "Personal biographical material including articles and speeches," Biographical Sketch D, 1964, 7 pp., box 82, AMK-AJA Papers. In a carbon copy of speech notes (Feb. 4, 1941), Kross wrote that "Accidental circumstances drove me into the work of the then Women's Night Court as the Chairman of the Legal Committee of the Church of the Ascen[s]ion" (box 1 [1910–1974], Addresses, articles, speeches for radio and television, 1953–1963, fol. "Notes 1941," AMK-AJA). She did not describe the "accidental circumstances."

68. Rev. Grant wrote her a glowing recommendation, saying that Kross won the "admiration" and "friendship" of all who worked with her (Grant to Mayor John F. Hylan [copy], Jan. 8, 1918, box 76, AMK-AJA). The Krosses had three daughters, the first of whom, Esther, died at age five. Kross's official biography (box 82, fol. 2, "Biographical Sketch D, 1964," 7 pp., AMK-AJA).

69. See "Women in Our Courts," *Women Lawyers' Journal* 4, no. 7 (Apr. 1915): 52, describing a "mass meeting" prompted by anger over the replacement of five female probation officers with men at salaries $300 higher. See also AMK (unsigned) to Dr. Percy S. Grant, May 20, 1919, box 76 (no folder), AMK-AJA; "New York's First Woman Magistrate Mixes Justice with Common Sense," *Literary Digest* (Feb. 21, 1920): 24–26; and Mary Weston Cottle, "Women in the Legal Profession," *Women Lawyers' Journal* 4, no. 8 (May 1915): 60.

70. In the *NYT* for 1921: "Women 40 Per Cent of Republican Vote" (Oct. 26); "Women Politicians Tilt in Town Hall" (Oct. 28). Marshall's "Women's Political Debate Is Tabasco, Paprika, Cayenne, and Mixed Hisses and Jeers" (*Evening World*, Oct. 28, 1921) includes evocative drawings of the participants. See also "Boos, Cheers, Jeers in Women's Debate on Choosing Mayor," *Herald*, Oct. 28, 1921. Also for subsequent paragraphs.

71. "Women Politicians Tilt in Town Hall," *NYT*. Also the source for the following paragraph.

72. "Women Outline Campaign for March Election," *Tribune*, Feb. 5, 1918; "Here's Woman Ready to Run; Miss Stephenson May Yet Be Secretary of State," *BDE*, June 20, 1918.

73. See interviews in the *BDE*: "Mrs. Falco Picks a Man as Campaign Chairman," July 1, 1921, and Edward Titus, "Mrs. Pratt, Coming Alderman from Silk Stocking District, Tells of Her Aims," June 21, 1925. On women's support for women candidates solely because of sex, see "Organization Men in Queens Smile over Opposition," *BDE*, Sept. 15, 1918. Democratic women complained more than Republicans about "untrained" women, even for such minor posts as election official: "TWV," *BDE*, Oct. 3, 1918.

74. Ida B. Sammis was also elected to the assembly in 1918, but as she ran from Suffolk County I am not profiling her here. See Petrash, *Long Island and the Woman Suffrage Movement*, chap. 11.

75. "Bachelor of the Laws," *NYT*, June 11, 1895, lists her as one of ten women and sixty men. See Isabella Mary Pettus, "The Work of the Woman's Law Class, New York University," *Women Lawyers' Journal* 1, no. 3 (Nov. 1911): 20–22, and Phyllis Eckhaus, "Restless Women: The Pioneering Alumnae of New York University School of Law," *New York University Law Review*, 66 (Dec. 1991): 1996–2013. For Lilly's career as a lawyer, see the *BDE* of 1917: "Judge Makes Her Doff Hat" (Sept. 19) and " 'Tipperary' Echoes in Hall of Justice" (Sept. 20); in the *NYT* for 1920: "Sues on Tipperary Sales" (May 13) and "Loses 'Tipperary' Suit" (June 24). In her oral history, Rebecca Hourwich Reyher says of women's hats: "At that time [the 1910s] you didn't go out bare headed, you wore a hat once you left the house" ("Search and Struggle for Equality and Independence," 39).

76. In the *NYT*: "Democrats Name a Woman: Miss Mary M. Lilly Nominated for the Assembly," Aug. 2, 1918; "Women Begin Campaign for Tammany Ticket," Oct. 16, 1925; "Mrs. Mary F. [*sic*] Lilly, Noted Lawyer, Dies," *NYT*, Oct. 12, 1930. In the *BDE* for 1918: "TWV" (Oct. 12, Nov. 26, Dec. 11), "Women Democrats of State and City Form Federation" (Oct. 20). In the *Tribune*: Emma Bugbee, "Politicians Worried about How Women Will Act at Polls Tuesday" (Nov. 3, 1918), "Gayety Rules Albany on Eve of Inaugural" (Jan. 1, 1919); "Kings County Women Have Good Time Up at Albany," *BDE*, Jan. 2, 1919.

77. Edith Moriarty, "With the Women of Today," *Olean Times Herald*, Jan. 8, 1919; "Move in Albany for Milk Inquiry," *NYT*, Jan. 14, 1919; in the *BDE* for 1919: H. J. B., "Two Women Legislators Making Their Presence Felt in Albany" (Jan. 19); "Mrs. Lilly's Election Bill" (Jan. 28); in the *Tribune* of 1919: "Mrs. Lilly Offers Bill to End Death Penalty" (Jan. 14); "Mrs. Lilly Files Bill to Legitimize War Babies" (Feb. 5); Denis Tilden Lynch, "Our Women Lawmakers in the Assembly" (Mar. 2). Also, "The Log of a Woman Legislator," *Woman Citizen* 4, no. 1 (June 7, 1919): 9.

78. In the *NYT* for 1919: "Friends Honor Mrs. Lilly" (May 18); "Republican Women Work for Primary" (July 5); "Union Answers Mrs. Lilly" (Aug. 18); "Citizens Union Hits Woman Candidate" (Nov. 3); "Mrs. Lilly Upholds Her Two Salaries" (Nov. 4). See also "Democrats Talk of Making Mrs. Lilly Assembly Leader," *Tribune*, May 12, 1919, and "The Defense of Mrs. Lilly" (editorial), *BDE*, Nov. 4, 1919. In 1919, Lilly's sister Marguerite Krecker, also a suffragist and Democrat, ran for an open seat on the board of aldermen; by May she was the only woman left in that race, but she lost ("TWV," *BDE*, Apr. 12 and May 19, 1919).

79. On Mamie Colvin, "Woman Candidate for Congress First of Sex in State," *Evening World*, Mar. 4, 1918; " 'Win the War' an Issue for Women," *Middletown Times-Press*, Mar. 5, 1918; and "Democrats Win in Elections," *Poughkeepsie Eagle-News*, Mar. 6, 1918. Anna George wrote that Colvin brought more attention to the cause of Prohibition than ever before and that she was a "fine campaign speaker" and that despite her loss "New York women are proud of her" ("Women as Voters in New York State," *Union Signal*, Mar. 28, 1918, 7). On Charlotte Smith, see "Women Look Over Many Candidates," *Sun*, Feb. 22, 1918. On Clara A. Rodger, "Woman

Named County Clerk by Whitman," *Tribune*, Nov. 3, 1918; "Mrs. Rodger, First Woman County Clerk of Queens, A County Clerk's Daughter," *Evening World*, Nov. 5, 1918.

80. Socialists nominated labor organizer Ella Reeve Bloor for lieutenant governor, pacifist educator Jessie Wallace Hughan for secretary of state, minimum wage activist Mollie Scheps Rumpler for state senate, and labor reformer Gertrude Weil Klein for the assembly. Klein won a seat on the city council in 1941. Of four major party woman candidates for the assembly in the 1918 primary, only one, former antisuffragist Republican Kate Farrer Southmayd, was on the organization ticket; the others—Democrats Lillian E. Kiefer, Julia Eppig, and Florence Dougherty—entered as "antiboss" (i.e., anti-Tammany) candidates. On women's defeats in their first year as voters, see "Women's Ticket Failed," *NYT*, Mar. 21, 1918; "Women Vote Tuesday for First Time for State Candidates," *BDE*, Sept. 1, 1918; "Women May Decide Today's Primaries," *NYT*, Sept. 3, 1918. On other candidates, see in the *BDE* for 1918: "Here's Woman Ready to Run; Miss Stephenson May Yet Be Secretary of State" (June 20); "Woman Candidate for County Clerk" (July 1); "TWV" (July 10, Aug. 5, 18, 31, Sept. 5, Oct. 1); "Should Women Be Put in Public Office?" (Sept. 29). Stephenson ran for magistrate in 1921, as did Jeanette Brill: "TWV," *BDE*, Mar. 16, 1921. In May 1929 Mayor Jimmy Walker appointed Brill to the Brooklyn bench: see "Mrs. Brill Says 'O.K.' after First Day as a Judge," *BDE*, June 4, 1929. After his first mayoral victory, he ignored Democratic women party workers' pleas for "plums": "100 Democratic Women in City Demanding 'Plums' of Tammany," *Herald-Tribune* (hereafter *H-T*), Nov. 22, 1925.

81. See "Woman Candidate for Governor," *Evening World*, Sept. 13, 1918; "Alfred Smith's Plurality over Whitman 14,842," *Rochester Democrat and Chronicle*, Dec. 31, 1918; "Socialist Labor Ticket Out," *BDE*, Mar. 19, 1925; "Socialists Nominate Woman for Mayor," *NYT*, June 9, 1929; "Brooklyn Woman Picked for Socialist-Labor Mayor," *BDE*, June 9, 1929; "Socialist-Labor Nominee Says She Doesn't Want to Be Mayor under Capitalism," *BDE*, June 10, 1929; "Socialist Labor Nominee Led Enright by 646; Mrs. Johnson Congratulated after Election," *NYT*, Nov. 7, 1929. Her party nominated her for the US Senate in 1934. Herbert M. Merrill (letter to the *NYT*, May 17, 1935) noted that New York Socialists had long been nominating women for office, including Carrie W. Allen for secretary of state in 1910, Bertha H. Mailly for the same office in 1912, and Anna A. Malay for governor in 1912.

82. Joan Moody, "What Will They Do with It?," *Everybody's Magazine* 41, no. 5 (Nov. 1919): 113. Three other New York City women ran for US House seats in 1918: Republican Sadie Kost and Democrats Clara B. Mann and Elizabeth Arthur. See "Six Women Aspire to Congress Seats in This Election," *Tribune*, Nov. 4, 1918.

83. On Cook, see Mary E. Dreier Papers, Arthur and Elizabeth Schlesinger Library on the History of Women, Radcliffe College (hereafter, MED-SL), box 7, fol. 101.

84. See Marion Dickerman, "An 'Uplifter' and a Political Machine," *The Survey*, Jan. 3, 1920, 362–64; Mary Dreier's memoir of the campaign, in Marion Dickerman

Papers, box 2 ("Correspondence"), fol. 10, FDR Library. Dickerman described Dreier as "young and beautiful, with eyes the color of cornflowers and cheeks pink with the fire that burned within her for a cause she believed right." Many memoirs refer to Dreier's blue eyes, e.g., Justine Wise Polier, who said workers called her "the blue-eyed goddess of the working woman" (Oral History, FDR Library, 3); Rose Schneiderman described her as "a beauty," with "honey-colored hair and large blue eyes which could express great anger at conditions under which women had to work and live" (*All for One* [New York: Paul S. Eriksson, 1967], 79). See chap. 3 for more on the WJLC.

85. "After the defeat of our legislation" (remarks delivered at an event honoring Marion Dickerman, n.d.), MED-SL, box 5, fol. 68. On a Friday the 13th (1961?), Dreier wrote to Dickerman, "You were a gallant fighter, and though Speaker Sweet won, he, for the first time, had to work hard and if it had not been for the unwillingness of the Temperance Union ladies to join with us, we would have won. Anyway, we had a great time" (fol. 105, "Marion Dickerman"). See also, in the *Tribune* for 1919: "Red Cross Nurse to Run against Speaker Sweet" (July 27); "Woman Candidate Indorsed" (Aug. 4); "New York's 1919 Crop of Women Candidates for Office" (Oct. 19). See also Dickerman's Scrapbook for the 1919 Campaign, "Women in Politics" (3 folders), Marion Dickerman Papers, FDR Library; Blanche W. Cook, *Eleanor Roosevelt*, vol. 1 (New York: Viking, 1992), 242; and Kenneth S. Davis, *Invincible Summer: An Intimate Portrait of the Roosevelts Based on the Recollections of Marion Dickerman* (New York: Atheneum, 1974), 7 (Davis calls Dickerman "the first woman ever to run for the New York legislature," which she was not).

86. In the *NYT* for 1919: "Woman Hopes for Election as Judge" (Oct. 5); "Runs Her Campaign on a Coal-Hole Basis" (Oct. 20); Hildegarde Hawthorne, "A Woman Candidate for Judge" (Oct. 26); "Rembaugh or Hoyer?" (Oct. 28); "Miss Rembaugh Has Hope" (Nov. 5). Also, "Women Serve Tea in Old-Time Saloon," *Evening World*, Oct. 22, 1919; in the *Tribune* for 1919: Denis Tilden Lynch, "Women in Politics for an Unbossed Judiciary" (Nov. 2) and "Women in Public Office" (editorial, Nov. 13); and "Politics and the Woman," *Woman Citizen* 4 (Nov. 15, 1919): 476–77.

87. On Campbell, see Pauline Snowdon, "Empire Friendly Shelter Need Aid," *Chicago Defender*, Apr. 19, 1919; Thelma E. Berlack, "Grace Campbell First in Harlem to Tackle Problem of Unmarried Mother," *Amsterdam News*, Feb. 20, 1929; "Harlem Women Organize to Win Seat in Congress," *Philadelphia Tribune*, Nov. 30, 1933 (where Dr. Julia Coleman Robinson lists Campbell as one of almost thirty Harlem women with a "special degree of fitness for high public service"). Also, Julie Gallagher, *Black Women & Politics in New York City* (Urbana: University of Illinois, 2012), 29–30, and see chap. 4 for Campbell on the framing of Harlem women. For more on Baright, see "Why I Would Be a Judge," *New Castle Herald*, June 26, 1915. Also, "Maj. R. S. Allyn Wins Aldermanic Race," *BDE*, Jan. 10, 1920; in the *NYT* for 1920: "Woman for Senator Is Named by Labor" (May 31) and "Five Women

Are Candidates for U.S. Senate" (Oct. 17); "Artificial Leg Beat Her for Assembly, Says Miss Kipper," *BDE*, June 5, 1921; "When Women Seek Office," *NYT*, Oct. 23, 1921; "Tammany Women to Drive for 1,000 Members in Boro," *BDE*, Dec. 6, 1925. On Schneiderman's race, see her *All for One*, 146–47.

88. "First Impressions of a Woman Voter," *NY Age*, Mar. 16, 1918.

89. In this era Harlem's population was still 70 percent white.

90. "Negro to Oppose Woman," *NYT*, Aug. 30, 1919; "New York's 1919 Crop of Women Candidates for Office," *Tribune*, Oct. 19, 1919; "Miss Smith, Assemblyman, Won on Her War Record," *Tribune*, Nov. 6, 1919; "3rd Anniversary of Women's Rep[ublican]. League," *NY Age*, July 16, 1921. The *Times* noted that both "whites" and "negroes" supported Smith's candidacy.

91. "New Divorce Bill Put in at Albany," *BDE*, Jan. 14, 1920; "Expel Socialist Assemblymen by an Overwhelming Majority after Debate Lasting All Night," *Oneonta Star*, Apr. 2, 1920; "State Bonus Bill Passed," *NYT*, Apr. 24, 1920; "Woman in Assembly an Adept in Sports," *Sun and Herald*, May 2, 1920; "Battle over Legalizing of 2.75 Beer Sale . . .," *Rochester Democrat and Chronicle*, Apr. 20, 1920; "Victory Hall Bill Signed," *Evening World*, Apr. 28, 1920; "TWV," *BDE*, Jan. 13 and Feb. 11, 1921; "New York News Items in Brief," *Sun and Erie County Independent*, Feb. 3, 1921; "Court May Decide on Validity Bonus Bill," *Olean Times Herald*, Aug. 31, 1921; "Court Overthrows Soldier Bonus Act in Divided Ruling," *NYT*, Sept. 1, 1921.

92. "Republican Women of Harlem Hosts at 'Turkey Festival,'" *NY Age*, Dec. 25, 1920; "Won't Give Up Feminine Frills, Assemblywoman Tells Vassar Students," *Poughkeepsie Eagle-News*, Jan. 13, 1921; "Smith and Roberts Named for Reelection," *NY Age*, Aug. 13, 1921; "Women Hold Meeting," *NY Age*, Oct. 22, 1921; "Citizens Union Fails to Endorse Miss Smith," *Tribune*, Oct. 26, 1921; "Two Good Terms Deserve Third, Says Miss Smith," *Tribune*, Oct. 30, 1921; "Mayor Hylan Is Reelected," *NYT*, Nov. 9, 1921. The *Tribune*, which had referred to her as the "girl member of the New York State Legislature," said she lost by a "heavy majority" ("Republicans Keep Control of Assembly," Nov. 10, 1921). Dr. Elizabeth Van Rensselear Gillette, a Schenectady surgeon, joined Smith in the assembly in 1920 but was also defeated for re-election. No woman won a seat in the assembly in 1921.

93. See "TWV" columns of 1921, especially June 27, July 1, July 20, Aug. 12; also, in the *BDE* of 1921: "Mrs. Falco's Campaign" (Sept. 4); "Mrs. Falco Defeats Gorman by 200 in Aldermanic Fight" (Sept. 14); "Queer Turn of Odds in Contest between Mrs. Falco and Larney" (Nov. 4); "TWV" (Nov. 5); "Miss Mathews Is Only Woman to Win in City Office Race" (Nov. 9); "TWV" (Nov. 10). "TWV's" editor wondered whether women would "have the courage" to place another woman in nomination anytime soon.

94. In the *BDE* for 1921: "TWV" (Jan. 18); Esther A. Coster, "Miss Annie Mathews, Who Has Won Success at a Man's Job, Eschews Mannish Manners" (Nov. 8),

"Club Women Honor Woman Register" (Nov. 27); "Annie Mathews, Ex-City Aide, Dies," *NYT*, Oct. 25, 1959. Four years later Mathews ran against another female opponent, Ida Slack, former president of the New York City Federation of Women's Clubs. Mathews won again and served until she retired ("TWV," *BDE*, Sept. 22, 1925).

95. In the *Pittsburgh Courier* for 1924: "Race Woman, Candidate for Legislature, Favors Lower Rents in Harlem" (Aug. 24) and "Interest Keen in Harlem as Primary Day Approaches" (Sept. 13); and "New York," *Baltimore Afro-American*, Sept. 15, 1934. Some sources identify Bessye J. Bearden, a Harlem Democratic Party activist, as "elected" to Manhattan's Fifteenth School District Board, but she was appointed; in 1935 she was appointed deputy collector of internal revenue: see "Mrs. Bessye Bearden Named to School Board 15th District," *NY Age*, Feb. 9, 1924; the Bessye J. Bearden papers at the Schomburg Center for the Study of Black Culture (NYPL) are ambiguous on this point. On Carter and Bolin, see chap. 6. Alma Crosswaith, wife of Harlem Socialist Frank Crosswaith, had previously run for alderman. Two other Socialists, Jane P. Morgan and Layle Lane, ran for the US Senate and Congress, respectively.

96. "Vital Records," *BDE*, May 23, 1918, noted the death of a baby daughter from pneumonia; also, Eunice Fuller Barnard, "A Lone Woman Sits with the Aldermen," *NYT*, Sept. 25, 1927.

97. In the *NYT*: "Women Plan Party Rally" (May 12, 1920); "Tours for Women Speakers" (Oct. 24, 1920); "Ogden Mills Names Aids" (Oct. 11, 1922). Also, "N.Y. Delegates to Saratoga Unbound," *Sun and Herald*, July 20, 1920; "TWV," *BDE*, Oct. 8, 1920, noted her fundraising; Oct. 14, her elector status. On the leadership fight see "Republicans Plead with Insurgents," *NYT*, Feb. 16, 1924; this contest lasted until after the primary: see, e.g., "Coleman Wins Fight for the Leadership of the 15th District," *NYT*, Apr. 2, 1924 (Pratt sided with Coleman).

98. Formed in 1922, the Women's Democratic Union (WDU) opposed newspaperman William Randolph Hearst's attempt to unseat Governor Smith. It remained active throughout the 1920s in support of Smith's legislative initiatives; in 1932 the women's division of the National Democratic Committee absorbed it.

99. For Pratt doing nothing for suffrage, see Barnard interview; "Women Celebrate Suffrage Victory," *Sun and Herald*, Aug. 28, 1920, includes her as participating in the 1920 celebration of the Nineteenth Amendment. For suffragist efforts to find a Democratic woman opponent, see *NYT* for 1925: "Mrs. John T. Pratt Is Boomed for Alderman to Succeed Falconer in Silk Stocking District" (May 12); "Mrs. J. T. Pratt to Be First Woman Alderman; 'Silk Stocking District' to Support Her" (June 5); "Women Candidates for Alderman Urged" (June 8); "Woman Rejects Aldermanic Chance" (June 18); "Seek Woman to Run in Aldermanic Race" (June 21). On men's opposition to women's political participation, see Sarah Schuyler Butler, "Women Who Do Not Vote," *Scribner's* 76 (Nov. 1924): 529–33.

100. In the *BDE* for 1925: "Mrs. Pratt for Alderman" (editorial, June 5); Edward Titus, "Mrs. Pratt, Coming Alderman from Silk Stocking District, Tells of Her Aims" (June 21); Esther A. Coster, "Mrs. Pratt Crashes Portals of New York's Board of Aldermen" (Nov. 22); for 1926, " 'Real Fellow,' Says Board of Mrs. Pratt after Trial as City's First Alderwoman" (Apr. 7); for 1928, Lillian Sabine, "The Lady from New York" (Dec. 9).

101. "Women in Tribute to Mrs. J. T. Pratt," *BDE*, Nov. 19, 1925; Coster's profile cites Pratt's valuing "party solidarity" in national matters; in *NYT* for 1926: "Pratt Meets First Defeat" (Jan. 13); "Protest Rejection of Alderman Pratt" (Feb. 3); "She Can Take Care of Herself" (Feb. 4).

102. See, e.g., in the *NYT*: "Mrs. Pratt Demands Ousting of Kohler" (Aug. 17, 1927); "Mrs. Pratt Renews Attack on Kohler" (Aug. 10, 1928). Charles L. Kohler was Walker's budget director.

103. Two other women, also named Ruth, joined Pratt in Congress in 1929: Ruth Bryan Owen (William Jennings Bryan's daughter) and Ruth Hanna McCormick (daughter of President McKinley's political manager, Mark Hanna, and widow of US senator Medill McCormick). "I am back of Hoover heart and soul," Pratt said in December 1928, before the Depression hit (quoted in Sabine, "The Lady from New York").

104. See Esther Coster's "ten reasons why women should be candidates for office" ("TWV," *BDE*, Aug. 18, 1921).

105. "Women Orators Win Election Crowds Easier Than Men Do," *BDE*, Oct. 31, 1920, and "Campaign's Final Rush," *NYT*, Oct. 31, 1920.

CHAPTER 3

1. Emma Bugbee, "The Mystery of Woman as a Political Force," *Tribune*, Dec. 7, 1919, and following quotations.. On Bugbee, see Glen Fowler, "Emma Bugbee, 93; Reporter 55 Years," *NYT*, Oct. 10, 1981.

2. Louise M. Young, *In the Public Interest: The League of Women Voters, 1920–1970* (New York: Greenwood Press, 1989), 46; Lilly is quoted in "The Log of a Woman Legislator," *Woman Citizen* 4, no. 1 (June 7, 1919): 9.

3. "Reminiscences of Frances Perkins," CCOH, I, part 3, 399–401. Also, see my "Women's Political Choices after Suffrage: The Women's City Club of New York, 1915–present," *New York History* 62, no. 4 (Oct. 1990): 417–34 and "The Tradition of Women's Voluntary Political Associations and the Women's City Club of New York," *Papers of the Women's City Club of New York* (microfilm ed.), introduction. Attorney Dorothy Kenyon called the club's mansion the "round house" in a letter to Mrs. Herbert Sternau, Mar. 25, 1965 (box 55, fol. "Women's City Club," Dorothy Kenyon Papers, Sophia Smith Archives, Smith College). See in the *NYT*: "Women's City

302 • Notes to pages 68–72

Club Has New Quarters" (June 16, 1918); "Park Av. Building Sold by Women's City Club" (Feb. 6, 1937). A modern office building replaced it.

4. The US Children's Bureau, founded in 1912 at the urging of Lillian Wald and Florence Kelley, established the first reliable birth registration system. See Kriste Lindenmeyer, *A Right to Childhood. The U.S. Children's Bureau and Child Welfare, 1912–1946* (Urbana: University of Illinois Press, 1997).

5. "Reminiscences of Frances Perkins," CCOH, I, part 3, 401–12.

6. "Women's City Club Opens Maternity Center," *BDE*, Sept. 3, 1917; Downey, *The Woman behind the New Deal*, 69–71.

7. By 1924 the WJCC consisted of twenty-one organizations with a total membership of twelve million women. See Jan Doolittle Wilson, *The Women's Joint Congressional Committee and the Politics of Maternalism, 1920–30* (Urbana: University of Illinois Press, 2007).

8. Margaret Doane Fayerweather to the *NYT*, May 18, 1921; "TWV," *BDE*, Aug. 2, 1921; "Maternity Measure Approved by House," *NYT*, Nov. 20, 1921. For an analysis of Sheppard-Towner and its impact on women's professional lives, see Robyn Muncy, *Creating a Female Dominion in American Reform, 1890–1935* (New York: Oxford University Press, 1991), chap. 4.

9. Louisiana, Massachusetts, and Rhode Island also rejected Sheppard-Towner. Mary Guthrie Kilbreth and J. S. Eichelberger led the "Woman Patriots"; see "Miss Mary Kilbreth, Opposed Suffrage," *NYT*, June 28, 1957, and Susan Goodier, *No Votes for Women: The New York State Anti-Suffrage Movement* (Urbana: University of Illinois, 2013), 119–20 passim. Also, Wilson, *The Women's Joint Congressional Committee*, 57–58; Narcissa Cox Vanderlip, "'Human Side' of Maternity and Infancy Law Is Considered," letter to the *NYT*, Feb. 5, 1923 and for subsequent quotation. The amount each state received depended on the percentage of its rural population.

10. For this and following paragraph: Hilda R. Watrous, "Narcissa Cox Vanderlip: Chairman, New York State League of Women Voters 1919–1923" (Foundation for Citizen Education, 1982), 21–23; many newspapers commented on these events, e.g., in the *NYT* for 1921: "Miller Tells League of Women Voters It Is a Menace to Our Institutions" (Jan. 28); "Women's League Replies to Miller" (Jan. 29); and "Miller Still Firm against Sex Groups" (Feb. 9, 1922). Several Republican women agreed with Miller: Pauline Sabin, Rosalie Loew Whitney, and Grace Vanamee protested a "sex line" in politics ("Prominent Suffragists Uphold Miller's Stand," *Tribune*, Jan. 29, 1921).

11. Her *NYT* obituary makes no mention of her political activities (Mar. 6, 1966). See her "Regular Meeting of United Organizations Held May 8, 1923," box I-25, fol. "Meetings," and box I-24 ("United Organization for the Sheppard-Towner Bill, 1922–23"), NCV. Blanche Wiesen Cook first alerted me to these papers, which are appended to those of her husband.

12. "Women Urge State to Aid Mothers," *NYT*, Mar. 9, 1922; "Finds Country Baby in Greatest Peril," *NYT*, Mar. 10, 1922; S. Josephine Baker, MD, DPH, "The Sheppard-Towner Bill" (n.d.), fol. "Printed Material" and an anonymous note saying, "'They say' Dr. Baker would get all the money" (n.d.), box I-25, fol. "Misc. Documents," NCV; "82,549 Babies Saved," *NYT*, Apr. 26, 1922 (covering a dinner honoring Baker's twenty years in public service). See also "Appoints Dr. Baker in State Health Department," *Rochester Democrat and Chronicle*, Apr. 30, 1922, and "Woman Doctor Gets Federal Post," *Evening Tribune*, Dec. 13, 1923. In her memoir *Fighting for Life* (New York: MacMillan Company, 1939), Baker barely mentions Sheppard-Towner, and then only to express disappointment in suffrage's meager accomplishments (200–201). On her pursuit of Mallon, see Judith Leavitt, *Typhoid Mary: Captive to the Public's Health* (Boston: Beacon Press, 1996). In 1922 she accepted consultancies on child health with the state department of health and in 1923 with the US Department of Labor.

13. "Federal Midwifery" (editorial), *NYT*, Jan. 24, 1922.

14. Vanderlip, "'Human Side' of Maternity and Infancy Law Is Considered."

15. Mrs. Frank A. Vanderlip (FAV) to [blank], Feb. 23, 1922; to all State Senators and Assemblymen, Feb. 23, 1922; to various senators, Feb. 27, 1922 (box I-24, fol. "NCV"); "Regular Meeting of United Organizations Held May 8, 1923" (box I-25, fol. "Meetings"). Also, "Miller Demands State Home Rule," *NYT*, Jan. 22, 1922.

16. "Mrs. W. G. Mitchell, Suffragette, Dies," *NYT*, July 28, 1960; "Woman Candidate for Assembly No Believer in Swivel-Chair Politics," *Evening Telegram*, Aug. 23, 1918; "Women Will Continue Campaign to Save Babies of New York State," *Oneonta Star*, Apr. 10, 1922; "Reminiscences of Nathan Straus Jr.," CCOH. Her letters to Senator Straus, Feb. 26; Grace Greene, Mar. 15; Mrs. Joseph Rieger, Dunkirk, Mar. 12; Mrs. H. Edward (Ethel) Dreier, Mar. 22, are in NCV, box I-24, fol. "Betty Wakeman Mitchell."

17. "Regular Meeting of [UO] . . . May 8, 1923," NCV, box I-25, fol. "Meetings."

18. All of these letters went out on May 5, 1923 (NCV, box I-24, fol. "Betty Wakeman Mitchell").

19. See Carolyn M. Moehling and Melissa A. Thomasson, "The Political Economy of Saving Mothers and Babies: The Politics of State Participation in the Sheppard-Towner Program," *Journal of Economic History* 72, no. 1 (Mar. 2012): 75–103. In the twenty-first century, American maternal death rates have once again become a source of concern: see http://www.npr.org/2017/05/12/528098789/u-s-has-the-worst-rate-of-maternal-deaths-in-the-developed-world (accessed Aug. 24, 2017).

20. Dorothy Kirchwey Brown, "The Sheppard-Towner Bill Lobby," *Woman Citizen* 5 (Jan. 22, 1921): 907–8.

21. For this and following paragraphs on the trial, see newspapers including the *NYT*, *BDE*, and *Bronx Home News* (Oct. 9–24, 1936). See my "Rhetoric, Strategy, and Politics in the New York Campaign for Women's Jury Service, 1917–1975"

(*New York History* 82, no. 1 [Winter 2001]: 53–78) and the New York City League of Women Voters Papers (hereafter, NYCLWV), box 42, fol. "Jury service."

22. Holly J. McCammon, *U.S. Women's Jury Movements and Strategic Adaptations* (Cambridge: Cambridge University Press, 2012), 38. On Grilli, see Ada Patterson, "The New Triumphs of Women Lawyers," *Wilmington Morning Star*, Dec. 3, 1918; for Grilli's writ, see "Woman Jury Issue Now Before Court," *BDE*, Dec. 5, 1919; "Court Gets Plea to Allow Women to Act as Jurors," *Tribune*, Dec. 10, 1919.

23. In the *NYT*: "Women as Jurors Called a Failure" (Apr. 29, 1923); "Jury Duty Denied to Women in State" (Mar. 28, 1924); "Women Plead for Right to Serve on Juries; Retort Sharply to Men at Albany Hearing" (Mar. 5, 1931).

24. In the *NYT*: "Women Plead Right to Serve on Juries" (Feb. 23, 1926); "Women as Jurors Called a Failure" (Apr. 29, 1923); "Lehman and Ward Urge Women Jurors" (Feb. 28, 1930); for the Brooklyn poll, Esther Coster, "Battle on Between Women's Factions over Jury Duty," *BDE*, Dec. 21, 1924; Graves was quoted in the *Knickerbocker Press*, Feb. 15, 1928.

25. Esther Coster, "Battle on between Women's Factions over Jury Duty," *BDE*, Dec. 21, 1924.

26. Esther Coster, "Opposition to Acceptance of Women as Jurors Lessens Yearly as Bill Is Pressed," *BDE*, Feb. 23, 1928.

27. John P. McCarthy to Gov. Herbert H. Lehman, May 11, 1937; Mr. & Mrs. Owens, Mr. & Mrs. Thomas, Mr. and Mrs. Hirsch to Gov. Lehman (Bill Jacket, chap. 513, Laws of 1937, NYS Library, Albany); also, "347 Brooklyn Women Ready to Serve as Jurors—31 Say It Is Not a Woman's Job," *BDE*, June 15, 1924; *Knickerbocker Press*, Mar. 25, 1937.

28. "TWV," *BDE*, Mar. 17, 1924; Sept. 11, 1928.

29. The Caroline Klein Simon Papers, Schlesinger Library (hereafter, CKS-SL) provide a full record of Simon's career.

30. Isabelle Keating (later, Savell), "Woman Victor Didn't Wait for the Returns," *BDE*, Nov. 8, 1933; "Miss Byrne to Seek Aid for Idle from Assembly," *H-T*, Nov. 10, 1933; Mabel Parker Smith, "Girl Legislator, with No Bill Reported, Asks No Favors of Masculine Assembly Colleagues," *Middletown Times Herald*, May 1, 1934 (this article calls Byrne the state's second assemblywoman, and Rhoda Fox Graves the first, which was not correct, as Byrne herself pointed out in the *H-T* article, cited previously).

31. In 1945 Todd became deputy New York State commissioner of commerce, a post she held until the end of Thomas E. Dewey's governorship in 1954. In the *NYT*: "Wide Revolt Indicated" (Sept. 21, 1933); "Republicans Gain 8 Assembly Seats" (Nov. 8, 1933); "Woman to Fight Thayer" (May 18, 1934); "Mrs. Graves, First Woman in State Senate, Is Independent on Home and Other Issues" (Nov. 7, 1934).

32. Alma Lutz, "The Case for Women Jurors," *Independent Woman* (National Federation of Business and Professional Women's Clubs), Jan. 1936; Mildred Adams, "Women Knock Loudly at the Jury Box," *NYT*, Mar. 29, 1936.

33. "Assembly Passes Women Jury Bills," *NYT*, Mar. 27, 1935.

34. "Girl Mother Who Killed Baby Freed," *BDE*, Oct. 23, 1936.

35. Bill Jacket, chap. 513, Laws of 1937. "State's First Women Jurors Spurn Cigars, Demand Ice Cream—and Win," *BDE*, Aug. 29, 1937; "Harlemite Is among First Women Jurors," *NY Age*, Oct. 16, 1937.

36. In the *NYT* for 1937: "Jury Law Termed a 'Sop to Women'" (May 22); "Women's Fitness to Rule Debated" (May 23); Kathleen McLaughlin, "Clubwomen Gauge Legislative Gains as Season Comes to Close" (May 30). "Form Schools for Woman Jurors in New York," *Independent Woman,* Sept. 1937, 276, 294. Exemptions later proved problematic, as they provided employers with a disincentive to release women to perform a civic duty considered "optional." Teachers and civil service workers lost salaries when on jury duty, a grievance that came up in testimony to government officials during the modern women's movement: *Women's Role in Contemporary Society: The Report of the New York City Commission on Human Rights, September 21–25, 1970* (New York: Avon Books, 1972), testimony of Rose Aronoff, 561–63.

37. Esther Coster, "Battle on Between Women's Factions over Jury Duty," *BDE*, Dec. 21, 1924.

38. Linda Kerber, *No Constitutional Right to Be Ladies: Women and the Obligations of Citizenship* (New York: Hill and Wang, 1998), chap. 4. New York lawyers Dorothy Kenyon and Pauli Murray were prominent players in this outcome.

39. See Schneiderman, *All for One*, 254.

40. Clara M. Beyer, *History of Labor Legislation for Women in Three States* (US Women's Bureau, Bulletin No. 66, 1929), 66–119.

41. Grace Phelps, "More about Special Labor Laws for Women," *Tribune*, Jan. 26, 1919.

42. See "Women Fail to Agree on Welfare Measures," *NYT*, Mar. 6, 1919; "Miss Wren and Miss McCormick Clash over Bills Designed to Aid Women Workers," *BDE*, Mar. 6, 1919; "Women Workers' Platform," *The Survey* 41 (Mar. 15, 1919): 868–69. For the transcript, see Mark A. Daly, "Hearing on Labor Bills Develops an Unexpected Opposition of Women to Passage of Proposed Acts," *The Monitor: Official Publication of Associated Manufacturers and Merchants (of New York State),* 5, no. 10 (Mar. 1919): 1–41, accessed Mar. 23, 2016, https://books.google.com/books?id=ZZJDAQAAMAAJ&pg=RA9-PA1&dq#v.

43. For this and subsequent quotations, see Daly, "Hearing on Labor Bills," 2.

44. The WLEO women would go to Oswego in the fall to campaign against Marion Dickerman, a proponent of sex-specific labor laws. See "TWV," *BDE*, Oct. 8, 1919.

45. Daly, "Hearing on Labor Bills," 12–15. Wren was not always consistent on the issues of protecting women. In the jury service campaign, she argued that women needed

"special protections" and should enjoy "automatic exemption." See Esther Coster, "Battle on between Women's Factions over Jury Duty," *BDE*, Dec. 21, 1924.

46. Renamed the New York State Association Opposed to Woman Suffrage after its postsuffrage restructuring, the group associated suffrage with political radicalism. See Goodier, *No Votes for Women*, 13, 118–20 passim.

47. See Kathryn K. Sklar, Florence Kelley, and Landon R. Y. Storrs, *Civilizing Capitalism: The National Consumers' League, Women's Activism, and Labor Standards in the New Deal Era* (Chapel Hill: University of North Carolina Press, 2000).

48. Daly, "Hearing on Labor Bills," 29–30. Mark Daly wrote that Kelley's testimony "engendered a smoldering anger that such a bald attempt to intimidate the legislature should be possible" (41). "Report and Protest," *Woman Citizen* 4 (Apr. 3, 1920): 1067ff, states that Daly and Bewley were close "pals" and Bewley had sponsored a "living wage" bill in order to kill it.

49. Daly, "Hearing on Labor Bills," 32.

50. Beyer, *History of Labor Legislation*, 95. McCormick was active in women's court reform.

51. See in the *Tribune* of 1919: "B.R.T. [Brooklyn Rapid Transit] Offers Women's Jobs to Ex-Soldiers" (May 18) and "Women on Cars Flay Reformers" (May 20); and in the *BDE* of 1919: "Scab Labor and Bolsheviki Seen in New Women's Laws" (May 1); "Nixon Starts Probe of B.R.T.'s Action Dismissing Women" (May 20); "B.R.T. Women Agents Seek Lewis' Help" (June 20). Also, New York (State), *Labor Laws and Legislation* (Albany, NY: Department of Labor, 1925), 49; Elizabeth Faulkner Baker, *Protective Labor Legislation, with Special Reference to Women in the State of New York* (New York: Columbia University, 1925), 143–44, 371; and Alice Kessler-Harris, *Gendering Labor History* (Urbana: University of Illinois Press, 2006), 84, 234.

52. The debate can be followed in the *BDE*'s "TWV" columns of Apr. 7 and 10, 1923; Feb. 26, 1924; Feb. 3, 1925; Mar. 12, 1926; and Apr. 3, 1926.

53. Mastick-Shonk restricted women's workweek to forty-eight hours (eight hours a day, six days a week) but with many exceptions. See "TWV," *BDE*, Oct. 8, 1927, Oct. 13, 1928; and The Woman Voter (byline), "Labor Department Worried over Administration of New Working Law for Women," Dec. 25, 1927. In 1940, the Federal Wage and Hour Act set a forty-hour workweek, with time and half for overtime, as "basic" for *all* workers.

54. See Susan Ware, *Partner and I: Molly Dewson, Feminism, and New Deal Politics* (New Haven, CT: Yale University Press, 1987), 101.

55. Ware, *Partner and I*, chap. 7. New York women worked closely with Elizabeth Brandeis, then secretary of the Washington, DC, minimum wage board at the time of the national case; Frances Perkins; Josephine Goldmark; and Clara Beyer.

56. Natalie H. McCloskey, "Why Special Laws for the Working Woman," *Tribune*, Jan. 12, 1919.

57. For this and subsequent quotations, see McCloskey, "Why Special Laws." See also Ellen Dubois, *Harriot Stanton Blatch*, chap. 8, and Nancy Woloch, *A Class by Herself: Protective Laws for Women Workers, 1890s–1990s* (Princeton, NJ: Princeton University Press, 2015) for discussions of the complexities of sex-specific labor laws and the limitations of the "entering wedge" argument.

58. Eunace Fuller Barnard, "When New York Gave Woman the Vote," *NYT Magazine*, Nov. 6, 1927.

59. Barnard, "When New York Gave Woman the Vote"; "Browning Case Aids Marriage Age Bill," *NYT*, Mar. 13, 1927, reported on the league women's frustrations over the bills they had failed to get passed.

60. On Byrne and the Brooklyn clinic, see Ellen Chesler, *Woman of Valor: Margaret Sanger and the Birth Control Movement in America* (New York: Simon and Schuster, 1992), chap. 8.

61. David Kyvig, *Repealing National Prohibition* (Kent, OH: Kent State University Press, 2000).

62. For an earlier attempt at government reorganization, see "Women Claim Civil Service Plums Fall to Men," *BDE*, June 8, 1913, which tells of attorney Anna Hochfelder's early effort to promote civil service reorganization.

63. The post of attorney general remained elective and the number of executive departments dropped to nineteen. See Perry, *Belle Moskowitz*, chap. 7; Caro, *The Power Broker*, chap. 6.

64. The Council of Jewish Women, Women's City Club, New York State League of Women Voters, New York City and State Federations of Women's Clubs, National Civic Federation, Consumers' League, Woman's Municipal League, and United Neighborhood Workers all promoted state reorganization.

CHAPTER 4

1. Emma claimed she met Oscar in 1910, when, separated from her first husband, "playboy" Julian Walton Swift (allegedly a grandson of Gustavus Franklin Swift, founder of Chicago's Swift and Company), she had fled to London. After several years of a secret romance with Oscar, who financed her divorce, they married on Dec. 31, 1914. See "Mrs. Hammerstein's Own Story," *Philadelphia Inquirer Magazine*, July 13–Aug. 17, 1930 (a six-part autobiographical series).

2. Vincent Sheean, *Oscar Hammerstein I: The Life and Exploits of an Impresario* (New York: Simon and Schuster, 1956), 342–44. Famed lyricist Oscar Hammerstein II was Oscar I's grandson.

3. In the *NYT*: "Julian W. Swift Has a Midnight Wedding" (May 19, 1909); "Explain Stock Transfer" (Jan. 4, 1918); "Oscar Hammerstein Is Seriously Ill" (July 29,

1919); "O. Hammerstein, Long in Coma, Dies" (Aug. 2, 1919); "Daughters Control Hammerstein Stock" (Sept. 20, 1919); "Sue Hammerstein's Widow" (Apr. 11, 1920); "Manhattan Opera House Is Auctioned" (June 23, 1921); "Hammerstein Case Up" (Jan. 13, 1922); "Hammerstein Troth Put under a Cloud" (July 20, 1922); "Hammerstein Explains" (Nov. 10, 1922); "Bankruptcy Sales" (Jan. 2, 1923); "Tells Opera Plans" (Mar. 24, 1926); "Mrs. O. Hammerstein to Give French Opera" (Apr. 5, 1926); "Mrs. Hammerstein Sues" (May 5 and Sept. 23, 1926; May 16, 1928). Also, Russell S. Sims's over-two-thousand-word illustrated piece, "On a Park Bench Listening for the Stars That Sing No More," *Durham Morning Herald*, Nov. 5, 1922 (widely reprinted). The *Tribune* also followed Hammerstein's fate, e.g., "Artists Balk, but Faithful 128 Hear Out Hammerstein Benefit" (Nov. 14, 1922).

4. Hammerstein gave a variety of explanations for having accepted the thirty dollars: see in the *H-T* for 1930: "Tells of Offer to 'Frame' Mrs. Emma Hammerstein" (June 6); "Hammerstein's Widow Guilty, Court Decides" (June 7).

5. For this and subsequent paragraphs on the case, see in the *NYT* for 1930: "Mrs. Hammerstein Seized" (May 13); "Bails Mrs. Hammerstein" (May 14); "Mrs. Hammerstein Heard" (May 21); "Hammerstein Case Off" (May 23); "Hear Mrs. Hammerstein" (May 30); "Mrs. Hammerstein Is Found Guilty" (June 7). Also, in the *BDE* for 1930: "Baldwin Hints State Quiz of Appeals Board" (May 29); "Women Protest Conviction of Hammerstein's Widow" (June 6). On Marie Lassell's Women's Forum, "Plan Forum Where Woman Can Make Herself Heard," *BDE*, Dec. 8, 1928.

6. In the *NYT* for 1930: "Mrs. Hammerstein Gets Step-Son's Aid" (June 10); "Court Fixing Inquiry May Go to Prisons" (Oct. 16); "Mrs. Hammerstein Cleared" (Oct. 23); "Mrs. Hammerstein on Relief" (Nov. 13); "Mrs. Hammerstein Balked" (Nov. 16). In the *BDE*: "Hammerstein Vagrancy Guilt Voided by Court" (Oct. 22, 1930); "Mrs. Hammerstein Joins Jobless Apple Sellers" (Nov. 17, 1930); "Arthur Hammerstein Sued by Step-Mother" (Aug. 28, 1931); "Mrs. Hammerstein Gets $25 a Week" (May 25, 1934). Also, "Mrs. Hammerstein In," *Sun*, Nov. 7, 1930. For photographs of her selling apples, see "Hammerstein Widow Sells Apples," *Jamestown Evening Journal*, Nov. 20, 1930; "Once Wealthy, Now Apple Seller," *Elmira Star-Gazette*, Nov. 24, 1930. She spent her last years in Syracuse, and when she died (Jan. 14, 1946) she left an estate of less than $5,000: "Widow of Impresario Wills Estate to a Friend," *Syracuse Post-Standard*, Apr. 6, 1946.

7. "Justice Whitman" (editorial), *NYT*, July 20, 1907. See Mae C. Quinn, "Revisiting Anna Moscowitz Kross's Critique of New York City's Women's Court: The Continued Problem of Solving the 'Problem' of Prostitution with Specialized Criminal Courts," *Fordham Urban Law Journal* 33, no. 2 (2005): 665–726; George E. Worthington and Ruth Topping, *Specialized Courts Dealing with Sex Delinquency: A Study of the Procedure in Chicago, Boston, Philadelphia, and New York* (New York: F. H. Hitchcock, 1925), chap. IV.

8. "Women's court" and "women's night court" were synonymous until 1919, when under pressure from social workers and women's organizations the court ended its night sessions. In the *NYT* for 1907: "Night Police Court a Step Nearer" (Mar. 13); "A Night Court Assured" (editorial, June 19); "Justice Whitman" (July 20).

9. Worthington and Topping, *Specialized Courts*, 292ff.

10. A "sociological" observer told the *Times* that "bad home conditions, lack of employment, trust in some man" had gotten most defendants in trouble ("Sad Human Drama Played Nightly in Women's Court," *NYT Magazine*, Sept. 11, 1910). For Blackwell's Island, see http://www.correctionhistory.org/html/chronicl/nycdoc/html/blakwel1.html (accessed July 9, 2016).

11. Katharine Wright, "Sightseers End Women's Night Court," *Tribune*, Aug. 11, 1918; Frederick H. Whitin, "The Women's Night Court in New York City," *Annals of the American Academy of Political and Social Science* 52 (Mar. 1914): 181–87; John P. Peters, "The Story of the Committee of Fourteen of New York," *Journal of Social Hygiene* 4, no. 3 (July 1918): 347–88; Willoughby C. Waterman, *Prostitution and Its Repression in New York City, 1900–1931* (New York: Columbia University Press, 1932).

12. See New York State Laws of 1910, chap. 659, "Clause 79"; "Sad Human Drama," which said that women doctors were not always available to conduct the exams; Anna Moscowitz, "The Women's Night Court," *Medico-Legal Journal* 33, no. 9 (Dec. 1916): 2–7; "Scores Women's Court," *NYT*, Mar. 4, 1916.

13. See in the *NYT* for 1910: "Suffragettes Start Fight on New Court" (Sept. 2); Dock letter (signed L. L. D., Sept. 3); "New Attack on Page Law" (Nov. 19); "Women Win in Court" (Nov. 26). Also, in *The Survey*, "Clause 79 Is Held Unconstitutional" (1910), 416, and "The End of Clause 79" (1911), 552.

14. Alice Smith ran the probation system for over two decades; according to Whitin ("The Women's Night Court"), the magistrates generally took her advice. In the *NYT* for 1911: "To Uphold New Courts" (Jan. 11); "Are the Men's and Women's Night Courts to Go?" (editorial, Feb. 12); and for 1912: "Women Visit Night Court" (Mar. 30). On Jones, see Susan Goodier, *No Votes for Women*, 59–62. For Menken's view, see her "The Passing of the Women's Night Court in New York City," *The Survey*, Oct. 12, 1918, 41–42.

15. In the *NYT* for 1912: "Woman Lawyer at Night Court" (Jan. 11); "When Women Plead in the Night Court" (Feb. 4); and in the *BDE*, "Women in Trouble Find a Friend in Miss McKeen" (Jan. 21, 1912). Helen McKeen was a Bryn Mawr and NYU Law School graduate.

16. "The Night Court for Women in New York City," *Women Lawyers' Journal* 5, no. 2 (Nov. 1915): 9; Quinn, "Revisiting Anna Moscowitz Kross's Critique."

17. "Hard for Women in Night Courts," *Rochester Democrat and Chronicle*, Nov. 13, 1916; "Assail Court for Women," *NYT*, May 20, 1916. Mitchell's poem is in *The Book of New York Verse*, ed. Hamilton Fish Armstrong (New York: G. P. Putnam's Sons, 1917).

18. See "Vice Charge Promises Shake-up," *Evening Journal*, Jan. 24, 1917; "Will Hear Court Grafting Charge," *Tribune*, Jan. 25, 1917;. On June 26, 1917, Moscowitz wrote publicly to Mayor John Purroy Mitchel: "the evil will remain so long as the vice question is handled by the police" (AMK-SS, box 2, fol. 3).

19. Worthington and Topping (*Specialized Courts,* 324) quote McAdoo's 1915 *Annual Report*. Bridget Bennett writes: "Harris is generally remembered as being a self-promoting and vulgar man of great talent and energy but with dubious taste," http://www.anb.org/articles/16/16-02056.html (accessed June 6, 2016).

20. Frank Harris, "New York Night Court for Women," Nov. 1916; "The American Inquisition," Feb. 1917; "The Night Court Inquisition," Mar. 1917; "The Night Court Inquisition," May 1917; "The Passing of the Night Court," June 1917; "The Night Court Inquisition," Aug. 1917; "The Infamous Night Court," Aug. 1919, all in *Pearson's Magazine*, vols. 37–38. Moscowitz preserved marked-up copies in her scrapbooks (AMK-AJA, box 438 Scrapbooks).

21. Simon, "Speech," Robert A. Taft Institute meeting, C.W. Post College of Long Is. Univ., Dec. 7, 1964, carton 1, CKS-SL. In addition to Paul and Stevens, the arrested suffragists included Elsie Hill, Lucy Maverick, Beatrice Castleton, and Minna Schein (Mrs. Max) Bodenheim. "Society Slumming to End Night Court for Women Here," *Evening World*, Apr. 12, 1917; "End Women's Night Court," *NYT*, June 29, 1918; "Urges Night Court Action," *NYT*, July 31, 1918; Katharine Wright, "Sightseers End Women's Night Court," *Tribune*, Aug. 11, 1918 (includes photos of Whitman, Alice Smith, and McAdoo); "6 Anti-Wilson Suffragists Are Arrested Here," *Tribune*, Mar. 5, 1919; "End of Night Court to Be Blessing to Women, Says Judge," *Tribune*, Apr. 13, 1919; "New Women's Court Today," *NYT*, Apr. 21, 1919.

22. In the *Tribune* for 1919: "Judge Tells Girls to Sue Policeman for False Arrest" (June 18); "Hylan Ordered Inquiry into Girls' Arrest" (June 19); "Swann Will Fix Blame in Girls' Arrest" (June 20); "Woman Lawyer to Try Accused Girls Hereafter" (June 24); "Woman Says Inspector Daly Shields Sleuth" (June 28); "Girl Convicted on Detective's Word Is Freed" (July 31); "Mancuso Resents 'Unfair Criticism' in Edwards Case" (Aug. 4). In the *NYT* for 1919: "Judge Rosalsky Criticises Magistrate; Sets aside Night Court Conviction" (June 18); "Court Vindicates another Woman" (June 27). Also, "Magistrate Mancuso Not to Sit in Women's Court," *Evening World*, Aug. 2, 1919. According to "The Scandal of the Women's Court in New York City" (*The Shield*, official organ of London's Association for Moral and Social Hygiene January 1931), it was this "false arrest" that led the association to reject Frederick Whitin's suggestion that London set up a women's court. On Rosalsky, see "Otto Rosalsky, Jurist, Dies at 63," *NYT*, May 12, 1936, and an editorial praising his thirty-one years on the bench.

23. "Brooklyn Women Protest Arrest of Innocent Girls," *BDE*, June 29, 1919; "Girl Is Freed in 2 Minutes after Retrial," *Tribune*, July 3, 1919; "Mrs. Talbot-Perkins Urges

Need of Public Defender for Poor Girls in Women's Court," *BDE*, Oct. 2, 1927. On Meyer, see Goodier, *No Votes for Women*, 51 passim.

24. Emma Bugbee, "Hopeful Scenes in the Woman's Court under Improved Conditions," *Tribune*, July 6, 1919; William C. Kranowitz for the *Tribune*: "New Assistant District Attorney to Women's Court Is for Unstrained Mercy" and "Accused Women Swear by Miss District Attorney" (July 13 and Sept. 14, 1919); "Manhattan Portia Declares for Justice in Women's Court," *American Hebrew & Jewish Messenger*, July 18, 1919; "Woman Defends Police Crusade against Her Sex," *Evening World*, July 23, 1919. A year later, women "court attendants" were authorized ("Women to Get Posts in Court as Attendants," *Evening World*, Oct. 22, 1920).

25. "Mayor Appoints Mrs. Jean Norris City Magistrate," *Evening World*, Oct. 27, 1919; "Hylan Appoints Woman to Magistrates' Bench," *Tribune*, Oct. 28, 1919; "Mrs. Jean H. Norris Appointed to Bench," *NYT*, Oct. 28, 1919; "Woman Judge Talks on the Women's Court," *Tribune*, Dec. 14, 1919; "Woman Succeeds Curran," *NYT*, Jan. 3, 1920. See also Mary Weston Cottle, "Women in the Legal Profession," *Women Lawyers' Journal* 4, no. 8 (May 1915): 60, and "New York's First Woman Magistrate Mixes Justice with Common Sense," *Literary Digest*, Feb. 21, 1920, 24–26. In 1930 Mayor Walker renewed her appointment ("Walker Renames Two Magistrates," *NYT*, July 1, 1930).

26. Thyra Espenscheid, in "She Wanted to Be a Circus Rider, but Became a Judge," *BDE*, Sept. 7, 1924; the article describes Norris's approach to cases and contains a sketch of her "on the bench." Also, "The Revolver Was Loaded," *BDE*, May 9, 1899; "Teacher-Mother Decision Pleases Suffragists," *BDE*, Mar. 7, 1913. Thanks to Mae Quinn for sharing with me her draft essay, "Fallen Woman (Re)Framed: Judge Jean Hortense Norris, New York City – 1900–1950."

27. Rose Falls Bres published a study of discrimination against women, *Law and the Woman*, https://archive.org/details/lawwoman00bres (accessed Sept. 12, 2016), and *Maids, Wives and Widows: The Law of the Land and of the Various States as It Affects Women* (New York: E. P. Dutton, 1918), in which she called Norris "one of the best known women lawyers at the New York Bar" and noted that Carrie Chapman Catt employed her to "place the proper legal safeguards around the million dollars left by Mrs. Frank Leslie to the cause of woman suffrage." For Bres's critique of Norris as a magistrate, see "Change in Law Asked to Help Accused Girls," *Tribune*, Feb. 20, 1920. On Lersner, see "Woman's Vice Court 'Railroads' Girls to Jail, Is Charge," *New Castle Herald*, Mar. 26, 1920; "Gotham Court Helps Girls to Get New Start," *Wilkes-Barre Times-Leader*, May 3, 1920; "Demand Jury Pass on Women's Cases," *NYT*, May 8, 1920.

28. Billie Holiday (with William Dufty), *Lady Sings the Blues* (Garden City, NY: Doubleday, 1956), unpaginated at https:books.google.com/books?isbn=0307786161 (accessed Apr. 4, 2018). Also, "Magistrate Norris Criticizes Sessions Court for Reversals," *Tribune*, Feb. 18, 1920; "Jean Norris Defends

Bonding House Link; Severe in Vice Cases," *NYT*, Feb. 12, 1931. Investigative re-
porter Milton MacKaye repeats Norris's conviction figures in *The Tin Box Parade: A
Handbook for Larceny* (New York: R. M. McBride, 1934). Burton W. Peretti,
*Nightclub City: Politics and Amusement in Manhattan* (Philadelphia: University
of Pennsylvania Press, 2007), shows that Norris's prostitution cases disproportionately concerned black women (127–31). Cheryl D. Hicks, *Talk with You like a
Woman* (Chapel Hill, NC: University of North Carolina Press, 2010),, 173ff., says
Norris lacked sympathy for black girls, but in 1927 Norris worked with the Urban
League to find a "trained colored social worker" for the women's court to assist
with youthful "sex offenders," especially those from the South who lacked local support. See, e.g., in the *NY Age* for 1927: "Judge Norris Is Guest of Harlem Women
at Lunch" (Apr. 16), "Work for Women's Federation" (editorial, Apr. 23); "Judge
Norris on Woman Worker in City Day Courts" (May 7); "Urban League Auxiliary
Asked to Supply Woman Worker in Family Court" (May 14).

29. In the *NY Age* for 1924: "Notorious Stool Pigeon for Police Engaged in Trapping
Decent, Hard-Working Girls" (July 5); "Stool Pigeon Still at Dirty Work" (July 12);
"Stool Pigeon Sends Girl to Welfare Island" and "Charles Dancey, Alleged Police
'Stool Pigeon' Is Held in Tombs for Assault" (Aug. 2); "East Siders Vow Vengeance
against Stool Pigeon Who 'Framed' Woman" (Aug. 9).

30. Also in the *NY Age* for 1924: "Stool Pigeon Dancey, out on Bail on Serious Charge
Still Perniciously Active" (Aug. 23); "Dancey Indicted by Grand Jury" (Sept. 13);
"Dancey Jailed on Larceny Charge" (Sept. 20); "Threats Sent the Age Editor
Anonymously" (Oct. 4); "Dancey out Again and at Old Tricks; Girls Are Warned"
(Oct. 11); "Judge Rosalsky Scores Unmercifully the Jury Which Freed Chas.
Dancey" (Nov. 15).

31. In the *NY Age* for 1925: "Charles Dancey Attacks Judge Francis McQuade" (Feb.
14) and "Women Victims of Alleged Frameup by Police Stool Pigeon Freed by
Court" (Oct. 17); also, the paper's editorial, "Framing Women in Harlem" (Dec.
6, 1930).

32. In the *NY Age*: Grace P. Campbell, "Women Offenders and the Day Court" (Apr.
18, 1925) and "Tragedy of the Colored Girl in Court" (Apr. 25, 1925). Campbell
represented the Urban League as a probation officer in the court of general sessions,
was acting parole officer for black female prisoners at the state prison in Auburn,
New York, and founded and supervised the Empire Friendly Shelter of New York.
Since 1917 a member of the municipal parole commission, in 1923 she was appointed to the Fifteenth District school board.

33. St. Clair's letters appeared as *Amsterdam News* advertisements, Sept. 4, 1929.
Admired for her entrepreneurial and feisty character, St. Clair, a resident of
Harlem's famous "Sugar Hill" district, hoped to arouse the "colored race" to
protest police brutality and defend their civil rights; she was considered one of
Harlem's leading political activists. See Shirley Stewart, *The World of Stephanie*

*St. Clair: An Entrepreneur, Race Woman and Outlaw in Early Twentieth Century Harlem* (New York: Peter Lang, 2014). TVONE's "Celebrity Crime Files" produced a documentary about her life ("Lady Gangster") in 2014 (available on YouTube).

34. The Brooklyn women's night court, established in October 1916, became a day court in 1927. Brooklyn political activist Rebecca C. Talbot-Perkins visited it weekly and organized clubwomen to give aid to the "girls." In the *BDE*, see "Clubwomen Aid Girls Taken to the Night Court" (letter, July 14, 1917); "Women's Day Court Opened by McAdoo; Night Court Passes" (June 7, 1927).

35. Selma Warlick, "New Brooklyn Woman's Court," *BDE*, Aug. 2, 1931,

36. Born in 1889, McCormick went to St. Lawrence University, studied pedagogy for intellectually disabled children at Dartmouth College, and then went to Brooklyn Law School. She passed the bar in 1913 and got a job as a factory inspector for the state's department of labor. After the 1917 suffrage victory Republican district attorney Harry E. Lewis appointed her assistant district attorney; in 1922 newly elected district attorney Charles J. Dodd, a Democrat, replaced her with another Brooklyn Law School graduate and a Democrat, May Patterson. See almost weekly articles in the *BDE* from 1928 onward. See also "Brooklyn Court Called Faulty," *NYT*, Sept. 12, 1929; "Adams Street 'Rat-Hole' Scored by Women Who Seek New Court Site," *Brooklyn Standard Union*, Oct. 25, 1930; and Isabelle Keating, "Woman's Court Shift Effected," *BDE*, Aug. 6, 1934.

37. The survey took place from Nov. 19 to 24 and was limited to the seven district magistrates' courts in Manhattan and the five "special" Manhattan courts: family, women's (which also covered the Bronx), traffic, homicide, and municipal term (where officials brought cases against citizens who violated government rules and codes).

38. "Magistrates Courts in the Borough of Manhattan. A Study of Some Features," a joint publication of the WCC and CC, Jan. 1929, 11 pp., carton 14, fol. Women's City Club, CKS-SL. Its examination of the five special courts showed that, in all but traffic, the flow of cases was low; traffic was "so disorganized as to be a mere melee of human beings." Also, a typed draft of Simon's article for the WCC's bulletin on the investigation's origins and methods.

39. Of course, the clubs lacked authority to probe any of the more serious allegations against the courts. For Thomas's comment, see Norman Thomas and Paul Blanshard, *What's the Matter with New York: A National Problem* (New York: MacMillan, 1932), 122. In the *NYT* for 1929: "Says He Can't Spur Late Magistrates" (Feb. 5); "City Magistrates" (editorial, Feb. 5). On the importance the WCC gave to its report, see Alice Cogan, "Those Amazing Women," *BDE*, Mar. 21, 1936, and Eva v. B. Hansl, "Club to Celebrate 20 Years of Work," *NYT*, Mar. 8, 1936.

40. "Gamblers Hunted as Rothstein Lies at Point of Death," *BDE*, Nov. 5, 1928; "Sensational Breaks in Rothstein Murder Worrying Tammany," *BDE*, Sept. 28,

1929; "Proof in Gambler's Files," *NYT*, Sept. 28, 1929. Vitale got the loan to buy stocks on margin, a common practice before the crash in October. The murder reminded New Yorkers of the 1912 murder of gambler Herman Rosenthal. Damon Runyon later immortalized Rothstein as Armand Rosenthal in *Guys and Dolls,* and F. Scott Fitzgerald used him as a model for Meyer Wolfsheim in *The Great Gatsby.*

41. At the time, the appellate division could not initiate an investigation of inferior courts on its own but had to wait for charges to be preferred, a limitation not lifted until spring 1930. See in the *NYT* for 1930: "City Club Supports Fearon-Post Bill" (Mar. 25), which Roosevelt signed on Apr. 17. On the Vitale dinner hold-up, see in the *NYT* for 1929: "Seven Bandits Hold Up 50 at Dinner to Vitale" (Dec. 8); "7 of Vitale Guests Had Police Records, Whalen Declares" (Dec. 13); "Vitale Must Tell M'adoo of Dinner" (Dec. 14); "Vitale Recognized Ex-Crooks at Dinner" (Dec. 17); "Court Authorizes Bar to Investigate Conduct of Vitale" (Dec. 20); "Vitale Will Fight Whalen's Charges" (Dec. 21); "Light in Vitale Case Due at Police Trial" (Dec. 23); "Vitale Says Pistol Was Found in Street and Handed to Him" (Dec. 29).

42. In the *NYT* for 1930: "Says Vitale Freed a Confessed Thief" (Jan. 6); "Whalen Is Sifting Report Vitale Met Murder Fugitive" (Jan. 7); "Demands Mayor Sift" (Jan. 10); "City Inquiry Bill Goes in at Albany; Covers 3 Branches" (Feb. 4); W. A. Warn, "Assembly Majority to Assail Walker" (Mar. 24) and "City Inquiry Bill Vetoed" (Mar. 30). By late January, some New York City officials were taking action, but none effectively. See in the *NYT* for 1930: "Crain and M'adoo Map Court Inquiry" (Jan. 23); "Bail 'Night Riders' Exposed by Crain" (Jan. 24); "Tuttle Seeks to Aid City Bond Inquiry" (Jan. 29). *Herald-Tribune* journalist Denis Tilden Lynch summarizes the Vitale "case" in *Criminals and Politicians* (New York: MacMillan, 1932), 87–94.

43. Milton MacKaye, "Politicians Maneuver Boldly in Court under Magistrate 'Racket,'" *NY Evening Post*, Jan. 10, 1930.

44. In the *NYT* for 1930: "Bar Asks Vitale Removal on Corruption Charges" (Feb. 16); "Sees Incompetence in the Low Courts" (Feb. 24); "Vitale Says He Made $165,000 in 4 Years While on the Bench" (Mar. 13); "Vitale Removed by Court over the Rothstein Loan; Scored for Incompetence" (Mar. 14).

45. In the *NYT* for 1930: "Thomas Backers Join in a Civic Committee" (Mar. 30); "Urge City Workers to Help Bare Graft" (Sept. 22) provides a full list of participants.

46. The SPUC, which had given character witness at her trial, paid for Crow's appeal. The Brooklyn Heights Public Forum, a civic discussion group, had sponsored the SPUC's formation. Other SPUC women leaders included former policewoman Mary Hamilton; Dr. Sophia P. Harned (a club leader on municipal public welfare and health issues), Dr. L. Adele Cuinet (Republican Party activist), and Helen P. McCormick (former assistant district attorney and head of Catholic Big Sisters). The Brooklyn Women's Hoover-Curtis Constitutional Committee also defended Crow. Press reports sometimes spelled her last name "Crowe" and her first as "May"

or "Mae." In the *BDE* for 1930: "Nurse Accuses Cop of 'Vice' Frameup" (June 15); "Nurse Found Guilty of Vagrancy after Frameup Charge" (Aug. 23).

47. See Milton MacKaye's *New Yorker* "Profile" of Roosevelt (Aug. 15, 1931, 18–22; Aug. 22, 1931, 24–29) for a sensitive portrait of Roosevelt's political "tight-rope" walk. Eleanor Roosevelt called these articles "the fairest and the best" on her husband she had ever seen ("Milton MacKaye Dies," *Washington Post*, Mar. 23, 1979). See William B. Northrop and John B. Northrop, *The Insolence of Office: The Story of the Seabury Investigation* (New York: G. P. Putnam's Sons, 1932), 5. In the *NYT* for 1930: "Tuttle Now Sifting Cotter Mine Stock" (June 10); "Tuttle Subpoenaes Ewald and Healy" (June 11); "Ewald Indicted with Five for Fraud in Mine Project; To Be Asked to Quit Bench" (July 8); "Ewald Off Bench; Faces Tax Inquiry" (July 9); "Ewald Quits the Bench; Now Faces State Charge of Falsifying His Records" (July 15); "Warrant Is Sought for Healy's Arrest" (July 31); "Bar Asks Governor to Act on Charges Judgeships Are Sold" (Aug. 17).

48. Herbert Mitgang, *Man Who Rode the Tiger. The Life of Judge Samuel Seabury and the Story of the Greatest Investigation of City Corruption in This Century* (New York: Norton, 1979), 167–68. The newspapers covered the disappearance in hundreds of articles, and the Crater story still reappears in fiction and nonfiction set in the early years of the Great Depression. For a concise summary of all the court-related scandals of the preceding years, see C. G. Poore, "Scandals Arising over Judgeships," *NYT*, Aug. 24, 1930.

49. See Mitgang, *Man Who Rode the Tiger*, 76. Mary M. Stolberg, *Fighting Organized Crime: Politics, Justice, and the Legacy of Thomas E. Dewey* (Boston: Northeastern University Press, 1995), quotes Frances Perkins describing Seabury as having an "arrogant" and "disdainful" face and looking like a Roman emperor strutting into the Circus Maximus (24).

50. In the *NYT* for 1930: "Magistrate M'Adoo Dies Suddenly at 76" (June 8); "Corrigan Demands 'Wild' Charges End" (Oct. 23).

51. Polly Adler, *A House Is Not a Home* (New York: Rhinehart, 1953), 166.

52. Mitgang, *Man Who Rode the Tiger*, chap. 9. Stolberg says politicians convinced citizens that gangsters "levied hidden taxes through payoffs" (*Fighting Organized Crime*, 3–4). Olvany, whose law firm made a fortune from Tammany "contracts," was forced out in 1929.

53. Thomas and Blanshard, *What's the Matter with New York*, 42.

54. See "Mrs. C. P. Clivette, Civic Leader Here," *NYT*, June 23, 1951, and on Merton's work as an artist, http://www.clivette.com/ (accessed Oct. 22, 2016). On the Clivettes' "Bohemian" life, see Albert Parry, *Garrets and Pretenders: A History of Bohemianism in America* (New York: Covici, Friede Publishers, 1933), 311–12 (Parry makes no mention of Catherine's political activism). On the narcotics issue, Clivette worked closely with antidrug crusader Sarah Graham-Mulhall, who had served as deputy commissioner of the New York State Department of Narcotic

Drug Control under Governor Smith; published the popular *Opium, The Demon Flower* (New York: H. Vinal, 1926); and in 1928 founded the World Anti-Narcotic Union. See "Opens World Drive on Drug Traffic," *NYT*, Mar. 8, 1928.

55. "Assails False Arrests," *NYT*, Oct. 9, 1930.

56. "Assails False Arrests" and "Waldman Charges Lower Courts Are Full of Corruption," *BDE*, Oct. 9, 1930. "The Scandal of the Women's Court in New York City" (*The Shield*, Jan. 1931) identified Hammerstein's conviction as the cause of the Seabury investigation.

57. On Hochfelder, see "Police Department O.K.'s League of Women Voters," *BDE*, June 12, 1923 and Kerry Segrave, *Policewomen: A History* (Jefferson, NC: McFarland, 2014), 155. "Hammerstein's Widow Appears in Court," *World News Service*, May 20, 1930, mentions Julius Hochfelder's role in the case. For Corrigan's response to the clubwomen, see "Warns of Reforms in Morality Laws," *NYT*, Oct. 25, 1930; "Women Ask Law to Prosecute Men for Immorality," *BDE*, Oct. 25, 1930. On Lewinson, see "Ruth Lewinson, 84, an Ex-Official for County Lawyers Association," *NYT*, Dec. 4, 1979; on Olive Stott Gabriel, see Bres, *Maids, Wives and Widows*, 36. On Corrigan's imposing a higher bail, see "3 Vice Squad Cops Held by Corrigan on Women's Story," *BDE*, Nov. 10, 1930.

58. In the *NYT* for 1930: "Got $20,000 to Free 900 in Vice Cases, Prosecutor Confesses, Exposing Ring" (Nov. 25); "Innocent Girls Arrested" (Nov. 27).

59. For this and following, see "Acuna Protection Cost City $40, 984," *BDE*, June 24, 1932. Details of his testimony can be followed in dozens of *NYT* stories in fall 1930, e.g., "Innocent Girls Arrested" (Nov. 27), "Mulrooney Starts Vice Squad Shake-up by Demoting Seven" (Nov. 29).

60. "Framing the Innocent" (editorial), *BDE*, Nov. 29, 1930; "13 Policemen Identified as 'Framers' in Vice Cases; Victims Tell of Brutality," *NYT*, Dec. 4, 1930. On McHugh's fate, see "Cop Accused by Informer," *Syracuse Journal*, Dec. 3, 1930; "Trial Halted; Officer Dead," *Brooklyn Standard Union*, Nov. 18, 1931: McHugh died of "neuritis" at the age of twenty-eight the night before his trial.

61. In the *NYT* for 1930: "Civic Leaders Join Mayor to Keep Firm Curb on Vice" (Dec. 24); "Informer May Face Perjury Charges" (Dec. 26). The women leaders attending the meeting with Walker included Madeleine (Mrs. Sidney C.) Borg, Jane M. Hoey, and Lillie Skiddy (Mrs. Willard) Parker (all advisers to the city's bureau of crime prevention), Stella Miner (Girls Service League), Caroline Slade (LWV), and Clara (Mrs. Ordway) Tead and Minnie Dunlop (WCC).

62. In the *NYT* for 1930: "Forty Lawyers Face 'Fixer Ring' Charges; Wider Inquiry Looms" (Dec. 25); "Hearing on Goodman Ordered by Seabury; Vice Verdict Upset" (Dec. 27); Adler, *A House Is Not a Home*, 179.

63. In the *NYT* for 1931: "77 Minor Girls Imprisoned Unlawfully by 7 Judges; Corrigan Acts to Free All" (Jan. 9); "Mayor Acts to Free 71 Imprisoned Girls" (Jan. 14).

64. On advertising agency J. Walter Thompson's "celebrity endorsement" campaign for Fleischmann's yeast, see Kerry Segrave, *Endorsements in Advertising: A Social History* (Jefferson, NC: McFarland, 2005), 68. In the *NYT* for 1931: "Source of $100,000 Banked by Simpson Studied by Kresel" (Jan. 18); "Silbermann to Face Dismissal Hearing; Jailed Minors Lose" (Feb. 1); "Judge Norris Faces Bail Bond Inquiry" (Feb. 6); "Jean Norris Defends Bonding House Link; Severe in Vice Cases" (Feb. 12); "Two Magistrates Face Hearing Today" (Feb. 13); "Lt. Kenna Banked $237,235, . . . Jean Norris 'Fixed' Record" (Feb. 14); "Move to Prosecute Judge Norris Fails" (Feb. 25). See also Karen Berger Morello, *The Invisible Bar: The Woman Lawyer in America: 1638 to the Present* (Boston: Beacon Press, 1986), 227–30.

65. In the *NYT* for 1931: "Jean Norris Faces New Inquiry Today" (Feb. 26); "Charge Jean Norris Defied Court Order" (Feb. 27); "Judge Norris Got $1,000 for Yeast Ad" (Feb. 28); "Breakdown Is Bared in Probation Bureau" (Mar. 27); "Seabury to Demand Magistrates Norris and Silbermann Go" (May 20); "Removal of Judge Norris Is Demanded by Seabury; Her Trial Set for June 4" (May 29).

66. Her removal made national news. In the *NYT* for 1931: "Acts Misconstrued, Judge Norris Says, Fighting Removal" (June 4); "Changing of Record to Temper Severity Laid to Mrs. Norris" (June 24); "Mrs. Norris Admits She Convicted Girl without Evidence" (June 25); "Mrs. Norris Ousted as Unfit for Bench; Guilty on 5 Charges" (June 26). Also, "Magistrate Norris Removed," *BDE*, June 26, 1931, an editorial praising the removal.

67. On Knapp, see Lauren Kozakiewicz, "Political Episodes, 1890–1960: Three Republican Women in Twentieth Century New York State Politics" (PhD diss., State University of New York at Albany, 2006).

68. "Women Lawyers Defend Sex in Norris Ouster," *Salem (Ohio) News*, July 7, 1931 (widely reprinted). Though she hesitated to interfere in appointments, in 1929 Eleanor Roosevelt had written admiringly of Norris to Mayor Walker: "I am very fond of Judge Norris and think her an extremely conscientious and able person" (Mrs. Franklin Roosevelt to Mayor Walker, Nov. 6, 1929, box 8, Eleanor Roosevelt Papers, Correspondence 1928–32, FDR Library). There is no evidence she commented on Norris's ouster.

69. "J. Walter Thompson Company," *Fortune* 36, no. 5 (Nov. 1947): 226, as cited in Segrave, *Endorsements*, chap. 4, note 24.

70. Esther A. Coster, "Kresel Held Prehistoric for View That Women Are Unfit for Profession," *BDE*, Jan. 4, 1929.

71. Pauline Mandigo, "Plea for Another Woman to Succeed Mrs. Norris," *NYT*, July 3, 1931. On Mandigo's career, see "Pauline Mandigo, Publicist, Was 63," *NYT*, July 18, 1956. In a chapter "Lady Lawyers Stub Their Toes," Alexander L. Schlosser provides excerpts from Seabury's examination of Norris (211ff.) and calls Norris a highly qualified lawyer (*Lawyers Must Eat* [New York: Vanguard Press, 1933]).

72. "Big Fight Ahead for Norris Place," *Evening Post*, July 16, 1931, and in the *NYT* for 1931: "Six Women Contend for Bench Vacancy" (June 28); "Urge Woman Be Put in Jean Norris Post" (May 31); "20 Women Seeking Norris Post on Bench" (July 16); "Mayor Picks a Man for Norris Vacancy" (July 30); "Walker Swears in Five Magistrates" (Aug. 1). An effort the previous December to appoint Lena Madesin Phillips to the magistracy had also failed: see Lena Madesin Phillips to Mrs. Roosevelt, Dec. 10, 1930, in which she thanked Roosevelt for presenting her case to Mayor Walker and Commissioner Curry (fol. "P," box 9, Eleanor Roosevelt Papers, Correspondence 1928–32, FDR Library).

73. On Norris's suit, see the *NYT* for 1933: "Producers of Play Sued by Jean Norris" (Feb. 19); "Reply in Mrs. Norris's Suit" (Feb. 21); "'Four O'Clock' Suit Settled" (May 24); Brooks Atkinson's review (Feb. 14).

CHAPTER 5

1. Governor Roosevelt enjoyed the 1931 Inner Circle satires so much that he preserved the words to the "tin box" and other songs: "1929–33 Political Files," fol. 16, box 23, The Roosevelt Family Papers Donated by Children, FDR Library. Kaufman's parody appeared in *The Nation* 134 (June 15, 1932): 676–77; see Herbert Mitgang, *Once Upon a Time in New York: Jimmy Walker, Franklin Roosevelt, and the Last Great Battle of the Jazz Age* (New York: Free Press, 2000), 154–56, for a longer excerpt. James Wyman Barrett, the last city editor of the *World*, attributed the limerick about Acuna to Stanley Walker, *H-T* city editor, who probably recited it at the 1931 Inner Circle dinner ("Political Targets Riddled by Quips of Inner Circle," *H-T*, Mar. 8, 1931). Barrett says his own staff added verses about an "innocent lass ensnared in the toils of the law through Mapocha's machinations," setting them to the 1928 "hit" tune, "The Gay Caballero."

2. John Dewey, "The Government of New York City," in *The Later Works, 1925–1953*, vol. 9: *1933–1934*, ed. Jo Ann Boydston and Abraham Kaplan (Carbondale: Southern Illinois University Press, 1981), 363–64.

3. See Northrop and Northrop, *The Insolence of Office*, chap. XIV: "Doctor Doyle."

4. In the *NYT* for 1931: "Woman Vice Case Witness Found Strangled in Park; Her Lawyer Is Arrested" (Feb. 27); "Daughter Ends Life over Gordon Murder" and "Shamed by Scandal, Girl's Diary Says" (Mar. 4).

5. See Peretti, *Nightclub City*, 139–40, and Adler, *A House Is Not a Home*, 31, 42, 87, 96, 145, 166–74, and chap. 6 (Rachel Rubin, who edited a modern version of Adler's memoir, calls it "a remarkable account of New York's cultural history, a knowing and innovative immigrant tale, a significant meditation on sex and the marketplace," xi).

6. On Brooklyn, see "Politics Is Hunted in Brooklyn Courts," *NYT*, July 6, 1931.

7. Northrop and Northrop, *The Insolence of Office*, chap. X; many articles in the *NYT* between January and early July 1931, and his obituary, "J. Silbermann Dies; Ex-Magistrate, 69" (May 18, 1947).

8. Northrop and Northrop, *The Insolence of Office*, chaps. XII and XIV; in the *NYT* for 1931: "40 Witnesses Vanish in Vice Frame-Ups" (Feb. 8); "Roosevelt Orders Inquiry on Crain after City Club Demands His Removal for Misfeasance in Prosecuting Graft" and "Crain Record Scored by Public Leaders" (Mar. 8); "Crain to Be Cleared but Scored as Lax in Seabury Report" (Aug. 30).

9. Fiorello La Guardia, *The Making of an Insurgent* (New York: J.B. Lippincott, Co., 1948); Ray T. Tucker, "The Roughneck of Congress," *North American Review* 228/5 (Nov., 1929): 541-47. Howard Zinn, *La Guardia in Congress* (Ithaca: Cornell University Press, 1958).

10. For this and following paragraph, see in the *NYT* for 1931: "Demand for City-Wide Inquiry Grows" (Mar. 12); "Charges against Walker Given to Governor Here; His Removal Demanded" (Mar. 18); "Civic Groups Flock to Join Vigilantes" (Mar. 21); "150 Lawyers Aiding Inquiry Movement" (Mar. 24). Founder of the Bureau of Municipal Research, which sought to apply scientific management to urban government, in 1931 Allen was director of an institute for public service; his charges against Walker are in Records of the Governor of the State of New York, 1929–1932 (Franklin D. Roosevelt), microfilm, reel no. 114, FDR Library. Schieffelin, a Republican, ran Schieffelin & Co., a wholesale drug business, and chaired the Citizens Union for thirty-two years.

11. Letters to the Governor from March 1931, in Records of the Governor of the State of New York, 1929–1932, microfilm, reels no. 114–15, FDR Library.

12. Northrop and Northrop, *The Insolence of Office*, chap. XXIV. On Oct. 11 and 15, the *BDE* published charts of how much money politicians and vice squad members had accumulated and their "explanations."

13. The daily press reported voluminously on these events; Mitgang's *Once Upon a Time* provides a lively, informed, and perceptive narrative (chaps. 9–12).

14. In the *BDE* for 1930: "Vice Squad Detectives Accused by Society" (Sept. 28); "Women Throng Court to Hear 'Frameup' Case" (Dec. 9); "New Trial Given Nurse Charging Framed Arrest" (Dec. 26); "Mulrooney Orders 2 Cops Be Quizzed in Vagrancy Case" (Dec. 30); and in the *NYT* for 1930: "No Police Stool Pigeons" (Oct. 27); "Hearing on Goodman Ordered by Seabury; Vice Verdict Upset" (Dec. 27); "Seabury Inquiry 'Illegal,' City's Counsel Charges; Corrigan Shifts 150 Aides" (Dec. 30). The two dismissed officers were reinstated two years later: *NYT*: "Police Department" (Aug. 14 and Sept. 25, 1931); "Court Overrules Mulrooney in Two Vice Case Rulings" (Feb. 28, 1933); "Vice Squad Men Win Appeals" (Mar. 1, 1933).

15. "Seek Framed Girls' Freedom," *Troy Times*, Dec. 11, 1930; "Roosevelt Pardons Six Women 'Framed' by Police Vice Ring," *NYT*, Dec. 23, 1930; for Clivette's response, "Court's Reversal in Vice Case Hints Brooklyn Inquiry," *BDE*, Dec. 27,

1930. On Mary Hamilton, see Mary Jane Aldrich-Moodie, "Staking Out Their Domain: Women in the New York City Police Department, 1890–1935" (PhD diss., University of North Carolina/Chapel Hill, 2002), passim.

16. For this and following, see Hochfelder to Mayor Walker, Dec. 24, 1930, fol. corr. 1930 "W" (for "women"), Papers of Mayor James J. Walker, New York City Municipal Archives (hereafter, NYCMA). For the appointees to assist the Crime Prevention Bureau, see "Women's Clubs Act to End Vice Spies," NYT, Feb. 7, 1931. Also, see "Walker, 'Shocked,' Asks Drive on Vice," NYT, Mar. 5, 1931, for a report on this group's first meeting. See in the NYT for 1930: "Crain Acts to Jail Vice Ring Grafters" (Nov. 30); "Six More Policemen Stripped of Shields; M'Quade under Fire" (Dec. 7); "Graft on Gambling Laid to the Police by 'Policy Queen'" (Dec. 9); "Brodsky to Testify on Income Today" (Dec. 12); "High Tammany Men Named by Kresel in Inquiry on Funds" (Dec. 22); "Roosevelt Pardons Six Women 'Framed' by Police Vice Ring" (Dec. 23).

17. Lazansky is the same judge who, in 1919, had denied a petition for women's jury service. In the BDE for 1930: "Brooklyn Bar Considers Quiz on Magistrates" (Dec. 28); "Mulrooney Orders 2 Cops Be Quizzed in Vagrancy Case" (Dec. 30); and for 1931: "Plan to Call on Roosevelt for Quiz Here" (Jan. 4); "Padding Expenses in Nurse's Arrest Is Laid to 2 Police" (Feb. 26). In the NYT for 1931: "City-Wide Inquiry Mapped by Republicans at Albany; Governor to Get Measure" (Jan. 4); "Governor to Reveal Policy Tomorrow on City Inquiries" (Jan. 6); "77 Minor Girls Imprisoned Unlawfully by 7 Judges; Corrigan Acts to Free All" (Jan. 9); "Lazansky Bars B'klyn, Queens Court Probes" (Jan. 19); "Extend Court Quiz, Governor Is Urged" (Feb. 15: contains text of the SPUC petition); "Act for Wider Inquiry" (Feb. 16); "Court Inquiry Fund Asked" (Feb. 17); "Brooklyn Inquiry Near" (Feb. 18); "Governor for Court Quiz Here; Demands Facts of Lazansky" (Feb. 19: contains text of Roosevelt's letter to Lazansky); "Roosevelt Acts to Force a City-Wide Court Inquiry" (Feb. 20); "Brooklyn Inquiry Opposed by Court" (Feb. 28); "Governor, Vexed by Bench Rebuff, Drops Quiz Here" (Mar. 7).

18. "Report on Vice Awaited by Women as Basis of Court Reform Program," H-T, Mar. 1, 1931.

19. Only the sudden death of Clivette's husband in May slowed her down. See "Demands Men Be Held in Immorality Cases," BDE, Jan. 6, 1931, and dozens of almost daily subsequent articles reporting on her speeches, including "Mrs. Clivette Asks Pistols for Women," BDE, Mar. 10, 1931. Dr. Sophia Harned, SPUC treasurer and vice chair of the Alliance of Brooklyn Women's Clubs, had called Corrigan's characterization of women, which he made before some three thousand members of the NYCFWC, "insulting" ("Corrigan Speech Insult to Women, Says Dr. Harned," BDE, Jan. 15, 1931).

20. See "Score Use of Stool Pigeons," Sun, Feb. 6, 1931; "Women's Clubs Act to End Vice Spies," NYT, Feb. 7, 1931; "Report on Vice Awaited by Women," H-T, Mar. 1, 1931.

21. In the *NYT* for 1931: "Bar 'Unknown Man' in Vice Arrests" (Mar. 13) and "Mulrooney Replaces Entire Vice Squad; A New General Order Bars Informers to Cure Abuses Revealed by Seabury" (Apr. 12); "Abolish Vice Squad and 'Stool Pigeons' in Drastic Shake-up," *BDE*, Apr. 12, 1931.

22. "Co-Leader of Healy Indicates Judges Make Gifts for Jobs," *NYT*, Apr. 16, 1931.

23. In 1931: "Leaders Must Live," *BDE*, Apr. 16; "Miss Mathews Sticks to Guns on Job Gifts," *BDE*, Apr. 16; "A Frank Lady" (editorial), *NYT*, Apr. 17; "Paid Political Leaders" (letter), *NYT*, Apr. 20; "Sales Technique," *Time Magazine* 17, no. 17 (Apr. 27, 1931): 18.

24. Mary Simkhovitch to the Editor, *NYT*, Mar. 18, 1931.

25. See in the *NYT* for 1931: "Committee of 1,000 Speeds Inquiry Job" and "1,200 to Aid City Inquiry," which includes a detailed membership list (Apr. 17); S. J. Woolf, "A Veteran Crusader Surveys the City" (May 3). Also, in the *BDE* for 1931: Ralph H. Dryer, "Bootlegging Corrupts City, Says William Jay Schieffelin" (May 17). Among the women members of Schieffelin's committee were, in addition to Dublin, Kenyon, Lexow, and Whitney, women discussed previously in this book, such as Mary Dreier, Ruth Lewinson, Alice Duer Miller, Bertha Rembaugh, Mary K. Simkhovitch, and Lillian Wald.

26. Daniel O. Prosterman, *Defining Democracy: Electoral Reform and the Struggle for Power in New York City* (New York: Oxford University Press, 2012), 40; Mitgang, *Man Who Rode the Tiger*, 200–201; Dewey, "The Government of New York City," 381. In the *NYT*: "Seabury to Demand Wide Court Reform" (Jan. 11, 1931); for 1932: "To Break Tammany Grip" (Jan. 25); "Civic Leaders Back Seabury on Reform" (Jan. 26); "The Reforms Urged by Seabury" (Mar. 28); "Seabury Endorses a Minority Voice" (Nov. 26, 1935).

27. Reminiscences of Genevieve Beavers Earle (hereafter, GBE-CCOH), 18; "Walker Reviews Record in Office," *NYT*, Apr. 11, 1929.

28. In the *NYT* for 1929: "Republican Women Hear Party Advised" (Jan 13); "Strikers Visit City Hall" (Apr. 18); "Record Majority for Walker Foreseen" (May 19); "Mrs. Pratt Assails Regime of Walker" (June 7). In the *Chicago Defender*: on Bearden, "'Invaluable Advice Given' Says Writer" (Oct. 19, 1929); "Mayor Opens Harlem's New Health Center" (Nov. 22, 1930); "Thousands at Courthouse" (May 26, 1932).

29. Walker would later deny he made the "more or less shocked" wisecrack: see Frank Emery, "Rose to Power on Chessboard of Tiger Chiefs," *BDE*, Sept. 2, 1932 (a cogent summary of Walker's political career). In the *NYT*: "Mulrooney Starts Vice Squad Shake-up by Demoting Seven" (Nov. 29, 1930); "Walker, 'Shocked,' Asks Drive on Vice" (Mar. 5, 1931).

30. Quoted in Mitgang, *Man Who Rode the Tiger*, 185.

31. For early twentieth-century women's leadership in corrections reform, see Beard, *Woman's Work in Municipalities*, chap. VIII.

32. Murray had helped Detroit, Cleveland, and Atlanta establish women's divisions in police departments. To assist Murray, Whalen also appointed Matilda Van

Axen Hamill, a former investigator for New York Life Insurance and widow of Assemblyman Peter J. Hamill. The three "Negro" women were Araminta W. Anthony, Marguerite J. C. Tiller, and Anne W. Forrester. See State of New York, *Report of the Crime Commission 1928* (Albany: J. B. Lyons, 1928); Aldrich-Moodie, "Staking Out Their Domain," 337–38; and in the *NYT* for 1930: "Picks Woman to Aid New Crime Bureau" (Jan. 22); "Miss Murray Begins Work in Crime Bureau" (Jan. 23); "Mrs. Hamill Gets Post in New Police Unit" (Jan. 24); Virginia Pope, "New Police Bureau Aims at Prevention of Crime" (Feb. 2); "Five Made Policewomen in Bureau to Aid Youth" (Apr. 4); "10 Women Get Police Jobs" (Apr. 13).

33. Whalen's deployment of baton-swinging policemen against unemployed workers and his view that "There is plenty of law at the end of a nightstick" had aroused protests. He resigned at the end of May, saying he had agreed to only a year. See Grover Whalen's memoir, *Mr. New York* (New York: Putnam, 1955), chaps. XIII–XIV, and in the *NYT*: "Whalen Takes Over Police Post Today" (Dec. 18, 1928); "Whalen Is Silent on Ouster Move" (Mar. 18, 1930); "Won't Resign, Says Whalen after a Talk with Mayor" (Mar. 22, 1930); "Mulrooney Heads Police; 34 Years on the Force; Whalen Farewell Today" (May 21, 1930).

34. Additon was only the city's second woman to hold such a rank. The first was former probation officer Ellen O'Grady, appointed in 1918 by Mayor Hylan in response to women's groups' demands that he do more to protect young girls. On Feb. 11, 1917, young Ruth Cruger had gone to a Bronx motorcycle shop to pick up her sharpened ice skates and never came home. Convinced she had "eloped," the police dropped the case. Her parents hired attorney and investigator Grace Humiston, who soon found Cruger's body under the shop's basement floor and exposed the shop's laundering of money that traffic cops took from motorists. O'Grady lasted only a year, resigning when Police Commissioner Richard E. Enright insisted on protecting friends implicated in sex crimes. On Humiston and Cruger, see Brad Ricca, *Mrs. Sherlock Holmes* (New York: St. Martin's Press, 2017) on the case's role in the 1921 mayoral election, see in the *NYT*: "Whitman Will Keep Hands Off Police" (Jan. 30, 1918); "Will Add 12 Women to Regular Police" (May 21, 1918); "Enright to Resign, Says High Official" (Apr. 7, 1920); "Hylan-Hearst Men Get Out, the Hour I Get In, Says Curran" (Nov. 3, 1921); "J.C. Hackett Back in New Police Job" (Oct. 19, 1922). On O'Grady, see Djuna Barnes, "Woman Police Deputy . . ." (*Sun Magazine*, Mar. 24, 1918); and the works of Aldrich-Moodie, Claire Bond Potter, and Andrea Friedman.

35. In the *NYT*: "Miss Additon Made Crime Bureau Head" (Oct. 12, 1930); "Miss Additon to Be Sixth Deputy" (June 20, 1931); "Miss Additon Takes New Police Office" (June 23, 1931, photo of Mulrooney swearing her in); "Woman Police Deputy Gets at Crime Source" (July 12, 1931); "Mulrooney Pleads for Crime Bureau" (Jan. 20, 1934).

36. "Woman Police Deputy Gets at Crime Source," *NYT*, July 12, 1931.

37. Additon, "The Crime Prevention Bureau of the New York City Police Department," in Sheldon and Eleanor Glueck, *Preventing Crime* (1936) (New York: McGraw-Hill, 1936), 215–36.

38. For this and following paragraph, see: "Statement of Miss Henrietta Additon, Deputy Police Commissioner, in Charge of the Crime Prevention Bureau of the New York City Police Department," in *Hearings before a Subcommittee of the Senate Committee on Commerce: Pursuant to S. Res. 74, A Resolution Authorizing an Investigation of the Matter of So-Called "Rackets" with a View to Their Suppression* (73rd Cong., 2nd session), vol. 1, part IV, New York Hearings, November 23–24, 1933, 646–54. See also Aldrich-Moodie, "Staking Out Their Domain," 350ff., on the CPB's investment in recreational outlets, especially for boys; girls received much less attention. Additon wrote frequently on recreation and crime prevention, e.g., "Leisure and Crime Prevention," *Recreation* 27, no. 10 (Jan. 1934): 458–59, 487.

39. "Crime Bureau's Value Weighed," *Sun*, Jan. 12, 1934, and in the *NYT* for 1934: "City May Abolish the Crime Bureau" (Jan. 13); "Mulrooney Pleads for Crime Bureau" (Jan. 20); "Anti-Crime Bureau Put on Probation" (Feb. 28).

40. In the *NYT* for 1933: "Big Drop in Crime Here, Bolan Finds" (June 16); "166 City Play Sites Urged By Police" (June 20); "Playground Funds Asked" (Dec. 22); and in the *BDE*: "Boy with Sleigh Injured by Car" (Dec. 29, 1933); "Boy, 8, Borrows Auto, Takes Pal for Spin through Coney" (Jan. 19, 1934). Also, "Crime Prevention" (*NYT*, Feb. 28, 1934); "Ride Hitchers Lectured" (*NYT*, June 29, 1934); "Parents Urged to Cooperate with Crime Prevention Bureau" (*NY Age*, July 21, 1934).

41. Madeleine (Mrs. Sidney) Borg and Lillie (Mrs. Willard) Parker were the two leaders. See "Crime Bureau's Value Weighed," *Sun*, Jan. 12, 1934; "Women Voters Rally Marks Budget Drive," *BDE*, Feb. 14, 1934; "Pay $5 Graft for CWA Job to Politician," *BDE*, Feb. 16, 1934; "La Guardia Plans More Pay Slashes," *NYT*, Mar. 2, 1934. O'Ryan's visit to the Brooklyn unit of the CPB had left him "favorably impressed with the personality and zeal" of the staff: see in the *NYT* for 1934: "Crime Bureau Staff Impresses O'Ryan" (Jan. 25) and "Mayor and Medalie Study Crime Bureau" (Mar. 8). Hurst's letter to "Fiorello," June 21, 1934, is in fol. "Fannie Hurst," La Guardia Papers, microfilm ed., reel no. 501 (hereafter, LaG-NYCMA).

42. The charter amendment authorizing Additon's post did not make it civil service, which meant it was politically vulnerable; see Alfred J. Kahn, *Police and Children: A Study of the Juvenile Aid Bureau of the New York City Police Department* (New York: Citizens' Committee on Children, 1951), 13. Valentine was no friend of the CPB's founder, Grover Whalen, who had ended Valentine's effort to run an anti–racketeering and corruption squad and then "exiled" him to Queens. See Lewis Valentine, *Night Stick: The Autobiography of Lewis J. Valentine* (New York: Dial Press, 1947), chap. 7. Appointed September 26, 1934, Valentine

remained commissioner for eleven years, longer than any of his predecessors, and was one of La Guardia's most trusted allies.

43. In the *NYT* for 1934: "Miss Additon out as Police Deputy" (Sept. 28) and "La Guardia Hostile, Miss Additon Says" (Sept. 29); in the *H-T* for 1934: "Miss Additon Quits Post of Police Deputy" (Sept. 28); "A Loss to the City" and "Miss Additon Says La Guardia Hindered Work" (Sept. 29). The CPB was soon renamed the juvenile aid bureau ("Anti-Crime Bureau Renamed by Mayor," Oct. 17), a name suggested by settlement leader Lillian Wald.

44. See in the *NYT* for 1934: "Valentine to Reorganize Crime Bureau; Personnel and Expenses Will Be Reduced" (Sept. 30); "Valentine Is Urged to Aid Crime Bureau: 70 Social Agencies Join In" and "Miss Additon's Retirement" (Oct. 1); "Pleads for Crime Bureau: Welfare Council Opposes Further Cut in Its Appropriation" (Oct 25); "Miss Mulrooney out of Old Crime Bureau" (Dec. 29).

45. Rebecca Rankin, ed., *New York Advancing: A Scientific Approach to Municipal Government; An Accounting to the Citizens by Departments and Boroughs of the City of New York, 1934–1935* (New York: Municipal Reference Library, 1936), 179. The website of today's PAL puts the program's roots in the New York Police Department but makes no mention of Additon. See http://www.palnyc.org/history/ (accessed Dec. 22, 2016).

46. Valentine, *Night Stick*, 278–79, 285. Alfred J. Kahn, professor at Columbia University School of Social Work, reported on the juvenile aid bureau in 1951 for the New York Citizens' Committee for Children and gave full credit to Additon for PAL (*Police and Children*, 14).

47. In the *NYT* for 1940: "Henrietta Additon to Head Bedford" (Mar. 14); "Footnotes on Headliners" (Mar. 17); "Tribute Planned to Miss Additon" (Mar. 24); "Miss Additon Is Guest" (Mar. 29); "Honored by the A.W.A." (Apr. 21); and for 1942: "Juvenile Aid Unit Will Be Abolished" (Apr. 18); "Fight Is Continued for Juvenile Bureau" (Apr. 23); "Preventing Juvenile Crime: Proposed Elimination of Aid Bureau Here Is Viewed as Backward Step" (Apr. 23).

48. In the *NYT*: "City Plans Fight on Delinquency" (Mar. 4, 1954); "Miss Additon 'Retires'" (editorial, Dec. 23, 1957, praising her "courage and good humor"); Austin MacCormick, professor of criminology at the University of California at Berkeley, credited her with establishing "a sound philosophy and practical procedures which police departments in other cities could and did use as models," and compared her favorably to other outstanding female penologists, such as Miriam Van Waters of Massachusetts and Edna Mahan of New Jersey ("Miss Additon Praised," Jan. 9, 1958); on Melchionne, see "High Police Post Goes to Woman" (Oct. 29, 1963). New York newspapers did not carry an obituary, but a death date, March 1, 1973, appears at http://www.locateancestors.com/ddition/ (accessed Apr. 23, 2018).

49. For the early part of Kross's life and career, see chap. 2. Cathy FitzGerald and Jennifer Lopez, "This Month in History: A Mighty Outraged Woman," *Hearsay*

(New York City Law Department Newsletter), August 2009. My thanks to Mae Quinn for sharing this article.

50. Before letting Brill go, La Guardia gave her a thirty-day appointment to replace another female judge, Jane Bolin, who was going on maternity leave (Bolin was the nation's first African American female judge, whom La Guardia appointed in 1935). Lehrich was the first woman member of the *Yale Law Journal*; she was made an assistant corporation counsel in 1935 and had served the board of estimate since 1938; Vincent Richard Impellitteri, Democratic mayor when Lehrich's ten-year term came up for renewal, did not renew her. In the *BDE*: "Board Appoints Mrs. Lehrich" (Apr. 7, 1938); "Mrs. Brill Holds to Hope She'll Keep Bench Post" (May 1, 1941), "A Place for Mrs. Brill" (May 6, 1941); in the *NYT*: "2d Woman Named as a Magistrate" (July 1, 1941); "Jeanette G. Brill, Ex-Magistrate, 75" (Mar. 31, 1964); "Frances Lehrich, 92, Lawyer and Magistrate" (Dec. 29, 1992).

51. Referring to how his mayoral campaign would be conducted, La Guardia said, "This will be no high school debate or pink tea party" ("Rule of Curry Is Only Issue of LaGuardia," *H-T*, Sept. 15, 1933). "O'Brien Is Named to Succeed Burr," *BDE*, Apr. 9, 1920; "Murphy Turns Down Surrogate Cohalan," *NYT*, Aug. 17, 1922; "Welcome New Judges in Many Courtrooms," *NYT*, Jan. 3, 1923; "Morgan Trust Examiner," *NYT*, Aug. 4, 1924; "Anna M. Kross, O'Brien Woman Leader, Good Cook, but Tends to Political Pot First," *Evening Post*, Nov. 2, 1933; "Mayor's Wife Honored," *NYT*, Jan. 6, 1933; "O'Brien Gives Jobs to 3 on Last Day," *NYT*, Dec. 31, 1933.

52. Untitled luncheon speech at Teachers College, Columbia University, July 26, 1945 (box 48, General Correspondence; Reports; Nearprint, 1945–1949, fol. "1945," AMK-AJA Papers). See also in the *NYT*: "Pick Carty on Jury in Plasterers' Case" (Apr. 13, 1923: the executives were charged with hampering the city's construction industry with strikes and other tactics); "70,000 Work People Clients for Woman" (July 22, 1923); "Union Fights Injunction" (Jan. 21, 1924); "Plasterers' Union Freed of Charges" (June 4, 1924); "Rain Fails to Dim Tammany Rallies for John W. Davis" (Sept. 10, 1924); "McKee Committee Formed" (Oct. 12, 1925); "Miss Byrne Named County Register" (July 3, 1931). Goldstein was a Republican who became a city magistrate in 1931 and in 1939 was elected a New York County General Sessions judge.

53. Zoe Beckley, "Honest, Sympathetic and Able Counsel Sought, 80,000 Men Pick Woman," *Mail*, Oct. 25, 1923.

54. Ann Wythe, "Mrs. Kross—Counsel of 37 Unions! The Story of the Woman to Whom Turn the Plasterers, Machinists, Painters, Plumbers and Other Skilled Workers When Legal Advice Is Wanted," *BDE*, Nov. 25, 1923.

55. "Women Ask Court Appointment for One of their Sex," *Tribune*, Dec. 28, 1922; "Women Rivals for Children's Bench Vacancy," *Evening World*, Dec. 28, 1922; "Portias Would Sit in Judgment if Hylan Just Says the Word" ("Big Black Scrapbook"

[my designation], box x-438, AMK-AJA). On Craig, later the first woman elected a New York County Municipal Court justice, see "Law as a Career for Women Urged," *NYT*, Nov. 10, 1935. The children's court judgeship carried a salary $2,000 more than a magistrate ($8,000). The anecdote about the Moskowitz's "advice" to Kross is in Voorsanger, "Everybody's Judge," 228.

56. Voorsanger, "Everybody's Judge," 238.

57. Mitgang, *Man Who Rode the Tiger*, 198–99 passim, covers the ins and outs of O'Brien's last-minute appointments, though with no mention of women's hopes. Kross was appointed to an unexpired term, which ran until June 30, 1940. See "Woman's Place Is on the Bench, Says Domestic Relations Candidate," *Evening Post*, Sept. 15, 1933. On her appointment, see "O'Brien Gives Jobs to 3 on Last Day," *NYT*, Dec. 31, 1933; "Tammany Ends 16-Year Rule over City Hall," *H-T*, Dec. 31, 1933 (includes photo of O'Brien swearing Kross in).

58. Zelda Popkin, *Open Every Door* (New York: E. P. Dutton, 1956), 188; Isabelle Keating, "3d Woman Judge Has a 'Lot to Live Down,'" *BDE*, Jan. 3, 1934; Voorsanger, "Everybody's Judge," 4, 275.

59. See for this and following, Keating, "3d Woman Judge."

60. Zelda Popkin, "Magistrate Kross Attacks the Present Method of Dealing with Vice Cases," n.p., n.d., but from early 1934 ("Big Black Scrapbook," AMK-AJA).

61. "Women's Court Abolition Urged by Mrs. Kross," *H-T*, Jan. 14, 1934.

62. Popkin, *Open Every Door*, 191.

63. As a young lawyer, Anna Moscowitz had made essentially the same proposal to Mayor John Purroy Mitchel. Her "Report on 'Prostitution and the Women's Court,'" submitted to The Mayor, Hon. F. H. La Guardia, by Magistrate Anna M. Kross (box 61, AMK-AJA), was a full-blown study and proposal for action. For press coverage, see the *NYT* for Mar. 9, 1935: "Mrs. Kross Gives Data to Grand Jury on Court Vice Ring" and "Mrs. Kross Favors Social War on Vice."

64. "Mayor Studies Kross Proposals on Vice Control," *H-T*, Mar. 9, 1935; "Mrs. Kross Favors Social War on Vice," *NYT*, Mar. 9, 1935. Special prosecutor Thomas Dewey used wiretaps to implicate gangster "Lucky" Luciano in prostitution rings.

65. The women made twenty-eight visits to twenty-one courts from mid-February to the end of March 1936. "Women's City Club Group Assails 'Noisy. Flippant' Women's Court," *H-T*, July 6, 1936.

66. Harry J. Benjamin, "Prostitution: In Some of Its Medico-Psychological Aspects and an Attempt at Its Practical Solution," *Medical Review of Reviews*, Sept. 1935, off-print in AMK-AJA. The only qualification he made about Kross's report (he had read about it only in the newspapers) was that it nowhere *justified* prostitution. He would never use such terms as "offenders" and "rehabilitation."

67. Anna M. Kross, "Memorandum on Immediate Changes in the Procedure of the Women's Court," fol. 19: "Committee to Study Women's Court," reel no. 22, LaG-NYCMA.

68. Popkin, *Open Every Door*, 196.

69. Voorsanger, "Everybody's Judge," 271–75. Kross's friend, writer Janet Mabie, referred to her refusal to sit in women's court in a Sept. 7, 1938, letter to Bill O'Brien of the *World-Telegram*, copy in box 79, "New York Supreme Court, First Judicial District (Manhattan and the Bronx). Correspondence; Reports. 1938," AMK-AJA.

70. Voorsanger, "Everybody's Judge," 274; on Hines, who was prosecuted and convicted in 1939, see Stolberg, *Fighting Organized Crime*, chap. 10.

71. Mae Quinn explores Kross's innovative courts in "Anna Moscowitz Kross and the Home Term Part: A Second Look at the Nation's First Criminal Domestic Violence Court," *Akron Law Review* 41 (2008): 733–62. See also "Just Bring Us Peace in Our House," *New Yorker*, Dec. 11, 1954, 44ff., a long unsigned piece on Kross's home term court; for the abolition of the Social Service Bureau, see Voorsanger, "Everybody's Judge," 290–91.

72. See John M. Murtagh and Sara Harris, *Cast the First Stone* (New York: McGraw-Hill, 1957) and Murtagh, "Problems and Treatment of Prostitution," *Correction* (New York State Department of Correction) 23, no. 3 (Jan.–Feb. 1958): 3–6, with a response by Beatrice S. Burstein, member of the New York State Commission of Correction, 3–8, 34. Also, "Murtagh Asks End of Women's Court," *NYT*, July 27, 1951, and Quinn, "Revisiting Anna Moscowitz Kross's Critique," 688–94.

73. Adler, *A House Is Not a Home*, 198.

74. Adler, *A House Is Not a Home*, 199.

75. "240 in Vice Squads Shifted to Spur Racket Campaign," *NYT*, Mar. 6, 1935.

76. Between March and May 1935, all of the city's newspapers gave wide coverage to these events. The two lawyers Kross named ridiculed the idea of a "ring" and said they were hired because of their successful practices ("Dodge Will Force Lawyers to Talk in Racket Inquiry," *NYT*, Mar. 10, 1935). The US government later seized Adler's bail to pay an income tax debt.

77. In the *NYT* for 1936: "$435,000 Bail Set for Ten as Heads of City Vice Ring" (Feb. 4); "Lucania Convicted with 8 in Vice Ring on 62 Counts Each" (June 8); "Bribery Is Bared in Vice Ring Trial; 2 Face Disbarment" (June 9). Also, "Crime Experts Blame Police for Vice Rings," *BDE*, June 14, 1936; and two undated articles by Dorothy Dunbar Bromley for the *World-Telegram* from 1936 in Kross's scrapbooks: "Law Itself Branded Vice Racket Cause" and "Hits Woman's Court as Vice Racket's Aid."

78. In the *BDE*: Jane Corby, "Reforming Modern Girl Not Such Hard Task as It Was, Asserts Jane Corby" (Dec. 12, 1934); "Asks for Return of Woman's Court to This Borough" (Mar. 13, 1935); "La Guardia Gets New Protest on Women's Court" (June 30, 1935); "For a Women's Court in Brooklyn" (editorial, July 26, 1935); A. I. Schnipelsky, "Changes Urged in Boro Courts" (Sept. 21, 1935); "Ask Mayor to Back Women's Court Here" (Feb. 29, 1936); Alice Cogan, "Woman

Judge Hits Boro's Clubwomen on Reform Laxity" (Nov. 8, 1936). Also, "Helen P. M'Cormick Dies in Brooklyn," *NYT*, Feb. 22, 1937 (she died following surgery at age forty-seven). Attorney Sarah Stephenson took over her post but soon resigned because of the press of business ("Miss Stephanson [*sic*] Resigns," *BDE*, Aug. 11, 1937).

79. In the *BDE*: "Goldstein Would Segregate Wayward Minor and First Cases" (Mar. 30, 1935); "Men in Vice Raid Called to Testify" (Apr. 22, 1935); "Mayor in Court Starts Vice Quiz" (Sept. 1, 1936); "Mayor Cites Growth of City Subway Line" (Oct. 21, 1937).

80. For this and following, see "Launch Campaign to Rid Harlem of Vice," *Chicago Defender*, Mar. 23, 1935; "Negro Magistrate Scores Men Caught in Disorderly House," *NY Age*, Sept. 19, 1936. On the failed attempt of the Committee of Fourteen to win judicial approval of a "customer" law in the early 1920s, see Thomas Mackey, *Pursuing Johns: Criminal Law Reform, Defending Character, and New York City's Committee of Fourteen, 1920–1930* (Columbus: Ohio State University Press, 2005).

81. "Law as a Career for Women Urged," *NYT*, Nov. 10, 1935. Other speakers at this event included Judge Genevieve Cline (US Customs Court), Jane Todd (Westchester County's assemblywoman), Doris Byrne (Bronx County's assemblywoman), Bertha Schwartz (assistant state attorney general), Magistrate Jeanette Brill, settlement leader Mary K. Simkhovitch (then the only woman on the New York City Housing Authority), and other women leaders in philanthropy, welfare work, and civic activism. For the SPUC claiming credit for having spurred the investigations, see Margaret Mara, "Bay Ridge Woman Devotes Life to Solving Troubles of Others," *BDE*, Dec. 16, 1931.

CHAPTER 6

1. Earle preserved a carbon copy of the play; an amateur writer of both poetry and prose, she may have written much of it. See box 2, fol. 25, Genevieve Beavers Earle Papers, Municipal Archives of the City of New York (hereafter, GBE-NYCMA); and appendix for the full text. All in-text quotations from this version. The photograph of the "Women of the La Guardia Administration" comes from this event.

2. In 1936 Magda Fontanges was a young French reporter, rumored to be having an affair with Italian dictator Benito Mussolini.

3. Going to "star-gazing conferences" was an insult La Guardia hurled at officials who talk "definitions" instead of action; see, e.g., "La Guardia Urges Straus to Start Housing Jobs Now," *NYT*, Nov. 19, 1937.

4. The removal of policemen from the juvenile aid bureau was a dig at Additon's insistence that "real cops" do preventive work with youth. The "fat, moth-eaten matrons" remark may refer to a planned modernization: see Milton Bracker and Remie

Lonse, "Streamlining the Policewoman," *NYT*, Mar. 26, 1939, where the authors wrote disparagingly of "bulky" matrons.

5. Considering the pushcarts on the Lower East Side a cause of congestion and health hazards, La Guardia was determined to eliminate them.

6. The custodian issue was a second dig at Additon, this one concerning her reluctance to violate custodial labor contracts.

7. "Camp La Guardia" was a rehabilitation farm for homeless men ("City Camp Marks First Anniversary," *NYT*, May 12, 1935).

8. "La Guardia Invites Women's 'Nagging,'" *Ithaca Journal*, Dec. 7, 1937. This is the only press report I have found on the dinner event.

9. See George Martin, *CCB: The Life and Century of Charles C. Burlingham, New York's First Citizen 1858–1959* (New York: Hill & Wang, 2005). Also, Charles Culp Burlingham Papers, Harvard Law School (hereafter, CCB-Harvard), boxes 5–6 (Fusion 1933).

10. Fiorello La Guardia, *The Making of An Insurgent* (New York: J. B. Lippincott, 1948); Ray T. Tucker, "The Roughneck of Congress," *North American Review* 228, no. 5 (Nov. 1929): 541–47; Howard Zinn, *La Guardia in Congress* (Ithaca, NY: Cornell University Press, 1958).

11. "Women to Make Active Fight for La Guardia," *Tribune*, Oct. 17, 1919.

12. In the *Tribune* for 1919: "Secret Budget Attacked by Maj. La Guardia" (Oct. 14); Dennis Tilden Lynch, "Women in Politics for an Unbossed Judiciary" (Nov. 2); "Women Take Babies, Dogs, and Husbands to Polls" (Nov. 5); "$5,269 Spent by Women" (Nov. 22). On military personnel not getting their naturalization papers in time to vote, see "Registration Sets New High Record," *NYT*, Oct. 12, 1919; on La Guardia's recall of women's contribution to his 1919 victory, see "TWV," *BDE*, Aug. 18, 1921, and "Mayor Makes Plea for Morris Votes," *NYT*, Oct. 28, 1936.

13. "Devoy to Become La Guardia's Aid," *NYT*, Dec. 21, 1919.

14. "Forsakes Society for Political Job," *Tribune*, Jan. 11, 1920.

15. "La Guardia Names Miss Delafield as His Secretary," *Tribune*, Dec. 21, 1919; "Two Women 'Hang Up Hats' and Start Work for City," *Tribune*, Jan. 3, 1920; Edith Moriarty, "With the Women of Today," *Sandusky Star*, Jan. 27, 1920.

16. "La Guardia Flays Traction Directors for Transit Mixup," *BDE*, Feb. 9, 1921; "Kings G.O.P. Women May Not Co-operate," *BDE*, June 24, 1921, and "Another Fusionist Quits," *NYT*, July 25, 1921. "The Woman Voter" columns from August to September 1921 covered women's support (or lack thereof) for La Guardia, as do longer articles in the *Tribune*.

17. "Mrs. Gooderson Honored at Lunch by G.O.P. Workers," *BDE*, Oct. 27, 1929.

18. (Sources in this note apply to this and previous paragraph.) See "Gooderson Quits Fire Department after 51 Years," *BDE*, Feb. 16, 1930, regarding Gooderson's husband, a firefighter whom Tammany mistreated. In the *NYT* for 1929: "LaGuardia's Foes Are Losing Ground" (July 26); "Republicans Seek Ticket Head Today" (July

29); "City Republicans Name La Guardia to Head Ticket as Mrs. Pratt Quits" (Aug. 2). In the *BDE* for 1929: "Who's Who in the Campaign—Mrs. May M. Gooderson" (Aug. 13); "Women Will Back Bennett in Race" (Sept. 12); "Democrat Claims for City Scored by Mrs. Gooderson" (Sep. 17); "La Guardia Will Lose, Mrs. Woodruff Predicts" (Sept. 18); "Mrs. Gooderson Lauds La Guardia" (Sept. 26); " 'Gentlemanly Talk' of Past Not Way to G.O.P. Victory, Is Belief of Mrs. Gooderson" (Oct. 4); "Best Chance Now to Clean Up, Says Mrs. Gooderson" (Nov. 1). On the Housewives' League, see in the *NYT*: "Women Will Rout Crooked Tradesmen" (Dec. 18, 1911); "La Guardia Scores High Price of Bread" (Oct. 13, 1929); and in the *BDE*, "Walker Shields 'Food Monopoly,' Says LaGuardia" (Oct. 13, 1929). On African American support for La Guardia, see "Walker Scored for Rome 'Jim-Crow,'" *Amsterdam News*, Oct. 23, 1929.

19. See Kevin C. Murphy, "Lost Warrior: Al Smith and the Fall of Tammany Hall," part II, accessed Aug. 21, 2012, http://www.kevincmurphy.com/alsmith.htm. My thanks to Kevin Murphy for calling my attention to his work on this topic.

20. The women's names appear in "'Peace Committee,' Led by Burlingham, Chooses Independent Republican to Run against O'Brien," *H-T*, Aug. 4, 1933. Garing was a Queens party leader appointed vice chair of the Republican state committee.

21. Alva Johnston, *New Yorker*, July 1, 1933, 18–21; July 8, 1933, 17–20, and "Ex-Mayor O'Brien Dies at Home at 78," *NYT*, Sept. 23, 1951; Mitgang, *Once Upon A Time*, 218.

22. In the *Amsterdam News* for 1933: "Mckee Holds Top of Poll" (Oct. 18); "De Priest Will Aid La Guardia Monday" (Oct. 25); "La Guardia Friend of Negro, De Priest Says" (Nov. 1); "Maria Lawton Will Lead Fusion Forces" (Oct. 11).

23. Davie (Mrs. Preston L.) later opposed the New Deal and in 1940 led the women's Wendell Willkie campaign: see "After Four Years" (*New Yorker*, Oct. 19, 1940, 18–19). In the *NYT* for 1933: "Fusion Rally Held by Society Women" (Aug. 11); "Mrs. Sabin Opens Fusion Campaign" (Oct. 4); "A 'Challenge' to M'Kee" (Oct. 10).

24. "La Guardia's Reply to McKee's Keynote Address," *NYT*, Oct. 14, 1933.

25. In the *BDE* for 1933: "Women Fusion Members Start Crusade Today" (Oct. 10); "Fusion Bridge-Tea" (Oct. 13); for McKee's retort, "Untermyer Is Attacked as 'Public Enemy'" (Oct. 26). In the *NYT* for 1933: "Text of McKee's Address Opening His Campaign" (Oct. 12); W. A. Warn, "Republicans Plan Fight" (Oct. 15); "M'Kee Is Assailed as Anti-Feminist" (Oct. 26).

26. In the *NYT* for 1933: "LaGuardia Sees Victory" (Nov. 3); "Work of Women for Fusion Gets Ingersoll Praise" (Nov. 4); James A. Hagerty, "M'Kee Runs Second" (Nov. 8).

27. Neither Burlingham's private papers (CCB-Harvard) nor La Guardia's clippings scrapbook, box 27A2, fol. 02 FHL–Election Campaign, La Guardia-Wagner Archives, La Guardia Community College (hereafter, LaG-Archives), show interest in women as potential appointees.

28. See the following, all on Mar. 21, 1934: "Women in City Jobs Show How to Be Brief," *NYT*; "Brooklyn Women Honored at Arts, Industries Rally," *BDE*; "17 Speeches in an Hour," *Sun*. The honorees were Pearl Bernstein, secretary of the board of estimate; Sarah S. Dennen, secretary of the Parks Department; Rosalie Loew Whitney, deputy license commissioner; Lucille L. Kraft, secretary of the Department of Water Supply, Gas, and Electricity; Helen Springer, secretary to the board of aldermen; Sophie L. C. Battistella, investigator for the board of aldermen; Mrs. Charles F. Murphy, secretary of the borough of Brooklyn; Margaret W. Barnard, director of District Health Administration in the Health Department; Sophie Olmstead, examiner for the commissioner of accounts; Mary K. Simkhovitch, member of the housing authority; Mary Frasca, one of Mayor La Guardia's secretaries; Alma W. Fraas, secretary of the Health Department; Frances Foley Gannon, deputy markets commissioner; Anna Moscowitz Kross, city magistrate; Justine Wise Tulin, assistant corporation counsel; and Henrietta Additon, head of the Crime Prevention Bureau. On Gannon, see Kathleen M. M'Laughlin, "Consumer Service Likely to Resume," *NYT*, Nov. 7, 1937.

29. Alice Cogan, "Rosalie Whitney Joins Ranks of Women City Jurists; Thirty of Her Sex Now Hold Important Municipal Jobs," *BDE*, Dec. 29, 1935. For Whitney's antiracketeering crusade see the *H-T* for 1930: "Woman Leads Laundry War on Racketeer" (May 5); "Boycott Turned on Racketeers in Laundry Field" (May 13); "Laundry Body, Called Racket, Dissolves Self" (July 4); "Anti-Racketeer Agencies Urged by Mrs. Whitney" (Sept. 4); "An Ultimatum Is Ignored" (editorial, Sept. 7). In *Criminals and Politicians* (New York: MacMillan, 1932), Denis Tilden Lynch (who reported on the crusade for the *H-T*) says the laundry owners did not follow Whitney's advice (203–9). On her early appointments, see "Levine Is Out, Paul Moss Gets License Post," *H-T*, Jan. 19, 1934; "Mayor Appoints 14 to High City Posts; 2 Women on List," *NYT*, Dec. 15, 1935.

30. (Sources in this note apply to this and previous paragraph.) La Guardia's threat not to reappoint Tulin presaged his treatment of Anna Kross, whom he also threatened with nonrenewal because she had "defied" him. For the Burlingham-Frankfurter story, see a 1982 oral interview conducted by Dr. Ernest Goldstein in Tulin-Polier's papers, SL (fol. 3). See also, in the *NYT*: "Compensation Cases Reformed by City" (Mar. 22, 1934); Justine Wise Tulin, "Workmen's Compensation Comes Up for Revision" (Feb. 10, 1935); "Mrs. Tulin Named Justice by Mayor" (July 8, 1935); "Mrs. Tulin Is Sworn In" (Sept. 15, 1935); Edward Hudson, "Justine Wise Polier Is Dead; A Judge and Child Advocate" (Aug. 2, 1987). Also, "Windels Gives 10 Staff Jobs," *BDE*, Jan. 2, 1934; Dorothy Kilgallen, "'No Hero,' Says Woman Judge Taking Oath," *Evening Journal*, July 9, 1935; "Mrs. Tulin Sits as Judge; Bars 'Lady Justice' Title," *Brooklyn Times Union*, Aug. 5, 1935; "LaGuardia Aid Flays Johnson for Job

Delay," *Post*, Aug. 28, 1935; "'Work or Jail' Kicks Back at Johnson," *Evening Journal*, Aug. 28, 1935 (which called Tulin the "Portia of the Fusion Administration").

31. It is possible that Tulin thought of these activities as either silly or too time-consuming. See Cogan, "Rosalie Whitney"; "Mayor Halts Licensing of Pinball Game," *H-T*, June 9, 1935. Others listed include judges Justine Wise Tulin, Anna Moscowitz Kross, Jeanette Brill, and Agnes Craig; Dorothy Kenyon (who took Whitney's place in licenses), May Gooderson (director of sanitary education, Department of Sanitation), Pearl Bernstein (secretary, board of estimate), Dr. Margaret Barnard (director, district health centers), Dr. Marion Loew (tuberculosis clinics), Alma Fraas (secretary to Dr. John Rice), Mary Frasca (handling the mayor's "social service problems"), Mitzi Somach (mayor's secretary), Lucile Kraft (secretary, Department of Water Supply, Gas, and Electricity, who has "done much to shape the policy of the department"); three assistant corporation counsels (Frances Lehrich, Alice Trubin, and Rose Schnephs); Esther Nichols (secretary to Paul Windels, corporation counsel); three women aiding the president of the board of aldermen (Helen Springer, secretary; Sophia Battistella and Rose Miller, investigators); Sybil Stearns (director, Park Department concessions); Mary Upshaw (examinations director, Civil Service Commission); Charlotte Carr (director, Home Relief Bureau); Sarah Dennen (director, Women's Division of the Works Progress Administration); Grace Gosselin (assistant director, Works Division,); Genevieve Earle, charter commission (nonsalaried); and Sophie Olmsted (examiner, department of accounts and the "eyes and ears of the Mayor").

32. PB-AJC, 38–42.

33. PB-AJC, 30–34, 38–39, 43–44, 78.

34. On Kenyon, see in the *H-T*: "Woman License Official Sworn" (Dec. 20, 1935); "Mayor for New Vice Laws but Opposes Licensing of Prostitutes" (June 18, 1936); "Mayor to Start His 2d Term in Seabury Home" (Dec. 31, 1937); and in the *NYT*: "Mayor Appoints 14 to High City Posts; 2 Women on List" (Dec. 15, 1935); "University Women Stress Education" (May 9, 1936).

35. "Social Plan Urged to End Vice Racket," *NYT*, June 17, 1936.

36. For this and subsequent paragraph, see "Social Plan Urged to End Vice Racket."

37. Dorothy Kenyon to Mayor La Guardia, Aug. 24, 1936 (box 49, fol. 22, Dorothy Kenyon Papers, Sophia Smith Archives, Smith College). Also, in the *NYT*: "Churches Demand End of Burlesque" (Apr. 29, 1937); "Burlesque Shows of City Are Shut as Public Menace" (May 2, 1937). On the burlesque controversies, see Peretti, *Nightclub City*, 116–19, 164–67, and Andrea Friedman, *Prurient Interests: Gender, Democracy, and Obscenity in New York City, 1909–1945* (New York: Columbia University Press, 2000), 156–57 on women's organizations opposed to censorship.

38. Peretti, *Nightclub City*, 165. Kenyon's *NYT* obituary quotes her (without source) saying that burlesque offered "the only beauty in the lives of ice men and messenger

boys." As this view contradicts her position in 1936, either she changed her mind or the *NYT* got it wrong ("Judge Dorothy Kenyon Is Dead; Champion of Social Reform, 83," *NYT*, Feb. 14, 1972).

39. "La Guardia Names New Commission to Draft Charter," *NYT*, Jan. 13, 1935.

40. GBE-CCOH, 8; Earle, "A Portrait of an Amateur" [1926], box 13, fol. XXXIII (Biographical Sketches), GBE-Col; Harriette Oliver Forbes, "Genevieve Beavers Earle, A Profile," *Kappa Alpha Theta Magazine,* Nov. 1938, 8–9, MN59002, Scrapbooks, frames 215–16, GBE-NYCMA; speech, "Occupations for Women: V. Municipal Housekeeper."

41. GBE-CCOH, 11–12.

42. Letter of appointment from Mayor Mitchel, Oct. 8, 1918, GBE-NYCMA, box 1, fol. 3, item no. 110; GBE-CCOH, 17–18.

43. GBE-CCOH, 21.

44. Prosterman, *Defining Democracy*, passim.

45. The act passed in August 1934 separated PR from that of a new charter so as to prevent the defeat of a charter should PR fail. City newspapers covered these issues in innumerable articles.

46. Between 1915 and 1948 twenty-two American cities adopted PR, including Ashtabula, Ohio (1915); Boulder, Colorado (1917); Kalamazoo, Michigan (1918); Sacramento, California; and West Hartford, Connecticut (1921). The largest city to adopt by 1921 was Cleveland, followed by Cincinnati (1925), Hamilton (1926), and Toledo and Wheeling (1935). A drive for PR in Los Angeles failed in 1913, and in 1922 the California Supreme Court ruled PR a violation of the state constitution; the same happened in Philadelphia. Hopkins, Minnesota, adopted it in 1948, and although seven cities in Massachusetts ultimately adopted PR (Cambridge still has it), Boston won an exclusion.

47. The Merchants Association of New York, "Proportional Representation for New York City," Mar. 9, 1937.

48. Women's City Club of New York, "A Primer on Proportional Representation and Charter Revision," June 1936. See also in the *NYT*: "Primer on Charter Is Issued by Club" (Sept. 13, 1936) and Anne Petersen, "Civic Groups Face the P.R. Issue Again" (Sept. 1, 1938).

49. See Prosterman, *Defining Democracy*, 75–77, on PR supporters' ambivalence regarding women. A sample ballot sent out by the Proportional Representation League listed four ranked candidates: three men and one woman, "Jane Roe," who won fourth place (box 46, fol. 2A, Proportional Representation League Records, 1900–1965 [hereafter, PR League]). The League of Women Voters also did not promote the idea of women candidates in the PR campaign: box 10, fol. "Apportionment, Proportional Representation 1932–47 League Materials," NYCLWV.

50. Goetz later spearheaded the fight to prevent an amendment to make PR unconstitutional. See "Paul Windels to Discuss Charter at Women's City Club Tomorrow,"

*H-T*, Nov. 22, 1936 (photo of Goetz), and "Mrs. N. S. Goetz, Welfare Worker," *NYT*, Nov. 3, 1953.

51. See GBE-CCOH, 25–33; for her views on a city manager, see box 5, fol. III (Publicity), GBE-Col.; some of her publicity materials are in box 13, fol. XXXIII, GBE-Col.

52. Kathleen Barber, in *A Right to Representation: Proportional Election Systems for the Twenty-First Century* (Columbus: Ohio State University Press, 2000), discusses similar challenges in Ohio and says that Florence Allen, former suffragist and League of Women Voters activist who was an Ohio Supreme Court judge, helped validate the method (55ff.).

53. In the *NYT* for 1936: "Wigwam Is 'Unanimous'" (Oct. 28) and "New Election Plan Assailed by Smith" (Oct. 31).

54. Chamber of Commerce of the State of New York, "Proportional Representation: What It Is and How It Works in New York City," 9–12. See Frederick Shaw, *The History of the New York City Legislature* (New York: Columbia University Press, 1954), 171, 209. For Martha Byrne's comment, see Marie Frugone's "Talk about Politics," *BDE*, July 18, 1937.

55. Barry W. Seaver, *A True Politician: Rebecca Browning Rankin, Municipal Reference Librarian of the City of New York, 1920–1952* (Jefferson, NC: McFarland, 2004), chap. IV, 99, 130–31; "Rebecca Rankin, Librarian, Dies: Municipal Reference Branch, Chief Aided City Officials," *Daily News*, Mar. 3, 1965.

56. Seaver, *A True Politician*, prologue.

57. Seaver, *A True Politician*, 102; Murray Davis, "Woman Holds Vital City Library Post," *Telegram*, June 5, 1947; "Text of City's Measures to Levy Sales, Utility and Inheritance Taxes," *NYT*, Nov. 28, 1934.

58. Seaver, *A True Politician*, 126; *New York Advancing: A Scientific Approach to Municipal Government. An Accounting to the Citizens by the Departments and Boroughs of the City of New York, 1934–1935. F. H. La Guardia, mayor* (New York: Municipal Reference Library, 1936), ix–x; and Elizabeth La Hines, "City's 'Biographer' Faces a New Task," *NYT*, Oct. 16, 1938.

59. *New York Advancing*, 1–19.

60. *New York Advancing*, 166, 267, 217, 272, 279, and 282.

61. Rankin tried to get the book adopted as a civics textbook, but the board of education refused, calling it a "political campaign book" for La Guardia. In the *NYT*: W. R. Conklin, "Fusion Tells City's Story: New York's First Year Book Reports on Many Routine and Unusual Activities" (Sept. 13, 1936); "Educators Cold to City Year Book" (Oct. 21, 1936); "School Heads Deny Ban on Year Book" (Oct. 22, 1936). Also "Year Book of City Meets School Snag," *BDE*, Oct. 21, 1936, and Seaver, *A True Politician*, 130–31.

62. In the *NYT*: "Mayor's Book Popular: 'New York Advancing' Now Is in Its Second Printing" (Mar. 19, 1937) and Elizabeth La Hines, "City's 'Biographer' Faces a

New Task" (Oct. 16, 1938). Seaver, *A True Politician*, 132–33. Two more editions followed in 1939 and 1945.

63. Seaver, *A True Politician*, 146, 155; *New York Advancing*, 69.

64. (Sources in this note apply to this and previous paragraph.) Her name as editor was visible, but in print smaller than La Guardia's and at the bottom of the page. Seaver, *A True Politician*, 124, 128. She considered herself a "woman of the administration" and was present at the dinner honoring Judge Whitney (*BDE*, Dec. 29, 1935). For the *NYT* editorial on her retirement, see "The Big City's Librarian" (May 27, 1952). In retirement, Rankin lobbied for the Library Aid Bill, which in March 1950 increased money for state public library operations for the first time in over a hundred years. After she moved to Dobbs Ferry, she organized and got state funding for the Westchester County Library System. See Seaver, *A True Politician*, chap. VI and conclusion.

65. Cheryl Lynn Greenberg, *"Or Does It Explode?" Black Harlem in the Great Depression* (New York: Oxford University Press, 1997).

66. See *Mayor La Guardia's Commission on the Harlem Riot of March 19, 1935, Complete Report*, ed. Richard E. Rubenstein and Robert M. Fogelson (New York: Arno Press, 1969), copied from an account in the July 18, 1936, edition of the *Amsterdam News*. Other black members of the mayor's commission were Dr. Charles Roberts, chairman, and Hubert T. Delaney, tax commissioner (La Guardia's first high-level African American appointment). Other white members were attorneys Morris Ernst and Arthur Garfield Hayes; Col. John J. Grimley of the 369th Infantry; and the Reverend William R. McCann. E. Franklin Frazier, Howard University's professor of sociology, directed the commission's studies.

67. Barbara Sicherman and Carol Hurd Green, ed., *Notable American Women: The Modern Period* (Cambridge, MA: Harvard University Press, 1986), q.v. "Carter, Eunice Hunton," 141–42.

68. Julie Gallagher, *Black Women & Politics*, 59–61. In the *Amsterdam News* for 1934: "Eunice Carter Office Seeker" (July 28); "Eunice Carter Club Launched by Women" (Sept. 22: sponsors included Louise H. Johnson [chair], Fannie Austin, Marion Moore Day, Laura S. Gibbs, J. Ida Jiggetts, Jeanette M. Johnson, Winonah Bond Logan, Effa Manley, Mary E. Oliver, Ollie Porter, Ruth Logan Roberts, journalist Thelma Berlack-Boozer, Amanda Smith, Ferol Smoot, and Miss E. Haden); T. E. B. [Thelma Berlack-Boozer], "The Feminist Viewpoint: Give Eunice Carter a Chance" (Oct. 13); "Mammoth Republican-Fusion Mass Meeting" (Oct. 27); "Making Your Vote Count" (editorial, Oct. 27); Edgar T. Rouzeau, "Local Candidates Launch Final Drive for Votes" (Nov. 3); "Stephens and Andrews Win" (Nov. 10).

69. "Eunice Carter Has Busy Time: Assembly Candidate Is Qualified for Job," *Amsterdam News*, Nov. 3, 1934; on Speaks, see Gallagher, *Black Women & Politics*, 63–65.

70. In the *Amsterdam News*: T. E. B., "An Open Letter to Stephens" (Nov. 10, 1934); Edgar T. Rouzeau, "Pope Billups, Johnson, Dench in Bitter Fight" (Nov. 2, 1935); "Ex-Assemblyman Goes to Trial" (Dec. 18, 1937). H. B. Webber, "Ex-Assembly-Man Stephens Exonerated," *Chicago Defender*, Dec. 25, 1937.

71. In the *Amsterdam News* for 1935: "Mayor's Committee under Fire" (Mar. 30); "Mrs. Carter Seen as Only Negro Appointee" (Aug. 10). Also, in the *New Journal and Guide* (Norfolk) for 1935: "Woman Named N. Y. Vice Probe Assistant" (Aug. 10); Lillian Johnson, "The Feminine Viewpoint: Orchids to Mrs. Carter" (Aug. 17).

72. Stolberg, *Fighting Organized Crime*, 122ff.; William Donati, *Lucky Luciano: The Rise and Fall of a Mob Boss* (Jefferson, NC: McFarland, 2010), 110, 112; Edgar T. Rouzeau, "Eunice Carter's Sleuthing Lands Two Racketeers," *Pittsburgh Courier*, Jan. 23, 1937; "Dewey Names Two," *Amsterdam News*, Jan. 1, 1938; "Born in Atlanta," *Amsterdam News*, Aug. 15, 1942; "I Earn $5,500 Per Year," *Afro-American*, Mar. 5, 1938; and in the *Amsterdam News*: "Eunice Hunton Carter Resigns D. A.'s Staff" (Jan. 6, 1945) and "Negro Woman Sent Lucky Luciano Away" (Mar. 1, 1947).

73. "Four Women Get Honors at Smith," *NYT*, June 21, 1938. In the *Amsterdam News*: "Women Battle for Dewey in Boro Campaign" (Oct. 29, 1938); Thelma Berlack-Boozer, "Women Spent No Dull Months in Year About to Terminate" (Dec. 31, 1938); Roy Wilkins, "Watchtower" (Aug. 12, 1939).

74. Jacqueline A. McLeod, *Daughter of the Empire State: The Life of Judge Jane Bolin* (Urbana: University of Illinois Press, 2011), 41. See in the *NYT*: "First Negro Woman Gets City Law Post," (Apr. 8, 1937); David Margolick, "At the Bar" (May 14, 1993). In the *Chicago Defender*: "Jane Bolin Begins Job as New York Justice" (Aug. 5, 1939); "For a Very Pleasant Day in Court—See New York's Judge Jane Bolin" (Sept. 30, 1939).

75. In the *Amsterdam News* for 1936: "Gird for Closing Conflict in Campaign" (Oct. 31); "Andrews and Justice Return to Assembly" (Nov. 7). Also, "Democrats Called Unfriendly to Race at Big Mass Meeting Held by Women at Mother Zion Church," *NY Age*, Oct. 31, 1936.

76. This was the court that the young Anna Kross had urged the city to establish when she was an assistant corporation counsel in the early 1920s.

77. "First Negro Woman Gets City Law Post," *NYT*, Apr. 8, 1937; Thomas Kessner (*Fiorello La Guardia*, 372) cites Katherine Hildreth (special examiner, New York City Children's Court), "The Negro Problem as Reflected in the Functioning of the Domestic Relations Court of the City of New York" (June 1934).

78. Bolin had met Roosevelt during a campaign to save the Wiltwyck School, a home on the Hudson River for minority boys that was losing its funding. O'Dwyer reappointed Bolin, as did Mayors Lindsay (a Republican) and Wagner (a Democrat). On Wiltwyck, see http://www.columbia.edu/cu/lweb/archival/collections/ldpd_6262245/, accessed Apr. 16, 2018; also, McLeod, *Daughter of the Empire State*, 56–58, 63–64, chap. 5. Succeeding mayors Robert Wagner Jr. (Democrat) and John Lindsay

(Republican) reappointed Bolin. Also, see Judy Klemesrud, "For a Remarkable Judge, a Reluctant Retirement," *NYT*, Dec. 8, 1978; for the Brown-Isaacs bill, see Biondi, *To Stand and Fight*, passim. Justine Wise Polier (a few years after her first husband died, she married Shad Polier) worked with Bolin on establishing Wiltwyck and then, along with Judge Hubert Delaney, was on the forefront of campaigns to end racial discrimination and sectarianism in the treatment of children in the justice system.

79. In the *NYT*: "Mayor Appoints 14 to High City Posts; 2 Women on List" (Dec. 15, 1935) and Klemesrud, "For a Remarkable Judge."

80. McCleod, *Daughter of the Empire State*, 59–60. See also Constance Baker Motley, *Equal Justice under Law: An Autobiography* (New York: Farrar, Straus and Giroux, 1998), 35, where Motley also refers to Eunice Hunton Carter as helping her visualize herself as a lawyer.

81. For Mizelle's recollection, see New York State, "Jury Pool News," Spring 2007, 3, accessed Feb. 28, 2017, http://nysl.cloudapp.net/awweb/guest.jsp?smd=1&cl=all_lib&lb_document_id=62984.

82. Handwritten draft of Herrick's letter to an unknown corr., n.d. (box 1, fol. 2, Elinore Morehouse Herrick Papers, Schlesinger Library [hereafter, EMH-SL]).

83. Elinore Morehouse Herrick, "Labor's Responsibility for Full Productivity," *Advanced Management* 12, no. 1 (Mar. 1947): 14–19 (box 10, EMH-SL); "Mrs. Herrick Tells College Girls to Get Jobs at Factory Machines," *H-T*, Mar. 10, 1935.

84. Herrick, "No Life for a Lady" (unpublished memoir), box 10, fol. 154, EMH-SL.

85. All of the following anecdotes and quotations about her first lobbying experience come from an eleven-page chapter in the aforementioned manuscript memoir entitled "Horrors—A Lobbyist!"

86. "Experience Record of Elinore Morehouse Herrick," box 1, fol. 1, EMH-SL; Elinore M. Herrick, "Report to the Mayor," n.d. (after 1935, she wrote it as Director, NLRB, District 2). See also Elinore M. Herrick, "The National Labor Relations Act," *Annals of the American Academy of Political and Social Science* 248 (Nov. 1946): 82–90.

87. Dorothy Dunbar Bromley, "Mrs. Herrick of the Labor Board," *Harper's Magazine* 183 (Oct. 1941): 501–11.

88. On her work for the ALP (an affiliate of New York State's "Labor's Non-Partisan League"), see "Mrs. Herrick Gets Leave to Aid Roosevelt," *H-T*, Aug. 3, 1936; box 2, fol. 25 (Misc. Papers), EMH-SL; and box 3, fols. 49–52, for more details.

89. "Labor Board Methods Held Spur to Strikes," *Washington Evening Star*, Jan. 5, 1940; "Mrs. Herrick Tells House Inquiry of Protest on N. L. R. B. 'Ogpu,'" *H-T*, Jan. 6, 1940; "Mrs. Herrick, Accused, Holds Up Edison Tally," *H-T*, Apr. 6, 1940; "C.I.O. Move to Oust Mrs. Herrick Begun," *NYT*, Apr. 10, 1940.

90. New York newspapers published hundreds of articles on various aspects of Herrick's career. Her papers (EMH-SL) contain rich records from her Todd Shipyard work (box 5); on her postwar advocacy of women's work lives see Herrick to Marguerite Mooers Marshall, Feb. 26, 1943 (box 2, fol. 23) and Elinore M. Herrick, "What

about Women after the War?," *NYT*, Sept. 5, 1943; her anti-Communism of the early 1950s (box 7, e.g., "Notes for Washington Trip, Testimony, Senate Internal Security Committee, June 4, 1953); and John Kelso, "Woman's Blunt Comments on NLRB Amaze Senators," *Boston Sunday Post*, June 7, 1953. Also, in the *H-T* for 1942: "Women Named to Draft Laws for War Work" (Oct. 19); "Todd Will Hire Women at Its Hoboken Yard" (Nov. 8); "Mrs. Herrick Sees Women in Industry to Stay" (Nov. 21); and "Women's Board Advising State on Labor Quits" (Aug. 9, 1943). Also, in the *NYT*: "Mrs. Herrick Quits NLRB Post to Join Shipyard Company" (Aug. 30, 1942); "Mrs. Herrick's New Field" (editorial, Sept. 2, 1942); "Mrs. Herrick Quits Paper" (Feb. 11, 1955); "Elinore Herrick, Labor Aide" (Oct. 12, 1964).

91. On her views on women, see in the *H-T*: "Women Executives List Vocational Experiences" (Oct. 23, 1934); "Women Learn How to Get Jobs of Government" (Mar. 31, 1935). "Women in Politics See Merit Barred," *NYT*, Mar. 31, 1935.

92. Rosenberg's obituary, *NYT*, May 10, 1983; biographical entries in *Current Biography* for 1943, 1951; Susan L. Tananbaum, "Anna Lederer Rosenberg," accessed Mar. 5, 2017, https://jwa.org/encyclopedia/article/rosenberg-anna-marie-lederer; Christy L. Thurston, "Rosenberg, Anna Marie Lederer," accessed Mar. 7, 2017, http://www.anb.org/articles/06/06-00797.html; her oral history, CCOH; "Outgoing Directrix," *New Yorker*, Sept. 15, 1945, 20–21; "Anna M. Rosenberg—She Sells Intuitions," *Fortune* 50, no. 5 (Nov. 1954): 74. See also Jacqueline McGlade, "Establishing Mediation as Enterprise: The Career of Anna Rosenberg," *Business and Economic History* 25, no. 1 (Fall 1996): 242–51; and my essay in *Notable American Women* (2004), 555–56. Her collection at the Schlesinger Library is small; in 1982 she told Diane Sawyer that she had burned her correspondence with President Roosevelt (videotape, Papers of Anna Rosenberg Hoffman, SL).

93. After divorcing her husband in 1962, she married Paul Gray Hoffman, a progressive Republican, first Marshall Plan administrator, and then head of the Ford Foundation. She called herself Anna R. Hoffman thereafter.

94. (Sources in this note apply to this and previous paragraph.) "Mrs. Rosenberg Succeeds Straus," *NYT*, Sept. 16, 1934.

95. Section 213 of the Economy Act (1932) mandated that in staff reductions "married persons" with spouses in government should be fired first and discouraged hiring spouses of government workers; some businesses followed suit. See John Thomas McGuire, "'The Most Unjust Piece of Legislation': Section 213 of the Economy Act of 1932 and Feminism during the New Deal," *Journal of Policy History* 20, no. 4 (2008): 516–41.

96. *Time Magazine*, Nov. 20, 1950, 23; Charles Grutzner, "World Troubles Rest on 'Miss Government,'" *BDE*, Nov. 15, 1936.

97. Richard W. Steele, "The Pulse of the People. Franklin D. Roosevelt and the Gauging of American Public Opinion," *Journal of Contemporary History* 9, no. 4 (1974): 208, 210. Anna K. Nelson says Rosenberg traveled to Washington

almost weekly for working lunches or dinners with FDR: "Anna M. Rosenberg, an 'Honorary Man,'" *Journal of Military History* 68, no. 1 (2004): 133–61; Diane Sawyer interview.

98. For this and following paragraphs, see S. J. Woolf, "A Woman Sits in Judgment for NRA," *NYT Magazine*, Mar. 31, 1935 (includes Woolf's charcoal drawing of Rosenberg).

99. "Busiest Woman in U.S.: Anna Rosenberg Runs Country's Manpower," *Life Magazine*, Jan. 21, 1952, 79–87. In her interview with Diane Sawyer (recorded a year before she died), Rosenberg said FDR sent her on this mission in July 1944, but FDR had already signed the legislation on July 22, so she may have gotten the year wrong. In his memoir, *Working with Roosevelt* (New York: Da Capo Press, 1972), Rosenman twice mentions Rosenberg as one of FDR's informal contacts who influenced his policies and speeches (301, 356). See also Eric Pace, "Anna Rosenberg Hoffman Dead; Consultant and 50's Defense Aide," *NYT*, May 10, 1983.

100. She was the first civilian recipient of the "Medal of Freedom" (Oct. 29, 1945); in 1947 she was the first woman to receive the US Medal for Merit. For a newsreel clip announcing her Department of Defense appointment, see https://www.you-tube.com/watch?v=1h8eWJv14gk (accessed March 6, 2017). For the "facial" anecdote, see Henry Mitchell, "Homage to a 'Perfect American,'" *Washington Post*, Nov. 20, 1980 (George Marshall's centennial).

101. Alfred E. Smith made a similar comment about Belle Moskowitz, saying, "She demonstrated that participation by women in public life does not involve any sacrifice of their essential feminine qualities. . . . She was no doubt a womanly woman, but I saw no difference between the processes of her mind and the way the best men's minds work." See my *Belle Moskowitz*, "Appendix," 220–21.

102. Diane Sawyer interview.

CHAPTER 7

1. City newspapers reported extensively on the count in almost daily articles for a month after Nov. 2.

2. In the *NYT* for 1937: "25 Council Seats Are Sought by 211" (Oct. 6); "Mrs. Earle Chides Women on Votes" (Nov. 29).

3. See in the *BDE* for 1937: [Frugone], "Talk about Politics" (July 18, 25, Aug. 1) and "With Women's Clubs" (Aug. 18); "Expect Dark Horses to Enter Eagle's City Council Contest," (July 23) an article on the *BDE*'s "unofficial" popularity contest for council; "Women Candidates Favored" (Sept. 4).

4. McCann, "Women Join City Election Fight," n.p., Aug. 7 (clipping in Scrapbooks, frame 146, MN59002, GBE-NYCMA). Her list included Genevieve Earle, along with Ethel Dreier (La Guardia fundraiser and former president of the WCC),

Agnes Leach (LWV), Jane Smith Cramer (organizer of juror schools), Jane Norman Smith (NWP), Mary Dreier (WTUL), Marie Frugone, Harriet Laidlaw (WSP), and many more. Dorothy Dunbar Bromley, "Women Seek Justice in Party Politics" and "Labor Party Women Explain Male Slate," *World-Telegram*, Oct. 19 and 27, 1937.

5. In the *NYT* for 1937: "Seabury Backs 33 for City Council" (Sept. 27); Anne Petersen, "Women Nominees Few but Notable" (Oct. 10); "Nominees Backed by Citizens Union" (Oct. 21); "19 Choices Listed for City Council" (Oct. 25); "Mrs. W. F. Williams, Queens Civic Leader" (Apr. 8, 1950); "Mary K. Simkhovitch," *NY Age*, Oct. 30, 1937.

6. "14 Women Seeking Council Posts," *NYT*, Oct. 24, 1937: also mentioned were Lewinson; Deutsch; Vera Montgomery (publisher of the *Yorkville Advance* and American Labor Party nominee, who later withdrew); Frances Reder Ruskin (a nonpracticing lawyer, Democratic county committeewoman); Helen Martin (organizer of women for John Hylan); and, from Brooklyn, Mary O'Brien (an independent Democrat), Wren, Doyle, and Knopping. The candidates from Queens included Rachel Williams, Grace B. Daniels (a fusionist whose father Silas B. Browning had fought the Tweed ring), and Pearl E. O'Connor (manager of her father's newspaper, the *Irish Advocate*). Earle complained newspapers reported her speeches but never quoted her words (Harriette Oliver Forbes, "Genevieve Beavers Earle, a Profile," *Kappa Alpha Theta Magazine,* Nov. 1938, 8–9, MN59002, Scrapbooks, frame nos. 215–16, GBE-NYCMA).

7. Emma Bugbee, "14 Women for the City Council: New Voting System Heartens Feminists to Dare the Ballot," *H-T*, Oct. 24, 1937; Dorothy Dunbar Bromley, "La Guardia Needs Full Ticket," *World-Telegram*, Nov. 1, 1937.

8. "Mrs. Earle Chides Women on Votes," *NYT*, Nov. 29, 1937; "Although Defeated, Butler Wins Great Moral Victory," *NY Age*, Dec. 4, 1937. In Brooklyn, Amy Wren came closest to Earle, but had only 5,429 votes at the seventh count. In Manhattan, Ruth Lewinson had 22,776 votes by November 18 to Deutsch's 13,011 and Simkhovitch's 12,071. In Queens, Grace Daniels had only 6,725 by the third count, Rachel Williams 5,884. See in the *NYT* for 1937: "40 Are Eliminated in P. R. Vote Count" (Nov. 15); "The Count in City Council Race" (Nov. 18); "End of P. R. Count Near in 2 Boroughs" (Nov. 21); "Manhattan to End P.R. Count Today" (Nov. 22); "P. R. Count in Bronx under Way Again" (Nov. 23); "Tammany Elects 3 of 6 Councilmen in Manhattan Race" (Nov. 24); "Full Council List to Be Known Today" (Nov. 30); "Democrats Elect Council Majority" (Dec. 1).

9. Warren Moscow, "P. R. Is Seen Vindicated by Analysis of Votes," *NYT*, Dec. 5, 1937; Prosterman, *Defining Democracy*, 90 ff. The *Amsterdam News* claimed that, since black voters scattered their votes among a number of candidates running borough-wide, a black candidate could not accumulate enough votes to win; see, e.g., "A Flop in New York," Oct. 1, 1938.

10. Copy of the citation, Jan. 27, 1937 (box 13, fol. XXXIII, GBE-Col.). I have corrected minor typographical errors in these quotations.

11. See GBE-CCOH, 42; a copy of her speech, Jan. 27, 1937 (box 14, fol. XLII, GBE-Col.); Earle to La Guardia, Feb. 2, 1937, box 14, fol. XLI, "Correspondence, 15 Sept. 1917-3 Jan. 1938," GBE-Col; in the *BDE* for 1937: "Mrs. Earle Honored for Civic Services" (Jan. 8); "Tribute Paid to Mrs. Earle" (Jan. 27); "Mrs. Earle Is Proclaimed 'Queen of Kings' at Presentation of Medal" (Jan. 28), as well as several editorials. For her work during the Depression, see in the *BDE*: "Name Mrs. Earle to Aid in Block Relief Work Here" (Feb. 18, 1932) and "A Well-Deserved Tribute" (editorial, May 28, 1933).

12. E.g., in the *BDE* for 1937: "Child Toil Foes Mass Demands for Ratification" (Feb. 22); "La Guardia Names Four to Committee on City Planning" (Mar. 1); "Mrs. Earle's Candidacy" (endorsement editorial, Aug. 25).

13. Prosterman writes that Earle's election so fascinated the press that reporters treated her "akin to an exotic zoo animal" (*Defining Democracy*, 98). See in the *BDE*: "Mrs. Earle Has Long Record in Civil Service" (Sept. 26, 1937); "Mrs. Earle Hunts Pheasants as Surcease from Politics" (Nov. 29, 1937); Virginia Clemmer, "Mrs. Earle's 'Wild Oat'" (Aug. 14, 1939). Also, "Thumbnail Portrait of Genevieve Earle," *Daily News*, Oct. 18, 1937, and Helen Ewing, "Ex-Councilwoman Talks to Fireplace Literary Club," *Patchogue Advance*, Feb. 9, 1950, http://nyshistoricnewspapers.org/lccn/sn86071739/1950-02-09/ed-1/seq-15/, accessed May 3, 2017. An online recording of her voice is at http://thisibelieve.org/essay/16524/ (accessed May 8, 2017).

14. GBE-CCOH, 39. She first stated these views in "The Lighter Side of Campaigning (as a woman sees it)," *Alumnae Bulletin* (Adelphi College Alumnae Association) 8, nos. 21–22 (Feb.–May 1938), 2, 4.

15. Ernest L. Meyer, "As the Crow Flies" (*Post*, n.d., but before the 1937 election), who also listed Stanley Isaacs (president of United Neighborhood Houses), Philip Schiff (Madison House headworker running for the assembly against a man who had opposed the child labor amendment), Edward Corsi (former headworker of Haarlem House), Ingersoll (former headworker at Maxwell House), and Reuben Lefkowitz (former worker at Henry St. Settlement). See also "Use Political Power, Woman Leader Urges," *News*, Jan. 17, 1937; Anne Petersen, "Mrs. Earle Eager to Serve the City," *NYT*, Sept. 12, 1937; "G.O.P.-Labor Alliance Seen in City Council," *BDE*, Dec. 8, 1937; Oliver Pilat, "The Lady Who Tells Them Off," *Evening Post* [1943], all in Earle's scrapbook.

16. Clemmer, "Mrs. Earle's 'Wild Oat.'"

17. In the *BDE*: "Dumbness a Menace, Avers Mrs. W. P. Earle" (May 3, 1931); Isabelle Keating, "Declares Cuts Curtail Best in Government" (Feb. 12, 1933) and "Mrs. Earle Quits Ideal for Practical Politics" (Sept. 25, 1933); and Katherine Blanck, "Daughter to Cast First Vote in Mother's Favor" (Oct. 10, 1941). Also, "Favors

'No-Man's Land' Drama in Government, Mrs. Earle Cites Formula for Woman Voter," *NYT*, June 4, 1931; Emma Bugbee, "Mrs. Earle to Seek Re-election to Council in Her Own Name," *H-T*, Oct. 2, 1939.

18. GBE-CCOH, 46; "G.O.P.-Labor Alliance Seen in City Council," *BDE*, Dec. 8, 1937. For the "spats" story, see, e.g., Murray Davis, "Woman of Firsts Puts City First," *World-Telegram*, June 6, 1947.

19. In the *BDE* for 1937: "Mrs. Earle for La Guardia" (June 19, where she claims he had thus far appointed eighty-three women); "Mrs. Earle Supports La Guardia" (letter to the editor, Aug. 7).

20. All newspaper references for the campaign are to 1937 unless otherwise noted; they are on microfilm MN59002, "Scrapbooks," GBE-NYCMA, "Mrs. Earle Stresses Pension Reform as She Files Petitions," n.p., n.d. (fragment); "Brooklyn Women Fusionists Launch Crusade to Drive Degenerate Out of the Subways," *BDE*, Aug. 31; O[liver]. R. Pilat, "Men, Beware Ballot, There's Feminine Chicanery Afoot," *Evening Post*, Aug. 31. On transit police, see in the *NY Amsterdam News* for 1949: "Ask Probe of New York City Administration" (Jan. 15); "Cites Need for More Subway Police in City" (Sept. 3).

21. In the *BDE* for 1937: "Mrs. Earle supported as Qualified for Election to the City Council" (letter to the editor, Sept. 1); Bromley's articles ran from midsummer through November 1939: "More Women Urged to Run for Office"; "City Politics a Puzzle to One Woman Voter"; "Woman Candidate Interested in Charter"; "A Wife Proves Women Can Serve City."

22. GBE-CCOH, 40–41.

23. Earle, "The Lighter Side of Campaigning," 4.

24. "Silly Municipal Laws Are Flayed by Morris," *BDE*, Dec. 12, 1937; "Only Councilwoman, She Studies for Job," *Daily News*, n.d. (early 1938); Bromley, "Strike a Balance," *Post*, June 10, 1938.

25. "County Reform Pressed," *NYT*, Dec. 2, 1935; F. H. La Guardia to the City Council, Dec. 5, 1938 (MN59001, frame 475, GBE-NYCMA).

26. "Sidelights of the Week," *NYT*, Dec. 11, 1938.

27. "Mrs. Earle Up All Night with Respectable Men, Police Tell Frantic Mate of 'Lady Councilman,'" *BDE*, Dec. 21, 1938. Also, Genevieve Beavers Earle, "Behind the Scenes in the N.Y.C. Council from a Woman's Point of View," *Alumnae Bulletin* (Adelphi College Alumnae Association) 10, no. 27 (Mar. 1940), 2 An editorial supporting county reorganization, "A Reform Too Long Delayed" (*NYT*, Dec. 8, 1938), called hundreds of county jobs "utterly useless . . . overmanned . . . political flotsam and jetsam." On the cost of street name changes, see Robert K. Straus, *In My Anecdotage* (Santa Barbara, CA: R. K. Straus, 1989), 205.

28. Office of the Minority Leader, "Press Release," letter to the Honorable William A. Carroll (Chairman, Committee on General Welfare, City Council), and "Statement in Support of Earle County Reorganization Bills," June 26, 1940 (frames

477ff., MN59001, GBE-NYCMA). Also, in the *NYT* for 1940: "Mrs. Earle Presses Bills" (June 29); "County Job Bills Opposed by Mayor" (Aug. 24).

29. Citizens' Non-Partisan Committee, "County Reform: Why We Need It and How to Get It" (frames 515ff., MN59001, GBE-NYCMA). Also, in the *NYT* for 1941: "Board Approves Two County Bills" (Aug. 29) and "Reform Bill Wins" (Nov. 5). The referendum created one city-wide sheriff and register appointed by the mayor on the basis of a civil service exam. See also "Brooklyn's Best Bets" (editorial), *Evening Post*, Oct. 11, 1941.

30. GBE-CCOH, 52, 55.

31. [F. P. A.], "The Conning Tower," *Post*, June 18, 1938.

32. "The Council Closes Its Door" (editorial), *NYT*, Jan. 18, 1940.

33. Straus, *In My Anecdotage*, 208–9. The *NYT* for 1940 carried many articles on the controversy, e.g., "Council Demands Russell Rejection" (Mar. 16); "Russell Is Ousted by Court as Unfit" (Mar. 31); "Post for Russell Cut from Budget at Mayor's Order" (Apr. 6). Also, see John Dewey and Horace Meyer Kallen, eds., *The Bertrand Russell Case* (New York: Viking Press, 1941).

34. Sophia Steinbach, "Woman of Social Service Skill Pushes Reform in City Council," *Christian Science Monitor*, Mar. 11, 1940. Earle received a draft of this article (written end January 1940) and corrected it (box 13, fol. XXXIII, GBE-Col.).

35. For this and following quotations, see: GBE-CCOH, 48, 52–55, 58–64, 68–69, 72, 75–78, 80, 113–15. Oliver Pilat, in "The Lady Who Tells Them Off," *Evening Post* [1943], refers to Gibbs as "brilliant." See also "Secretary Sees Boss Sworn In," *Afro-American*, Jan. 10, 1942 (photo of Gibbs observing Earle's swearing in for her third term); "Emily Gibbes [*sic*] Gets Position," *NY Amsterdam News*, June 8, 1940. Councilmen Earle especially admired Robert K. Straus, an independent Democrat; Stanley Isaacs, a Republican and widely admired public servant and housing advocate (Manhattan borough president 1938–42 and council member 1942–62); and Hugh Quinn (from Queens, who did a "creditable job" on building codes). She also expressed appreciation of Gertrude Weil Klein, ALP member from 1942 to 1945 until she lost her ALP endorsement and ran as an independent, when she was defeated. Goaded by the majority Democrats, Klein erred (Earle thought) in overdefending La Guardia.

36. GBE-CCOH, 61, 113. See Thomas Kessner, *Fiorello La Guardia*, on the decline of progressive reformers' support for La Guardia (546–48) and Hart's investigation (548–49); also, in the *NYT* for 1943: "The Council's Witch Hunt" (June 19); "Herlands in Clash over City Inquiry" (June 25); "Final Hart Report Is Full of Charges" (Dec. 24).

37. Her sufferings from neuritis loomed large in her papers (see, e.g., "Winter Solstice," her prose narrative about her illness, no. 34–35, GBE-NYCMA); she broke her hip in 1949. In the *NYT*: "W.P. Earle Jr. Dies; A Park Champion" (July 8, 1940); "Mrs. Earle, Former Councilman, Dies in Blaze at Bellport Home" (Mar. 7, 1956).

38. Cleveland Rodgers to Mrs. Earle, Jan. 11, 1937 (fol. XLI, "Correspondence, 15 Sept. 1917–3 Jan. 1938," GBE-Col.); the same folder contains letters from women similar to Rodgers's. Heffernan's characterization is in "Heffernan Says: Rita Casey Adds Color to Municipal Campaign," *BDE*, Nov. 1, 1941. Dorothy Dunbar Bromley, "Genevieve Earle Called Bulwark of City Council," *H-T*, Oct. 17, 1943, quotes Burlingham.

39. In the *H-T* for 1956: "Mrs. Genevieve B. Earle" (Mar. 8); Mrs. Donald Hutchinson, Mrs. Ralph B. Morris, Mrs. Lewis Steiger, "Tribute to Mrs. Earle" (Mar. 14); and Seth S. Faison, "City Council: Return to Old System Is Urged in Elections" (Aug. 11, 1957). In the *NYT*: "Mrs. Earle, Former Councilman, Dies in Blaze at Bellport Home" (Mar. 7, 1956); Stanley M. Isaacs, "In Defense of P. R." (Mar. 29, 1958).

40. Unless otherwise noted, all correspondence cited on Kross's race comes from 1938 and is in box 79, "New York Supreme Court, First Judicial District (Manhattan and the Bronx). Correspondence; Reports. 1938," AMK-AJA. All other information on the race comes from newspaper articles, many of which (not all identified) were in a scrapbook in box x-439. Kross kept every clipping, letter or carbon copy, and scrap of notepaper from this campaign, indicating how important it was to her. Supreme court justices earned twice as much ($25,000) as magistrates (*Post* editorial, May 19, 1938). For Boss Murphy's chastisement, see Emma Bugbee, "She Storms a New Gate for Women," *H-T*, Nov. 6, 1938.

41. Kross to "Zelda" [Popkin], July 7.

42. "A Woman for the Supreme Court" (editorial), *H-T*, Aug. 24.

43. Lynch, "Woman in State Supreme Court: Advocates Point to Mrs. Kross," *H-T*, Aug. 28, 1935. Kross thanked "Mrs. Ogden Reid" in letters of Sept. 1 and 21 and Oct. 22. Fifteen women lawyers had founded the New York Women's Bar Association in 1936.

44. Maud E. Smith to Kross, Sept. 16; McIntosh to Kross, n.d. (end Oct.); Kross to William Bolger (McIntosh's campaign manager), Oct. 28; Kross to Father Divine, Oct. 21; Kross to Daniel L. Reed, Oct. 13. For Divine's endorsement and those of others, see "Back Kross Candidacy," *NYT*, Oct. 16 1936.

45. "Leaders Endorse Candidacy of Magistrate Anna Moscowitz Kross for State Supreme Court," *National Negro News*, Oct. 5, [1938]. The gambling stories are in the *NYT* for 1936: "Court Denounces 'Snooping' Police" (July 20); "11 Women's Arrest Draws Court's Ire" (Oct. 19); "Quotations of the Week" (Oct. 20); and Ted Poston, "Judge Kross Gets Pot of Votes in Harlem Club Raid," *Post*, [Oct. 6, 1938]. La Guardia disapproved of her release of "gamblers": "Mayor Assails Anna Kross, Who 'Frees Gamblers, Rebukes Police," *Mirror*, Aug. 30, 1943.

46. Lena Madesin Phillips to Anna, Sept. 14; Helen Probst Abbott to Kross, Sept 22; Kross to Abbott, Sept. 27. In the *NYT* for 1938: "Mrs. Kross Starts Campaign for Bench" (Sept. 10); "Backs Magistrate Kross" (Sept. 15); "Miss Lewinson Backed" (Sept. 16); "Magistrate Kross" (endorsement editorial, Sept. 20). In the *H-T* for

1938: "Second Woman Is Candidate for Supreme Court" (Sept. 25); "Magistrate Kross Opens Headquarters" (Sept. 28).

47. For quotations in this and following paragraphs, see: Constance [Sporborg] to Marion [Mrs. Malcolm Parker MacCoy] and Kross, n.d. ("Sunday," probably Sept. 11); Anna to Constance, Sept. 12; Kross to Miss Dorothy Kenyon, Oct. 4. On Sporborg, see "Mrs. William Sporborg, 81, Dies; Leading Clubwoman 30 Years," *NYT*, Jan. 3, 1961. Kross to Miss Mabel Russell, Sept. 10; Kross to Janet Mabie, Sept. 10, 18.

48. William Harvey Smith (Attorney at Law) to Judge Kross, Sept. 20; "Wormser Calls Mrs. Kross Fit for State Court," unidentified clipping, Oct. 21; Mrs. [Constance] William Dick Sporborg, Chairman, Citizen's Judiciary Committee for the election of Anna Moscowitz Kross, to Mrs. Roosevelt, Oct. 30. In the *NYT* for 1938: "To Aid Magistrate Kross" (Oct. 8); "Labor Backs Mrs. Kross" (Oct. 9); editorial endorsement (Sept. 20). Also, "Statement by Magistrate Anna M. Kross," n.d., box 82, fol. 12, AMK-AJA; and for La Guardia's endorsement: Emma Bugbee, "She Storms a New Gate," *H-T*, Nov. 6 1938.

49. Kross to Mrs. Harry H. Thomas, N.Y.C. Federation of Women's Clubs, Oct. 21; Kross to Laura Berrien, Oct. 22, telegram; Mary O'Toole to Judge Kross, Nov. 3.

50. "Route of the Motorcade," Thurs., Nov. 3 (carbon copy included in her correspondence on the race); Emma Bugbee, "She Storms a New Gate."

51. Voorsanger, "Everybody's Judge," 274–75; "Democrats Gain Places on the Bench," *NYT*, Nov. 9 1938; "Statement by Magistrate Anna M. Kross," n.d., box 82, fol. 12, AMK-AJA; "Tabulated Election Results for New York State Officers," *H-T*, Nov. 10 1938.

52. Fay S. Paul [President, Independent Welfare League, Inc.] to Judge Kross, Nov. 9; Kross to Judge Mary O'Toole, Nov. 30.

53. Kross to Fannie [Hurst], Nov. 13. She made similar points to others: see Kross to La Guardia (Dear Friend), Nov. 14; Kross to Mrs. Goodman Richard Davis, Nov. 14; Kross to Dr. Robert W. Searle [General Secretary, The Greater New York Federation of Churches; Rev., D.D.], Nov. 14.

54. "Woman Urged for Bench," *NYT*, Dec. 20, 1938; in the *H-T*: "Woman Chosen as Tammany's Court Nominee" (Oct. 7, 1939); "Woman Justice to Be Inducted on City Bench" (Jan. 1, 1940); "Woman Justice Calls Her Work Social Service... Tells Humanitarian Aims" (Jan. 3, 1940); "Begins Her Work, on the Municipal Court Bench" (portrait, Jan. 3, 1940); Tom O'Hara, "Birdie Amsterdam to be in N. Y. State Court Race" (Sept. 18, 1957); Emma Bugbee, "Birdie Amsterdam Voted to State Supreme Court" (Nov. 7, 1957).

55. For this and subsequent quotations, see: *NYT*: "Bar Group Votes to Admit Women" (May 12, 1937); "Bar Group Turns to Noted Women" (Oct. 24, 1937); "Justice Bolin in Bar Unit" (Apr. 14, 1943). The twelve were law partners Dorothy Straus and Dorothy Kenyon (then first deputy commissioner of licenses), Catherine

Noyes Lee, Susan Brandeis (Supreme Court justice Louis Brandeis's daughter), Edna Rapallo (her family's fourth generation to practice law), Rosalie Loew Whitney (by then justice in the court of domestic relations), Mary-Chase Clark (granddaughter of Episcopal Bishop Philander Chase), Mary H. Donlon (Cornell University trustee, state constitutional convention candidate), Emelyn Laura Mackenzie, Margaret Mary J. Mangan, Margaret May Burnet (special assistant to the US attorney general), and Julia van Dernoot (Hunter College trustee, member of the city's board of higher education). Anna Kross may have been too bitter to apply. On their exclusion from the association's library, see Charles C. Burlingham to Emelyn L. MacKenzie, Mar. 19, 1930: "I am sorry to say that there is a ruling against giving women the use of our library" (CCB-Harvard, box 1, fol. 9).

56. In the *NYT* for 1937: Kathleen McLaughlin, "Business Women Pledge Jury Duty" (May 23); "Equal Labor Pacts Sought by Women (June 7); "Zonta Urges Right of Women to Work (June 25); "Women Hail Gain on 'Section 213a'" (July 11); "Congress Repeals Federal Job Law" (July 23); "The Women March" (editorial, July 24); Kathleen McLaughlin, "Women Push Fight for Full Equality" (July 24); Winifred Mallon, "Empty Triumph for Women Revealed in Repeal of Section 213" (Oct. 17).

57. "Doris Byrne Sworn in as Flynn's Assistant," *H-T*, May 18, 1937; "Doris Byrne Honored," *NYT*, Dec. 12, 1937. In the *NYT* for 1937: "Only 6 Women Win Convention Posts" (Dec. 19); Anne Petersen, "Dramatic Innovations Mark Year's Record of Women's Clubs" (Dec. 26).

58. Gallagher, *Black Women & Politics,* 62–65.

59. "Women Voters in Last Session," *BDE*, May 21, 1937.

60. On Rooney, see "Woman Seeks Council Post," *Sun*, Oct. 27, 1939, which says she was inspired to run by her aunt Margaret Rooney, a Democratic coleader in the Fourteenth AD, and by listening to city council broadcasts; on Klein, see "Gertrude W. Klein, 93, Councilwoman in 40's," *NYT*, July 30, 1986; on Casey, "Heffernan Says: Rita Casey Adds Color to Municipal Campaign," *BDE*, Nov. 1, 1941; on Schwartz, in the *H-T*, "Fourteen Women Seek Seats in City Council" (Nov. 4, 1945) and "Bertha Schwartz Is Dead; Bronx Municipal Justice" (Oct. 17, 1961); also, "Women Candidates for the City Council," *NY Sun*, Nov. 5, 1945. In 1946 the Democratic committee in Queens selected Fourth AD coleader Mae V. Gallis to replace James A. Phillips, who had resigned: "Queens Woman Joins City Council," *NYT*, Feb. 6, 1946. Doris I. Byrne would hold a temporary council seat to fill a war vacancy.

61. Simon [S.] W. Gerson, *Pete: The Story of Peter V. Cacchione, New York's First Communist Councilman* (New York: International Publishers, 1976), 84.

62. Gerson, *Pete,* passim; see Prosterman on Gerson in *Defining Democracy,* 202–3.

63. Benjamin J. Davis, *Communist Councilman from Harlem: Autobiographical Notes Written in a Federal Penitentiary* (New York: International Publishers, 1969).

On Stuyvesant Town's discriminatory policies, see Martha Biondi, *To Stand and Fight: The Struggle for Civil Rights in Postwar New York City* (Cambridge, MA: Harvard University Press, 2003), 121–36.

64. GBE-CCOH, 80–81; Prosterman, *Defining Democracy*, chap. 6.

65. For this and following paragraphs see: "Young Democrats Urge Repeal of PR," *NYT*, Aug. 3, 1947; H. R. Moskovit (State President, Young Democrats of New York), "Against PR" (letter to the editor), *NYT*, Aug. 25, 1947; "P.R.'s Latest" (editorial), *World-Telegram*, Nov. 19, 1945; "Council Election Proves Again That P.R. Should Be Abolished," *BDE*, Nov. 19, 1945; between Oct. 27 and 30, 1947, four *NYT* editorials, "The Record on P.R." Also, see Straus, *In My Anecdotage*, 216; Dorothy Detzer (National Executive Secretary, WILPF) to Elsie S. Parker (Assistant Secretary, National Municipal League), June 26, 1934 (box 35A, fol. "Women's International League for Peace and Freedom," PR League); "Women's Club Delegates against PR 3 to 1; Three Counts Are Taken at Stormy Session," *NYT*, Nov. 1, 1947. For contemporary summaries of opposition arguments, see Richard S. Childs, *Civic Victories: The Story of an Unfinished Revolution* (New York: Harper & Brothers, 1952), 244–45; Gerson covers the last days of PR from a leftist perspective: 181ff.

66. In the *NYT* for 1939: "City Elections Held Challenge to Women Here" (Oct. 8); Anne Petersen, "6 Women Ask Public Support at City Polls" (Nov. 5); "P.R. Poll Held a Boon to City" (Nov. 19). Also, "8 Council Candidates Tell Views to Women," *H-T*, Nov. 1, 1939; "May Seek Referendum for Repeal of P.R.," *Post*, May 10, 1947; Earle, "Should New York City Vote to Abolish PR?," *Republican Review Forum*, May 1947; "Issues on P.R. Fight Discussed by Mrs. Earle and Mrs. Davie," *H-T*, Nov. 2, 1947.

67. Prosterman, *Defining Democracy*, chap. 6; "Results of Citywide and Local Races," *NYT*, Nov. 4, 1965.

CHAPTER 8

1. Fanny Hurst, *Lonely Parade* (New York: Harper, 1942), 283. Hurst's other main characters were Kitty ("Kits"), modeled on interior decorator Elsie de Wolfe (later, Lady Mendl), with whom Marbury had a long love affair, and Sierra ("High Sierra"), a settlement worker based on philanthropist Anne Morgan (financier J. P. Morgan's daughter). See Brooke Kroeger, *Fannie: The Talent for Success of Writer Fannie Hurst* (New York: Times Books, 1999), 76, 302–3; on Marbury, see Rebecca W. Strum, "Elisabeth Marbury, 1856–1933: Her Life and Work" (PhD diss., New York University, 1989).

2. "Women Extolled and Then Chided," *NYT*, Nov. 9, 1959; "Statement for a Conference Organized by the Women's Unit in Governor Rockefeller's Office for Nov. 13–14, 1971," carton 23, CKS-SL.

3. The Hurst-La Guardia correspondence is on microfilm roll no. 501, LaG-NYCMA: Hurst to La Guardia, Nov. 9 and Dec. 1, 1933; June 21, 1934; La Guardia to Hurst, Dec. 4, 1933.

4. Hurst to La Guardia, Mar. 19, 1943, LaG-NYCMA.

5. Hurst to La Guardia, Mar. 28 and Dec. 13, 1943; June 8 and Nov. 30, 1944, LaG-NYCMA.

6. In the *NYT* for 1938: Kathleen McLaughlin, "Women Advance in Party Councils during 20 Years as Voters" (Sept. 25) and "Women Efficient in Saratoga Roles" (Sept. 28); and on Kennedy: "Woman to Have Big Task at Republican Convention" (May 28, 1940). McLaughlin named many other New York City "first mates," e.g., Democrats Agnes Leach (platform committee), Frieda Miller (now Governor Lehman's commissioner of labor), Alice Campbell Good (since 1936 national committeewoman from New York State), Anna M. Rosenberg, Dorothy Straus, Dorothy Schiff Backer, Nancy Cook, Anna Kross, and Ruth Lewinson; and Republicans Ruth Baker Pratt, Mrs. T. Channing Moore of Bronxville (a delegate to the state constitutional convention), Natalie Couch (assembly journal clerk), Mary C. Lawton (chair, Negro women Republicans), and Helen Varick Boswell.

7. Kathleen McLaughlin, "Women 'Nominate' Mrs. F. D. Roosevelt," *NYT*, Oct. 16, 1938.

8. In 1944, Miller became director of the Women's Bureau of the US Department of Labor, a post she held until 1953. McLaughlin, " 'Spade Work' Done for 2 Candidates" (Oct. 30, 1944); "Women Show Gain in State Offices" (Nov. 12, 1944); "New Pioneering for Mrs. Graves" (Jan. 1, 1939).

9. Both the *NYT* and the *H-T* covered the congress, e.g., "Woman's Centennial Session Ends," *NYT*, Nov. 28, 1940. The congress's program is at https://babel.hathitrust. org (accessed Apr. 8, 2018).

10. That any Belle Moskowitz papers were saved at Connecticut College in New London was thanks to inspiration from Beard's project: see my "Critical Journey: From Belle Moskowitz to Women's History," in *The Challenge of Feminist Biography*, ed. Sara Alpern et al. (Urbana: University of Illinois Press, 1992), 83–84. Also, Anke Voss-Hubbard, " 'No Documents, No History': Mary Ritter Beard and the Early History of Women's Archives," in *Perspectives on Women's Archives*, ed. Tanya Zanish-Belcher, with Anke Voss (Chicago: Society of American Archivists, 2013), 31–56; Martha Swain, *Ellen Woodward: New Deal Advocate for Women* (Jackson: University Press of Mississippi, 1995), 157–59.

11. Cynthia Harrison writes that polls in the early 1940s showed support for women's equal pay but not their political power: *On Account of Sex: The Politics of Women's Issues, 1945–1968* (Berkeley: University of California Press, 1988), 57–58. See in the *NYT*: McLaughlin, "What Women Have Done with the Vote" (Nov. 24, 1940);

"Women Politicians Scored in Debate" (Oct. 30, 1940); Dougherty, "It's a Man's Game, but Woman Is Learning" (Nov. 3, 1946).

12. In the *NYT*: Wolfgang Saxon, "Birdie Amsterdam, 95, a Pioneer for Female Judges in New York" (July 10, 1996); "Selected by La Guardia for Brief Term on Bench" (May 2, 1941); John Erskine, "The World Will Belong to the Women" (Mar. 14, 1943); "Doris Byrne Takes Court Post" (Aug. 17, 1948); "Doris I. Byrne, 70, of Criminal Court," (June 29, 1975—when the state reorganized special sessions in 1962, Byrne became a judge on the criminal court). Also, Walter Lister Jr., "Mayor Names Doris Byrne to Special Sessions," *H-T*, Jan. 12, 1950; Gladys Priddy, "Woman Named Vice-Chairman of G. O. P. Group," *Chicago Tribune*, June 22, 1944.

13. Cited earlier, preface, note 2. All but Whaley had been, were, or soon would be judges.

14. David McConnell, "Record List of Women Seek Office," *H-T*, Oct. 16, 1957.

15. "Campaign for City Council Presidency, 1957," CKS-SL; my essay on Simon at https://jwa.org/encyclopedia/article/simon-caroline-klein, accessed July 13, 2017; Caroline Simon interview, Women's City Club, Dec. 22, 1988 (in author's possession); "Lady Candidates," *NY Age*, Aug. 3, 1957; Mildred Murphy, "Mrs. Simon's Day Is a Full 17 Hours," *NYT*, Oct. 29, 1957; Bert Quint, "Mrs. Simon a Fighting Candidate," *H-T*, Sept. 23, 1957; and Emma Bugbee, "Mrs. Simon in a Final Vote Drive," *H-T*, Oct. 31, 1957.

16. Caroline Simon interview, Women's City Club; Ann Meuer, "Mrs. Simon Gets State Court Post," *NYT*, Aug. 7, 1963.

17. See Robert F. Kennedy to Mrs. Kross, Apr. 18, 1966 (box 84, "Subject File Correspondence," AMK-AJA), in which he praised her preventive and rehabilitative work, and "Resume of Achievements 1954-65," City of New York, Department of Correction, 42 pp. (box 82, AMK-AJA). Kross's experimentation with specialized courts likely influenced Judith Kaye, the first woman to sit on the New York Court of Appeals, who advocated "problem-solving" courts that sought alternatives to punishment, such as treatment programs for substance abuse. See David Margolick, "Cuomo Selects First Woman for High Court," *NYT*, Aug. 12, 1983; on her "problem-solving courts," see Judith S. Kaye, "Making the Case for Hands-On Courts," *Newsweek*, Oct. 11, 1990, 13.

18. Quinn, "Revisiting Anna Moscowitz Kross's Critique," 695–96. Quinn argues that, in many ways, the "Midtown Community Court," established in the early 1990s to control sex work in midtown Manhattan, repeated the same "sordid history" of the old women's court: it reduced the visibility of prostitution but did nothing to end it. On the customer legislation of the modern era, see in the *NYT*: Emanuel Perlmutter, "State Is Urged to Prosecute Both Prostitute and Customer" (Nov.

24, 1964), a discussion of a proposed "customer law," and " 'Prostitute' Arrests 2 as Would-be Patrons" (Nov. 30, 1972).

19. In the *NYT* for 1939: "Miss Kenyon Gets Aid" (Sept. 16), "Justice Kenyon on Three Tickets" (Sept. 19). See Philippa Strum, "Dorothy Kenyon, Senator Joseph McCarthy's First Case," accessed June 27, 2015, http://www.historyweekly.com/dorothy-kenyon-senator-joseph-mccarthys-first-case/; Linda Kerber, *No Constitutional Right to Be Ladies* (New York: Hill and Wang, 1999), 199.

20. Gallagher, *Black Women & Politics*, 63–65, 68–71.

21. "Women in Politics," *H-T*, Feb. 6, 1947; Gallagher, *Black Women & Politics*, 74–83.

22. Gallagher, *Black Women & Politics*, 106–13; Jennifer Scanlon, *Until There Is Justice: The Life of Anna Arnold Hedgeman* (New York: Oxford University Press, 2016), 76ff., 81ff., and chap. 9.

23. In 1951, when attorney Ruth Whitehead Whaley became secretary of the board of estimate, she too mentored Murray by giving her her caseload: Caroline Ware to Pauli Murray, Nov. 10, 1949, in *Pauli Murray & Caroline Ware: Forty Years of Letters in Black & White*, ed. Anne Firor Scott (Chapel Hill: University of North Carolina Press, 2006), 49; Rosalind Rosenberg, *Jane Crow: The Life of Pauli Murray* (New York: Oxford University Press, 2017), 182–83, 187–89. Also, news articles from 1949: "Pauli Murray Lauded for Social Vision," *Amsterdam News*, Oct. 29; Betty Granger, "Women at Home," *Age*, Nov. 5; "Local Democrats Run Wild," *Amsterdam News*, Nov. 12; "New York," *Chicago Defender*, Nov. 19.

24. "Mayor's Appointments," *Amsterdam News*, June 2, 1951; "43 Negroes and Puerto Ricans Eye State Offices," *Amsterdam News*, Nov. 1, 1952; Gallagher, *Black Women & Politics*, 103–5; and Biondi, *To Stand and Fight*, 221.

25. On Motley, see her *Equal Justice under Law*, and *Reminiscences* (CCOH). On Chisholm, see her *Unbought and Unbossed* (Boston: Houghton Mifflin, 1970) and Barbara Winslow, *Shirley Chisholm, Catalyst for Change, 1926–2005* (Boulder, CO: Westview Press, 2014).

26. On Jones's support for Motley, see John C. Walter, *The Harlem Fox: J. Raymond Jones and Tammany, 1920–1970* (Albany: State University of New York Press, 1989), 166–70.

27. In the *NYT*: "Democrats Designate 1st Woman to Run for Congress in Brooklyn" (July 16, 1949); "Brooklyn Woman Sent to Congress" (Nov. 9, 1949); Wolfgang Saxon, "Edna Kelly, Congresswoman from Brooklyn, Is Dead at 91" (Dec. 17, 1997).

28. See Alan H. Levy, *The Political Life of Bella Abzug 1920–1976* (Lanham, MD: Lexington Books, 2013); Elizabeth Holtzman with Cynthia L. Cooper, *Who Said It Would Be Easy? One Woman's Life in the Political Arena* (New York: Arcade Publishers, 1996), ix.

29. "Ruth Messinger," *Jewish Women's Archive*, accessed November 8, 2018, https://jwa.org/encyclopedia/article/messinger-ruth; "Miriam Bockman, Groundbreaking

Manhattan Democrat, Dies at 86," *NYT*, June 29, 2018); the documentary *Geraldine Ferraro: Paving the Way*, directed by Donna Zaccaro (Dazzling Media, 2014).

30. Susan Brinson, *Personal and Public Interests: Frieda B. Hennock and the Federal Communications Commission* (Westport, CT: Praeger, 2002); "Hennock, Frieda," in *Notable American Women/The Modern Period*, ed. Barbara Sicherman and Carol Hurd Green (Cambridge, MA: Harvard University Press, 1980); and "Frieda Hennock Simons Dead; Lawyer, 55, Had Been on F.C.C.," *NYT*, June 21, 1960.

31. Mary Gardiner Jones, *Tearing Down Walls: A Woman's Triumph* (Lanham, MD: Hamilton Books, 2008), 205–6, 211; and her oral history, http://www.ftc. gov/about-ftc/our-history/oral-histories/oral-histories/oral-history-interview-mary-gardiner-jones (accessed Apr. 23, 2014). Also, Patricia Sullivan, "Mary Gardiner Jones, 89; First Female Commissioner of Federal Trade Commission," *Washington Post*, Jan. 7, 2010.

32. See Esther Peterson and Winifred Conkling, *Restless: The Memoirs of Labor and Consumer Activist Esther Peterson* (Washington, DC: Caring Pub., 1995); Cynthia Ellen Harrison, *On Account of Sex: The Politics of Women's Issues, 1945–1968* (Berkeley: University of California Press, 1988), passim; Brigid O'Farrell and Joyce L. Kornbluh, *Rocking the Boat: Union Women's Voices, 1915–1975* (New Brunswick, NJ: Rutgers University Press, 1996); Lawrence B. Glickman, *Buying Power: A History of Consumer Activism in America* (Chicago: University of Chicago Press, 2009), chap. 9. Glickman identifies Peterson, after Ralph Nader, as "the leading consumer advocate of the postwar era" (27).

33. Eve Garrette, *A Political Handbook for Women* (New York: Doubleday, Doran and Company, 1944), 180–88.

34. See Mattie Quinn, "The City Councils Where Women Are Least Represented," Aug. 24, 2017, accessed Sept. 3, 2017, http://www.governing.com/topics/poli-tics/gov-nyc-city-council-women.html. The council now has a total of fifty-one members.

## APPENDIX

1. The script lists only the last names of the performers and the carbon copy did not make all names legible; where I could find first names, I included them. Mentioned are Mildred (Mitzi) [Somach], his confidential secretary who worked for only a dollar a year and walked out on him after a "bitter quarrel" ("La Guardia Aide Quits After a Row," *NYT*, Apr. 30, 1940; photo); Lewis Valentine, police commissioner; Robert Moses, parks commissioner; Joseph Goodman, water, gas, and electricity commissioner; Russell Forbes, Purchase Department; S. S. Goldwater, hospitals commissioner; John L. Rice, health commissioner; Henry Curran, deputy mayor; Sophia A. Olmsted, legal staff, commissioner of accounts office; Magda

(Fontanges), a young French reporter who had an affair with Benito Mussolini in 1936; B. Charney Vladeck, general manager, *Jewish Daily Forward*, elected to the council in 1937, as was Joseph Clark Baldwin, a Republican from Manhattan; Newbold Morris, Republican, former alderman, elected president of the New York City Council, served 1937–45; Peter Chieffo (long-time custodian of city hall); Joseph E. Kinsley, Bronx Democrat, elected to the city council 1937; Genevieve B. Earle, Republican councilman from Brooklyn; Robert K. Straus[s], city fusionist councilman.

Some terms: Wasserman[n]s (New York State's compulsory premarital blood tests for syphilis, no longer used); Croton Dam (supplies water to New York City); "tzoros" (Yiddish for "troubles"); Bennett Field (small airport in Brooklyn); Leacock stories (Canadian humorist Stephen Leacock); Traffic Part ("Part"—refers to a "part" of a court dedicated to a special issue or problem); Moses's boys (the men working for parks moved into juvenile aid, so that police could focus on crime); Delehanty Institute (secretarial school); pushcarts (La Guardia built enclosures for peddlers' pushcarts to end traffic and sanitation issues); T.B. – V.D. – D.T. (tuberculosis, venereal disease, delirium tremens); parisi-tology (study of parasitic organisms); Altman's mental cases (refers to a charge by controversial alienist Dr. Emil Altman, chief medical examiner of New York City schools, that a significant number of city teachers were "mental cases"); Lyons Residence Bill (proposed by James J. Lyons, Bronx borough president, requiring six months' residency and citizenship to qualify for relief; both the LWV and WCC opposed and La Guardia vetoed it); P. R. (proportional representation); St. Franklin (Franklin Roosevelt); Ma Simkhovitch (Mary K. Simkhovitch, settlement leader and La Guardia appointee to the housing authority); Post (Langdon W. Post, tenement house commissioner); St. Fio (Fiorello La Guardia).

# SELECT BIBLIOGRAPHY

PRIMARY SOURCES

*Manuscript Collections*

Bearden, Bessye J. Schomburg Center for Research in Black Culture, New York Public Library.

Burlingham, Charles Culp. Harvard University Law School.

Catt, Carrie Chapman. Library of Congress Microfilm Edition.

Dewson, Mary. Franklin D. Roosevelt (FDR) Library.

Dreier, Ethel Eyre. Sophia Smith Archives, Smith College.

Dreier, Mary Elisabeth. Arthur & Elizabeth Schlesinger Library on the History of Women, Radcliffe College.

Earle, Genevieve Beavers. Municipal Archives of the City of New York.

Earle, Genevieve Beavers. Rare Books and Manuscripts, Butler Library, Columbia University.

Governor of the State of New York, 1929–1932, Microfilmed Records, FDR Library.

Hay, Mary Garrett. Rare Books & Manuscripts Division of the New York Public Library.

Herrick, Elinore Morehouse. Arthur & Elizabeth Schlesinger Library on the History of Women, Radcliffe College.

Kenyon, Dorothy. Sophia Smith Archives, Smith College.

Kross, Anna M. Jacob Rader Marcus Center of the American Jewish Archives, Cincinnati Campus, Hebrew Union College Jewish Institute of Religion.

Kross, Anna M. Sophia Smith Archives, Smith College.

La Guardia, Fiorello. La Guardia-Wagner Archives, La Guardia Community College.

La Guardia, Fiorello. Municipal Archives of the City of New York.

Lane, Layle. Schomburg Center for Research in Black Culture, New York Public Library.

New York City League of Women Voters. Rare Books and Manuscripts, Butler Library, Columbia University.

New York State League of Women Voters. Rare Books and Manuscripts, Butler Library, Columbia University.

Polier, Justine Wise. Arthur & Elizabeth Schlesinger Library on the History of Women, Radcliffe College.

Proportional Representation League, 1900–1965. Rare Books and Manuscripts, Butler Library, Columbia University.

Roosevelt, Anna Eleanor. FDR Library.

Roosevelt Family Papers Donated by the Children of Franklin D. and Eleanor Roosevelt. FDR Library.

Rosenberg, Anna (Hoffman). Arthur & Elizabeth Schlesinger Library on the History of Women, Radcliffe College.

Simkhovitch, Mary Kingsbury. Arthur & Elizabeth Schlesinger Library on the History of Women, Radcliffe College.

Simon, Caroline Klein. Arthur & Elizabeth Schlesinger Library on the History of Women, Radcliffe College.

Vanderlip, Narcissa Cox (in the Frank A. Vanderlip Papers, Series I). Rare Books and Manuscripts, Butler Library, Columbia University.

Wadsworth, James W., Jr. Manuscripts Division, Library of Congress.

Walker, Mayor James J. New York City Municipal Archives.

Women's City Club of New York. Microfilm ed., University Publications of America, 1989–90.

Women's City Club of New York, 1915–2011. Archives & Special Collections, Hunter College Libraries, Hunter College (CUNY), New York.

*Oral Histories*

Columbia Center for Oral History Archives: William Harvey Allen, Genevieve Beavers Earle, Constance Baker Motley, John Lord O'Brian, Frances Perkins, Charles Poletti, Ruth Baker Pratt, Anna Rosenberg, Nathan Straus Jr., James W. Wadsworth Jr.

Max, Pearl Bernstein. 1984. American Jewish Committee Oral History Collection, New York Public Library.

Max, Pearl Bernstein. 1988. Women's City Club Oral History Project, in author's possession.

Polier, Justine Wise. 1977. Franklin Delano Roosevelt Library.

Reyher, Rebecca Hourwich. 1977. "Search and Struggle for Equality and Independence." Accessed June 23, 2016. http://digitalassets.lib.berkeley.edu/rohoia/ucb/text/struggle4equalit00reyhrich.pdf.

Simon, Caroline Klein. 1988. Women's City Club Oral History Project, in author's possession.

*Published Primary Sources*

Addams, Jane. *Twenty Years at Hull House*. New York: MacMillan, 1910.

Adler, Polly. *A House Is Not a Home*. New York: Rhinehart, 1953.

Baker, Elizabeth Faulkner. *Protective Labor Legislation, with Special Reference to Women in the State of New York*. New York: Columbia University, 1925.

Baker, S. Josephine. *Fighting for Life*. New York: MacMillan, 1939.

Barnes, Djuna. "Woman Police Deputy Is Writer of Poetry." *Sun Magazine*, Mar. 24, 1918.

Beard, Mary Ritter. *Woman's Work in Municipalities*. New York: D. Appleton, 1915.

Beyer, Clara M. *History of Labor Legislation for Women in Three States*. US Women's Bureau, Bulletin No. 66. 1929.

Blatch, Harriot Stanton, and Alma Lutz. *Challenging Years: The Memoirs of Harriot Stanton Blatch*. New York: G. P. Putnam's Sons, 1940.

Bres, Rose Falls. *Maids, Wives and Widows: The Law of the Land and of the Various States as It Affects Women*. New York: E. P. Dutton, 1918.

Brill, Jeanette G., and E. George Payne. *The Adolescent Court and Crime Prevention*. New York: Pitman Publishing, 1938.

Catt, Carrie Chapman, and Nettie Rogers Shuler. *Woman and Politics—The Inner Story of the Suffrage*. New York: Scribner & Sons, 1926.

Childs, Richard S. *Civic Victories: The Story of an Unfinished Revolution*. New York: Harper & Brothers, 1952.

Chisholm, Shirley. *Unbought and Unbossed*. Boston: Houghton Mifflin, 1970.

Curran, Henry. *From Pillar to Post*. New York: Charles Scribner's Sons, 1941.

Dewey, John. "The Government of New York City." In *The Later Works, 1925–1953*. Vol. 9, *1933–1934*, edited by Jo Ann Boydston and Abraham Kaplan, 363–64. Carbondale: Southern Illinois University Press, 1981.

Garrette, Eve. *A Political Handbook for Women*. New York: Doubleday, Doran, 1944.

George, Anna P. "Women as Voters in New York State." *Union Signal* 45–46 (Mar. 28, 1918): 7.

Glueck, Sheldon and Eleanor. *Preventing Crime*. New York: McGraw-Hill, 1936.

Goldman, Emma. *Living My Life*. New York: A. A. Knopf, 1931.

Graham, Frances W., and Georgeanna M. Remington Gardenier. *Two Decades: A History of the First Twenty Years' Work of the Woman's Christian Temperance Union of the State of New York*. 1894. Accessed December 4, 2016. https://www.gutenberg.org/ebooks/20811.

Hapgood, Norman, and Henry Moskowitz. *Up from the City Streets: Alfred E. Smith*. New York: Harcourt, Brace, 1927.

Haskell, Oreola Williams. *Banner Bearers: Tales of the Suffrage Campaigns*. Geneva, New York: W. F. Humphrey, 1920.

Hays, Will. *The Memoirs of Will H. Hays*. New York: Doubleday, 1955.

*History of Woman Suffrage*. Vol. 6, edited by Ida Husted Harper. New York: National American Woman Suffrage Association, 1922.

Jones, Mary Gardiner. *Tearing Down Walls: A Woman's Triumph*. Lanham, MD: Hamilton Books, 2008.

Kellor, Frances. "Women in British and American Politics." *Current History* 17 (Feb. 1923): 831–35.

La Guardia, Fiorello. *The Making of An Insurgent*. New York: J. B. Lippincott, 1948.

[Laidlaw, Harriet Burton]. *Organizing to Win by the Political District Plan: A Handbook for Working Suffragists*. New York: National American Woman Suffrage Association, 1914.

Lynch, Denis Tilden. *Criminals and Politicians*. New York: MacMillan, 1932.

MacKaye, Milton. *The Tin Box Parade: A Handbook for Larceny*. New York: Laugh Club, 1934.

MacPhail, Elizabeth C. "Survey of Women Lawyers in Public Office." *Women Lawyers Journal* 40, no. 4 (Fall 1954): 26–30, and 41, no. 1 (Winter 1955): 22–24.

*Mayor La Guardia's Commission on the Harlem Riot of March 19, 1935, Complete Report*. Edited by Richard E. Rubenstein and Robert M. Fogelson. New York: Arno Press, 1969 (reprint).

McCaffrey, George H. "Proportional Representation in New York City." *American Political Science Review* 33 (Oct., 1939): 841–52.

Menken, Alice D. "The Passing of the Women's Night Court in New York City." *The Survey*, Oct. 12, 1918, 41–42.

Miner, Maude E. *Slavery of Prostitution: A Plea for Emancipation*. New York: MacMillan, 1916.

Moley, Raymond. *Tribunes of the People: The Past and Future of the New York Magistrates' Courts*. New Haven, CT: Yale University Press, 1932.

Moscowitz, Anna. "The Night Court for Women in New York City." *Women Lawyers' Journal* 5, no. 2 (Nov. 1915): 9.

Moscowitz, Anna. "The Women's Night Court." *Medico-Legal Journal* 33, no. 9 (Dec. 1916): 2–7.

Motley, Constance Baker. *Equal Justice under Law: An Autobiography*. New York: Farrar, Straus and Giroux, 1998.

Murtagh, John M., and Sara Harris. *Cast the First Stone*. New York: McGraw-Hill, 1957.

Nathan, Maud. *The Story of an Epoch-Making Movement*. New York: Doubleday, 1926.

New York, State of. *Report by Laurence M. D. McGuire of the Factory Investigating Commission, Transmitted to the Legislature Mar. 4, 1915*. Albany: J. B. Lyon, 1915.

Northrop, William B., and John B. Northrop. *The Insolence of Office: The Story of the Seabury Investigation*. New York: G. P. Putnam's Sons, 1932.

Peters, John P. "The Story of the Committee of Fourteen of New York." *Journal of Social Hygiene* 4, no. 3 (July 1918): 347–88.

Peterson, Esther, and Winifred Conkling. *Restless: The Memoirs of Labor and Consumer Activist Esther Peterson*. Washington, DC: Caring Pub., 1995.

*Plunkitt of Tammany Hall: A Series of Very Plain Talks on Very Practical Politics, Recorded by William L. Riordan*. Edited by Terrence J. McDonald. Boston: Bedford Books of St. Martin's Press, 1994.

Popkin, Zelda. *Open Every Door*. New York: E. P. Dutton, 1956.

Pringle, Henry F. *Alfred E. Smith: A Critical Study*. New York: Macy-Masius, 1927.

Rankin, Rebecca, ed. *New York Advancing; A Scientific Approach to Municipal Government. An Accounting to the Citizens by the Departments and Boroughs of the City of New York, 1934–1935*. F. H. La Guardia, mayor. New York: Municipal Reference Library, 1936.

Rembaugh, Bertha. "Problems of the New York Night Court for Women." *Women's Law Journal* 2, no. 2 (Aug. 1912): 45.

Riis, Jacob. *How the Other Half Lives: Studies among the Tenements of New York*. New York: Charles Scribner's Sons, 1890.

Roosevelt, Eleanor. *Autobiography*. New York: Harper, 1961.

Roosevelt, Eleanor. *It's Up to the Women*. New York: Frederick A. Stokes, 1933.

Schlosser, Alexander L. *Lawyers Must Eat*. New York: Vanguard Press, 1933.

Schneiderman, Rose, with Lucy Goldthwaite. *All for One*. New York: Paul S. Eriksson, 1967.

Seabury, Samuel. *Final Report of Samuel Seabury, Referee, The Investigation of the Magistrates' Courts in the First Judicial Department and the Magistrates Thereof, and of Attorneys-at-Law Practicing in Said Courts. Supreme Court, Appellate Division, First Judicial Department*, Mar. 28, 1932. New York: Arno Press, 1974 (reprint).

Simkhovitch, Mary Kingsbury. *Here Is God's Plenty: Reflections on American Social Advance*. New York: Harper & Bros., 1949.

Simkhovitch, Mary Kingsbury. *Neighborhood: My Story of Greenwich House*. New York: Norton, 1938.

Simkhovitch, Mary Kingsbury. "The Settlement's Relation to Religion." *Annals of the American Academy of Political and Social Science* 30, no. 3 (Nov. 1907): 62–67.

Smith, Alfred E. *Up to Now: An Autobiography*. New York: Viking Press, 1929.

Stevens, Doris. *Jailed for Freedom*. New York: Liveright, 1920.

Straus, Robert K. *In My Anecdotage*. Santa Barbara: R. K. Straus, 1989.

Thomas, Norman, and Paul Blanshard. *What's The Matter with New York: A National Problem*. New York: MacMillan, 1932.

Valentine, Lewis. *Night Stick: The Autobiography of Lewis J. Valentine*. New York: Dial Press, 1947.

Wald, Lillian D. *The House on Henry Street*. New York: H. Holt, 1915.

Wald, Lillian D. *Windows on Henry Street*. Boston: Little, Brown, 1934.

Waterman, Willoughby C. *Prostitution and Its Repression in New York City, 1900–1931*. New York: Columbia University Press, 1932.

Whalen, Grover. *Mr. New York*. New York: Putnam, 1955.

Whitin, Frederick H. "The Women's Night Court in New York City." *Annals of the American Academy of Political and Social Science* 52 (Mar. 1914): 181–87.

Worthington, George E., and Ruth Topping. *Specialized Courts Dealing with Sex Delinquency: A Study of the Procedure in Chicago, Boston, Philadelphia, and New York*. New York: F. H. Hitchcock, 1925.


*Unpublished Primary Sources*

Voorsanger, Henriette M. "Everybody's Judge: Anna Moscowitz Kross" (typescript).


*Newspapers and Journals*

*Baltimore Afro-American*
*Brooklyn Daily Eagle*
*Brooklyn Standard Union*
*Chicago Defender*
*Chicago Tribune*
*Everybody's Magazine*
*Literary Digest*
*New York Age*
*New York Amsterdam News*
*New York Daily News*
*New York Evening Mail*
*New York Evening Post*
*New York Evening Telegram*
*New York Evening World*
*New York Globe*
*New York Herald*
*New York Herald-Tribune*
*New York Mirror*
*New York Sun*
*New York Times*
*New York Tribune*
*New York World-Telegram*
*New Yorker Magazine*
*Philadelphia Tribune*
*Rochester Democrat and Chronicle*
*The Survey*
*Time Magazine*
*The Woman Citizen*
*The Women Lawyers' Journal*

SECONDARY SOURCES

Abu-Lughod, Janet L. *Race, Space, and Riots in Chicago, New York, and Los Angeles.* New York: Oxford University Press, 2007.

Aldrich-Moodie, Mary Jane. "Staking Out Their Domain: Women in the New York City Police Department, 1890–1935." PhD diss., University of North Carolina/Chapel Hill, 2002.

Andersen, Kristi. *After Suffrage: Women in Partisan and Electoral Politics before the New Deal.* Chicago: University of Chicago Press, 1996.

Antler, Joyce. *The Journey Home: How Jewish Women Shaped Modern America.* New York: Schocken, 1997.

Argersinger, Jo Ann E., ed. *The Triangle Fire: A Brief History with Documents.* Boston: Bedford/St. Martin's, 2009.

Babcock, Barbara. *Woman Lawyer: The Trials of Clara Foltz.* Stanford, CA: Stanford University Press, 2011.

Baker, Paula. *The Moral Frameworks of Public Life: Gender, Politics, and the State in Rural New York, 1870–1930.* New York: Oxford University Press, 1991.

Barber, Kathleen L. *A Right to Representation: Proportional Election Systems for the Twenty-First Century.* Columbus: Ohio State University Press, 2000.

Barber, Kathleen L. *Proportional Representation and Election Reform in Ohio.* Columbus: Ohio State University Press, 1995.

Barry, Kathleen. *Susan B. Anthony: A Biography of a Singular Feminist.* New York: New York University Press, 1988.

Basch, Norma. *In the Eyes of the Law: Women, Marriage, and Property in Nineteenth-Century New York.* Ithaca, NY: Cornell University Press, 1982.

Berry, Mary. *Why ERA Failed: Politics, Women's Rights, and the Amending Process of the Constitution.* Bloomington: Indiana University Press, 1988.

Biondi, Martha. *To Stand and Fight: The Struggle for Civil Rights in Postwar New York City.* Cambridge, MA: Harvard University Press, 2003.

Bordin, Ruth. *Woman and Temperance: The Quest for Power and Liberty, 1873–1900.* Philadelphia: Temple University Press, 1981.

Boris, Eileen. *Home to Work: Motherhood and the Politics of Industrial Homework in the United States.* New York: Cambridge University Press, 1994.

Brandt, Allan. *No Magic Bullet: A Social History of Venereal Disease in the United States since 1880.* New York: Oxford University Press, 1985.

Bredbenner, Candice L. *A Nationality of Her Own: Women, Marriage, and the Law of Citizenship.* Berkeley: University of California Press, 1998.

Brinson, Susan. *Personal and Public Interests: Frieda B. Hennock and the Federal Communications Commission.* Westport, CT: Praeger, 2002.

Brodsky, Alyn. *The Great Mayor: Fiorello La Guardia and the Making of the City of New York.* New York: St. Martin's Press, 2003.

Brown, Nikki. *Private Politics and Public Voices: Black Women's Activism from World War I to the New Deal*. Bloomington: Indiana University Press, 2006.

Burner, David. *The Politics of Provincialism: The Democratic Party in Transition, 1918–1932*. New York: Knopf, 1968.

Campbell, Nancy. *Using Women: Gender, Drug Policy, and Social Justice*. New York: Routledge, 2000.

Caro, Robert. *The Power Broker: Robert Moses and the Fall of New York*. New York: Knopf, 1974.

Carson, Mina. *Settlement Folk: Social Thought and the American Settlement Movement*. Chicago: University of Chicago Press, 1990.

Chapman, Mary. *Making Noise, Making News: Suffrage Print Culture and U.S. Modernism*. New York: Oxford University Press, 2014.

Chesler, Ellen. *Woman of Valor: Margaret Sanger and the Birth Control Movement in America*. New York: Simon & Schuster, 1992.

Clapp, Elizabeth J. *Mothers of All Children: Women Reformers and the Rise of Juvenile Courts in Progressive Era America*. University Park: Pennsylvania State University Press, 1998.

Connelly, Mark Thomas. *The Response to Prostitution in the Progressive Era*. Chapel Hill: University of North Carolina Press, 1980.

Cook, Blanche Wiesen, ed. *Crystal Eastman on Women and Revolution*. New York: Oxford University Press, 1976.

Cook, Blanche Wiesen. *Eleanor Roosevelt*. Vols. 1–2. New York: Viking, 1992, 1999.

Cott, Nancy F., ed. *A Woman Making History: Mary Ritter Beard through Her Letters*. New Haven, CT: Yale University Press, 1991.

Cott, Nancy F. *The Grounding of Modern Feminism*. New Haven, CT: Yale University Press, 1987.

Czitrom, Daniel. *New York Exposed: The Gilded Age Police Scandal That Launched the Progressive Era*. New York: Oxford University Press, 2016.

Dahlberg, Jane S. *The New York Bureau of Municipal Research: Pioneer in Government Administration*. New York: New York University Press, 1966.

Daniels, Doris Groshen. *Always a Sister: The Feminism of Lillian D. Wald*. New York: Feminist Press at the City University of New York, 1989.

Daniels, Doris Groshen. "Building a Winning Coalition: The Suffrage Fight in New York State," *New York History* 60, no. 1 (1979): 59–80.

Davis, Allen F. *Spearheads for Reform: The Social Settlements and the Progressive Movement*. New York: Oxford University Press, 1967.

Davis, Kenneth S. *Invincible Summer: An Intimate Portrait of the Roosevelts Based on the Recollections of Marion Dickerman*. New York: Atheneum, 1974.

Downey, Kirstin. *The Woman behind the New Deal: The Life of Frances Perkins, FDR's Secretary of Labor and his Moral Conscience*. New York: Nan A. Talese/Doubleday, 2009.

Dreier, Mary E. *Margaret Dreier Robins: Her Life, Letters, and Work*. New York: Island Press Cooperative, 1950.

DuBois, Ellen Carol. *Harriot Stanton Blatch and the Winning of Woman Suffrage*. New Haven, CT: Yale University Press, 1997.

Dye, Nancy Schrom. *As Equals and as Sisters: Feminism, the Labor Movement, and the Women's Trade Union League of New York*. Columbia: University of Missouri Press, 1980.

Eldot, Paula. *Governor Alfred E. Smith: The Politician as Reformer*. New York: Garland, 1983.

Finan, Christopher M. *Alfred E. Smith, The Happy Warrior*. New York: Hill and Wang, 2002.

Fitzpatrick, Ellen. *Endless Crusade: Women Social Scientists and Progressive Reform*. New York: Oxford University Press, 1990.

Flexner, Eleanor. *Century of Struggle: The Woman's Rights Movement in the United States*. Cambridge, MA: Harvard University Press, 1959.

Freedman, Estelle B. *Maternal Justice: Miriam Van Waters and the Female Reform Tradition*. Chicago: University of Chicago Press, 1996.

Freeman, Jo. "'One Man, One Vote; One Woman, One Throat': Women in New York City Politics, 1890–1910." *American Nineteenth-Century History* 1, no. 3 (Autumn 2000): 101–23.

Freeman, Jo. *One Room at a Time: How Women Entered Party Politics*. Lanham, MD: Rowman & Littlefield, 2000.

Friedman, Andrea. *Prurient Interests: Gender, Democracy, and Obscenity in New York City, 1909–1945*. New York: Columbia University Press, 2000.

Gallagher, Julie. *Black Women & Politics in New York City*. Urbana: University of Illinois, 2012.

Garrett, Charles. *The La Guardia Years, Machine and Reform Politics in New York City*. New Brunswick, NJ: Rutgers University Press, 1961.

Gerson, Simon [S.] W. *Pete: The Story of Peter V. Cacchione, New York's First Communist Councilman*. New York: International Publishers, 1976.

Giddings, Paula. *Ida: A Sword among Lions, Ida B. Wells and the Campaign against Lynching*. New York: Amistad, 2008.

Gilfoyle, Timothy. *City of Eros: New York City, Prostitution, and the Commercialization of Sex, 1790–1920*. New York: W. W. Norton, 1992.

Ginzberg, Lori. *Elizabeth Cady Stanton: An American Life*. New York: Hill and Wang, 2009.

Ginzberg, Lori. *Untidy Origins: A Story of Woman's Rights in Antebellum New York*. Chapel Hill: University of North Carolina Press, 2005.

Glendon, Mary Ann. *A World Made New: Eleanor Roosevelt and the Universal Declaration of Human Rights*. New York: Random House, 2001.

Glickman, Lawrence B. *Buying Power: A History of Consumer Activism in America.* Chicago: University of Chicago Press, 2009.

Golway, Terry. *Machine Made: Tammany Hall and the Creation of Modern American Politics.* New York: W. W. Norton, 2014.

Goodier, Susan. *No Votes for Women: The New York State Anti-Suffrage Movement.* Urbana: University of Illinois, 2013.

Goodier, Susan, and Karen Pastorello. *Women Will Vote: Winning Suffrage in New York State.* Ithaca, NY: Cornell University Press, 2017.

Gordon, Felice D. *After Winning: The Legacy of New Jersey Suffragists, 1920–1947.* New Brunswick, NJ: Rutgers University Press, 1986.

Gordon, Linda. *Woman's Body, Woman's Right: A Social History of Birth Control in America.* New York: Penguin, 1976.

Greenberg, Cheryl Lynn. *"Or Does It Explode?" Black Harlem in the Great Depression.* New York: Oxford University Press, 1997.

Griffith, Elisabeth. *In Her Own Right: The Life of Elizabeth Cady Stanton.* New York: Oxford University Press, 1984.

Gustafson, Melanie S. *Women and the Republican Party, 1854–1924.* Urbana: University of Illinois Press, 2001.

Gustafson, Melanie S., Kristie Miller, and Elisabeth I. Perry, eds. *We Have Come to Stay: American Women and Political Parties, 1880–1960.* Albuquerque: University of New Mexico Press, 1999.

Hareven, Tamara K. *Eleanor Roosevelt: An American Conscience.* Chicago: Quadrangle Books, 1968.

Harrison, Cynthia. *On Account of Sex: The Politics of Women's Issues, 1945–1968.* Berkeley: University of California Press, 1988.

Hart, Vivien. "Feminism and Bureaucracy: The Minimum Wage Experiment in the District of Columbia." *Journal of American Studies* 26, no. 1 (1992): 1–22.

Harvey, Anna. *Votes without Leverage: Women in American Electoral Politics, 1920–1970.* Cambridge: Cambridge University Press, 1998.

Hicks, Cheryl D. *Talk with You Like a Woman: African American Women, Justice, and Reform in New York, 1890–1935.* Chapel Hill: University of North Carolina Press, 2010.

Higginbotham, Evelyn Brooks. "In Politics to Stay: Black Women Leaders and Party Politics in the 1920s." In *Women, Politics, and Change,* edited by Louise A. Tilly and Patricia Gurin, 199–220. New York: Russell Sage Foundation, 1990.

Hobson, Barbara Meil. *Uneasy Virtue: The Politics of Prostitution and the American Reform Tradition.* New York: Basic Books, 1987.

Hoffert, Sylvia. *Alva Vanderbilt Belmont: Unlikely Champion of Women's Rights.* Bloomington: Indiana University Press, 2012.

Ingalls, Robert P. "New York and the Minimum-Wage Movement, 1933–1937." *Labor History* 15, no. 2 (Spring 1974): 179–99.

Jack, Zachary Michael. *March of the Suffragettes: Rosalie Gardiner Jones and the March for Voting Rights*. San Francisco: Zest Books, 2016.

Josephson, Matthew and Hannah. *Al Smith: Hero of the Cities, A Political Portrait Drawing on the Papers of Frances Perkins*. Boston: Houghton Mifflin, 1969.

Kahn, Alfred J. *Police and Children: A Study of the Juvenile Aid Bureau of the New York City Police Department*. New York: Citizens' Committee on Children, 1951.

Kerber, Linda K. *No Constitutional Right to be Ladies: Women and the Obligations of Citizenship*. New York: Hill and Wang, 1998.

Kerber, Linda K. *Toward an Intellectual History of Women: Essays*. Chapel Hill: University of North Carolina Press, 1997.

Kerber, Linda K. *Women of the Republic: Intellect and Ideology in Revolutionary America*. Chapel Hill: University of North Carolina Press, 1980.

Kerr, Thomas J., IV. "New York Factory Investigating Commission and the Progressives." PhD diss., Syracuse University, 1965.

Kessler-Harris, Alice. *Gendering Labor History*. Urbana: University of Illinois Press, 2006.

Kessler-Harris, Alice. "Where Are the Organized Women Workers?" *Feminist Studies* 3, no. 1/2 (1975): 92–110.

Kessner, Thomas. *Fiorello La Guardia and the Making of Modern New York*. New York: Viking, 1991.

Keyssar, Alexander. *The Right to Vote: The Contested History of Democracy in the United States*. New York: Basic Books, 2009.

Kozakiewicz, Lauren. "Political Episodes, 1890–1960: Three Republican Women in Twentieth Century New York State Politics," PhD diss., State University of New York at Albany, 2006.

Kroeger, Brooke. *Fannie: The Talent for Success of Writer Fannie Hurst*. New York: Times Books, 1999.

Kyvig, David. *Repealing National Prohibition*. 2nd ed. Kent, OH: Kent State University Press, 2000.

Lash, Joseph P. *Eleanor and Franklin: The Story of Their Relationship*. New York: Norton, 1971.

Leavitt, Judith. *Typhoid Mary: Captive to the Public's Health*. Boston: Beacon Press, 1996.

Lemons, J. Stanley. *The Woman Citizen: Social Feminism in the 1920s*. Charlottesville: University Press of Virginia, 1990.

Lerner, Michael A. *Dry Manhattan: Prohibition in New York City*. Cambridge, MA: Harvard University Press, 2009.

Levy, Alan H. *The Political Life of Bella Abzug 1920–1976*. Lanham, MD: Lexington Books, 2013.

Lindenmeyer, Kriste. *A Right to Childhood: The U.S. Children's Bureau and Child Welfare, 1912–1946*. Urbana: University of Illinois Press, 1997.

Logan, Andy. *Against the Evidence: The Becker-Rosenthal Affair.* New York: McCall Publishing, 1970.

Mackey, Thomas C. *Pursuing Johns: Criminal Law Reform, Defending Character, and New York City's Committee of Fourteen, 1920–1930.* Columbus: Ohio State University Press, 2005.

Martin, George. *CCB: The Life and Century of Charles C. Burlingham, New York's First Citizen 1858–1959.* New York: Hill & Wang, 2005.

Martin, George. *Madam Secretary, Frances Perkins.* Boston: Houghton Mifflin, 1976.

May, Vanessa H. *Unprotected Labor: Household Workers, Politics, and Middle-Class Reform in New York, 1870–1940.* Chapel Hill: University of North Carolina Press, 2011.

McCammon, Holly J. *The U.S. Women's Jury Movements and Strategic Adaptations.* Cambridge: Cambridge University Press, 2012.

McLeod, Jacqueline A. *Daughter of the Empire State: The Life of Judge Jane Bolin.* Urbana: University of Illinois Press, 2011.

Mitgang, Herbert. *The Man Who Rode the Tiger. The Life of Judge Samuel Seabury and the Story of the Greatest Investigation of City Corruption in This Century.* New York: Norton, 1979.

Mitgang, Herbert. *Once Upon a Time in New York: Jimmy Walker, Franklin Roosevelt, and the Last Great Battle of the Jazz Age.* New York: Free Press, 2000.

Monoson, S. Sara. "The Lady and the Tiger: Women's Electoral Activism in New York City before Suffrage." *Journal of Women's History* 2, no. 2 (Fall 1990): 100–135.

Morello, Karen Berger. *The Invisible Bar: The Woman Lawyer in America: 1638 to the Present.* Boston: Beacon Press, 1986.

Muncy, Robyn. *Creating a Female Dominion in American Reform, 1890–1935.* New York: Oxford University Press, 1991.

Murphy, Kevin C. "Lost Warrior: Al Smith and the Fall of Tammany Hall." Accessed August 21, 2012. http://www.kevincmurphy.com/alsmith.htm.

Musto, David F. *The American Disease: Origins of Narcotic Control.* New York: Oxford University Press, 1987.

Nelson, Anna Kasten. "Anna M. Rosenberg, an 'Honorary Man.'" *Journal of Military History* 68, no. 1 (2004): 133–61.

Neumann, Caryn E. "The End of Gender Solidarity: The History of the Women's Organization for National Prohibition Reform in the United States, 1929–1933." *Journal of Women's History* 9, no. 2 (1997): 31–51.

O'Farrell, Brigid. *"She Was One of Us": Eleanor Roosevelt and the American Worker.* Ithaca, NY: Cornell University Press, 2010.

O'Farrell, Brigid, and Joyce L. Kornbluh. *Rocking the Boat: Union Women's Voices, 1915–1975.* New Brunswick, NJ: Rutgers University Press, 1996.

Orleck, Annelise. *Common Sense & A Little Fire: Women and Working-Class Politics in the United States, 1900–1965.* Chapel Hill: University of North Carolina Press, 1995.

Patterson, James T. "Mary Dewson and the American Minimum Wage Movement." *Labor History* 5, no. 2 (Spring 1964): 134–52.

Payne, Elizabeth Anne. *Reform, Labor, and Feminism: Margaret Dreier Robins and the Women's Trade Union League.* Urbana: University of Illinois Press, 1988.

Peretti, Burton W. *Nightclub City: Politics and Amusement in Manhattan.* Philadelphia: University of Pennsylvania Press, 2007.

Perry, Elisabeth Israels. *Belle Moskowitz: Feminine Politics and the Exercise of Power in the Age of Alfred E. Smith.* New York: Oxford University Press, 1987.

Perry, Elisabeth Israels. "Rhetoric, Strategy, and Politics in the New York Campaign for Women's Jury Service, 1917–1975." *New York History* 82, no. 1 (Winter 2001): 53–78.

Perry, Elisabeth Israels. "Training for Public Life: Eleanor Roosevelt and Women's Political Networks in New York in the 1920s." In *Without Precedent: The Life and Career of Eleanor Roosevelt,* edited by J. Hoff-Wilson and M. Lightman, 28–45. Bloomington: Indiana University Press, 1984.

Perry, Elisabeth Israels. "Women's Political Choices after Suffrage: The Women's City Club of New York, 1915–Present." *New York History* 62, no. 4 (October 1990): 417–34.

Perry, Lewis. *Civil Disobedience, An American Tradition.* New Haven, CT: Yale University Press, 2013.

Petrash, Antonia. *Long Island and the Woman Suffrage Movement.* Charleston, SC: History Press, 2013.

Pivar, David J. *Purity and Hygiene: Women, Prostitution, and the "American Plan," 1900–1930.* Westport, CT: Greenwood Press, 2002.

Potter, Claire Bond. *War on Crime: Bandits, G-Men, and the Politics of Mass Culture.* New Brunswick, NJ: Rutgers University Press, 1998.

Prosterman, Daniel O. *Defining Democracy: Electoral Reform and the Struggle for Power in New York City.* New York: Oxford University Press, 2012.

Quinn, Mae C. "Anna Moscowitz Kross and the Home Term Part: A Second Look at the Nation's First Criminal Domestic Violence Court." *Akron Law Review* 41 (2008): 733–62.

Quinn, Mae C. "Revisiting Anna Moscowitz Kross's Critique of New York City's Women's Court: The Continued Problem of Solving the 'Problem' of Prostitution with Specialized Criminal Courts." *Fordham Urban Law Journal* 33, no. 2 (2005): 665–726.

Ricca, Brad. *Mrs. Sherlock Holmes: The True Story of New York City's Greatest Female Detective and the 1917 Missing Girl Case that Captivated a Nation.* New York: St. Martin's Press, 2017.

Robertson, Nancy Marie. *Christian Sisterhood, Race Relations, and the YWCA, 1906–46.* Urbana: University of Illinois Press, 2007.

Rogow, Faith. *Gone to Another Meeting: The National Council of Jewish Women, 1893–1993.* Tuscaloosa: University of Alabama Press, 1993.

Rosen, Ruth. *The Lost Sisterhood: Prostitution in America, 1900–1918*. Baltimore: Johns Hopkins University Press, 1984.

Rosenberg, Rosalind. *Beyond Separate Spheres: The Intellectual Roots of Modern Feminism*. New Haven, CT: Yale University Press, 1982.

Rosenberg, Rosalind. *Jane Crow: The Life of Pauli Murray*. New York: Oxford University Press, 2017.

Rule, Wilma. "Electoral Systems, Contextual Factors and Women's Opportunity for Election to Parliament in Twenty-Three Democracies." *Western Political Quarterly* 40, no. 3 (1987): 477–98.

Rymph, Catherine E. *Republican Women: Feminism and Conservatism from Suffrage through the Rise of the New Right*. Chapel Hill: University of North Carolina Press, 2006.

Savell, Isabelle Keating. *Ladies' Lib: How Rockland Women Got the Vote*. New City, NY: Historical Society of Rockland County, 1979.

Scanlon, Jennifer. *Until There Is Justice: The Life of Anna Arnold Hedgeman*. New York: Oxford University Press, 2016.

Schaffer, Ronald. "The New York City Woman Suffrage Party, 1909–1919." *New York History* 43, no. 3 (July 1962): 269–87.

Schick, Thomas. *The New York State Constitutional Convention of 1915 and the Modern State Governor*. New York: National Municipal League, 1978.

Schultz, Jamie. "The Physical Is Political: Women's Suffrage, Pilgrim Hikes and the Public Sphere." *International Journal of the History of Sport* 27, no. 7 (May 2010): 1133–53.

Scott, Anne Firor. *Natural Allies: Women's Associations in American History*. Urbana: University of Illinois Press, 1991.

Scott, Anne Firor, ed. *Pauli Murray & Caroline Ware: Forty Years of Letters in Black & White*. Chapel Hill: University of North Carolina Press, 2006.

Seaver, Barry W. *A True Politician: Rebecca Browning Rankin, Municipal Reference Librarian of the City of New York, 1920–1952*. Jefferson, NC: McFarland, 2004.

Shaw, Frederick. *The History of the New York City Legislature*. New York: Columbia University Press, 1954.

Sklar, Kathryn Kish. *Florence Kelley and the Nation's Work: The Rise of Women's Political Culture, 1830–1900*. New Haven, CT: Yale University Press, 1995.

Skolnik, Richard. "Civic Group Progressivism in New York City." *New York History* 51, no. 4 (July 1970): 411–39.

Slayton, Robert A. *Empire Statesman: The Rise and Redemption of Al Smith*. New York: Free Press, 2001.

Stansell, Christine. *American Moderns: Bohemian New York and the Creation of a New Century*. New York: Henry Holt, 2000.

Stein, Leon. *The Triangle Fire*. New York: Carroll & Graf, 1962.

Stivers, Camilla. *Bureau Men, Settlement Women: Constructing Public Administration in the Progressive Era*. Lawrence: University Press of Kansas, 2000.

Stolberg, Mary M. *Fighting Organized Crime: Politics, Justice, and the Legacy of Thomas E. Dewey*. Boston: Northeastern University Press, 1995.

Storrs, Landon R. Y. *Civilizing Capitalism: The National Consumers' League, Women's Activism, and Labor Standards in the New Deal Era*. Chapel Hill: University of North Carolina Press, 2000.

Swain, Martha. *Ellen Woodward: New Deal Advocate for Women*. Jackson: University Press of Mississippi, 1995.

Terborg-Penn, Rosalyn. *African-American Women in the Struggle for the Vote, 1850–1920*. Bloomington: Indiana University Press, 1998.

Tetrault, Lisa. *The Myth of Seneca Falls: Memory and Women's Suffrage Movement, 1848–1898*. Chapel Hill: University of North Carolina Press, 2014.

Van Voris, Jacqueline. *Carrie Chapman Catt: A Public Life*. New York: Feminist Press at the City University of New York, 1987.

Walter, John C. *The Harlem Fox: J. Raymond Jones and Tammany, 1920–1970*. Albany: State University of New York Press, 1989.

Ware, Susan. *Beyond Suffrage: Women in the New Deal*. Cambridge, MA: Harvard University Press, 1981.

Ware, Susan. *Partner and I: Molly Dewson, Feminism, and New Deal Politics*. New Haven, CT: Yale University Press, 1987.

Watrous, Hilda R. "Narcissa Cox Vanderlip: Chairman, New York State League of Women Voters 1919–1923." New York: Foundation for Citizen Education, 1982.

Wellman, Judith. *The Road to Seneca Falls: Elizabeth Cady Stanton and the First Woman's Rights Convention*. Urbana: University of Illinois Press, 2004.

Whalen, Bernard, and Jon Whalen. *The NYPD's First Fifty Years: Politicians, Police Commissioners, and Patrolmen*. Lincoln, NE: Potomac Books, 2014.

Williams, Mason B. *City of Ambition: FDR, La Guardia, and the Making of Modern New York*. New York: W. W. Norton, 2013.

Wilson, Jan Doolittle. *The Women's Joint Congressional Committee and the Politics of Maternalism, 1920–30*. Urbana: University of Illinois Press, 2007.

Winslow, Barbara. *Shirley Chisholm, Catalyst for Change, 1926–2005*. Boulder, CO: Westview Press, 2014.

Woloch, Nancy. *A Class by Herself: Protective Laws for Women Workers, 1890s–1990s*. Princeton, NJ: Princeton University Press, 2015.

Young, Louise M. *In the Public Interest: The League of Women Voters, 1920–1970*. New York: Greenwood Press, 1989.

Zahniser, J. D., and Amelia R. Fry. *Alice Paul: Claiming Power*. New York: Oxford University Press, 2014.

Zinn, Howard. *La Guardia in Congress*. Ithaca, NY: Cornell University Press, 1958.

# INDEX

Kipper, Lucy, 61
Klein, Gertrude Weil, 236, 297n80
Klein, Leontine C., 60–61
Klein, Samuel H., 126–27
Kleinfeld, Philip M., 79–80
Klemesrud, Judy, 203–4
Knapp, Florence, 60–61, 121, 122, 248
Knopping, Helen, 215
Krecker, Marguerite, 296n78
Kresel, Isidor Jacob, 112–13, 118, 119, 121
Kross, Anna Moscowitz
  Adler case (1935) and, 152–53
  African American political supporters
    of, 228
  anti-prostitution efforts of, 147–50,
    151–52, 153–54
  as assistant corporation counsel for
    New York City, 227
  biographical background of, 54
  Church of the Ascension and,
    54–55, 102
  as commissioner of corrections for
    New York City, 248–49
  Dewey vice raids (1936) and, 153–54
  Hurst and, 232–33, 243–44
  Jewish identity of, 230
  Kenyon and, 229–30
  La Guardia and, 51–52, 54, 138, 148,
    149, 150–51, 154–55, 182, 184–85,
    228, 230–31
  Lehman and, 146–47
  mayoral election of 1921 and,
    54, 55–56
  mayoral election of 1932 and, 144
  mayoral election of 1933 and, 182
  McKee and, 144
  Motley and, 253
  as New York City magistrate, 138, 143,
    144–48, 150–51, 153, 202, 227
  O'Brien and, 144–45, 146–47, 151,
    182, 202, 227

  as plasters' union general counsel, 145
  Rosenberg and, 146–47, 209–10, 212
  Sabin and, 227
  Seabury investigations and, 149
  Silver family and, 103–4
  Smith and, 55, 145–47
  state supreme court campaign (1938)
    of, 150–51, 227–33, 245–46
  Tammany Hall and, 51–52, 114, 138,
    144, 145–47, 151, 209–10, 227,
    229–30, 232
  Women's Court of New York City
    and, 102, 103–4, 105–6, 114, 137,
    147–48, 150–52, 153, 154–55, 201,
    227, 228, 249
  on women's more prominent role in
    legal system by 1930s, 155
Kross, Isidor, 55

La Guardia, Fiorello
  Additon and, 138, 141–42, 143,
    184–85, 243–44
  African American voters and, 180–81,
    182–83, 202
  anti-prostitution campaigns and, 149,
    150, 154, 188
  appointment of New York City
    magistrates by, 144, 150–51,
    186–87, 201–2, 325n50
  Bernstein and, 11, 12, 187–88
  biographical background of, 177
  Board of Aldermen campaign (1919)
    by, 177, 178
  as Board of Aldermen president
    (1920–21), 177, 179
  burlesque show regulations, 189–90
  Carter and, 194, 198, 199, 200, 213
  charter reform in New York City and,
    156, 179–80, 190, 191
  city council election of 1937 and, 214,
    215–16, 218